D1293197

SHAKESPEARE IMPROVED

LONDON : HUMPHREY MILFORD
OXFORD UNIVERSITY PRESS

THOMAS BETTERTON

SHAKESPEARE IMPROVED

THE RESTORATION VERSIONS IN QUARTO AND ON THE STAGE

BY

HAZELTON SPENCER

CAMBRIDGE
HARVARD UNIVERSITY PRESS
1927

PRINTED AT THE HARVARD UNIVERSITY PRESS
CAMBRIDGE, MASS., U. S. A.

PREFATORY NOTE

THE object of this book is to tell the story of Shakespearean performance on the London stage from 1660, when the licensed theatres reopened, to 1710, when the great actor Betterton died and Drury Lane passed into the control of the first triumvirate, Wilks, Cibber, and Dogget. By that time all the plays had been produced which we now include under the general title of Restoration Drama. Poor George Farquhar's troubles were over. Congreve was alive, but as good as dead for all he mattered to the English stage. Steele had begun the *Tatler* the year before — a decade was to elapse before *The Conscious Lovers*. Throughout our study, then, 1710 is to stand as the terminal date for the Restoration theatre. It nearly coincides with the date which marks the end of the long sequence of independent Shakespeare Quartos, for Rowe published the first critical edition in 1709.

The notion of Shakespeare entertained by any age affords an index to its thought in general. If men re-create God in their own image, they are constantly remodelling their effigy of him whom they insist on regarding as the most God-like of men. *Après Dieu, il créa le plus.* I hope that without trespassing on sociological territory this volume may serve in some measure to illuminate the Restoration mind. More specifically, an examination of the place of Shakespeare on the stage focuses for the student current dramatic and theatrical ideas. And finally, as a third excuse for dealing so extensively with this subject, the present tendency of scholars to minimize the closing of the theatres (1642–1660) suggests the likelihood that now and again we may find in the Restoration a clue to the Elizabethan.

Professor Odell's *Shakespeare from Betterton to Irving* renders unnecessary any detailed treatment here of the mechanics of Restoration stagecraft. The present work falls naturally into two divisions. Part One will trace the history of Restoration performance, indicating as well the outlines of the general chronology of the stage, though without attempting to preserve due proportion between them and our more specialized concerns, or hesitating to include an occasional note designed to help solve some problem of Restoration stage history not directly relevant to Shakespeare. Part Two will examine the Quartos and all the extant stage versions of this period, with special attention to the adapted texts.

In writing this book I have been the recipient of numerous courtesies from the librarians of the Boston Public Library, where I have made extensive use of the magnificent Barton Shakespeareana; of the British Museum; and of the Library of Harvard University, which, already well provided with the Restoration texts, purchased for my use several more, and thus completed the collection of alterations now available in Boston and Cambridge. I have also to thank the editors of the *Publications of the Modern Language Association of America*, *Modern Philology*, and the *Review of English Studies* for permission to reprint portions of my articles in those journals.

My indebtedness to fellow-laborers in the Restoration vineyard has been constant; I have tried to be scrupulous in acknowledging it. Professors John Tucker Murray and Chester Noyes Greenough have offered many useful suggestions. So has Dr. Arthur Colby Sprague, also of Harvard. And like all Professor Kittredge's pupils, I am at this juncture embarrassed (as Ben Jonson, under similar circumstances, was not) by the difficulty of reconciling adequacy and seemliness in the expression of my grateful thanks.

H. S.

STATE COLLEGE OF WASHINGTON
October 1, 1927

CONTENTS

PART I

THE STAGE HISTORY OF THE PLAYS

PART II

THE RESTORATION TEXTS

ILLUSTRATIONS

PART I

THE STAGE HISTORY OF THE PLAYS

CHAPTER I

THE THEATRE RENASCENT

From the Reopening of the Licensed Theatres to the Organization of D'Avenant's Company (March, 1660–November 5, 1660)

THE dour fanaticism which in 1642 struck a death-blow to the stage made ever glorious by the exertions of Shakespeare and his great associates and successors had little direct effect on the development of the English drama. From Jonson through Middleton to Etherege and Shadwell the continuity of seventeenth-century comedy of manners flows on evenly enough; and in the serious drama the romances of Fletcher, if they do not fully account for the heroic plays of the Restoration, at least contain their seed. Had the Puritans not closed the theatres from 1642 to 1660, it seems unlikely that the subsequent course of the drama would have cut a channel materially different.

The theatre, on the other hand, was permanently affected by the closing and by the exile of the aristocracy, for during their Continental wanderings Charles and his courtiers became convinced of the superior merits of the picture-stage. In the opening years of the Restoration the platform of the Elizabethans was scrapped. It had been essentially a place for the actor to stand on and spout from — it was on the whole a rhetorical theatre that Shakespeare had written for. The pictorial stage which in 1661 replaced it brought into the English theatre a "sensual supply of sight and sound," as Colley Cibber, with finely scornful alliteration, described it, of which we are only now beginning to question the value. The aesthetes assumed, as they still do, that if your scenery is artful enough, it can make an audience forget it is in the theatre. Only one thing can do that — great acting. Unlike our own, the Restoration was an age of great acting. But only too like ours, it was an age of scenic pretension, delusion, and folly.

The court was also dissatisfied with the old English prejudice against women on the stage. The fair ones were performing on the politer boards of France, and the English exiles resolved to abolish the boy actresses and introduce the charms of desirable femininity into the London theatres. From their professional status these delightful ladies were frequently "erept," as old John Downes not unhappily terms it, "by the Force of Love." A number of the greatest nobles spent their choicer hours in a divided allegiance between the bottle and the society of the actresses. For Charles the theatres were a superb recruiting-ground. According to an unauthenticated story, "Old Rowley" carried Nell Gwyn away the first night he saw her act. And Downes tells us that little Molly Davis first attracted the King's interest when she sang "My Lodging it is on the Cold Ground": "She perform'd that so Charmingly, that not long after, it Rais'd her from her Bed on the Cold Ground, to a Bed Royal." [1]

The gap between the new theatre and the old is bridged in the person of Sir William D'Avenant, poet laureate and first Restoration adapter of Shakespeare. Shirley, though he lived till 1666, was not personally a factor in the revival of the drama, despite the frequent performance of his plays during the Restoration's first decade. Besides being poet and dramatist, D'Avenant was a practical man of the theatre. On March 26, 1639, a few months after his appointment to the laurel as Ben Jonson's successor, Charles I had granted him a patent to erect a playhouse; but after the death of Christopher Beeston, its manager, the Lord Chamberlain appointed D'Avenant (superseding Christopher's son, William) "Governor of the King and Queen's company acting at the Cockpit in Drury Lane." D'Avenant's intention may have been to build a new theatre expressly for the purpose of introducing opera with scenes into England, for his patent specifies that he is allowed not only to present plays but also to "exercise musick, musical presentments, scenes, dancing, or other the like, at the same or other hours, or times, or after plays are ended." [2]

If this were, as Mr. William J. Lawrence convincingly argues,[3] his purpose, D'Avenant abandoned it, perhaps because of financial obstacles; perhaps because he was promised at the Cockpit sufficient scope for his talents; perhaps, as Professor Joseph Quincy Adams suggests, because of opposition on the part of the proprietors of the other theatres and the owners of property adjacent to D'Avenant's proposed site. At any rate, on October 2, 1639, he signed an indenture promising not to erect his playhouse either in Fleet Street (which the document declares "inconvenient") or anywhere else without further permission.[4] Yet the terms of the patent remained valid; and twenty years later it was partly in consideration of the old grant "of my Royal Father" that Charles II confirmed D'Avenant's share in the theatrical monopoly.

During the Wars D'Avenant stood for the King; but later he made his peace with the Commonwealth, and in 1656 was allowed by the Puritan administration to produce a feebly dramatic effusion of declamation and music, now known as *The First Day's Entertainment at Rutland House*.[5] This modest and tentative performance was followed later in the same year by a much more ambitious production: *The Siege of Rhodes. Made a Representation by the Art of Prospective in Scenes, and the Story sung in Recitative Musick.*

The scenes, as Professor Odell points out,[6] were only pictures "hung before the audience to get it into an understanding of the 'locale' of the story." They consisted of permanent side-wings, and "shutters," or "flats," as we should call them, the latter running in grooves and clamping together in the middle of the stage to form a backing for the action. Behind them (as we learn from the sketches of the designer) there should have been "releive" scenes at the extreme rear of the stage, which would be rendered visible when the back shutters (in mid-stage) should be pulled apart.[7] A cross-section of this stage also shows borders hung from the ceiling, but probably these were not actually used. Nor could the "releive" scenes be employed effectively, since the stage was too shallow: it was only fifteen feet deep and eleven high.

The only change of scene possible was by drawing off the back shutters. The back scene, however, was not always changed to correspond with the action, and was, moreover, painted on so small a scale (the demands of perspective reduced it to seven and one half feet high by nine wide) that it had little realistic relation to the performers. The artist was John Webb, a pupil of Inigo Jones. We must, accordingly, not ascribe all the blame for the introduction of scenery to its vogue on the Continent; Webb had assisted Jones before the Wars in the staging of D'Avenant's court masque de luxe, *Salmacida Spolia*, in 1640. This constitutes, as Professor Odell declares, "a kind of royal descent from the court masque to the D'Avenant opera," though the fact remains that the modern drama owes its scenic embellishments not to the drama but to the opera of the seventeenth century.

The staging of *The Siege* was, historically considered, one of the most important dramatic productions ever made in London. Were it not that the piece was performed as an opera rather than as a regular play, we should have to grant it priority in introducing both scenery and actresses, for Ianthe was sung by Mrs. Coleman, who was not, however, strictly speaking, an actress.

These productions were made for the entertainment of the nobility and gentry at Rutland House in Aldersgate Street. But two years later, in 1658, D'Avenant was allowed to use the Cockpit in Drury Lane; the public was thus invited to performances in a regular theatre, though these were still not plays but "operas." [8] The new works were *The Cruelty of the Spaniards in Peru* and *The History of Sir Francis Drake.* On them the government seems to have looked with indulgence or even favor because they were anti-Spanish and anti-Catholic. Indeed, so thoroughly in its good graces does D'Avenant appear to have been, that several years after the Restoration of Charles, when Sir William was engaged in making operative his share in the theatrical monopoly granted to him and to Killigrew, Sir Henry Herbert, younger brother of the poet, and since 1623 Master of the Revels,[9] attacked him as having exercised that office

> to Oliuer the Tyrant, and wrote the First and Second Parte of Peru, acted at the Cockpitt, in Oliuers tyme, and soly in his fauour; wherein hee sett of the justice of Oliuers actinges, by comparison with the Spaniards, and endeavoured thereby to make Oliuers crueltyes appeare mercyes, in respect of the Spanish crueltyes; but the mercyes of the wicked are cruell.[10]

On the other hand, the more rigidly righteous viewed with alarm the renascence of dramatic entertainment. Writing on December 14, 1658, to her brother, Sir Richard Leveson, Rachell Newport gives unmistakable evidence that D'Avenant was obliged to proceed with caution: "It is thought," she says, "the Opera will speedily go down; the godly party are so much discontented with it." [11]

Whatever merit the Puritans saw in the political implications of *Drake* and *The Cruelty,* as dramas they were scarcely more than experiments. It was not till General Monk entered the city early in 1660 that the players regularly mounted the boards and made again accessible to the people of London their great dramatic heritage.

Monk reached London on February 3, 1660. "From the moment of his entry," says Green, "the restoration of the Stuarts became inevitable." The reaction was immediate, and the players were quick to take advantage of it. By the end of the following month, as Betterton's prompter, John Downes, informs us, a licensed company was established:

> In the Year 1659, General Monk, Marching then his Army out of Scotland to London. Mr. Rhodes a Bookseller being Wardrobe-Keeper formerly (as I am inform'd) to King Charles the First's, Company of Comedians in Black-Friars; getting a License from the then Governing State, fitted up a House then for Acting call'd the Cock-pit in Drury-Lane, and in a short time Compleated his Company.[12]

Since Downes's dates are Old Style this seems to fix the organization of Rhodes's company not later than March 24, 1660, though there had been earlier illegal performances at the Cockpit.[13]

His principal actor was Thomas Betterton, then about twenty-five years of age, and destined to become one of the greatest Shakespeareans ever vouchsafed to the theatre.[14] For the remainder of his long life he gave himself to the stage with complete devotion. His colleagues included many a rogue and rapscallion, and the ladies of the stage were most of them sad jades indeed. "Among this wild rout," testifies his biographer, "Thomas Betterton walked unspotted. I have not, in the course of extensive wading through the mud-heaps of Restoration satire, met with one derogatory allusion to him or to the great actress and good woman who was his wife." [15]

Whether Betterton had ever acted before Rhodes engaged him is not known. He appears to have taken his place at once as leading man, for during the brief existence of Rhodes's company he assumed such rôles as Pericles (which oddly enough seems to have been the first Shakespearean revival), Archas in Fletcher's *The Loyal Subject*, and Memnon in his *The Mad Lover*, Deflores in Middleton and Rowley's *The Changeling*, and Marullo in Massinger's *The Bondman*. *Hamlet* was probably not revived till the summer of 1661, when D'Avenant produced it with scenery at Lincoln's Inn Fields. Betterton then played the Dane, presumably for the first time. He was coached in the "business" of the part by D'Avenant, who had seen Taylor (Burbage's successor) act it before the Wars. Since it seems not unlikely that Taylor was instructed by Shakespeare himself, we have some warrant for believing the tradition of the rôle unbroken.

Forty-eight years after his first appearance as Hamlet, Betterton acted the Prince for the last (recorded) time. This performance was at the Haymarket on September 20, 1709, when he was well over seventy years of age. He had played Hamlet for half a century, and still the "town" would have no other.[16] Steele then praised him in the *Tatler*, as follows:

> Had you been to-night at the play-house, you had seen the force of Action in perfection: your admired Mr. Betterton behaved himself so well, that, though now about seventy, he acted youth, and by the prevalent power of proper manner, gesture, and voice, appeared through the whole drama a young man of great expectation, vivacity, and enterprize.

Here we have a striking endorsement of the historical critics' view of Hamlet as the beau ideal of active young-manhood, rather than a dream-sick weakling pining for the ministrations of Dr. Freud.

In person this great actor was better fitted to play a manly than an effeminate Hamlet; for he was not delicate but robust, inclining even to corpulence, as Colley Cibber tells us. He was not above middle height. Yet the testimony of his contemporaries agrees with the beautiful portrait by Sir Godfrey Kneller,[17] which shows in the man's poise a well-proportioned strength and dignity, and, despite the serenity of the face, a flashing blue eye that compels attention and respect.

In an age when the social status of the actor was still anything but desirable and the theatrical audience anything but decorous, Betterton's personality seems in his greatest rôle to have enforced a kind of exaltation on both sides of the footlights. Barton Booth, who played the Ghost to his Hamlet and succeeded him in many of his tragic rôles, said in later years, "When I acted the Ghost with Betterton, instead of my awing him, he terrified me. But divinity hung round that man!" [18]

He had [says Cibber] so just a sense of what was true or false Applause, that I have heard him say, he never thought any kind of it equal to an attentive Silence; that there were many ways of deceiving an Audience into a loud one; but to keep them husht and quiet was an Applause which only Truth and Merit could arrive at: Of which Art there never was an equal Master to himself. . . . He had so full a Possession of the Esteem and Regard of his Auditors, that upon his Entrance into every Scene he seem'd to seize upon the Eyes and Ears of the Giddy and Inadvertent! To have talk'd or look'd another way would then have been thought Insensibility or Ignorance.[19]

Such was the foremost Restoration interpreter of Shakespeare. His long and honorable career covers the whole of the period treated in this book, that is, from the reopening of the theatres to the accession of the Wilks-Dogget-Cibber management. When he died, in 1710, a new group of actors and dramatists was in possession of the stage. His death is therefore the logical terminus of a treatise on the Restoration theatre.

To return to Rhodes's company in the spring of 1660. Betterton played the leading male rôles and Edward Kynaston the heroines. Pepys tells us that on August 18, 1660, he saw Fletcher's *The Loyal Subject*, "where one Kinaston, a boy, acted the Duke's sister, but made the loveliest lady that ever I saw in my life." On January 7 of the year following Pepys saw him as Epicoene in Jonson's play, and declares that as the wife of Morose he was "clearly the prettiest woman in the whole house," and that after he had resumed masculine apparel he "likewise did appear the handsomest man in the house."

John Downes, for fifty years "book-keeper" (prompter) of the Bettertonian company, assures us that Kynaston "being then very Young made a Compleat Female Stage Beauty, performing his Parts so well, especially Arthiope [in D'Avenant's *The Unfortunate Lovers*] and Aglaura [in Suckling's play so entitled]. being Parts greatly moving Compassion and Pity; that it has since been Disputable among the Judicious, whether any Woman that succeeded him so Sensibly touch'd the Audience as he." [20] It is clear, from this and other opinions, that the acting of feminine rôles by boys in Shakespeare's time was not necessarily the squeaking farce that Cleopatra shuddered to contemplate.

Besides those mentioned by Downes, another of Kynaston's famous parts was Evadne in Fletcher's *The Maid's Tragedy*. Soon after this time, when the actresses had established themselves, he turned to male rôles with great success. Among those recorded by Downes are Peregrine in Jonson's *Volpone*, Antony in *Julius Caesar*, and Freeman in Wycherley's *The Plain Dealer*, while Cibber singles out for especial praise his King Henry IV. Still others of particular interest were Harcourt in Wycherley's *The Country Wife*, and Morat in Dryden's *Aureng-Zebe*. He outlived Betterton, though his retirement from the stage was much earlier.

The principal comedians of Rhodes's company were Cave Underhill and James Nokes. Among the former's early Shakespearean rôles Downes mentions the First Gravedigger, Gregory in *Romeo and Juliet*, and Feste. Underhill's is one of the longest theatrical careers on record, for he survived Betterton himself on the stage. Cibber tells us that he excelled

> in Characters that may be called Still-life, I mean the Stiff, the Heavy, and the Stupid . . . a Countenance of Wood could not be more fixt than his, when the Blockhead of a Character required it.[21]

Tony Aston says that this comedian "was more admired by the Actors than the Audience — there being then no Rivals in his dry, heavy, downright Way in Low Comedy . . . his Face very like the *Homo Sylvestris*, or Champanza." Late in his career Underhill created the famous rôles of Sir Sampson Legend in Congreve's *Love for Love*, and Sir Wilful Witwoud in *The Way of the World*.

James ("Nurse") Nokes became one of the best drawing-cards London has ever seen. He achieved his sobriquet by a smashing hit in *Caius Marius*, Otway's altered version of *Romeo and Juliet*. Among his more important parts were, besides the Nurse, Polonius, Sir Humphrey Noddy in Shadwell's *Bury Fair*, and the title rôles in the same author's *Squire of Alsatia* and Dryden's *Sir Martin Mar-all*.[22]

Downes names thirteen plays, mostly Fletcher's, acted by Rhodes's troupe. *Pericles* is the only Shakespearean title. In the name rôle Betterton was notably successful, for the old prompter includes it among five of the great actor's early parts to which he accords special praise. Apparently this production was the first revival of Shakespeare on the Restoration stage. But Downes is our only authority, and beyond this we know nothing about the production or the text employed. Probably it was Quarto 1635, after which the play was not printed separately till 1734.

Its choice by Rhodes's company as their sole Shakespearean offering seems strange. We must remember, however, Ben Jonson's scornful testimony to the vogue of the play on the old stage, and that the number of pre-Wars editions in quarto indicates popularity with Jacobean and Caroline readers. The play does not appear to have remained in the repertory after the organization of D'Avenant's company (largely composed of Rhodes's players), though it was among the plays to which for two months Sir William was granted exclusive rights.

Othello was probably the second revival. It appears eleventh (incorrectly numbered XII) in Downes's list of plays performed by the King's Company. It was produced not later than October 11, 1660, when Pepys saw it. Yet we cannot be certain that it was not acted much earlier, possibly before *Pericles*, just as we cannot be *certain* that Rhodes's company was actually operating before the "Old Actors" had resumed licensed performances.[23]

For Rhodes was not long without competition. His group of novices was soon playing against an excellent company of experienced actors, described by Downes as the "scattered Remnant of several of these [pre-Wars] Houses." They had organized some time in the spring or summer of 1660 and commenced acting at the old Red Bull, a large pre-Wars playhouse, partly open to the weather and quite inferior to the smaller and completely roofed Cockpit in Drury Lane, where Betterton and his colleagues held forth. Some of the Red Bull actors had been concerned in several of the unlicensed attempts to revive the stage before Monk's arrival, and it is not impossible that their organization was in being before Rhodes opened the Cockpit. Theatrical dates during the first years of the Restoration are extremely difficult. Throughout the present work the practice will be to accept for the production of plays and the erection of theatres and companies the first date for which authority can be cited, however attractive an earlier but hypothetical date may be.

In the *Royal Arbor of Loyal Poesie* of the old actor, Thomas Jordan, there is "A Prologue to a Comedy call'd *The Tamre Tam'd* [Fletcher's *The Woman's Prize*], June 25. 1660," which points to a performance at the Red Bull by the "Old Actors." There is also an epilogue "Spoken by the Tamer, a Woman," but that this refers to an actress seems unlikely.[24] Of the members of the Red Bull company, Hart and Mohun, who had played before the Wars, were important Shakespeareans.

Charles Hart had been an apprentice at the old Blackfriars theatre, where he had acted feminine rôles. He was perhaps the most brilliant product of the boy-actress school of training;

when he came, on the Restoration stage, into the full maturity of his powers, he assumed a long series of great characters which he seems to have acted with uniform dignity and force. If his range was less extensive than Betterton's, within it he was till his retirement recognized as the first actor of his time. Some of his most famous rôles were Othello, Brutus, Hotspur, Bussy d'Ambois in Chapman's play, Amintor in Fletcher's *The Maid's Tragedy*, and the title-rôle of the same author's *Philaster*, Mosca in Jonson's *Volpone*, and the title-rôle in his *Catiline*, Antony in Dryden's *All for Love*, Almanzor in his *The Conquest of Granada*, the title-rôle of his *Aureng-Zebe*, Manly in Wycherley's *The Plain Dealer*, and Horner in his *The Country Wife;* and, finally, as Downes enthusiastically asserts, Alexander in Lee's *The Rival Queens:*

> towards the latter End of his Acting; if he Acted in any one of these but once in a Fortnight, the House was fill'd as at a New Play, especially Alexander, he Acting that with such Grandeur and Agreeable Majesty, That one of the Court was pleas'd to Honour him with this Commendation; That Hart might Teach any King on Earth how to Comport himself.[25]

Michael Mohun [26] had been trained as a boy-actress before the Wars, but seems to have graduated to male rôles by 1642. He was an accomplished actor, and a great favorite with Charles. When this group of players got into difficulties it was usually Major Mohun who was deputed to pour their side of the case into the royal ear. Among Mohun's chief parts were Iago, Cassius, Face in *The Alchemist*, the title-rôle in *Volpone*, Melantius in *The Maid's Tragedy*, Maximin in Dryden's *Tyrannick Love*, Ventidius in his *All for Love*, and Pinchwife in Wycherley's *The Country Wife*.

The leading parts at the Red Bull were, however, at first in the hands of the veterans, Nicholas Burt and Walter Clun. Both had been boy-actresses at the Blackfriars before the Wars, though Burt had also played at the Cockpit, or Phoenix, under Beeston. He does not appear after 1678. Clun was killed by a robber on the night of August 2, 1664.[27]

John Lacy, afterwards notorious as the author and star of *Sauny the Scot*, a despicable adaptation of *The Taming of the Shrew*, was another of the leading lights of the Theatre Royal, which grew out of this company of Old Actors. We know little about him before the Restoration, except that, like Hart and Mohun, he had served in the Wars. Langbaine describes him as follows:

> An excellent comedian of the King's company . . . originally a Dancing Master,[28] of a rare Shape of Body, and good Complexion; was a Lieutenant and Quarter Master under Col. Gerrard, afterwards Earl of Macclesfield; he died, Sept. 17. 1681. King Charles the Second fancied him so much, as to have his Picture drawn in Three several Figures, in the same Table, as Teague in the Committee, Scruple in the Cheats, and Gallyard in the Varieties.[29]

Lacy wrote several successful original pieces. Whether he joined while this company was acting at the Red Bull, or later at Vere Street, is uncertain; probably it was at the latter theatre. He was the original Bayes of *The Rehearsal*. Another of his famous parts was Sir Politick Would-be in *Volpone*. Another was Falstaff, in which, according to Langbaine, he "never fail'd of universal applause." [30] Evelyn refers to Lacy (October 3, 1662) as "the famous Roscius or comedian"; on November 27 of the same year he saw *The Committee*, "where the mimic, Lacy, acted the Irish footman to admiration." Lacy was Pepys's favorite among the actors of the King's house; on May 21, 1662, the diarist characterizes his (title) rôle in *The French Dancing Master* as "the best in the world."

Mention should also be made of William Cartwright, the first Falstaff of the Restoration stage. And there were others, who strutted their brief hour, and, winning little enough of fame in their time, have long been forgotten even by the antiquarian.

Besides Rhodes's company and the Old Actors, a third

sprang up at the renovated Salisbury Court theatre, under William Beeston, son of the Christopher Beeston who had managed the Cockpit in Drury Lane before D'Avenant's pre-Wars régime there, and had acted with Shakespeare in the original production of Jonson's *Every Man in His Humour.* Like the Cockpit in Drury Lane, the Salisbury Court was one of the smaller, roofed, and "private" theatres.[31]

It is not unlikely that all three of these companies were organized and playing by the end of June, 1660. Pepys's first mention of a theatrical performance is on June 6; not till August 18 did he pay the first of his many visits to the playhouse.

Between these dates the Court took a hand in the theatrical renascence. On Thomas Killigrew and Sir William D'Avenant, both courtier-dramatists, Charles bestowed, as a reward for past services, a monopoly of the London theatres. The erection of two playhouses, "suppressing all others," was authorized by a warrant of July 19, 1660; and on August 21 the grant was made, on the ground that "Certaine persons" had performed plays containing

> much Matter of Prophanation, and Scurrility, soe that such Kind of Entertainments, which, if well Mannaged, might serue as Morall Instructions In Humanne life, As the same are now vsed, doe for the most part tende to the Debauchinge of the Manners of Such as are present at them, and are very Scandalous and offensive to all pious and well disposed persons.

That all three of the companies were performing by the date of this grant is certain from the language of two documents of the day before, August 20, 1660. The first of these is described in the *Calendar of State Papers* ("Domestic Series") as follows:

> The King to Sir William Wylde, Recorder of London, Sir Rich. Browne, Alderman, and other Justices of Peace. Is informed that companies assemble at the Red Bull playhouse St. John's Street,

at the Cockpit Drury Lane, and at another in Salisbury Court, and perform profane and obscene plays, &c. Orders their rigorous suppression under heavy penalties.

Dr. J. Leslie Hotson has discovered [32] that the original document is in D'Avenant's handwriting, but was never signed, and that accordingly the order was not despatched to the officers of enforcement. This fact does not, of course, alter its bearing on the existence of the three companies.

On the same day, Sir Henry Herbert ordered the granting of a petition to the King by John Rogers, a wounded veteran of the royal army. It had been referred to the Master of the Revels "to take such order therein, as shalbe agreable to Equety, without further trubling his Majesty." Rogers had obtained from General Monk "a Tolleration to erect a playhouse or to haue a share out of them already Tollerated, your Peticioner thereby vndertaking to Supres all Riotts, Tumults, or Molestacions," and now prayed the King for a confirmation of his little graft.

Sir Henry decided "it reasonable That the Petitioner should have the same Allowance weekly from your Playhouse which you doe allowe Other Persons for the same worke." His order was addressed "To the Actors of the Playhouses called the Red bull, Cockpitt, and Theatre in Salesbury Court, and to euery of them, in & about the Citties of London & Westminster," that is, to the Old Actors, Rhodes's company, and Beeston's company.[33] In Herbert's statement of his claims on July 11, 1662, he asserts that on August 11, 1660, the King's company (that is the Old Actors) covenanted to pay him £4 a week, and that similar sums were agreed to by Beeston and by Rhodes, presumably on the same date, though he fails to specify.[34]

Besides these three, there was one other theatre, the Cockpit at Whitehall Palace, by Genest confused with the Cockpit in Drury Lane. This confusion is partly untangled by Lowe.[35]

It arose because Pepys fails to distinguish (at least by name) between the two Cockpit theatres. But when he attends the royal theatre in the Palace he particularizes his method of gaining admittance, which was usually by courtesy of some one who had the entrée, as in his entry of October 2, 1662:

> Hearing that there was a play at the Cockpit (and my Lord Sandwich, who came to town last night, at it), I do go thither, and by very great fortune did follow four or five gentlemen who were carried to a little private door in a wall, and so crept through a narrow place and come into one of the boxes next the King's.

Lowe points out that this does not look like a performance at the Cockpit in Drury Lane, where surreptitious means of getting in would not have been necessary. Moreover, Pepys would hardly mention his "hearing that there was a play" if he were referring to a regular theatre. Genest, taking Pepys's entry of August 18, 1660, to describe a performance by the Old Actors at the Cockpit, assumes correctly that the diarist means the Cockpit in Drury Lane, but incorrectly that he saw the Old Actors. He is misled by Pepys's mentioning Kynaston, who at this early date was a member of Rhodes's company. Besides, the play Pepys saw, Fletcher's *The Loyal Subject*, was in their repertory, not that of the Old Actors. This mistake invalidates Genest's further contention, that Downes's accounts of seasons at the Cockpit in Drury Lane and at the Red Bull are incorrect, and that the Old Actors were in possession of the former theatre as early as August.

Lowe's conclusion that *all* the references by Pepys to the Cockpit are to the Whitehall theatre does not, however, appear to be sound. By his own test the entry for October 30, 1660, indicates that the diarist sometimes refers to the Drury Lane house, for on that day he went "to the Cockpit all alone." Furthermore, the very entry that puzzled Genest, that of August 18, 1660, points to the Drury Lane Cockpit. What led Genest astray was not, as Lowe supposes, his mistaking the theatre, but his assumption that, because Kynaston played, the company was composed of the Old Actors.

Mr. William J. Lawrence, whose researches are a constant inspiration to the student of the early theatres, suggests another test, the *time* of performances: those at the regular theatre were in the afternoon, those at the Palace in the evening. He contends that all the entries of 1660 refer to the Cockpit in Drury Lane, and the rest to the Cockpit in Whitehall Palace.[36] This conclusion is all the more attractive since it squares with the fact that Betterton, Pepys's favorite actor, was at the Cockpit in Drury Lane till November, 1660, when, as we shall see, D'Avenant launched his new company at Salisbury Court, whence in the following June he moved to Lincoln's Inn Fields.

The day after Herbert's order in behalf of Rogers, the royal grant to D'Avenant and Killigrew was issued. What happened between then and the following October is unrecorded; but if we consider the fraility of human nature and the infinite opportunities for disagreement among the managers of the three companies *de facto* and the two monopolists *de jure*, it is not difficult to conjecture that the month of September was one of wrangling.

The best working hypothesis rests on a document, dated October 6, 1660, found by Lowe among the Lord Chamberlain's records, constituting the King's Company of Comedians and naming not only Hart, Mohun, and the other members of the Red Bull company, but Betterton and Kynaston, who belonged to Rhodes's company.[37] Lowe regards it as certain that, some time after the patent of August 21 was issued to Killigrew and D'Avenant, the King, wearied of the squabbles between them, and between them and the managers, and between them and Herbert, and between the managers and Herbert, attempted to simplify what was undeniably a fairly complex situation, by ordering the organization of one company, which lasted till D'Avenant engaged some of its members to form a new one.

This view is substantiated by two of Herbert's documents. On October 8, 1660, he attempts to establish his authority over the Cockpit in Drury Lane. He asserts that permission to erect playhouses rests in his hands, and orders "Mister John Roades at the Cockpitt Playhouse in Drury Lane" to "attende mee concerning your Playhouse. . . . And to bring with you such Authority As you haue for Errecting of the said house Into a Playhouse, at your perill." [38] Rhodes's reply is endorsed on the document: "Warrant sent to Rhodes and brought backe by him the 10th of October 1660 with this Answer: That the Kinge did authorize Him."

Two days, then, after we know that the King's Company of Comedians had been formally established, Rhodes was still, paradoxically, on deck in the Cockpit. But five days later (October 13, 1660) we find the Old Actors in possession, doubtless joined by the leading members of Rhodes's company. On that date Herbert sent a complaint "To Mr. Michael Mohun, and the rest of the actors of the Cockpitt playhouse in Drury Lane," specifying that Killigrew and D'Avenant had made several remonstrances

> concerning the unusuall and unreasonable rates taken at your playhouse doores, of the respective persons of quality that desire to refresh or improve themselves by the sight of your morrall entertainments which were constituted for profitt and delight.[39]

It appears from the superscription of this document (Major Mohun being addressed at the Cockpit in Drury Lane) that the actors had obeyed the royal injunction and formed one company; but evidently the two patentees, though they may have been taking toll of the receipts, were not acting as "governors" of the theatre. It may seem unlikely that they would object to larger profits, but there was method in this apparent madness. "The said complaints," continues Herbert, "[were] made use of by the said Mr. Killigrew and Sir William Davenant as part of their suggestions for their pretended power, and for your late restrainte." Herbert concludes by ordering the players to charge only the old Blackfriars rates, and to send him all the old plays they intend to act, "that they may be reformed of prophanes and ribaldry."

Immediately on receiving this annoying evidence of the double threat of regulation by the patentees and by the Master of the Revels, the Cockpit players petitioned the King, as follows:

To the Kings most excellent Majestie.

The humble Petition of Michael Mohun, Robert Shatterell, Charles Hart, Nich. Burt, Wm. Cartwright, Walter Clun, and William Wintersell.[40]

Humbly sheweth,

That your Majesties humble petitioners, having been suppress[41] by a warrant from your Majestie, Sir Henry Herbert informed us it was Mr. Killegrew had caused it, and if wee would give him soe much a weeke, he would protect them against Mr. Killegrew and all powers. The complaint against us was, scandalous plays, raising the price, and acknowledging noe authority; all which ended in soe much per weeke to him; for which wee had leave to play, and promise of his protection: the which your Majesty knows he was not able to performe, since Mr. Killegrew, having your Majesties former grante, supprest us, until wee had by covenant obliged ourselves to act with woemen, a new theatre, and habitts according to our sceanes.[42] And according to your Majesties approbation, from all the companies we made election of one company; and so farre Sir Henry Herbert hath bene from protecting us, that he hath been a continual disturbance unto us, who were [united][43] by your Majesties commande under Mr. Killegrew, as Master of your Majesties Comedians; and we have annext unto our petition the date of the warrant by which wee were supprest, and for a protection against that warrant he forced from us soe much a weeke. And if your majestie be graciously pleased to cast your eye upon the date of the warrant hereto annext, your majestie shall find the date to our contract succeeded; wherein he hath broke the covenants, and not your petitioners, haveing abused your majestie in giveing an ill character of your petitioners, only to force a sum from their poor endeavours; who never did nor shall refuse him all the reseits and just profitts that belong to his place; hee having now obtained leave to arrest us, only to give trouble and vexation to your petitioners, hopeing by that meanes to force a summe of money illegally from us.

The premises considered, your petitioners humbly beseech your majestie to be gratiously pleased to signify your royal pleasure to the Lord Chamberlaine, that your petitioners may not bee molested in their calling. And your petitioners in duty bound shall pray, &c.[44]

In this document, then, appears the plain statement that one company had been organized. The obvious question is, why does not Betterton's name stand among those of the actors petitioning? But far too much has been made of its non-appearance. The title of the petition contains the names of seven of the actors; apparently there are only four signatures. A reasonable inference is that, though he had been at the head of Rhodes's company, Betterton's lack of experience ranked him far down in the scale when that company was absorbed by the Old Actors, or else that as early as the middle of October he had come to some agreement with D'Avenant and was not included in the plans for Killigrew's royal company of comedians, afterwards known as the Theatre Royal or the King's Company.

Professor Allardyce Nicoll is unwilling to accept this view, and propounds the theory that the united company "can have been nothing but a troupe selected for the Cockpit at Whitehall." [45] No one can with safety be dogmatic while attempting to turn this particular corner of theatrical history; yet is it not clear from the context of the actors' petition just cited (Mr. Nicoll excerpts but one sentence) that the indignant players are pleading for freedom from molestation in their daily calling, and do not refer to special performances at the Palace? The only pertinent objection raised by Mr. Nicoll is the old one that Betterton's name does not appear in the petition. But I believe he misconceives the situation when he suggests that "we can never trust one single MS. which contradicts all we know of the history of the stage." As we have seen, the documents hang together, not perfectly, but understandably; and as for what we know of the history of the stage during those weeks, we know nothing about it except what these documents tell us.

"We must presume," Mr. Nicoll continues, "that Herbert's mention of Mohun at the Cockpit is an error, or that some slight re-arrangement of the theatres had taken place." Passing over the second of these suggestions as a little vague, one may submit for Sir Henry Herbert that he was the last person in Restoration London likely to make a mistake of that sort.

While the united company acted at the Cockpit in Drury Lane, *Othello* was produced, presumably the second Shakespearean play to be revived.[46] It was probably performed in an unaltered text. Our record of this production (October 11, 1660) fails to indicate whether it was at the Cockpit at Whitehall Palace or in Drury Lane. Pepys is our authority, as follows:

> Here, in the Park, we met with Mr. Salisbury, who took Mr. Creed and me to the Cockpitt to see *The Moore of Venice* which was well done. Burt acted the Moore; [47] by the same token, a very pretty lady that sat by me, called out, to see Desdemona smothered.

Wheatley's note [48] asserts that this performance was at the Cockpit in Drury Lane, and I am inclined to agree with him. In his MS. history of the Restoration stage (Theatre Collection of Harvard University) John Payne Collier waxes facetious over the episode of "the very pretty lady." He professes to regard it as conclusive evidence that Desdemona was at this time played by a handsome youth, rather than by an actress.

But except for Burt we cannot be sure of the performers. Downes's cast represents a later revival. By the date which Pepys gives us, the union of the Old Actors with Rhodes's company had been decreed, but whether joint performances had been given is uncertain. Probably the leading parts, at least, were played exclusively by the Old Actors. That they should have waited till October to produce *Othello* seems strange, though this delay may be compared with the (apparently) much longer one in the case of *Julius Caesar*. It is not unlikely that *Othello* was among their first offerings when they reopened the Red Bull in the spring or summer, but in the absence of any record of its performance then [49] we must allow the honor of priority to *Pericles* at the Cockpit.

Othello was again presented by the Old Actors after their removal to Vere Street, Clare Market. The date of its first performance there was December 8, 1660, important because it probably marks the first appearance of a professional actress on the London stage.

Burt was the first Othello; Iago was probably acted by Clun; Cassio probably by Hart; Roderigo probably by Mohun, who fell heir to Iago in 1664, when Clun was killed. Downes gives the cast as it was shortly after this event: Cartwright, Brabantio; Burt, Othello; Hart, Cassio; Mohun, Iago; Beeston, Roderigo; Mrs. Hughes, Desdemona; Mrs. Rutter, Emilia. The play stands eleventh (incorrectly numbered XII) in Downes's list of "their Principal Old Stock Plays," acted 1663–1682. It was this cast that Pepys saw on February 6, 1669,[50] when he pronounced the play

> ill acted in most parts; Mohun, which did a little surprise me, not acting Iago's part by much so well as Clun used to do; nor another Hart's, which was Cassio's; nor, indeed, Burt doing the Moor's so well as I once thought he did.

Whether Hart had dropped out of the cast, or on the occasion of Pepys's visit had been obliged to absent himself while his understudy played Cassio, is uncertain. He afterwards succeeded to the title-rôle. The cast as it then was is given in the Players' Quarto of 1681. This was reprinted in 1687, 1695, and 1705; the cast was not changed, though after the union of

WILLIAM CARTWRIGHT

the companies in 1682 it was of course no longer up to date. The actors mentioned are: Lydal as the Duke; Cartwright, Brabantio; Griffin, Gratiano; Harris, Lodovico; Hart, Othello; Kynaston, Cassio; Mohun, Iago; Beeston, Roderigo; Watson, "Montanio"; and the notorious Jo Haynes as the Clown. The actresses were: Mrs. Cox, Desdemona; Mrs. Rutter, Emilia; Mrs. James, Bianca.

After the union of the two patent companies in 1682 Betterton produced a number of plays in which, because they were the property of the Theatre Royal, he had before been unable to appear. Among these was *Othello*, in the title-rôle of which he had great success. Steele describes in the *Tatler* his impersonation during the last decade of his career:

> I have hardly a notion that any performer of antiquity could surpass the action of Mr. Betterton in any of the occasions in which he has appeared on our stage. The wonderful agony which he appeared in, when he examined the circumstance of the handkerchief in *Othello;* the mixture of love that intruded upon his mind upon the innocent answers Desdemona makes, betrayed in his gesture such a variety and vicissitude of passions, as would admonish a man to be afraid of his own heart, and perfectly convince him, that it is to stab it, to admit that worst of daggers, jealousy. Whoever reads in his closet this admirable scene, will find that he cannot, except he has as warm an imagination as Shakespeare himself, find any but dry, incoherent, and broken sentences; but a reader that has seen Betterton act it, observes there could not be a word added; that longer speech had been unnatural, nay impossible, in Othello's circumstances. The charming passage in the same tragedy, where he tells the manner of winning the affection of his mistress, was urged with so moving and graceful an energy, that while I walked in the cloisters, I thought of him with the same concern as if I waited for the remains of a person who had in real life done all that I had seen him represent.

Downes places *The Moor of Venice* eighth on his list of eleven plays "Withdiversothers" revived after the union and acted 1682–1695.[51] The production by the united company was probably in 1683.[52] The play was very popular and remained a stock piece throughout the whole of the period we are concerned with. It seems to have been played on February 6, 1686.[53] Genest records a performance on February 19, 1704, at Little Lincoln's Inn Fields for Dogget's benefit; the beneficiary on this occasion gave his patrons additional entertainment free of charge in the form of "songs, dances, and comic dialogues." [54] *Othello* was played at the Haymarket on January 28, 1707, by a most distinguished cast, which included Betterton as Othello, Verbruggen as Iago, Booth as Cassio, and Mrs. Bracegirdle as Desdemona.[55] Cibber sometimes played Iago about this time. Wilks acted Othello, for the first time in England, at the Haymarket on June 22, 1710.[56]

Dr. Sprague gives me the following commentary by Sir John Perceval, who writes on September 20, 1709, to his cousin, Elizabeth Southwell:

> We should have languished for want of diversion but for *Othello*, which drew all the stragglers in town together, and our number was greater than I imagined. It was there I had an opportunity of seeing what gave me as much concern as the very play itself, I mean a flat insensibility in every lady, as if tenderness were no longer a virtue in your sex, whereas I own freely, had not Desdemona been very ugly, I had certainly pulled out my handkerchief. I can remember when the ladies were better natured; now, like Dutchwomen, they can talk of indifferent things at a time when the tenderest passions of their whole frame are called upon. But whether they affect to have it thought they have, or whether the war and the multitude of officers has at long run infused a more soldierlike genius or whether they have in earnest lost all feeling, for long use will produce that effect, I leave to others to determine; meanwhile I declare that they who cannot be moved at Othello's story so artfully worked up by Shakespeare, and justly played by Betterton, are capable of marrying again before their husbands are cold, of trampling on a lover when dying at their feet, and are fit to converse with tigers only. There will be another trial of them this night at *Hamlet*.[57]

But one should not take young men's reproaches of fair dames too seriously, particularly if they include references to hard hearts and lovers at the door of death.

That *Othello* is singled out for special condemnation as "a bloody farce" in Rymer's *Short View of Tragedy* (1693) is pretty good evidence of its popularity as played by the united patent company under Betterton. A few years later we learn on excellent authority that the play "is still often acted, and esteemed one of the best of our Author's Plays." [58]

Pericles and *Othello*, then, are the only Shakespearean plays which we can be certain were staged after the licensed companies commenced acting in the spring of 1660 and before the organization of D'Avenant's company on November 5 of that year. Shakespeare won his way slowly in the Restoration theatre. But, as we shall see, once D'Avenant and Betterton stage him at Lincoln's Inn Fields he begins to forge ahead to his unquestioned station as the foremost of the English tragic writers.

As for comedy, that was another story. And another story it remains to this day, despite the idolaters who would place *As You Like It* beside *Macbeth* and *Lear*, and above *Le Tartuffe* and *Candida*. It is highly creditable to our age that, while we cannot take the romantic comedies very seriously, we encounter only pure delight in Olivia's garden, and the magical "wood near Athens." Probably Shakespeare never intended us to find anything else there. But the Restoration critics bowed before the burly figure of the great god Ben. Their stage was not ample enough for the snarling comedies of Jonson and the gentle scenes of Shakespeare. Nor, apparently, is ours.

Notes to Chapter I

1. John Downes, *Roscius Anglicanus*, ed. Knight, p. 24.
2. Cf. Edmond Malone, "An Historical Account of the Rise and Progress of the English Stage," *The Plays of William Shakespeare*, ed. 1803, vol. iii, p. 99; and J. Q. Adams, *Shakespearean Playhouses*, pp. 425 f.
3. William J. Lawrence, "The Origin of the English Picture-Stage," *The Elizabethan Playhouse, and Other Studies, Second Series*, pp. 121–147.
4. Reprinted, Adams, *Shakespearean Playhouses*, pp. 428–430.
5. On the strength of a satirical ballad which he thinks describes Sir William's activities, Dr. J. Leslie Hotson concludes that D'Avenant carried on operations at a number of theatres several years before this. It is not impossible, perhaps, that this ballad satirizes the tall yarns with which D'Avenant put off his creditors. But see Dr. Hotson's unpublished Harvard dissertation (1923), *Sir William Davenant and the Commonwealth Stage*, pp. 187–204.
6. G. C. D. Odell, *Shakespeare from Betterton to Irving*, i, 97 f.
7. See the plans given by Lily B. Campbell, *Scenes and Machines*, pp. 224, 225; and by their discoverer, Mr. W. G. Keith, *Burlington Magazine*, April and May, 1914.
8. A letter of Oct. 15, 1658, asserts that "Sir William Davenant, the poet laureate, has obtained permission for stage plays, and the Fortune Play-house is being trimmed up." Hist. MSS Com., 12 (Appendix, part vii): 23.
9. That is, he had long been in charge of that office, the titular Master having farmed it out to him. By this time, however, Herbert was in possession of the title as well. J. Q. Adams, *The Dramatic Records of Sir Henry Herbert*, p. 8.
10. In Herbert's reply (July 11, 1662) to D'Avenant's petition for relief from his interference. Reprinted, Adams, *Dram. Rec.*, pp. 120–123.
11. Hist. MSS Com., 5: 146.
12. Downes, p. 17.
13. Professor Allardyce Nicoll (*A History of Restoration Drama*, pp. 269 f.) places the date of Rhodes's license between Feb. 4 and March 25, since the *Middlesex Records* (iii, 282) show that on the former date "Thomas Lillieston" was arrested for wrongfully playing at the Cockpit (or Phoenix). This actor is listed by Downes among the members of Rhodes's company, and was one of the signers of D'Avenant's articles of agreement on Nov. 5, 1660.
14. For more particular accounts of the actors mentioned in this work the reader should consult the *D. N. B.* (especially Joseph Knight's articles); Dr. Doran's *Annals of the Stage* (*Their Majesties' Servants*), ed. R. W. Lowe, 1888, vol. i, chs. 3–8; vol. ii, chs. 1–3; and Bellchambers's and Lowe's memoirs of the actors and actresses, Lowe's ed. of Cibber's *Apology*, ii, 319–371.
15. R. W. Lowe, *Thomas Betterton*, p. 56. But for an attack on Betterton see Robert Gould's venomous and contemptible "The Play-house, a

Satyr," *Works*, ed. 1709, ii, 250. I am afraid this passage refers to Betterton. Notice the reference to Betterton's tyrannical rule (p. 257), and to his wealth (p. 259).

16. Cf. Anthony Aston's *Brief Supplement to Colley Cibber, Esq; his Lives of the late Famous Actors and Actresses*, reprinted, Cibber, ii, 301.
17. In the National Portrait Gallery, London.
18. Thomas Davies, *Dramatic Miscellanies*, iii, 32.
19. Cibber, i, 109.
20. Downes, p. 19.
21. Cibber, i, 154 f.
22. Downes's account (p. 29) of this comedian's buffoonery in a command performance at Dover is especially interesting because of the paucity of references, hitherto noticed, to performances by the London actors outside the metropolis. Their first visit to Oxford seems to have been in July, 1661, when the Theatre Royal acted a number of plays on a stage in the yard of the King's Arms. (Anthony à Wood, *Life and Times*, ed. 1891–1900, i, 406.) In July, 1680, they played at a tennis court belonging to Wood's brother. (Ibid., ii, 490.) The Duke of York's players performed *Love in a Tub* at the Guildhall on July 8, 1669. (Ibid., ii, 165.) There is a reference to the Dover performances in a newsletter of May 17, 1670. Hist. MSS Com., 12 (Appendix, part vii): 70.
23. It is a curious coincidence that in his prologue to Charles D'Avenant's *Circe* Dryden selects these two plays for mention, as follows:

    "Shakespear's own Muse her *Pericles* first bore,
    The Prince of Tyre was elder than the Moore."

    Miscellany Poems, ed. 1684, p. 292. Cited in *Shakspere Allusion-Book*, ii, 303. *Circe* was produced in the spring of 1677.
24. Cf. Nicoll, *Restoration Drama*, p. 71; and Dr. Arthur C. Sprague, *Beaumont and Fletcher on the Restoration Stage*, p. 9, n. 2.
25. Downes, p. 16. Hart is frequently described (*e. g.*, by Joseph Knight in *D. N. B.*) as the grandson of Shakespeare's sister, Joan. Sir Sidney Lee does not allude to the question in his Life. Mr. Montague Summers (*Shakespeare Adaptations*, p. xxx) asserts that no proof of this relationship is forthcoming. I have not found any.
26. Pronounced, and often spelled, "Moon."
27. Mr. G. Thorn-Drury reprints, in his *A Little Ark Containing Sundry Pieces of Seventeenth-Century Verse*, "An Egley Upon the Most Execrable Murther of Mr. Clun, On of the Comedeans of the Theator Royal, Who was Rob'd and most inhumanely Kill'd on Tusday-night being the 2d of August, 1664, near Tatnam-Court, as he was Riding to his Country-house at Kentishtown."
28. Wheatley asserts that "Lacy was taught dancing by John Ogilby, but there is no evidence that he was a teacher of the art himself." Pepys's *Diary*, ed. Wheatley, ix, 140.
29. Langbaine–Gildon, *Lives and Characters of the English Dramatick Poets*, pp. 84 f. It is strange that Langbaine does not mention *Sauny*

the Scot among Lacy's works. (Cf. John Genest, *Some Account of the English Stage*, ii, 139.) This title is added by Gildon in the edition cited.

30. Gerard Langbaine, *An Account of the English Dramatick Poets*, p. 456.
31. William Beeston purchased the Salisbury Court house in 1652 and rebuilt it in 1660. Cunningham–Wheatley, *London Past and Present*, iii, 203 f.
32. Harvard dissertation, unpublished, p. 232.
33. Reprinted by Adams, *Dram. Rec.*, pp. 83, 84; Malone (1803), iii, 295–297, (*Var.*) iii, 244 f.; Halliwell-Phillipps, *A Collection of Documents*, pp. 17 f.
34. Adams, *Dram. Rec.*, pp. 120–123; Malone (1803), iii, 320–324, (*Var.*) iii, 265 f.
35. Lowe, *Betterton*, pp. 65 f. For the previous history of this portion of the Palace see Cunningham–Wheatley, *London Past and Present*, i, 437 f.; Adams, *Shakespearean Playhouses*, pp. 384–409. It is interesting to note that J. P. Collier in his MS. history of the Restoration stage (Theatre Collection, Harvard University) recognizes (pp. 21 f.) the possibility that Pepys sometimes refers to performances at Whitehall.
36. William J. Lawrence, "A Forgotten Restoration Playhouse," *Englische Studien*, xxxv, 284 f.
37. Lowe, *Betterton*, p. 68. This document is cited by Professor Nicoll as L. C. 5/137, p. 332. (*Restoration Drama*, p. 274.)
38. Adams, *Dram. Rec.*, p. 93; Malone (1803), iii, 304, (*Var.*) iii, 252; Halliwell-Phillipps, p. 26.
39. Adams, *Dram. Rec.*, pp. 93, 94; Malone (1803), iii, 305, 306, (*Var.*) iii, 252 f.
40. All members of the company of veterans that had opened at the Red Bull.
41. Cf. Herbert's reminder of that fact in his order of the same day (Oct. 13).
42. The relation of Killigrew to his company at this time was similar to that between D'Avenant and his during the following winter. In both cases the patentee was occupied in providing a new theatre. In the interim, as long as he received his share of the profits he was apparently willing to allow the actors to govern themselves. The suppression referred to by the actors was probably in September.
43. Thus Adams and Malone.
44. Adams, *Dram. Rec.*, pp. 94–96; Malone (1803), iii, 306–308, (*Var.*) iii, 254 f.; Halliwell-Phillipps, pp. 44 f. The date of this document is probably Oct. 13, 1660.
45. Nicoll, *Restoration Drama*, pp. 273, 274.
46. I am indebted to Dr. Sprague for several valuable references to the stage history of *Othello*.
47. Hart seems to have played Cassio at first but afterwards took over Othello, which became one of his greatest rôles. (Cf. Davies, *Dram-*

atic Miscellanies, i, 221.) Percy Fitzgerald (*New History of the English Stage*, i, 21) makes a curious slip when he says that Kynaston acted the Moor at this performance.

48. Pepys's *Diary*, ed. Wheatley, i, 241.
49. The undated list of Red Bull plays, which Malone wished to date "soon after the Restoration," includes *Othello*. But since this list may contain items acted before the theatres were licensed, or even before they were closed, we cannot state with certainty that *Othello* had been acted in the spring or summer. See Malone (1803), iii, 328; Adams, *Dram. Rec.*, p. 82.
50. Lowe (*Betterton*, p. 101) misprints February 7.
51. Downes, p. 40.
52. Genest, i, 402.
53. Hist. MSS Com. 12 (Appendix, part v): 104.
54. Genest, ii, 306. I do not attempt to list every performance of any of these plays after 1700. The reader may consult Genest, vol. ii, and, in the case of some adapted versions, Allardyce Nicoll, *Early Eighteenth Century Drama*, Appendix A.
55. Genest, ii, 364.
56. *Ibid.*, 454.
57. Hist. MSS Com., Egmont MSS, ii, 240.
58. Langbaine–Gildon, *Lives and Characters of the English Dramatick Poets* (*c.* 1699), p. 128.

CHAPTER II

GREAT INNOVATIONS

From the Organization of D'Avenant's Company to its Opening at Lincoln's Inn Fields (November 5, 1660–June, 1661)

THE authority by which the united company at the Cockpit was supposed to stifle competition derived from the monopoly assigned to D'Avenant and Killigrew on August 21, 1660. But that grant allowed two houses; and D'Avenant signed articles on November 5, 1660, with a number of the players, and organized a separate company, which was taken under the patronage of H. R. H. the Duke of York and became known, therefore, as "the Duke's," Killigrew's troupe of Old Actors being "the King's."

Betterton was leading man of the new company. All the members of Rhodes's troupe whom I have mentioned joined it, except Kynaston, who remained with the Old Actors, by this time submissive to Killigrew's authority. The reason for his choice is obvious. He was the best male interpreter of feminine rôles on the Restoration stage and found no difficulty in winning and holding an eminent place among the King's players. Betterton, however, having acted leading parts for Rhodes, was probably not enthusiastic over the prospect of playing second fiddle to Burt, Clun, Hart, and Mohun. He was doubtless glad of the opportunity to resume his old rank, even though it meant hitching his wagon to the fortunes of a new and distinctly experimental organization. Nor is it impossible that the elder actors may have been a little jealous of a youth who was clearly about to win, by his own natural gifts for acting, the rewards they had achieved by going through the theatrical mill.

On the day the articles were signed[1] Killigrew's troupe withdrew from the Cockpit in Drury Lane to their old haunts at the Red Bull. We have several lists of plays drawn up by Sir Henry Herbert in furtherance of his claims against the patentees for fees due his office; one of these contains a marginal note as follows: "Nouember '60. This is a List of plays acted by the Kings Companie at the Red Bull and the new house in Gibbon's Tennis Court near Clare Market."[2] The list begins:

Monday the 5. Nouember. '60.	Wit without money.
Tusday the 6. No.	The Traitor.
Wensday the 7. No.	The Beggers Bushe.
Thursday the 8 No.	Henry the fourthe. First Play Acted at the new Theatre.[3]

The King's Company, then, acted for three days at the Red Bull, probably because Vere Street was not ready for them. The latter was a much smaller house than the Red Bull; it was a made-over tennis court, in Vere Street, Clare Market, between Lincoln's Inn Fields and the Strand. Here the King's Company acted till 1663, when the first Theatre Royal in Drury Lane was built by them. It was not until they occupied the Drury Lane house that they made use of scenes. The authority for this statement is the *Historia Histrionica* of James Wright (1699), which makes it categorically:

Lovewit. Yes, presently after the Restauration, the King's Players Acted publickly at the Red Bull for some time, and then Removed to a New-built Play-house in Vere-Street, by Claremarket. There they continued for a Year or two, and then removed to the Theater Royal in Drury-lane, where they first made use of Scenes, which had been a little before introduced upon the publick Stage by Sir William Davenant at the Duke's Old Theater in Lincolns-Inn-fields, but afterwards very much improved, with the Addition of curious Machines, by Mr. Betterton at the New Theater in Dorset-Garden, to the great Expence and continual Charge of the Players.[4]

Mr. Lawrence confirms this statement, but remarks that he anticipates being asked "a somewhat ugly question": Why did Killigrew remove and fit up this new theatre (pronounced by Pepys, on November 20, 1660, to be "the finest play-house, I believe, that ever was in England") unless it was to have the advantages of scenery? Mr. Lawrence's answer, which he considers inadequate, is the greater accessibility of Vere Street. (The Red Bull stood in St. John's Street, Clerkenwell.[5]) But if we recall that the Red Bull was an old house, too large, and partly roofless, we have reasons enough for the removal.

In fact, the reputation of the Red Bull was none of the best, even before the Wars. It is also noteworthy that, when the Old Actors united with Rhodes's players in the fall of 1660, the combined companies elected to play at the Cockpit in Drury Lane, and not at the Red Bull. Mr. Lawrence may have overlooked this fact, for in describing Killigrew's removal to Vere Street he states that the King's players had been acting at the Red Bull for at least three or four months.[6] They appear rather to have been there but three days, November 5, 6, and 7, and to have moved on the eighth.[7] Evidently they returned to the Red Bull because Vere Street was not ready for them, and never intended that their stay there should be more than temporary. After their removal the Red Bull went down hill with great rapidity.[8]

From Herbert's list of this company's productions in 1660–1662 [9] we learn that, having opened their new theatre in Vere Street with *Henry IV*, they followed it on the next day (November 9, 1660) with "The merry wifes of Windsor," the first recorded performance of these plays on the Restoration stage.

Pepys saw *Henry IV* at this house on December 31, 1660, but was not pleased with it, perhaps, as he says, because he had the book. On June 4, 1661, he saw it again, and curtly pronounces it "a good play." It appears twelfth (incorrectly numbered XIII) in Downes's list of "Principal Old Stock

Plays" acted by the members of the Theatre Royal, 1663–1682, after, that is, their removal to Drury Lane. Only five actors are named: Wintersell, King Henry IV; Burt, the Prince; Hart, Hotspur; Cartwright, Falstaff; Shatterel, Poins. Doubtless this was the cast at Vere Street, as well. Pepys saw the play three times at Drury Lane: on November 2, 1667; January 7, 1668; and September 18, 1668.

Our only clue to which Part he saw comes in his entry for November 2, 1667:

> To the King's playhouse, and there saw *Henry the Fourth;* and contrary to expectation, was pleased in nothing more than in Cartwright's speaking of Falstaffe's speech about 'What is Honour?'

This identifies the play as *Part One;* and since there is nothing in Pepys's other references to indicate that he saw a different play, and from the absence of other records of performances, it seems probable that only *Part One* was acted during this period.

What the text was we do not know; probably it was the latest Quarto (1639). No Restoration Quarto was printed till 1700. The presumption is that the play was acted without alteration. The text of 1700 represents the Bettertonian stage version of that season. After the union of the companies in 1682 Betterton assumed the rôle of Hotspur, which he played with great success for a number of years. Apparently he appeared only in *Part One*.

As for *The Merry Wives* at Vere Street, Pepys saw it on December 5, and of the acting liked "the humours of the country gentleman and the French doctor," but not of any of the rest, Falstaff included. Both his subsequent verdicts (September 25, 1661, and August 15, 1667) were adverse, though the former may be discounted because he went against his own will, "such is the power of the Devil over me." According to Downes, this farce did not become a "Principal Old Stock Play"; he places it second in a list of twenty-one pieces which were acted at the Theatre Royal between 1663 and 1682. "These," he continues, "being Old Plays, were Acted but now and then; yet being well Perform'd, were very Satisfactory to the Town." To what extent it held the boards after the union is uncertain. According to the *Gentleman's Journal* for January, 1692,[10] it was acted on December 31, 1691.

After Betterton revived *Henry IV* during the season of 1699–1700, he brought out *The Merry Wives*. Downes records a performance on April 23, 1706, before Queen Anne. This was toward the end of Betterton's management. Downes gives the following cast: Betterton, Falstaff; Dogget, Sir Hugh; Verbruggen, Page; Powell, Ford; Pinkethman, "Dr. Cains"; Bullock, Host; Mrs. Barry, Mrs. Page; Mrs. Bracegirdle, Mrs. Ford; Mrs. Bradshaw, Anne Page.[11] In 1702 the play was altered by the critic, John Dennis. He entitled his version, which I shall discuss in a later chapter, *The Comical Gallant;* it failed to supersede Shakespeare's play.

Concerning the text used at the Theatre Royal, and afterwards by Betterton, we know nothing. Probably it was the unaltered Quarto of 1630, the last pre-Wars separate edition. Captain Jaggard observes that the Boston Public Library copy of this Quarto contains "numerous MS. stage directions, apparently contemporary." These are in fact only marginal notations of entrances and exits, which are not given at the proper points in the text, all the actors appearing in a scene being listed at its head.

Captain Jaggard notes two other texts of especial interest, an acting version (*c.* 1660) in MS, and a folio (text from the Third Folio) "with contemporary manuscript corrections and stage directions; apparently an old playhouse copy."[12] Both these were among the Shakespeareana of the fourth Earl of Warwick, now in the hands of an American collector, Mr. Henry C. Folger, of New York. Until they are made accessible to scholars we shall be in the dark concerning the acting of *The Merry Wives* during this period.

MARY DAVIS

ELIZABETH BARRY

MARGARET HUGHES

ELEANOR GWYN

About a week after the King's Company, under Killigrew, had opened at Vere Street,[13] the other company, soon to be known as the Duke's, under D'Avenant, began acting at the Salisbury Court theatre. The date usually given for their first performance is November 15, 1660, but I have never seen authority cited for it. The date appears to rest on a statement of Malone, which he probably based on a reference in Sir Henry Herbert's declaration in his action against Betterton.[14] Herbert charges the defendant with acting without license "10 new playes and 100 revived Playes" between November 15, 1660, and May 6, 1662, the date of Herbert's action. This seems to imply that the new company began to perform at Salisbury Court on November 15. Their agreement with D'Avenant already cited clearly indicates that this season was intended merely to occupy the interim till the new house in Lincoln's Inn Fields should be ready. D'Avenant was absorbed in his operatic preparations and probably paid little attention to his troupe, aside from collecting his daily share of the receipts. This company was to become more notable than the Old Actors in Shakespearean production. But for the moment D'Avenant appears to have avoided it, doubtless because he conceived that his success with it would depend on operatic innovations at his new theatre.

There is some doubt whether this company remained at Salisbury Court until they began rehearsals for the new theatre in Lincoln's Inn Fields. In Herbert's reply (July 11, 1662) to D'Avenant's petition for relief from his interference, the indignant Master of the Revels presents Clarendon, the Lord Chancellor, with an itemized statement of the fees he considers due him. Among these he demands the customary rake-off, or, as he terms it, "allowance," "for new and old playes acted by Sir William Dauenantes pretended company of players at Salisbury Court, the Cockpitt, and now at Portugall Rowe [in Lincoln's Inn Fields], from the 5th Novemb. 60. the tyme of their first conjunction with Sir William Dauenant."[15]

There are three possibilities, if Herbert is correct in his statement that D'Avenant's company acted at the Cockpit after November 5, 1660. The first is that after the agreement made on that date they remained at the Cockpit and gave performances there, very likely because the Salisbury Court theatre was not ready for them. This would account for the sudden return of the King's Company to the Red Bull, and their inconvenient season of three days at that house. Against this hypothesis is Herbert's selection (in his declaration against Betterton) of November 15 as the date of D'Avenant's commencing operations.[16] A second possibility is that the company came back to the Cockpit in Drury Lane for at least one special performance after they had set up at Salisbury Court. And a third is that Herbert is referring to special performances in the royal Cockpit at Whitehall. That he intended to collect fees for such performances is clear enough from the last item on his schedule of "allowances": "That rehearsall of plays to be acted at court, be made, as hath been accustomed, before the Master of the Reuells, or allowance for them."

Of these possibilities the last seems to me on the whole the most likely. If Herbert were referring to performances at the Cockpit in Drury Lane before the Salisbury Court house opened, the natural order of listing the theatres would give first place to the Cockpit. Furthermore, the silence of Pepys would be hard to account for, if D'Avenant's company had given a season there. Pepys was a regular patron of theirs, and records during this period frequent visits to Salisbury Court, but none to the Cockpit in Drury Lane. Finally, the sudden removal of the King's Company to the Red Bull may have been occasioned by the ousting of Beeston from Salisbury Court and his occupation of the Cockpit in Drury Lane, where we know that his troupe was acting a little later in the season. Probably, then, Herbert's reference to the Cockpit is to the Whitehall theatre.[17]

The fact is that, from November 5, 1660, when D'Avenant organized his company, till late in June, 1661, when he opened the new theatre in Lincoln's Inn Fields, we know almost nothing of its operations, except from Pepys; and several historians have at this point been completely mystified. Downes ignores the interim except, as we shall see, regarding the location of rehearsals for the new theatre. That rather hazy reference we must leave for later discussion, for we have still to touch upon several matters of importance which took place in December, 1660.

On the eighth of that month probably occurred the first appearance of a woman as a professional actress on the English stage. She was almost certainly Mrs. Hughes, afterwards Prince Rupert's mistress, and the part was undoubtedly Desdemona.[18] We know from a list of plays drawn up by Sir Henry Herbert, and already cited in connection with the removal of the King's Company to Vere Street, that "The moore of Uenice" was acted there on Saturday, December 8, for the first time that season.[19] We have, moreover, by the old actor, Thomas Jordan, "A Prologue to introduce the first Woman that came to Act on the Stage in the Tragedy, call'd 'The Moor of Venice.'"[20] Finally, Downes gives us a cast of the play with Mrs. Hughes as Desdemona.[21]

Unfortunately, this cast appears in a list of the "old stock plays" acted by the King's Company at Drury Lane and elsewhere after 1663. Downes's information about the Theatre Royal and its antecedents was derived, he tells us, "from Mr. Charles Booth sometimes Book-keeper there"; it is even more sketchy and unreliable than Downes's account of his own company. What is more serious than the later date of Downes's cast is the fact that it includes as Emilia the name of another woman, Mrs. Rutter; for both prologue and epilogue indicate that only one woman appeared. Evidently Downes's cast represents a later performance than the first; though it could not have been very late, since Burt is cast as the Moor and Hart as Cassio. Iago, moreover, was at first played by Clun, who had great success in the part,[22] but in Downes's cast it is assigned to Mohun. As a connecting link, therefore, Downes is not very satisfactory.

On the other hand, the date falls between limits definitely fixed by Pepys, for on January 3, 1661, he went "to the Theatre [that is, Vere Street], where was acted 'Beggar's Bush,' it being very well done; and here the first time that ever I saw women come upon the stage." On November 20, 1660, he had seen the same play at the same theatre.

The conjectural date of December 8 is also strengthened by a letter written exactly one week later by Andrew Newport to Sir Richard Leveson, in which it is casually remarked that "upon our stages we have women-actors, as beyond sea." [23]

On December 12, 1660, an edict of the Lord Chamberlain set aside certain of the "old plays" as the property of D'Avenant, and forbade actors to jump from one company to the other.[24] The plays reserved for Sir William were the following of Shakespeare's: *The Tempest*, *Measure for Measure*, *Much Ado About Nothing*, *Romeo and Juliet*, *Twelfth Night*, *Henry VIII*, *King Lear*, *Macbeth*, and *Hamlet;* and also Denham's *The Sophy* and Webster's *The Duchess of Malfi*. D'Avenant had, besides, the sole right for two months to *Pericles* and to Fletcher's *The Mad Lover*, *The Maid in the Mill*, *The Spanish Curate*, *The Loyal Subject*, and *Rule a Wife and Have a Wife*. He was also allowed the exclusive right to produce his own plays.[25]

The preponderance of Shakespearean items in this list is striking; it was D'Avenant's company, as we shall see, that became most active in producing Shakespeare, though their productions would, in some cases, hardly have been recognized by the author. The fact that on Sir Henry Herbert's list of plays produced, 1660–1662, by the King's Company there are only three of Shakespeare's has been cited by Malone, Professor Odell, and other writers as indicative of Shakespeare's lack of popularity.

That Shakespeare was less popular during the early years of the Restoration than either Fletcher or Jonson is undeniable; at least, not many modern commentators have cared to deny it, though one, Mr. Montague Summers, declares that "it may be broadly affirmed that the reasonable and reasoning love of the seventeenth century for Shakespeare hardly differed from the enthusiasm of the nineteenth century in degree." [26] In so far as it applies to the Restoration, this statement is very wide of the mark. It is true that Dryden and other critics not infrequently compliment Shakespeare in terms scarcely less ardent than their gratulatory epistles and addresses to each other. But their eulogies are commonly couched in the vaguest and most general terms. Dryden's famous characterization of Shakespeare as the man "who of all modern and perhaps ancient, poets had the largest and most comprehensive soul" is a striking and sonorous saying; but it means little, especially when compared with Dryden's other utterances. When he and his colleagues turn from phrase-making to detailed examination and criticism, there is much more of objection than of praise.

Yet the appearance of but three of Shakespeare's dramas in the repertory of the Theatre Royal is not of much significance, for in its revivals that house specialized in Fletcher and Jonson, leaving to D'Avenant's company the major portion of the Shakespearean field. After the opening of its new theatre the Duke's house became famous for two special activities, the staging of "operas" and the revival of Shakespeare with scenery.

Of the plays which the Old Actors did perform, their earliest productions, *Othello*, *Henry IV* (probably only *Part One*), and *The Merry Wives*, the first two seem to have been played rather frequently throughout their career, which ended with the union of the two companies in 1682.

As for the other Shakespearean productions of the Theatre Royal, they may perhaps be mentioned as logically at this point as anywhere, for while our only exact information specifies in each case performances later than the chronological limits of this chapter, we have no reason to suppose that it refers to the original revival. Sometime between the reopening of the theatres and the date hereafter mentioned the play first saw Restoration performance; but in what season we do not know. Since, then, we are for the moment concerned with the vogue of Shakespeare at the Theatre Royal, I shall group the rest of its presumably unaltered revivals here, though recognizing that I may or may not be anticipating the actual dates of production.

The Restoration audience enjoyed Falstaff — the "humour" character had more comic force than the romantic or the humane. But *A Midsummer Night's Dream* seemed mere unsuccessful silliness. To its performance we have but one reference. On September 29, 1662, Pepys went

> to the King's Theatre, where we saw 'Midsummer's Night's Dream,' which I had never seen before, nor shall ever again, for it is the most insipid ridiculous play that ever I saw in my life. I saw, I confess, some good dancing and some handsome women, which was all my pleasure.

I find no other mention of the acting of this play before 1692, when it was tortured into an opera, under the title of *The Fairy Queen*.

The performance seen by Pepys was of course at Vere Street. It was probably unaltered, though a good deal of unnecessary dancing may have been introduced. The text was probably an early Quarto; no separate edition was published during our period. Some of the low-comedy portions of the play had been popular while the theatres were closed, as one of the "drolls" ascribed to Robert Cox. This was sundry times reprinted as *The Merry Conceited Humours of Bottom the*

Weaver. Interest in it was not, however, sufficient to outweigh the inability of the Restoration to appreciate the other parts of Shakespeare's play. Pepys's statement, however, implies previous Restoration performances, and indicates expectation of subsequent ones.

Julius Caesar seems not to have been produced till late in the career of this company. Downes places it fourteenth and last (incorrectly numbered XV) in his list of "Principal Old Stock Plays" acted at the Theatre Royal 1663–1682. He gives the following cast: Bell, Caesar; Mohun, Cassius; Hart, Brutus; Kynaston, Antony; Mrs. Marshall, Calphurnia; Mrs. Corbett, Portia.[27] Pepys did not see it. Genest observes that "as Bell acted in this play, it must have been revived about 1671." [28] (This actor perished in the Drury Lane fire of 1672.) Langbaine (publishing in 1691) states that *Julius Caesar* was revived at the Theatre Royal about fifteen years before, that is, in 1676.[29] This date coincides with a reference, found by Professor Nicoll in the Lord Chamberlain's records, to a performance before the King on Monday, December 4, 1676; there was another on Monday, April 18, 1687.[30]

In Part Two of this volume we shall glance at the problem involved in the fact that two of the Restoration Quartos are undated. For the moment suffice it to say that the first separate edition under the Restoration did not appear till after the union of the two companies. The immediate cause of publication was doubtless renewed interest inspired by Betterton's revival. The text is practically unaltered, and this was doubtless the case with the production by the Theatre Royal before the union.[31]

The cast in the four editions I have examined is the same: Goodman, Caesar; Perrin, Octavius; Kynaston, Antony; Betterton, Brutus; Smith, Cassius; Griffin, "Caska"; Saunders, Trebonius; Bowman, Ligarius; Williams, Decius; Mountfort, Metellus; Carlile, Cinna; Percival, Artemidorus; Wiltshire,

Messala; Gillow, Titinius; Jevon, Cinna the Poet; Norris, Flavius; Underhill, Lee, Bright, Plebeians; Madam Slingsby, Calphurnia; Mrs. Cook, Portia. In Brutus, Betterton presented himself for virtually direct comparison with Charles Hart. Cibber gives a spirited description of his majestic assumption of this rôle:

> A farther Excellence in Betterton was, that he could vary his Spirit to the different Characters he acted. Those wild impatient Starts, that fierce and flashing Fire, which he threw into Hotspur, never came from the unruffled Temper of his Brutus (for I have more than once seen a Brutus as warm as Hotspur): when the Betterton Brutus was provok'd in his Dispute with Cassius, his Spirit flew only to his Eye; his steady Look alone supply'd that Terror which he disdain'd an Intemperance in his Voice should rise to. Thus, with a settled Dignity of Contempt, like an unheeding Rock he repelled upon himself the Foam of Cassius.[32]

Genest records several performances of *Julius Caesar* during the last few years of the Bettertonian period. On January 14, 1707, it was given a special subscription performance, "for the encouragement of the Comedians acting in the Haymarket, and to enable them to keep the diversion of plays under a separate interest from Operas." The superb cast, one of the finest that has ever played it, included Betterton as Brutus; Verbruggen, Cassius; Wilks, Antony; Booth, Caesar; Mills, Octavius; Keen, Casca; Bowen, Cinna; Husband, Decius; Bowman, Ligarius; Johnson, Bullock, Norris, and Cross, Plebeians; Mrs. Barry, Calphurnia; Mrs. Bracegirdle, Portia.[33]

The five plays, then, which we have just discussed were all acted at Killigrew's Theatre Royal, in assumably unaltered form. This company produced, as far as we know, but three other Shakespearean dramas before 1680. After that date and before the union of 1682 they staged three more, two of which, at least, died immediately.

There appears to have been a revival of *The Taming of the Shrew* at the Theatre Royal not later than 1663. In a list

(November 3) drawn up by Sir Henry Herbert as an account of his fees, the following entry appears: "Revived Play Tam-inge the Shrew . . . [£] 1." [34] This is the only reference I have found. The text used was doubtless that of the Quarto of 1631.

The farcical character, however, of many of the scenes in this play probably lent itself from the beginning to copious gagging and even alteration. By 1667 the process had continued so far as to erect one of the low comic parts into the principal, and even title, rôle; for a reference by Pepys on April 9 points to the altered version. These changes, I suspect, were not sudden, but the result of gradual tinkering with the text. Lacy seems to have been responsible for them, though whether he formally rewrote the play is not entirely certain. Its new title was *Sauny the Scot*. Grumio becomes a North-countryman and the chief character. Pepys was ill pleased, which is highly to his credit. He found it "but a mean play; and the best part, 'Sawny,' done by Lacy, hath not half its life, by reason of the words, I suppose, not being understood, at least by me." The play, however, became very popular.

My theory is that by 1663 Shakespeare's play had been staged by the Old Actors, probably not very seriously altered; but that gradually the text was tampered with till the new version was finally written down by Lacy. It was not printed till 1698, long after its author's death. This occurred before the union of the companies; the rôle fell long afterwards to Dogget and Bullock. Powell at that time acted Petruchio, and Margaret [Katherine] was among Mrs. Mountfort's parts. The first edition gives the following cast: Johnson, Woodall; Powell, Petruchio; Thomas, Geraldo; Harland, Tranio; Mills, Winlove; Pinkethman, Snatchpenny; Haynes, Jamy; Bullock, Sauny; Mrs. Verbruggen, Margaret; Mrs. Cibber, Biancha.

Lacy's version kept Shakespeare's from the stage till the time of Garrick, who presented instead a mangled three-act affair which lasted till well into the nineteenth century and is still occasionally undertaken by misguided amateurs.

As far as we know, Lacy's *Sauny* was the only violent alteration perpetrated by the Old Actors before the epidemic of 1678–1682. It was a *tour de force* designed not to "improve" an old masterpiece but to provide a low comedian with a fat part. Degrading as Lacy's amendments are, they can scarcely challenge Professor Odell's assertion that the blame for the practice of Shakespearean alteration lies chiefly at the door of D'Avenant and Betterton.[35]

Mr. Montague Summers attributes the comparative innocence of the King's Company to "the influence and judgement of Charles Hart," [36] whom he regards as a much better actor than Betterton. Without denying that Hart's taste may have been a factor, there is reason enough to be found in the natural conservatism of the older actors, who had been brought up in the pre-Wars companies and had there obtained their notions how Shakespeare should be handled. More to the point, perhaps, is the introduction of elaborate scenery by D'Avenant. It has wrecked many a performance of Shakespeare in our own time; to a large extent it was responsible for the violent treatment of D'Avenant's revivals.

Much later in their career the King's Company produced Dryden's *All for Love* (a challenge to *Antony and Cleopatra*), and Ravenscroft's *Titus Andronicus*. The latter seems to have attained some popularity; *All for Love* had an enormous vogue. Just before the union the Theatre Royal produced two adaptations by Tate, *Richard II* and *The Ingratitude of a Commonwealth*, the latter a version of *Coriolanus*. These worthless pieces were still-born. The last production by this company was D'Urfey's *Injured Princess*, a less objectionable alteration of *Cymbeline*. We shall consider these later performances at their proper points in our chronology.

Before we turn into the new year of 1661 and trace the

establishment of D'Avenant's company in its new theatre in Lincoln's Inn Fields, there remains only to note the continued existence of Beeston's company, which we abandoned at Salisbury Court in midsummer. This troupe is of little importance and may be dismissed briefly. It was theoretically wiped out by the D'Avenant–Killigrew grant of August 21, 1660. But on December 24 its leading actor, George Jolly, received a Christmas present from the King in the form of a license (flatly contradicting that grant) to build another London theatre.[37] During the course of the previous month the Lord Chamberlain had ordered Jolly and his company at the Cockpit to desist from playing till their quarrel with Beeston, their manager, should be adjusted.[38] Apparently, upon relinquishing the Salisbury Court theatre to D'Avenant, Beeston moved to the Cockpit in Drury Lane, which had been vacated by the Old Actors, as we have seen, immediately after the organization of D'Avenant's company. How long the Beeston–Jolly troupe lasted we do not know.[39]

We come to the new year (1661), then, with four companies in existence: the King's under Killigrew certainly at the theatre in Gibbons's Tennis Court, Vere Street, Clare Market; the other patent company, under D'Avenant, almost certainly at Salisbury Court; the Beeston–Jolly company, probably at the Cockpit in Drury Lane; and, lastly, a rag, tag, and bobtail troupe which seems to have been in existence at the Red Bull and perhaps was recruited from the remnant of Rhodes's now disbanded organization. The last two of these companies need concern us no further. Nor are the performances at the Nursery of importance.[40] From this time until the secession of 1695 the patent companies had a virtual monopoly of legitimate drama in London.

Leaving the Theatre Royal established at Vere Street, we have now to trace the fortunes of their younger rivals, under D'Avenant. And precisely at this point we come plump upon a puzzling reference to a *fifth* theatre. On January 29, 1661,

Pepys asserts that he "went to Blackfryers (the first time I ever was there since plays begun), and there . . . I saw three acts of *The Mayd in ye Mill* acted to my great content." Since this play of Fletcher's was one of those reserved for two months to D'Avenant, we can be reasonably sure that this performance was by his company. This particular entry of the diarist's has been productive of many misleading notes and is responsible for some of the obscurity which has enshrouded the operations of D'Avenant's company during these months. I think I have solved the problem, or, to put it more exactly, guessed the answer; but before propounding it I must present the rest of the evidence.[41]

Downes records a solitary aberration of D'Avenant's company from Salisbury Court, as follows:

> His Company being now Compleat, Sir William in order to prepare Plays to Open his Theatre, it being then a Building in Lincoln's-Inn Fields, His Company Rehears'd the First and Second Part of the Siege of Rhodes; and the Wits at Pothecaries-Hall: And in Spring 1662, Open'd his House with the said Plays, having new Scenes and Decorations, being the first that e're were Introduc'd in England.[42]

The reader should note in the first place that Downes says nothing about *performances* at Apothecaries' Hall.[43]

On Pepys's account of his visit to "Blackfryers" Miss McAfee makes this note: "Probably . . . a theatre in what was known as Cobham House, which stood in Water Lane, Blackfriars, on the site of Apothecaries' Hall before the Great Fire."[44] She follows Wheatley: "At Apothecaries' Hall, where Davenant produced the first and second parts of 'The Siege of Rhodes.' Downes says, in his 'Roscius Anglicanus,' that Davenant's company acted at 'Pothecaries Hall' until the building in Lincoln's Inn Fields was ready."[45] But, as we have seen, Downes says explicitly that D'Avenant went to Apothecaries' Hall for *rehearsals*.

As for the identification of Pepys's "Blackfryers" with this hall, Wheatley offers no reason for making it, while Miss McAfee says merely that Cobham House stood in Water Lane, Blackfriars. But what does Pepys himself say? "Went to Blackfryers (*the first time I was ever there since plays begun*)." Obviously, then, Pepys is referring to *a regular theatre*. Let us now compare his statement with the others in which he records first visits to playhouses:

1. Pepys's first visit to the Cockpit in Drury Lane, August 18, 1660: "to the Cockpitt play, the first that I have had time to see since my coming from sea."

2. Pepys's first visit to the Red Bull, March 23, 1661: "out to the Red Bull (where I had not been since plays come up again)."

3. Pepys's first visit to the King's house, Vere Street, Clare Market, November 20, 1660: "to the new Play-house near Lincoln's-Inn-Fields (which was formerly Gibbon's tennis-court) . . . and indeed it is the finest play-house, I believe, that ever was in England."

4. Pepys's first visit to the Duke's house in Lincoln's Inn Fields, July 2, 1661: "to Sir William Davenant's Opera; this being the fourth day that it hath begun, and the first that I have seen it."

5. Pepys's first visit to Killigrew's first Drury Lane theatre. He refers on September 24, 1662, and February 6, 1663 to its building. On May 7, 1663, he writes: "This day the new Theatre Royal begins to act with scenes the Humorous Lieutenant, but I have not time to see it." His first visit was on the next day: "to the Theatre Royall, being the second day of its being opened." He goes into some detail in criticizing the construction of the new house.

The reader must have been struck by the particularity with which Pepys mentions, in every one of these cases, either that it is his first visit, or that the house is new. I have purposely omitted, for the present, the account of his first visit to the Salisbury Court theatre; but I have listed every other. From the similarity of their phraseology, and the likeness of the "Blackfryers" reference to them, it seems reasonably clear that Pepys is there, too, referring to his first visit to some public playhouse. This could not have been the famous old

Blackfriars theatre, for that had been pulled down on August 5, 1655.[46]

As Pepys's first visit to D'Avenant's company at Salisbury Court, Miss McAfee gives [47] (though not in full) the entry for February 9, 1661: "To Whitefriars to the Play-house, and saw 'The Mad Lover,' the first time I ever saw it acted, which I like pretty well." Why Pepys mentions *Whitefriars* she explains with entire clearness:

> The term 'Whitefriars' is used to designate the quarter so-called (between Fleet Street and the Thames, east of the Temple), in which stood the Salisbury Court theatre, rebuilt in 1660, and not to designate the old Whitefriars theatre of the pre-Restoration period. It will be noted from a comparison of the entries for March 19 and March 26, [1661] that Pepys used the term 'Whitefriars' and 'Salisbury Court' interchangeably.[48]

Now if this were Pepys's first visit to the Salisbury Court theatre it would be his only entry of a first visit to a public playhouse in which he failed either to mention that fact or to describe the house as new. This discrepancy neatly coincides with our inability to explain Pepys's visit to a Blackfriars theatre. What more likely than that "Blackfriars" is a slip, on the part of the transcriber, the editors, or Pepys himself, for "Whitefriars" and that the entry of January 29, 1661, records his first visit to Salisbury Court?

Such a mistake would not be unnatural even for Pepys. Though the old theatre was no more, members of the old company were still active, and its tradition was the accepted standard in matters theatrical.[49] Moreover, it was to see D'Avenant's actors that Pepys went chiefly at this time, and presumably these were at Salisbury Court on this date. The reference is pretty clearly not to Apothecaries' Hall, but to a regular theatre. Why should the Duke's company have left Salisbury Court except for performances before the King at Whitehall, or to rehearse for the new theatre in Lincoln's Inn

Fields? That they played regularly at Salisbury Court during the late winter and spring is shown by Pepys's own record; for he went there repeatedly to see plays that were on D'Avenant's reserved list. He saw Massinger's *The Bondman* three times during this period (that is, November, 1660–June, 1661), and notes that "above all that ever I saw, Betterton do the Bondman best." He saw Fletcher performed several times, and his favorite actor again in the great rôle of Deflores in *The Changeling*. The dates of Pepys's visits during this period are: February 9, 12, 23, March 1, 2, 16, 19, 25, 26, April 1, 2, 6. To these I think we can safely add the visit on January 29 to the "Blackfryers" and the three acts of *The Maid in the Mill*.

As for the rehearsals at Apothecaries' Hall, we know nothing about them. January seems an odd season for them, since the new theatre opened late in June, 1661. For this latter date Downes incorrectly specifies 1662.[50] Perhaps he is also wrong on the time of the rehearsals.

D'Avenant must have been proud man that June afternoon,[51] for he saw the fruition of a purpose cultivated for twenty-odd years. However cordially one may detest the operatic innovations which he foisted on the English drama, one can entertain only admiration for Sir William's persistence and pluck.[52]

To the first volume of Professor Odell's *Shakespeare from Betterton to Irving* the reader should turn for an exhaustive study of the mechanics of the new stage. In view of that work the briefest of summaries is called for here, and only because on that stage Shakespeare's plays were for the first time subjected to the degradation of operatic embellishment.

Throughout the Restoration period scenic art made little technical advance over the old methods at Rutland House. The inner stage of the Elizabethans had become in expanded form the principal stage; the curtain and the proscenium were just in front of it; and all the scenery was confined to it. But the principal Elizabethan stage, the outer platform, remained, though reduced, in the form of an apron projecting into the audience. On each side of the apron, below the proscenium, were the permanent stage doors, probably four (though possibly but two); these highly unrealistic means of exit and entrance persisted well into the nineteenth century. Above each of the doors nearest the audience was a window which could be employed for balcony scenes.

Instead of using the curtain to hide a change of scenes the common practice was to "draw" the flats. These were sometimes at the extreme rear of the stage, but sometimes, when the action was on the apron, close to the proscenium. In the latter case cut-outs were occasionally used, through which a distant view might be simulated. Professor Odell offers an interesting, but not entirely conclusive, argument for the existence of box sets (three walls) on this stage. But since, as he acknowledges, we know that the eighteenth century confined itself to side-wings and left the introduction of lateral walls to the Victorian theatres, it seems hardly likely that this more realistic method of setting interiors was used on the Restoration stage. Drop scenes, on the other hand, were occasionally, though rarely, employed. Properties were elaborate in the case of the operatic spectacles, but for the legitimate drama were probably not extensive. Furniture, and indeed supernumeraries, were often painted on the flats. These were regularly drawn while the scene was in progress. The curtain itself seems ordinarily not to have been dropped between the acts.

The stage (as well as the house) was lighted by candles — chiefly in chandeliers suspended from the ceiling, but possibly with a row of footlights as well. How it was darkened is not certain. Mr. Odell suggests several possibilities. Perhaps the lights behind the proscenium were extinguished; perhaps the carrying of portable lights was conventionally accepted as signifying darkness; perhaps the chandeliers on the stage could be raised or pulled out into the wings.

However crude these methods of decoration may appear in an electrical age, they seemed highly refined to the playgoers of the Restoration. Scenes and lights became an end in themselves, just as in our own time the actual twiddling of radio dials appears to interest their owners far more than the music they "get" by their manipulations. The public flocked to D'Avenant's theatre as to a new toy, and from that day to this the spoken drama has had to contend with a meretricious interest engendered by its mere setting.

The relation of the new stage to the platform of the Elizabethans is admirably summed up by Mr. Lawrence in "The Origin of the English Picture Stage."

> The English picture-stage of the seventeenth and eighteenth centuries owed its distinctiveness to the concessions which had to be made in the beginning to the usages and prejudices of players habituated to the methods of the platform-stage. As created by D'Avenant it was a happy amalgam of the prime characteristics of the platform-stage and the masque-stage of the Caroline period. Permanent entering doors and balconies the players still required to have, but as the tiring-house disappeared with the introduction of scenery, the doors and balconies had to be brought to the front and placed on either side of the proscenium arch. The apron, so long a characteristic of our theatres, was apparently born of the physical limitations of the Duke's Theatre in Lincoln's Inn Fields. In a long, narrow house, where many of the audience were situated remote from the players, it was necessary that the stage should jut out as far as possible, so that the players might come well to the front to make themselves heard. . . .Where the players or singers of old, either for the purpose of being better heard or, in an ill-lit theatre, of being better seen, confined their acting to the forepart of the stage, the effect of the mounting must have been decorative rather than realistic. Since acting on the Restoration Stage was still largely an art of rhetoric, probably this was all that D'Avenant and Killigrew aimed at. To admit this is to expose the fallaciousness of the time-honoured contention that the introduction of scenery spelled the downfall of poetic drama. Scholars have allowed themselves to be deceived by a synchronization of events in

no wise inter-related. The truth is that the great seventh wave of Elizabethan poetico-dramatic impulse had reached high water mark considerably before the Civil War and the disruption of the theatres. With Shirley, the tide had begun to ebb.[53]

With the last of these contentions the present writer is in complete agreement. Few will be found of this stiff-necked and hard-boiled generation to deplore the passing of the poetic drama. We are thankful for Mr. Yeats, but prefer Augier, Ibsen, and Mr. Shaw to Bulwer, or even Browning. Yet the relation of scenery to the seventeenth-century decadence must not be dismissed quite so easily. D'Avenant's innovations had at least two evil effects on the Restoration drama and stage. In the first place, the popular lust for spectacle was systematically catered to as never before in English theatres; no longer was the play the thing — often, not even the acting. And second, the heavy expenditures for scenes and "machines" brought both houses so near the brink of ruin that both resorted to highly illegitimate means of increasing their patronage. All this ultimately had its effect on dramatic composition.

That this was recognized by discriminating, if over-conservative, contemporaries is shown by the following passage in the *Historia Histrionica* (1699) of James Wright:

> *Lovewit.* Which I admire at; That the Town much less than at present, could then maintain Five Companies, and yet now Two can hardly subsist.
>
> *Truman.* Do not wonder, but consider, That tho' the Town was then, perhaps, not much more than half so Populous as now, yet then the Prices were small (there being no Scenes). . . . It is an Argument of the worth of the Plays and Actors, of the last Age, and easily inferr'd, that they were much beyond ours in this, to consider that they cou'd support themselves meerly from their own Merit; the weight of the Matter, and goodness of the Action, without Scenes and Machines.[54]

Richard Flecknoe, who was not at all the moron sketched by Dryden's wicked pen, takes up this question specifically in "A Discourse of the English Stage" in his *Love's Kingdom* (1664):

> Now, for the difference betwixt our Theaters and those of former times, they were but plain and simple, with no other Scenes, nor Decorations of the Stage, but onely old Tapestry, and the Stage strew'd with Rushes, (with their Habits accordingly) whereas ours now for cost and ornament are arriv'd to the heighth of Magnificence; but that which makes our Stage the better, makes our Playes the worse perhaps, they striving now to make them more for sight, th[a]n hearing; whence that solid joy of the interior is lost, and that benefit which men formerly receiv'd from Playes, from which they seldom or never went away, but far better and wiser th[a]n they came.

This contemporary testimony of Flecknoe's, if somewhat counter to Mr. Lawrence's views, is even more damaging to Professor Odell's theory that scenery was not extensively used during the first decade of our period. Against Mr. Odell's conclusions is, moreover, the emphasis laid on scenery in the contracts, patents, and other documents relating to the theatres. That the artistic value of scenery became at once a subject of debate is shown by the Duke's Theatre prologue to D'Avenant's *The Wits*, the second production at Lincoln's Inn Fields. "There are some," says D'Avenant, who holds, of course, a brief for *décor:*

> who would the World perswade,
> That Gold is better when the Stamp is bad;
> And that an ugly ragged piece of Eight
> Is ever true in metal and in weight:
> As if a Guinny and Lovis had less
> Intrinsick vallue for their handsomeness.
> So divers, who outlive the former age,
> Allow the coorseness of the plain old stage;
> And think rich Vests and Scenes are only fit
> Disguises for the want of Art and Wit.

The evil effects of the passion for spectacle can be seen with perfect clearness in the acting versions in which Shakespeare's plays appeared on this stage. In many instances the authentic texts were driven from it by mangled adaptations got up with a view to the exhibition of mechanical ingenuity and scenic splendor. Not yet, though the Restoration adaptations (all but one) have yielded, are the restored plays entirely free from scenic excess. But the current tendency in Shakespearean production, whether from aesthetic virtue or financial necessity, is clearly toward simplicity.

Shakespeare aside, the American stage has been suffering lately from an overemphasis of its mechanical resources, like the Restoration stage, in imitation of Continental models. The movement began as a healthy reaction against the Child's Restaurant realism of the early twentieth century. Discontent is of course a hopeful sign; but the devotees of this new branch of the Fine Arts are making of it an esoteric cult. I suppose no one would be willing to abolish scenery entirely. Yet the fact remains that on our present stage the greatest masterpieces of our drama cannot be presented. They are still cut up and botched, in text and in structure — which means inevitably in characterization as well. Instead of striving to get back a little closer to the stage for which these great plays were written, the *précieux* who occupy themselves with the problems of lighting and scenery have run mad in the opposite direction. Lighting is now the most important factor in really artistic production, for the experts are not willing to make it serve the drama, but insist on playing with it. And the well-constructed dramatic review now begins with a paragraph or two on the dominant color-tone of the first set. We are slighting the human values, and our acting suffers — it too has become largely pictorial.

During the last decade ism has succeeded ism in the theatre, but the same false emphasis has been common to all. The heavy-handed literalism of Mr. Belasco has yielded on the one hand to a pretentious simplicity, on the other to the sheer craziness of expressionism. Behind both schools lurks the triumphant shade of Sir William D'Avenant, who put pictorialism on the English stage to stay. For the vital issue is not, and never was, realism versus impressionism, expressionism, or constructivism; but words versus materials, the actor versus the scene. I am well aware that this is not a popular thesis in these times, and accordingly refer the reader to the ablest plea on the right side: it is to be found in a recent volume by Mr. Frank Vernon, *The Twentieth Century Theatre*, one of the sanest essays on the stage ever written.

Mr. Vernon, I infer, is not subject to academic inhibitions; he becomes pleasantly profane on the subject of the eye versus the ear in the legitimate theatre. I am content to end this chapter with one of his milder purgative pills for a sick stage: "When the theatre receives 'decoration,' except in the most limited doses, it has indigestion." Or still better, with his version of a wise saying of Anatole France: "Be sure a single beautiful line has wrought the world more good than all the masterpieces of mechanism."

Notes to Chapter II

1. For the terms of the agreement see Adams, *Dram. Rec.*, pp. 96–100; Malone (1803) iii, 309–315, (*Var.*) iii, 257 f.; Halliwell-Phillipps, pp. 27 f. The document thus reprinted is a copy of the agreement, made for Herbert's use in his subsequent legal action against the patentees.
2. Adams, *Dram. Rec.*, pp. 116–118; Malone (1803) iii, 329–332, (*Var.*) iii, 273; Halliwell-Phillipps, pp. 34 f. According to Professor Adams the MS. reads "Gibbon's." The name was actually Gibbons.
3. Adams, *Dram. Rec.*, p. 116, reprints "Henry the fourthe. First Play. Acted at the New Theatre." According to the reprints of Malone and Halliwell-Phillipps, there is no point after "First Play."
4. James Wright, *Historia Histrionica*, reprinted, Lowe's ed. of Cibber, I, xxxi f.
5. See Cunningham–Wheatley, *London Past and Present*, iii, 153 f. For its previous history see Adams, *Shakespearean Playhouses*, pp. 294–309.
6. Lawrence, ii, 139.
7. See Herbert's list of plays acted by the King's Company 1660–1662 (Adams, *Dram. Rec.*, pp. 116 f.) Mr. Lawrence doubtless had in mind the first (Restoration) season at the Red Bull, which ended when the united company took over the Cockpit.
8. See, for example, Pepys's *Diary* for March 23, 1661, and the allusion in *The Playhouse to be Let* (Act I), D'Avenant's *Dramatic Works* (ed. Maidment and Logan), iv, 20.
9. Adams, *Dram. Rec.*, p. 116.
10. Dr. Sprague gives me this reference. (*Shakspere Allusion Book*, ii, 386.)
11. Downes, p. 47. Cf. Genest, ii, 307 f.
12. William Jaggard, *Shakespeare Bibliography*, p. 405.
13. There they acted till they built the first Drury Lane house in 1663. Dr. Sprague informs me that Dr. Edward Browne (Brit. Mus., Sloane MS. 1900. See Sprague, *Beaumont and Fletcher*, pp. 21–24; Hotson, *Studies in Philology*, xx, 433) saw *Hamlet* and *The Law against Lovers* at Lincoln's Inn Fields, and *Othello* at the Cockpit in Drury Lane. Browne's memoranda are not individually dated but appear to refer to performances in 1662. The reference to *Othello*, and the initials K. P., cited by Dr. Hotson, indicate that the King's Players went back to the Cockpit for a time. Perhaps repairs at Vere Street made this necessary, just as D'Avenant had to return to Salisbury Court for a few weeks while the stage of Lincoln's Inn Fields was being altered.
14. Malone (1803) iii, 316. In December, 1661, Herbert had won a similar case against Mohun and several other members of the King's Company. The verdict is referred to in a treaty of amity between Killigrew and Herbert drawn up June 4, 1662 (Adams, *Dram. Rec.*, pp. 113–115), and in a subsequent agreement by Killigrew to pay the costs of Herbert's suit against his own actors (Adams, *Dram. Rec.*, pp. 115, 116).

15. The whole document is reprinted as follows: Adams, *Dram. Rec.*, pp. 120–123; Malone (1803) iii, 320–324, (*Var.*) iii, 266 f.
16. Adams, *Dram. Rec.*, pp. 108–110; Halliwell-Phillipps, pp. 39 f.
17. Malone is vague on this point. He says: "On the 15th of Nov. 1660, Sir William D'Avenant's company began to act under these articles at the theatre in Salisbury-court, at which house or at the Cockpit they continued to play till March or April, 1662." Malone (1803) iii, 315 f. (The opening of the new theatre was actually in June, 1661.) On p. 332 Malone says that D'Avenant's company "after having played for some time at the Cockpit in Drury Lane, and at Salisbury Court, removed . . ."
18. See Lowe, *Betterton*, pp. 79–81. Mr. Lawrence (ii, 137) is not inclined to attach much weight to the Jordan reference, since Pepys gives us our first "definite foothold." The Newport letter (cited, p. 40) now affords an earlier one.
19. Adams, *Dram. Rec.*, p. 117; Malone (1803) iii, 329.
20. Quoted by Montague Summers (*Shakespeare Adaptations*, pp. xxii f.) from the rare collection *A Royal Arbor of Loyal Poesie*. Also by Malone (1803) iii, 135. H. G. Norton (*Shaks. Soc. Papers*, iv [1849], 140–142) gives, also by Thomas Jordan, "A Prologue to the Comedy call'd The Tamer Tamed [Fletcher's *The Woman's Prize*], June 24. 1660," which he quotes from *A Nursery of Novelties in Variety of Poetry*. I think no one has noticed that this date fell on a Sunday. Norton believed that this play "must have been performed at the Red Bull," though I find nothing in his citations to indicate whether it was at that theatre, the Cockpit in Drury Lane, or the Salisbury Court, except that the piece follows "'a Speech' made at the Red Bull on the very day preceding, reproving the auditors in the pit for rising and coming upon the stage before the play was ended." It is possible, but not certain, that there is in Jordan's Prologue a reference to this episode; which establishes, I suppose, a presumption in favor of the Red Bull. The piece is followed by "The Epilogue, spoken by the Tamer, a Woman." This has been taken to indicate the presence of an actress in the cast, but the language hardly substantiates this view. John Payne Collier (MS. *Hist. Rest. Stage*, p. 24 n.) points out that Pepys saw this play later, on Oct. 30, 1660, two months before, as he tells us, he saw the first woman come upon the stage.
21. Downes, pp. 6 f.
22. Pepys complains (Feb. 6, 1669) of what he considers the inferior acting of Mohun in the part. Clun was waylaid and killed by a robber in the summer of 1664.
23. Hist. MSS Com., 5: 158.
24. See Lowe, *Betterton*, pp. 75 f.
25. Professor Nicoll (*Restoration Drama*, pp. 315, 316) has discovered among the Lord Chamberlain's records two similar lists, which, however, were not drawn up till 1668, and will therefore be mentioned later.

26. Montague Summers, *Shakespeare Adaptations*, pp. xvii f. For a systematic study of the vogue of Fletcher see Dr. A. C. Sprague, *Beaumont and Fletcher on the Restoration Stage.*
27. Downes, p. 8.
28. Genest, i, 339.
29. Langbaine, *An Account of the English Dramatick Poets* (1691), p. 458.
30. Nicoll, *Dryden as an Adapter of Shakespeare*, p. 32.
31. See, however, Killigrew's letter suggesting alterations for *Julius Caesar*, in *Shakspere Allusion Book*, ii, 98–102.
32. Cibber, i, 103, 104.
33. Genest, ii, 363.
34. Adams, *Dram. Rec.*, p. 138.
35. Odell, i, 24, 41.
36. Montague Summers, *Shakespeare Adaptations*, p. xxx.
37. *Calendar State Papers* (Domestic Series), 1663–1664, p. 214; Fitzgerald, *New Hist.*, i, 26; Lowe, *Betterton*, p. 62 and n.; Lawrence, "A Forgotten Restoration Playhouse," *Englische Studien*, xxxv, 279–289; and Hotson's later and more authoritative article, "George Jolly, Actor-Manager: New Light on the Restoration Stage," *Studies in Philology*, xx, (Oct., 1923) 422–443. Dr. Hotson gives copious references to the German historians of the theatre who have established that George Jolly was from 1648 till 1659 leader of a troupe of English players in Germany, and that, as Mr. Lawrence surmised, he met Charles II there (at Frankfort Fair in 1655).
38. See Lowe, *Betterton*, p. 62.
39. See Hotson, in *Studies in Philology*, xx, 422–443.
40. With Mr. Lawrence's conclusion ("Restoration Stage Nurseries," Herrig's *Archiv*, New Series, xxxii, 301–315) that youngsters from the Nurseries acted at the regular theatres I am unable to agree. Pepys's entry for March 3, 1669, when he saw a play at the Duke's "acted only by the young people of the house," appears to refer to a performance by regular actors. This is Dr. Hotson's view (*Studies in Philology*, xx, 442). I had independently reached the same conclusion.
41. This attempt to resolve "The Blackfriars Mystery" appeared originally in *Modern Philology*, xxiv (Nov., 1926), 173–180.
42. Downes, p. 20. The date of the opening was actually 1661, as we shall see later.
43. Joseph Knight (preface to his edition of Downes, pp. xxiv f.) follows Cunningham's *Hand-Book to London* (cf. Cunningham-Wheatley, *London Past and Present*, i, 55) in stating that Apothecaries' Hall was not built till 1670, and in assuming the existence of an earlier structure. Professor Kittredge notes that the building in question was purchased by the Society of Apothecaries from Ann Lady Howard of Effingham in 1632 for a hall. It lasted till it was destroyed by the Fire of 1666. There was, therefore, an Apothecaries' Hall at the time mentioned by Downes. See C. R. B. Barrett, *The History of the Society of Apothecaries*, pp. 42–43, 77–78, 79 f.
44. Helen McAfee, *Pepys on the Restoration Stage*, p. 289, n. 1.

45. Pepys's *Diary*, ed. Wheatley, i, 312, n. 2. Professor Nicoll ends his discussion of the "wandering troupes" of the Restoration by noting that Pepys "mentions a performance at the Blackfriars" (*Restoration Drama*, p. 279); but later (p. 280) he omits this house from his list of "theatres already mentioned."
46. "Notes on London Churches and Buildings, A.D. 1631–1658," *Harrison's England*, vol. ii (New Shaks. Soc.), cited by Cunningham–Wheatley, *London Past and Present*, i, 201.
47. *Pepys on the Restoration Stage*, p. 302.
48. This use of "Whitefriars" for the Salisbury Court theatre is in fact not uncommon. See, *e. g.*, H. Moseley's letter of Aug. 30, 1660, to Sir Henry Herbert (Adams, *Dram. Rec.*, p. 90.)
49. Witness Herbert's order to the Cockpit players (Oct. 13, 1660) to reduce their prices to the old Blackfriars' scale. (Adams, *Dram. Rec.*, pp. 93, 94.) Also the references to Blackfriars plays in the Restoration play lists as reprinted by Professor Nicoll in his *Restoration Drama*. *E. g.* (p. 314): "Whereas Sr William Davenant, Knight hath humbly p^r^sented to us a proposition of reformeinge some of the most ancient Playes that were playd at Blackfriers . . ." (p. 315): "A Catalogue of part of His Ma^tes^ Servants Playes as they were formerly acted at the Blackfryers & now allowed of to his Ma^tes^ Servants at ye New Theatre."
50. On this point see Genest, i, 38; Lowe, *Betterton*, pp. 83, 84; Pepys for July and August, 1661; McAfee, p. 295, n. 1.
51. The hour for beginning performances varied during the period under discussion. At this date it was probably about three in the afternoon. By the end of the century, plays were advertised to begin promptly at five, and only a few years later at six. (Odell, i, 16–18.)
52. A momentarily puzzling reference to a theatre in Lincoln's Inn Fields occurs in Evelyn's *Diary* under date of Jan. 25, 1661: "After divers years since I had seen any play, I went to see acted The Scornful Lady, at a new theatre in Lincoln's Inn Fields." This play of Fletcher's is listed by Downes among the "old stock plays" of the Theatre Royal, and consequently could not have been seen in D'Avenant's theatre. The King's house in Vere Street, Clare Market, was near Lincoln's Inn Fields until newer buildings shut it off. Pepys himself refers, on Nov. 20, 1660, to "the new playhouse *near* Lincoln's Inn Fields (which was formerly Gibbon's tennis-court);" doubtless Evelyn refers to the same house. So does Dr. Edward Browne (Sprague, *Beaumont and Fletcher*, p. 22). This use by contemporaries of the same name for different theatres is typical of the difficulties that beset the historian of this period.
53. *Studies in the Elizabethan Playhouse, Second Series*, pp. 145–147.
54. Wright, *Historia Histrionica*, in Lowe's ed. of Cibber; see vol. i, p. xxvii.

CHAPTER III

THE TWO HOUSES

From D'Avenant's Opening at Lincoln's Inn Fields to the Union of the Companies (June, 1661–November 16, 1682)

THE success of the picture-stage was immediate. On the fourth of July, 1661, Pepys went to the other house; his report shows vividly enough what the public wanted:

> In the afternoon I went to the Theatre, and there I saw [Killigrew's] *Claracilla* (the first time I ever saw it), well acted. But strange to see this house, that used to be so thronged, now empty since the Opera begun; and so will continue for a while, I believe.

The new theatre stood in Portugal Row, on the south side of Lincoln's Inn Fields. It was known as the Duke's, being under the special patronage of James, as Killigrew's house was of Charles. It was also called the "Opera," a title which indicates the importance of D'Avenant's innovations. But it was referred to chiefly as the Theatre in Lincoln's Inn Fields. Like the Theatre Royal, it was a remodelled tennis court.

The more important of the actors who comprised the company have already been named; with the exception of Harris, they had been members of Rhodes's troupe at the Cockpit in Drury Lane. Harris began to act upon the opening in Lincoln's Inn Fields; among his parts were Horatio, Romeo, Macduff, Sir Andrew Aguecheek, Cardinal Wolsey, Truman Junior in Cowley's *Cutter of Coleman Street*, Duke Ferdinand in Webster's *The Duchess of Malfi*, Henry V in Orrery's play, Richmond in Caryl's *The English Princess*, and Ulysses in Dryden's *Troilus and Cressida*.

Downes records that the four principal actresses were boarded by D'Avenant at his own house. Foremost among

HENRY HARRIS AS CARDINAL WOLSEY

these was Mrs. Saunderson,[1] who became, about 1663, the wife of Betterton. Perhaps her greatest rôle was Lady Macbeth. She played Ophelia to her husband's Hamlet, and Juliet to Harris's Romeo. Other important parts were Queen Katharine in *Henry the Eighth*, the superb title rôle in *The Duchess of Malfi*, Ianthe in D'Avenant's *The Siege of Rhodes*, Princess Katharine in Orrery's *Henry V*, Belinda in Etherege's *The Man of Mode*, Evandra in Shadwell's *Timon*, Jocasta in Dryden and Lee's *Oedipus*, and Andromache in Dryden's *Troilus*. She survived Betterton, though she retired in 1694 on a pension of one pound a week from the company. "When she quitted the Stage,"says Cibber, "several good Actresses were the better for her Instruction."

The second woman was the unfortunate Mrs. Davenport, who played, among other parts, the Queen in *Hamlet*. Her betrayal by Aubrey de Vere, twentieth Earl of Oxford, is one of the most brutal escapades recorded of those rake-helly aristocrats. Another member of D'Avenant's company was the notorious Moll Davis, later a rival of Nelly Gwyn of the Theatre Royal, both as an exponent of "breeches parts" and as co-sharer in the affections of Charles. She it was who sang "My Lodging it is on the Cold Ground" with such charm and good fortune. Others of D'Avenant's actresses were Mrs. Long, the Duke of Richmond's mistress, and Mrs. Anne Gibbs, afterwards the wife of Thomas Shadwell.

About a year after the opening in Lincoln's Inn Fields the company was strengthened by the engagement of five new actors, two of whom became important members of it. Sandford was the foremost villain of his day and was so thoroughly identified with such parts in the mind of his public that, according to Cibber, they refused on one occasion to accept him miscast as a virtuous character. His person was to blame, not he; Tony Aston calls him "Round-shoulder'd, Meagre-fac'd, Spindle-shank'd, Splay-footed, with a sour Countenance, and long lean Arms." It was his hideous aspect that barred him from Thespian respectability. Thus, notes Cibber in an epigram that almost comes off, he was "admir'd by the Judicious, while the Crowd only prais'd him by their Prejudice."

Cibber attributes to Sandford's natural defects the vogue, among other actors of villains, for extravagance in make-up, and on Betterton's authority retails the famous witticism of the Merry Monarch at the expense of (probably) the Earl of Shaftesbury. Observing the frightful get-up of the murderers in *Macbeth*, Charles, who was notably dark-complexioned, turned gaily to the other occupants of his box and inquired, "Pray, what is the Meaning that we never see a Rogue in a Play, but, Godsfish! they always clap him on a black Perriwig? when it is well known one of the greatest Rogues in England always wears a fair one?" [2]

A curious rôle of Sandford's was Banquo's Ghost, Banquo in the flesh being played by Smith. He was the original Foresight in Congreve's *Love for Love*. Cibber says that, had this actor been at Drury Lane rather than among the seceders at Little Lincoln's Inn Fields when the famous alteration of *Richard III* was being produced, he would have offered Sandford the title rôle. That being out of the question, Cibber acted it, he asserts, as he thought Sandford would have done. Whether Master Colley is attempting to praise Sandford or himself at this point is not entirely clear. This actor retired about the end of the century, and seems to have died about 1704–1705.

To William Smith fell, besides Banquo, a number of excellent parts, among them Horatio, Cassius, Antonio in Webster's *The Duchess of Malfi*, Buckingham in *Henry VIII*, Colonel Bruce in Etherege's *The Comical Revenge, or Love in a Tub*, Courtall in his *She Would if She Could*, Sir Fopling Flutter in his *The Man of Mode*, Hector in Dryden's *Troilus and Cressida*, Young Marius in Otway's *Caius Marius*, Edgar in Tate's *Lear*, and Pierre in Otway's *Venice Preserved*. He eventually became

Betterton's second man. His career lasted from about 1663 to 1696.

Of the two great innovations that had transformed the English theatrical world, to Killigrew, as we have seen, belongs the credit of the first, the employment of actresses, though his priority was probably due merely to his opening his new theatre before D'Avenant was able to open his: the engagement of actresses had been on the cards from the beginning. D'Avenant had countered by adopting the same policy, and then proceeded to deliver a knock-down blow with his painted scenes. His fine company of youthful performers, who, if they lacked the finish of their rivals, had at their head one of the greatest actors the English stage has ever known, was all the rage.

Killigrew was not the sort of person to be tamely counted out. He began at once to lay plans for a new theatre and the employment of scenery. On December 20, 1661, he leased the ground on which he later erected the first Theatre Royal in Drury Lane. Doubtless he buzzed about the King, who probably disliked intervening in the bickerings of the theatres almost as much as he was bored by the graver concerns of government. Killigrew appears to have pestered him to such an extent that he determined to clarify the whole situation by issuing two new patents, one to Killigrew, the other to D'Avenant. Killigrew's was issued on April 25, 1662.[3] On January 15, 1663, a similar patent was granted to D'Avenant,[4] who had already found the stage at Lincoln's Inn Fields too narrow for his scene-mad mind. These documents mark the final step in the establishment of the theatrical monopoly, which with few and occasional exceptions controlled the performance of legitimate drama in London for nearly two centuries.

That D'Avenant was impatient with the limitations of his new stage we may infer from a reference by Pepys to alterations at Lincoln's Inn Fields within a few months of the opening of the new theatre. Indeed, in the prologue to the second part of *The Siege of Rhodes*, the first production at Lincoln's Inn Fields, there is a complaint against the inadequacy of that stage:

> But many Trav'lers here as Judges come;
> From Paris, Florence, Venice, and from Rome:
> Who will describe, when any Scene we draw,
> By each of ours, all that they ever saw.
> Those praising, for extensive bredth and height,
> And inward distance to deceive the sight.
> When greater Objects, moving in broad Space,
> You rank with lesser, in this narrow Place,
> Then we like Chess-men, on a Chess-board are,
> And seem to play like Pawns the Rhodian War.
> Oh Money! Money! If the WITS would dress,
> With Ornaments, the present face of Peace;
> And to our Poet half that Treasure spare,
> Which Faction gets from Fools to nourish War;
> Then his contracted Scenes should wider be,
> And move by greater Engines, till you see
> (Whilst you Securely sit) fierce Armies meet,
> And raging Seas disperse a fighting Fleet.

On October 21, 1661, Pepys went "to the Opera, which is now newly begun to act again, after some alteracion of their scene, which do make it very much worse." The play was D'Avenant's *Love and Honour*, listed by Downes fourth among the productions at Lincoln's Inn Fields. It seems likely that during the progress of the alterations the company returned to Salisbury Court. Pepys refers but once to a performance there later than April 6, 1661, and its date agrees with this hypothesis. On September 9, 1661, he saw Ford's *'Tis Pity She's a Whore* at this theatre.[5]

During the initial season at Lincoln's Inn Fields, D'Avenant staged several notable revivals of Shakespeare. Foremost in time and importance was his production of *Hamlet*. According to Downes, D'Avenant opened the new theatre with *The Siege of Rhodes*, which had the magnificent run, as it then was, of twelve days. Next came D'Avenant's own comedy, *The Wits*, which ran eight days; and then *Hamlet*. Downes fails to specify the run, but assures us that "no succeeding Tragedy for several Years got more Reputation, or Money to the Company than this."

In Thomas Betterton the title rôle found one of its greatest exponents. There is abundant testimony that this sterling actor gave an eloquent and moving interpretation of the part. Colley Cibber, who saw him play it many times, has left a vivid description of his bearing in the scene with the Ghost. (The testimony of Barton Booth has been cited above, p. 10.)

You have seen a Hamlet perhaps, who, on the first Appearance of his Father's Spirit, has thrown himself into all the straining Vociferation requisite to express Rage and Fury, and the House has thunder'd with Applause; tho' the mis-guided Actor was all the while (as Shakespear terms it) tearing a Passion into Rags [6] — I am the more bold to offer you this particular Instance, because the late Mr. Addison, while I sate by him to see this Scene acted, made the same Observation, asking me, with some Surprize, if I thought Hamlet should be in so violent a Passion with the Ghost, which, tho' it might have astonish'd, it had not provok'd him? for you may observe that in this beautiful Speech the Passion never rises beyond an almost breathless Astonishment, or an Impatience, limited by filial Reverence, to enquire into the suspected Wrongs that may have rais'd him from his peaceful Tomb! and a Desire to know what a Spirit so seemingly distrest might wish or enjoin a sorrowful Son to execute towards his future Quiet in the Grave? This was the Light into which Betterton threw this Scene; which he open'd with a Pause of mute Amazement! then rising slowly to a solemn, trembling Voice, he made the Ghost equally terrible to the Spectator as to himself! and in the descriptive Part of the natural Emotions which the ghastly Vision gave him, the boldness of his Expostulation was still govern'd by Decency, manly, but not braving; his Voice never rising into that seeming Outrage or wild Defiance of what he naturally rever'd. But alas! to preserve this medium, between mouthing and meaning too little, to keep the Attention more pleasingly awake by a temper'd Spirit than by meer Vehemence of Voice, is of all the Master-strokes of an Actor the most difficult to reach. In this none yet have equall'd Betterton.[7]

Betterton seems not to have acted in *Hamlet* before its production with scenes in 1661 at D'Avenant's "opera" in Lincoln's Inn Fields. From then on, for nearly fifty years, he played it constantly. Steele's tribute to the Hamlet of his old age has already been quoted (p. 9). Tony Aston did not, like Steele, find youth in Betterton's performance, but he concedes its excellence as well as its popularity.

I have often wish'd that Mr. Betterton would have resign'd the Part of Hamlet to some young Actor, (who might have Personated, though not have Acted, it better) for, when he threw himself at Ophelia's Feet, he appear'd a little too grave for a young Student, lately come from the University of Wirtemberg; and his Repartees seem'd rather as Apopthegms from a sage Philosopher, than the sporting Flashes of a Young Hamlet; and no one else could have pleas'd the Town, he was so rooted in their Opinion.[8]

As we have seen, *Pericles* was probably the only Shakespearean revival of Rhodes's company. *Hamlet* was among the plays reserved for D'Avenant by the order of December 12, 1660. It evidently held a prominent place on his list of projects for the new theatre. Though the contrary is often asserted, there is no record of its being acted while the company was at Salisbury Court; if it had been, Pepys would surely have seen it — his visits to that theatre in the late winter and spring of 1660–1661 were numerous.

The diarist saw *Hamlet* for the first time at Lincoln's Inn Fields on August 24, 1661: "To the Opera, and there saw *Hamlet, Prince of Denmark*, done with scenes very well, but above all, Betterton did the prince's part beyond imagination." Subsequent performances were seen by him on November 27 and December 5, 1661, May 28, 1663, and August 31, 1668. On the last occasion he was, as always, "mightily pleased with it; but, above all, with Betterton, the best part, I believe, that ever man acted." This may have been the view of most men of taste, yet a voice from the court is not so enthusiastic: on November 26, 1661, says John Evelyn, "I saw *Hamlet Prince of Denmark* played; but now the old plays beg[i]n to disgust this refined age, since his Majesty's being so long abroad."

Downes gives the cast:

> The Tragedy of Hamlet; Hamlet being Perform'd by Mr. Betterton, Sir William (having seen Mr. Taylor of the Black-Fryars Company Act it, who being Instructed by the Author Mr. Shaksepeur) taught Mr. Betterton in every Particle of it; which by his exact Performance of it, gain'd him Esteem and Reputation, Superlative to all other Plays Horatio by Mr. Harris; The King by Mr. Lilliston; The Ghost by Mr. Richards, (after by Mr. Medburn) Polonius by Mr. Lovel; Rosencrans by Mr. Dixon; Guilderstern by Mr. Price; 1st, Grave-maker, by Mr. Underhill: The 2d, by Mr. Dacres; The Queen, by Mrs. Davenport; Ophelia, by Mrs. Sanderson.[9]

The Quarto of 1676 (followed by those of 1683, 1695, and 1703) gives a later cast: "Claudius, Crosby; Hamlet, Betterton; Horatio, Smith; Marcellus, Lee; Polonius, Noake [*i. e.*, James Nokes]; Laertes, Young; Rosincraus, Norris; Guildenstern, Cademan; Fortinbras, Percival; Ostrick, Jeuan [*i. e.*, Jevon]; Barnardo, Rathband; Francisco, Floyd; Ghost, Medburn; Grave-makers, Undril [*i. e.*, Underhill] and Williams; Gertrard, Mrs. Shadwel; Ophelia, Mrs. Betterton." Later Ophelias were Mrs. Bracegirdle, Mrs. Mountfort, Mrs. Cross, Miss Santlow (afterwards Mrs. Barton Booth), and Mrs. Bradshaw. Not all these ladies were regularly in possession of the part, which was a favorite for benefit performances. Later Gertrudes were Mrs. Knight and Mrs. Porter. Wilks succeeded to the title rôle, which he occasionally acted during the last years of Betterton's career, when the veteran's appearances were less frequent. Booth played, at various times, Horatio, Laertes, and the Ghost.[10] The First Gravedigger was one of Cave Underhill's most celebrated parts. It was afterwards played by Dogget, who sometimes acted Polonius as well. Estcourt also played the Gravedigger.

Colley Cibber gives an account of the performance of January 15, 1708, on the occasion of the first appearance of the reunited company at Drury Lane. According to the Old Style, the year was, of course, 1707, during which England and Scotland had become one kingdom. Estcourt, who on this occasion doubled the Gravedigger and the Prologue in the Mouse Trap, inserted a line — apparently he had not been listening to the advice of Hamlet earlier in the scene. He read the prologue thus, according to Cibber:

> For Us, and for our Tragedy,
> Here stooping to your Clemency,
> *This being a Year of Unity,*
> We beg your Hearing patiently.

"This new Chronological Line," Cibber adds, "coming unexpectedly upon the Audience, was received with Applause, tho' several grave Faces look'd a little out of Humour at it." [11]

The text of the Restoration production was badly mangled, and must be reckoned among the altered versions, a fact that has escaped the notice of previous writers on this subject. I shall cite in Part Two (see pp. 178 ff.) of the work in hand a number of passages illustrative of the condition of the text, and also give my reasons for believing that D'Avenant himself was responsible for the revision.

About a month after *Hamlet*, D'Avenant revived *Twelfth Night*, Betterton exhibiting his remarkable versatility by playing Sir Toby Belch. The only other actors mentioned by Downes are Harris, Sir Andrew; Underhill, Feste; Lovel, Malvolio; Mrs. Gibbs, Olivia.[12] This assignment of parts is of some importance. Lovel was by no means a first-rate actor, and his selection for Malvolio, while Betterton and Harris played the two knights, shows where the emphasis went. The Malvolio-*simpático* of Mr. Sothern and others is undoubtedly a romantic invention. But one who has seen Mr. Max Montesole's exquisite performance may legitimately shudder to think what Cave Underhill must have done to the delicate rôle of Feste. The Viola is not even mentioned by Downes — a curious omission, which has by some scholars been taken as proof positive that the play was acted in an altered version. I should ordinarily infer the absence of an altered edition to imply that the play was acted unaltered. But the fact that the romantic comedies had no charm for the Restoration audience probably accounts for the failure to address the reading public. If the romantic plot were eradicated there would not be much left to print. Supposing that the play were thus altered, it is likely that a good deal of new buffoonery was interpolated *ad libitum*.

Without alteration *Twelfth Night* could have been no food for Restoration palates. On September 11, 1661, Pepys,

> walking through Lincoln's Inn Fields observed at the Opera a new play, "Twelfth Night," was acted there, and the King there; so I, against my own mind and resolution, could not forbear to go in, which did make the play seem a burthen to me, and I took no pleasure at all in it; and so after it was done went home with my mind troubled for my going thither, after my swearing to my wife that I would never go to a play without her.

Since Pepys saw the first performance of *Romeo and Juliet* on March 1, 1662, the order of the plays as given by Downes cannot be accurate. Accordingly we must recognize *Twelfth Night* as D'Avenant's second revival of Shakespeare. On Twelfth Day, January 6, 1663, Pepys saw it again "acted well, though it be but a silly play, and not related at all to the name or day." On January 20, 1669,[13] he saw it for the third and last (recorded) time "as it is now revived," but still found it "one of the weakest plays that ever I saw on the stage."

In the absence of any altered text we have only the clue afforded by Downes's failure to mention Viola, the Duke, Sebastian, and Antonio. These omissions look suspicious, and it is possible that the Orsino–Viola plot was cut completely. We can be certain that even if the letter were preserved, the spirit of Shakespeare's play was ruthlessly violated. There was not one separate edition, altered or unaltered, till 1703, when

Burnaby published his asinine *Love Betrayed*, which we shall be obliged to deal with later.

Pepys's references to *Twelfth Night* are often cited in his despite; unfairly, if the version he saw was violently altered. I have revised my earlier opinion of the probabilities, as follows. Downes says that *Twelfth Night* had a "mighty success." The emphasis of this performance was undoubtedly on the farcical rather than the romantic scenes. Pepys's references show that the play held the stage. If it had been acted lyrically and romantically it could never have done so in that age. Therefore, the chances are that the play underwent a considerable revision. In my opinion Pepys's comments are probably indicative of his superior taste. I find it hard to believe that one who insisted on perpetrating a musical setting of "To be or not to be" would have been insensible to the lyricism of *Twelfth Night* had its romantic scenes been presented.

Downes's failure to list certain characters is not, however, *prima facie* evidence that they were not acted. He does not mention the Nurse in his description of D'Avenant's production of *Romeo and Juliet* in 1662. Yet there can be little doubt that this rôle was performed by James Nokes with uproarious applause.

In the edict of December 12, 1660, certain plays (we have seen) were reserved for D'Avenant's company (see p. 40). These, according to the Lord Chamberlain's records, Sir William proposed "to reform and make fit for the Company of Actors appointed under his direction and command." The first of the revivals of 1662 was one of his most distorted versions. It was produced at least as early as February 18, when Pepys informs us he saw "'The Law against Lovers,' a good play and well performed, especially the little girl's (whom I never saw act before) dancing and singing."

What Pepys actually saw was a mangled version of *Measure for Measure*, into which D'Avenant has introduced Benedick and Beatrice from *Much Ado about Nothing*. The saucy pair are woven into the plot with a laborious ingenuity worthy of a better cause; but, though they outwardly conform, they are hopelessly out of their native element. Downes lists *The Law against Lovers* among the "other Plays" (than the stock pieces) acted at Lincoln's Inn Fields, 1661–1665.[14] His failure to enlarge upon the performance is pretty good evidence that the play was not particularly successful. Professor Odell is doubtless right in suggesting that it never became popular, but his statement that he finds no record of its being acted again [15] overlooks Evelyn's mention of a performance before the King on December 17, 1662. A list of actors was not supplied when the play was printed. I should guess that Betterton played Angelo; and Harris, Benedick.

D'Avenant's next Shakespearean offering was *Romeo and Juliet*. Betterton acted Mercutio; Harris, Romeo; and the future Mrs. Betterton, Juliet. Price played Paris, and Richards, Friar Lawrence. Sandford and Underhill made the most of Sampson and Gregory. Downes does not tell us who played the Nurse; doubtless it was James Nokes, who afterwards performed that part in Otway's adaptation. In spite of Downes's mention of "Count Paris's Wife" in a now unprintable anecdote, it appears that *Romeo and Juliet* was at first acted unaltered.

This tragedy was acted on March 1, 1662, when Pepys went

to the Opera, and there saw *Romeo and Juliet* the first time it was ever acted; but it is a play of itself the worst that ever I heard in my life, and the worst acted that ever I saw these people do, and I am resolved to go no more to see the first time of acting, for they were all of them out more or less.

The play was revived at least once after its production, as we learn from Downes:

The Tragedy of Romeo and Juliet, was made some time after into a Tragi-comedy, by Mr. James Howard, he preserving Romeo and Juliet alive; so that when the Tragedy was Reviv'd again, 'twas Play'd Alternately, Tragical one day, and Tragicomical another; for several Days together.

On the whole I am inclined to accept this plan as one of the most valuable, though neglected, contributions of the Restoration stage. What a boon to the theatrical public to-day if all "serious" plays now appearing did so in two versions! Then one could choose his evening according to his mood, and those whose lungs are only reasonably tickle of the sere would not attend the same performances as those who found humorous possibilities in the more harrowing moments of *He Who Gets Slapped*, *Anna Christie*, *Liliom*, *Mary Rose*, *John Ferguson*, *The Emperor Jones*, *Young Woodley*, and *Desire Under the Elms*. One doubts, however, whether an equal division would prove so satisfactory on our stage as it apparently did at Lincoln's Inn Fields.

In his account of Mrs. Holden's little infelicity Downes declares that "There being a Fight and Scuffle in this Play, between the House of Capulet, and House of Paris; Mrs. Holden Acting his Wife, enter'd in a Hurry," and so forth. Mr. Montague Summers suggests that the anecdote may refer to a performance of Howard's version.[16] To the present writer Downes's description of the fight seems to illuminate rather than to obscure the question of "Count Paris's Wife." Named in the cast (which Downes gives in the preceding paragraph), she is mystifying indeed; but does not the anecdote indicate that Downes's pen or memory slipped for Lady Montague? The reference may be to either of the versions. After all, these howlers of the ancient Downes are no worse than those we get from far nimbler wits in the classroom (and the newspapers) every day.

When D'Avenant's production of *King Lear* took place we do not know. Having noted the "Principal, which we call'd Stock-Plays" acted at Lincoln's Inn Fields, 1661–1665, Downes mentions a number of others, the success of which, we may presume, was not great enough to warrant their frequent revival. Among these he lists "The Tragedy of King Lear, as Mr. Shakespear Wrote it; before it was alter'd by Mr. Tate." [17] With one exception this is the only reference I have found to the production of *Lear* before Tate's version in 1681. Pepys is silent. But apparently Shakespeare's play *was* acted now and again, for Nell Gwyn saw it in June, 1675.[18]

There has been some speculation regarding the cast. Davies notes, in the 1789 edition of the *Roscius Anglicanus*, "Betterton, we must suppose, acted Lear." Waldron demurs: "Betterton being at this period a young man, it is more probable that Lear was performed by some Veteran: and that he did not represent the old Monarch 'till Tate's alteration was produced."[19] This suggestion has been taken over by several later writers, but there is not a shred of support for it. For one thing, D'Avenant's company had no veteran actors — these were all members of the other house. There can be little doubt that the rôle was acted by Betterton.

But the play probably met with scant applause; the Fool alone must have been a hopeless stumbling-block.[20] D'Avenant's production of Shakespeare's play was in fact its last for a century and a half. The text used was probably that of the Folios, since Quarto 1608 would have been too archaic, and we may suppose (as in the case of *Othello*) that Quarto 1655 did not find its way into the theatrical library. If Quarto 1 was used, it must have undergone a certain amount of modernization.

Another early revival of Shakespeare by the Duke's company occurred in 1663. This was *Henry the Eighth*, which Downes lists among the stock pieces of the Duke's company, 1661–1665. "This Play," he declares,

> by Order of Sir William Davenant, was all new Cloath'd in proper Habits: The King's was new, all the Lords, the Cardinals, the

Bishops, the Doctors, Proctors, Lawyers, Tip-staves, new Scenes: The part of the King was so right and justly done by Mr. Betterton, he being Instructed in it by Sir William, who had it from Old Mr. Lowen, that had his Instructions from Mr. Shakespear himself, that Idare and will aver, none can, or will come near him in this Age, in the performance of that part: Mr. Harris's, performance of Cardinal Wolsey, was little Inferior to that, he doing it with just such State, Port and Mein, that I dare affirm, none hitherto has Equall'd him: The Duke of Buckingham, by Mr. Smith; Norfolk, by Mr. Nokes; Suffolk, by Mr. Lilliston; Cardinal Campeius and Cranmur, by Mr. Medburn; Bishop Gardiner, by Mr. Underhill; Earl of Surry, by Mr. Young; Lord Sands, by Mr. Price; Mrs. Betterton, Queen Catherine: Every part by the great Care of Sir William, being exactly perform'd; it being all new Cloath'd and new Scenes; it continu'd Acting 15 Days together with general Applause.[21]

For the date of this gorgeous production Pepys is our authority. On December 10, 1663, he records that his shoemaker, Wotton, tells "of a rare play to be acted this week of Sir William Davenant's: the story of Henry the Eighth with all his wives." By December 22 the play had been acted, for on that date "I perceive the King and Duke and all the Court was going to the Duke's playhouse to see 'Henry VIII.' acted, which is said to be an admirable play." Two days later Captain Ferrers tells him "of the goodness of the new play of 'Henry VIII.' which makes me think long till my time [of vowed abstention from plays] is out." On January 1, 1664, he goes hotfoot

> to the Duke's house, the first play I have been at these six months, according to my last vowe, and here saw the so much cried-up play of "Henry the Eighth"; which, though I went with resolution to like it, is so simple a thing made up of a great many patches, that, besides the shows and processions in it, there is nothing in the world good or well done. Thence mightily dissatisfied.

The date of this production is thus fixed by Pepys as not later than December 22, 1663.

Whether the play was altered or not is uncertain. Lowe

is inclined to think it was, in view of Pepys's reference to D'Avenant and, especially, its expensive mounting.[22] Mr. Summers[23] and Mr. Kilbourne[24] think not, and I am inclined to agree with them. "The smart touch [of Pepys] about 'all his wives,'" suggests Mr. Summers, "is doubtless a mere bit of irresponsible and imaginative gossip."

The absence of any printed version is, in my opinion, strong evidence against the serious alteration of any play, especially if the production was notably successful. Since an altered text regularly superseded the previous Quarto on the stage, it became automatically the authoritative text of the players. It appears that when a new edition in Quarto was to be printed the players were appealed to by the publishers, as custodians of the latest and therefore the authentic stage text. But since no separate edition of *Henry the Eighth* appeared till 1732, the actors' text must have been excerpted from one of the Folios. The absence of a pre-Wars Quarto might account for the absence of a separate edition in the Restoration.

The play continued to hold the boards after the production of John Banks's popular "she-tragedy," *Anna Bullen*. A reference in Mrs. Behn's *The Lucky Chance*[25] (acted 1686–1687) shows that audiences were still supposed to be familiar with it. Genest records an interesting performance of *Henry the Eighth* at the Haymarket, on February 15, 1707, with the following notable cast: King Henry, Betterton; Wolsey, Verbruggen; Buckingham, Booth; Norfolk, Mills; Surrey, Cibber; Lord Sandys, Bullock; Queen Katharine, Mrs. Barry; Anne Bullen, Mrs. Bradshaw.[26] At Drury Lane, on March 11 of the following year, Betterton chose it for his benefit.[27] A still later performance of the King by Betterton took place at Drury Lane on January 26, 1709. The Wolsey was Keen; Booth again played Buckingham; Powell, Surrey; Cibber, Cranmer; and Johnson, Gardener; the other parts as before.[28] The play was certainly very popular,[29] even though it was not offered to the reading public of the Restoration in separate form.

Our first reference to the acting of *Macbeth* [30] on the Restoration stage is to be found in a list of plays drawn up by Sir Henry Herbert and dated November 3, 1663.[31] It includes the following item: "Revived Play. Mackbethe . . . [£] 1." [32] This reference agrees with Downes's assertion that, before its presentation at Dorset Garden with "new Cloath's, new Scenes, Machines, as flyings for the Witches; with all the Singing and Dancing in it," the play had been acted at Lincoln's Inn Fields. In the older theatre Pepys saw it on November 5, 1664, December 28, 1666, January 7, 1667, April 19, 1667, October 16, 1667, November 6, 1667, August 12, 1668, December 21, 1668, and January 15, 1669.

D'Avenant's alteration was published in quarto in 1674 "As it's now Acted at the Dukes Theatre." [33] Yet his name does not appear on the title page, nor was this play included in the posthumous folio of D'Avenant's works, published in 1673. There can, however, be little doubt that the text of 1674 represents the version referred to by Downes, who, as prompter of D'Avenant's company, could hardly be misinformed regarding its authorship. Moreover, as we shall see when we examine the text, the alterations are of precisely the same sort as those which disfigure D'Avenant's *The Law against Lovers*.

The first question, then, is, did Pepys see D'Avenant's version or an unaltered revival? Downes tells us that a special production of D'Avenant's version was made after the opening of the Duke's company at Dorset Garden. This event took place on November 9, 1671. Downes mentions five new plays acted there before *Macbeth*, and says besides that several stock plays were sandwiched in between the new ones. He describes *Macbeth* as follows:

> The Tragedy of Macbeth, alter'd by Sir William Davenant; being drest in all it's Finery, as new Cloath's, new Scenes, Machines, as flyings for the Witches; with all the Singing and Dancing in it:

The first Compos'd by Mr. Lock, the other by Mr. Channell and Mr. Joseph Preist; it being all Excellently perform'd, being in the nature of an Opera, it Recompenc'd double the Expence; it proves still [1708] a lasting Play.

Note, That this Tragedy, King Lear and The tempest, were Acted in Lincolns-Inn-Fields; Lear, being Acted exactly as Mr. Shakespear Wrote it; as likewise the Tempest alter'd by Sir William Davenant and Mr. Dryden, before 'twas made into an Opera.[34]

Genest asserts that *Macbeth* was acted at Lincoln's Inn Fields unaltered; but there is no warrant in Downes for this assumption.[35] On the contrary, the references of Pepys point with reasonable clearness to D'Avenant's version: [36]

[November 5, 1664]: with my wife to the Duke's house to a play, *Macbeth*, a pretty good play, but admirably acted.[37]

[December 28, 1666]: to the Duke's house, and there saw *Macbeth* most excellently acted, and a most excellent play for variety.

[January 7, 1667]: to the Duke's house, and saw *Macbeth*, which, though I saw it lately, yet appears a most excellent play in all respects, but especially in divertisement, though it be a deep tragedy; which is a strange perfection in a tragedy, it being most proper here, and suitable.

[April 19, 1667]: Here we saw *Macbeth*, which, though I have seen it often, yet is it one of the best plays for a stage, and variety of dancing and musique, that ever I saw.

The last three entries, at least, with their reference to "variety" and "divertisement" point to D'Avenant's alterations.[38] Thus 1663–1664 becomes our date for the production of *Macbeth* at Lincoln's Inn Fields,[39] and 1672–1673 for its revival with new trappings at Dorset Garden.

The Quarto of 1674, the first edition of D'Avenant's version, gives the names of only a few of the players: Macbeth, Betterton; Macduff, Harris; Banquo, Smith; Malcom, Norris; Duncan, Lee; [40] Lennox, Medbourne; Donalbain, Cademan; Seward, Husband; Seyton, Bickerstaffe; Fleance, Mrs. B. Porter; murderers, Fairbank and Cross; Lady Macbeth, Mrs. Betterton; Lady Macduff, Mrs. Long; Ghost of Banquo, Sandford. It is highly remarkable that Banquo and his gory shade were performed by different actors. Did Smith and Sandford quarrel for the part, and compromise by splitting it? Probably Waldron's solution is the right one: "Sandford's countenance," he suggests, "was naturally formed to inspire terror; while the representative of the living Banquo had, as was necessary, a placid mein." [41]

Concerning Betterton's performance of *Macbeth*, I find little testimony. That Pepys admired it is shown by his entry of October 16, 1667, when he was discontented with its performance by an understudy. Of Mrs. Betterton's success as Lady Macbeth, Colley Cibber tells us; he writes of performances shortly after he joined the company, that is, in the early nineties:

> Mrs. Betterton, tho' far advanc'd in Years, was so great a Mistress of Nature that even Mrs. Barry, who acted the Lady Macbeth after her, could not in that Part, with all her superior Strength and Melody of Voice, throw out those quick and careless Strokes of Terror from the Disorder of a guilty Mind, which the other gave us with a Facility in her Manner that render'd them at once tremendous and delightful.[42]

Genest records several interesting performances of *Macbeth* in the last decade of Betterton's career.[43] On December 27, 1707, the distinguished company at the Haymarket acted *Macbeth* with the following cast, perhaps the finest that has ever played it: Macbeth, Betterton; Macduff, Wilks; Banquo, Mills; Duncan, Keen; Lennox, Booth; [44] Seyton, Cory; Hecate, Johnson; Witches, Norris, Bullock, and Bowen; Lady Macbeth, Mrs. Barry; Lady Macduff, Mrs. Rogers.[45] The performance of all the witches by men shows how gradually women won their way on the stage. Betterton continued to act Macbeth till the end of his life. Genest notes his appearance in that rôle as late as December 17, 1709.[46] The Quartos after 1674 follow the first edition in their casts till the Quarto of 1710, which has: Macbeth, Betterton; Macduff, Wilks; Banquo, Mills; Malcom, Corey; Duncan, Keen; Donalbain,

Bullock, Jr.; Lennox, Griffin; Lady Macbeth, Mrs. Knight; Lady Macduff, Mrs. Rogers; Heccate, Mr. Johnson.

In tracing the Shakespearean revivals of the Duke's company we have reached only the season of 1663–1664. It will be remembered, on the other hand, that in examining the record of the King's Players we noticed their productions up to the union of the companies in 1682, since the dates of their first performances are in most cases uncertain. We found at the Theatre Royal the following plays actually staged: *Othello*, *1 Henry IV*, *The Merry Wives*, *A Midsummer Night's Dream*, *Julius Caesar*, *The Taming of the Shrew* (which gradually became *Sauny the Scot*), Dryden's *All for Love*, Ravenscroft's *Titus Andronicus*, Tate's *Richard II* and *Ingratitude* (*Coriolanus*), and D'Urfey's *Injured Princess* (*Cymbeline*).

Of these eleven plays, *All for Love* and *Titus* were not staged till 1677–1678, and *All for Love* is hardly an adaptation, anyway. The last three were produced just before the union — not earlier than 1680. Tate's pieces were, besides, flat failures. Of the plays pertinent to our inquiry, *The Merry Wives* was, according to Downes, acted "but now and then," and *A Midsummer Night's Dream* rarely, if ever, after its production; and of *Julius Caesar* what evidence we have points to production not long before 1671. That leaves active in their repertory throughout the sixties only *1 Henry IV* and *Othello* (in presumably unaltered form), and *Sauny the Scot*. And even if we count the late productions of this company, the only success of even a moderate description which we must add is Ravenscroft's *Titus*. *All for Love* is Dryden's, not Shakespeare's. Concerning the reception of *The Injured Princess* we have no information.

My contention that the Duke's rather than the King's was *par excellence* the home of Shakespeare during the rivalry of the two houses is sustained when their record is compared with the one just cited, though it is true their productions were chiefly adaptations. We have now noticed D'Avenant's revivals of *Hamlet*, *Twelfth Night*, *Measure for Measure* (in the form of *The Law against Lovers*), *Romeo and Juliet* (unaltered and in Howard's version), *King Lear*, *Henry VIII*, and *Macbeth*. Only seven plays, to be sure, but we have, I repeat, reached only the season of 1663–1664. We shall have seven other productions at the Duke's house to record during the years between 1664 and the union, several of them notably successful. Of the seven *early* productions, three (*Hamlet*, *Macbeth*, and *Henry VIII*) were big successes, probably more so than any of the Shakespearean productions of the Theatre Royal. The least popular were *The Law against Lovers* and *King Lear*, yet, as I have shown, even they were occasionally revived. *Twelfth Night* and *Romeo and Juliet* seem to have been at least moderate successes.

Meanwhile, Killigrew had opened his new theatre, a better house than the Duke's — it had been constructed especially for theatrical purposes. Standing between Drury Lane and Brydges Street, Covent Garden, it was referred to by either of the last two names; but, since its site has ever since been occupied by a Drury Lane theatre, historians have called it the First Drury Lane.[47] This house was also known as the King's and as the Theatre Royal. On the date of its opening Downes and Pepys again disagree, but Pepys is right in specifying May 7, 1663.[48]

Some time after the opening of its new theatre the King's Company was strengthened by the engagement of several new actors. An important accession was the mad wag, Jo Haynes, one of the most popular of all the Restoration comedians. His career lasted from 1672 to 1701.

According to Downes, seven actresses were members of the King's Company shortly after its opening in Drury Lane in 1663: Mmes. Corey, Ann Marshall (for several years the leading lady),[49] Eastland, Weaver, Uphill, and Knepp; besides Mrs. Hughes, whose first appearance, as Desdemona, we have already noticed. Knepp, or Knipp, was, of course, the fair frail friend of Mr. Pepys. She disappears from the bills after 1678.[50]

"Some few years," says Downes, after the advent of these ladies, came Mmes. Boutell, James, Rebecca Marshall, Rutter, Verjuice, and Reeves.[51] Mrs. Boutell, though ignored by Cibber, was an actress of importance. Among the rôles she created were Cleopatra in Dryden's *All for Love*, Statira in Lee's *The Rival Queens*, Mrs. Pinchwife in Wycherley's *The Country Wife* and Fidelia in his *The Plain Dealer*, Melantha in Dryden's *Marriage à la Mode*, Mrs. Termagant in Shadwell's *The Squire of Alsatia*, and Mrs. Fantast in his *Bury Fair*. Her last recorded performance was in 1697.[52]

Came also the captivating Nelly Gwyn. Her first appearance at Drury Lane was in 1665 — on the stage, that is, for she is said to have made her way from the pit, where she dispensed oranges. But her career as an actress was brief, and she excelled in prologues and epilogues, not as a Shakespearean. So we must be content to note that Charles (who was not squeamish about following Lacy, Hart, and Buckhurst, her successive protectors) took her from the boards in 1668, though she returned and played her last rôle, Almahide in *The Conquest of Granada*, in the winter of 1669–1670. She died in 1687.

It is in the autumn following the opening of the first Drury Lane theatre that we come upon Sir Henry Herbert's list (November 3, 1663) of plays for which he had collected, or proposed to collect, fees. It contains, among others, the following items:[53]

Revived Play	Taminge the Shrew	[£] 1
Revived Play.	Mackbethe	[£] 1
Henry 8.	Revived Play	[£] 1

Pepys did not see this production of the *Shrew*. He makes his first reference to that play on April 9, 1667, when he saw Lacy's version. Probably the production of 1663 was little altered.

It was acted, of course, at the Theatre Royal. *Macbeth*, produced at the Duke's house, was not seen by Pepys till November 5, 1664. *Henry VIII* was presented at Lincoln's Inn Fields in mid-December, 1663. The appearance of these titles in Herbert's list is not, of course, proof of production. But Pepys corroborates the actual performance of *Henry VIII* at that time, and thus strengthens the probability of the production of the *Shrew* and *Macbeth* also in 1663.[54]

Besides the performances of Shakespeare which we have noticed, the Theatre Royal continued to revive Fletcher and Jonson. About this time, however, the new dramatists begin to produce their plays. Before the company moved from Vere Street, Dryden's first play, *The Wild Gallant*, had been acted, probably on February 5, 1663.[55] Early in 1664 D'Avenant produced Etherege's epoch-making first play, *The Comical Revenge, or Love in a Tub.* Henry Norris, who later became one of the leading comedians, created the part of Lovis in this play. After a term with D'Avenant's company he went to Ireland, but returned, toward the end of the century, and set up again in London, where he earned the sobriquet of "Jubilee Dicky" by his success in Farquhar's *The Constant Couple.*

The trend toward rhyme appears in Etherege's play and in Sir Robert Howard's *The Indian Queen*, which was also acted at the Theatre Royal early in 1664. Dryden's first tragicomedy, *The Rival Ladies*, had been produced at the same theatre by mid-summer of that year. Not only does this play employ rhyme, but its dedication (to the Earl of Orrery) contains a defence of rhyme. During August, Orrery's ridiculous *Henry V*, all in rhyme, was acted at Lincoln's Inn Fields. This is an independent treatment, not an alteration of Shakespeare.

A month later (September 10, 1664) Pepys saw D'Avenant's *The Rivals*, an adaptation of *The Two Noble Kinsmen.*[56] An interesting revival about this time was Webster's great tragedy,

The Duchess of Malfi, with Betterton as Bosola, Harris as the Duke, Smith as Antonio, and Mrs. Betterton in the superb title rôle. Downes says that the initial run lasted eight days and that the play proved one of the best of the stock tragedies.

Late in the season of 1664–1665 the Theatre Royal acted Lacy's farce, *The Old Troop, or Monsieur Raggou,* which became extremely popular. Of greater artistic importance was the production there toward the end of the season of Dryden's *The Indian Emperour, or The Conquest of Mexico.* This play established the success of the new species of serious drama, the heroic tragedy, and also Dryden's reputation as a playwright. Though the vogue of the heroic play was brief, it influenced methods of Shakespearean representation, since many of the acting versions of D'Avenant, Dryden, and Tate tend toward the erection of the leading character into a spectacle of extravagance, and the artificial problems of love and honor are frequently worked into the plot.

On June 5, 1665, the Lord Chamberlain prohibited plays on account of the Plague. The closing was a hard blow to the newly resuscitated drama; the theatres did not reopen for nearly a year and a half, shortly after the Great Fire. On October 18, 1666, theatrical performances had been resumed at court, but not till November 20 was observed as a day of thanksgiving for the Plague's cessation were public performances undertaken.

In the spring of the following year Pepys saw Lacy's contemptible alteration, *Sauny the Scot,* or *The Taming of the Shrew,* acted at Drury Lane. This was on April 9. A month before, he had seen at Lincoln's Inn Fields, on "the coldest day that ever was remembered in England; and, God knows! coals at a very great price," Caryl's *The English Princess, or The Death of Richard III,* not an alteration of Shakespeare's play.

At least as early as November 7 of that year (1667), the Duke's company also staged one of the most outrageous, successful, long-lived, and impudent of all the Shakespearean adaptations, *The Tempest* of D'Avenant and Dryden, with its charming additions of a man who has never seen a woman, a monstrous sister of Caliban, and a sweet little supernatural playmate for Ariel. Betterton's severe illness that autumn kept him from acting till the following summer. Probably he had nothing to do with staging the most degraded of all the Restoration versions.

Rambling old Downes makes the following entry after his description of the sumptuous production of D'Avenant's *Macbeth* at Dorset Garden:

> Note, That this Tragedy, King Lear and the Tempest, were Acted in Lincolns-Inn-Fields; Lear, being Acted exactly as Mr. Shakespear Wrote it; as likewise the Tempest alter'd by Sir William Davenant and Mr. Dryden, before 'twas made into an Opera.[57]

Pepys saw the D'Avenant–Dryden *Tempest* eight times; his first visit was on November 7, 1667:

> at noon resolved with Sir W. Pen to go see "The Tempest," an old play of Shakespeare's, acted, I hear, the first day; and so my wife, and girl, and W. Hewer by themselves, and Sir W. Pen and I afterwards by ourselves; and forced to sit in the side balcone over against the musique-room at the Duke's house. . . . The house mighty full; the King and Court there: and the most innocent play that ever I saw; and a curious piece of musique in an echo of half sentences, the echo repeating the former half, while the man goes on to the latter; which is mighty pretty. The play no great wit, but yet good, above ordinary plays.

Pepys's reference to the echo song identifies the version he saw as the D'Avenant–Dryden comedy. His date agrees with the epilogue, as printed in 1670 and in subsequent editions, which begins:

> Gallants, by all good signs it does appear,
> That Sixty Seven 's a very damning year;

and with the Lord Chamberlain's warrant book, which mentions the performance of *The Tempest* on November 7, 1667.

This reference appears in a bill presented on behalf of Lady D'Avenant for plays acted by the Duke's company, 1666–1668, at court or in the presence of royalty at the public theatre. The popularity of *The Tempest* is indicated by payments of £10 each for such performances, on November 7, 14, and 26, 1667, and March 14 and April 13, 1668.[58] In fact, the success of this adaptation banished Shakespeare's play from the stage for many years, although it was itself modified, not long after its production, by Thomas Shadwell, who turned it into an "opera," which was launched after the removal of the Duke's company to Dorset Garden. Portions of the D'Avenant–Dryden amendments held the stage for a century and a half.[59]

Concerning the original performers Mr. Montague Summers, who reprints the play in his *Shakespeare Adaptations*, makes the following statement:

> No list of actors was printed with the piece, but we know that Henry Harris played Ferdinand;[60] Edward Angel, "an incomparable Comedian," Stephano;[61] Cave Underhill, Trincalo.[62] Moll Davis was also in the original cast, her rôle perhaps being Hippolito, for the "right Heir of the Dukedom of Mantua" was assigned to a woman, and "little Mis Davis" in breeches parts had already enraptured the town.[63] After she had left the stage she was succeeded in *The Tempest* by Mrs. Gosnell, who, *teste* Pepys, but ill supplied her place. Betterton himself did not appear in *The Tempest*.[64]

D'Avenant, co-author of this monstrous piece, died on April 7, 1668. Long before his death Sir William had planned a new theatre. His patent was now the property of Lady D'Avenant, and was administered for her by their son Charles. From this time on Betterton was doubtless in charge of the artistic end of the business, though for a while he shared his authority with Harris. The latter had attempted, in 1663, to set up as Betterton's superior, demanding a higher salary than any other member of the company. It was refused, and Harris deserted, expecting to join the Theatre Royal. The King would not allow this, and in a few months Harris returned to the Duke's house.

We have noticed the edict of December 12, 1660, in which certain plays were set aside as the exclusive property of D'Avenant's company. Professor Nicoll has found another document among the Lord Chamberlain's records, dated August 20, 1668, listing "Playes allowed to be acted by his Royall Highnesse ye Duke of Yorkes Comoedians," and including *Timon of Athens*, *Troyolus and Crisseida*, and *Three parts of H: ye 6.* Still another paper found by Mr. Nicoll, and undated (but among documents of about January 12, 1669), gives "Plays Acted at the Theatre Royall. A Catalogue of part of His Mates Servants Playes as they were formerly acted at the Blackfryers & now allowed of to his Mates Servants at ye New Theatre." The "New Theatre" is of course the Theatre Royal in Drury Lane.

The list of plays includes **The Winters Tale*, **King John*, *Richard the Second*, **The Gentlemen of Verona*, *The Merry Wives of Windsor*, **The Comoedy of Errors*, **Loves Labour Lost*, *Midsomer Nights Dreame*, **The Merchant of Venice*, **As you like it*, *The Tameing of ye Shrew*, **Alls Well yt ends well*, **Henry ye fourth*, *The Second part*, **Richard ye Third*, *Coriolanus*, *Andronicus*, *Julius Ceasar*, *The Moore of Venice*, **Anthony & Clopatra*, and *Cymbelyne*, besides many other Elizabethan plays, notably long lists of Jonson's and Fletcher's.[65] It does not appear that the eleven plays which I have starred were ever performed by the Old Actors. The others I have already mentioned.

About the year 1670, says Downes, the Duke's company "entertained" several new actresses. Important acquisitions were Mrs. Johnson, and Mrs. Mary Lee, née Aldrich, afterwards Lady Slingsby.

The new playhouse erected by Lady D'Avenant stood on the river, near Salisbury Court, Fleet Street, but was known chiefly as the Dorset Garden theatre, since its site was once occupied by a garden of the Earl of Dorset. Upon the reunion in 1682 Betterton removed to Drury Lane; but Dorset Garden was still used occasionally for opera and spectacle till 1709, when it was pulled down. After 1685, when upon the accession of James II his patronage was transferred to the Theatre Royal, the Duke's house became known as the Queen's.

It was opened on November 9, 1671, with Dryden's *Sir Martin Mar-all*. About a month later at Drury Lane the great man was held up to ridicule, and the bubble of the heroic drama effectively punctured, by the brilliant satire of *The Rehearsal*, in which Lacy, who created the part of Bayes, mimicked the Laureate's mannerisms, Dryden having been appointed D'Avenant's successor in that office.[66]

No sooner were the Duke's players established in their new theatre than the rival house was destroyed by fire. This disaster, which occurred on January 25, 1672, is described in a contemporary letter as follows:

> A fire at the King's play-house between 7 and 8 on Thursday evening last, which half burned down the house and all their scenes and wardrobe; and all the houses from the Rose Tavern in Russell Street on that side of the way to Drury Lane are burned and blown up, with many in Vinegar Yard; 20,000 l. damage. The fire began under the stairs where Orange Moll keeps her fruit. Bell the player was blown up.[67]

The fire is also mentioned in the Diary of the Earl of Anglesey:

> At eight of the clock the King's playhouse took fire, and most of that side of Russell Street and many other houses thereabout were burnt down, and we in Drury Lane and all about in great danger; but the Lord had mercy, and by great industry and blowing up houses the fire was overcome: I had no rest, but sat up almost all night, even till six in the morning. The Lord pardon sin, which brings judgements.[68]

This pious reflection is indicative of the survival of Puritan distrust of the theatre even in high places. It may be compared with the views of Robert Bowyer, who writes on December 27, 1670, to Robert Southwell of a disaster in a Dublin theatre:

Yesterday there being very many people at the playhouse the lofts fell down, three or four killed dead in the house, whereof a maid of Mr. Savage's was one. My Lord Lieutenant was hurt a little, one of his son's much hurt, the Countess of Clanbrasill ill hurt, very many wounded, some of which it is said cannot live. The play that was acted was Bartholemew Fair, in which it seems there is a passage that reflects upon a profession of holiness, and it is said when they were entering upon that part the scaffold fell.[69]

On February 26 the King's Company opened at the old Duke's house in Lincoln's Inn Fields. Their misfortune gave the younger actors a distinct advantage; but the veterans appear to have been more successful even after the fire. One reason for this was the greater experience of the King's Company, where the average of acting was probably higher at this time. The size of their theatre, moreover, seems to have become a burden to the Duke's company.

The new house in Dorset Garden was a spacious and handsome building, as the prints in Settle's *The Empress of Morocco* testify. The stage was larger and more elaborately equipped with scenic and mechanical devices than that of any previous English theatre. But the expense of the undertaking must have been, for those times, enormous, and there was war to the knife between the two houses.

The Duke's, in fact, was sorely in need of recruits. Several of the members of the original company under Rhodes had died; some of the actresses, in the suggestive phraseology of Downes, " by force of Love, were Erept the Stage." Several new performers were now engaged; the most important of these was the great Mrs. Barry, who became, when Mrs. Betterton retired, the leading woman of the company. She was not so famous for her Shakespearean rôles (Cordelia, Lady Macbeth, Lavinia, and others) as she was in the new drama; her Monimia and Belvidera were probably the greatest tragic

THE DORSET GARDEN THEATRE

successes achieved by any woman on the Restoration stage. To ope the sacred fount of sympathetic tears was her special talent, and she found ample opportunities in the dramas of Otway, Dryden, and Lee. Though she was preëminent as a tragedienne, she was also a graceful actress of comic rôles. Her last appearance was on the day after Betterton's final performance.

The most notable of the men who joined about the year 1672 was Anthony Leigh; his masterpiece was the title rôle in Dryden's *The Spanish Friar*. He was the favorite comedian of Charles, who used to refer to him as *his* actor. Another important acquisition was Joseph Williams, who, Downes tells us, "came in a Boy, and serv'd Mr. Harris." Among this actor's Shakespearean parts were Aeneas in Dryden's *Troilus and Cressida*, Sylla in Otway's *Caius Marius*, Henry VI in both of Crowne's adaptations, Edmund in Tate's *Lear*, the Second Gravedigger in *Hamlet*, and Decius Brutus in *Julius Caesar*. He created the important part of Polydore in Otway's *The Orphan*, and the title rôle in Lee's *Theodosius*. He disappears after 1699.

Other new members of the Duke's company were Bowman, Gillow, Jevon (Thomas Shadwell's brother-in-law), and Percival, whose daughter Susanna became one of the leading women. She married Will Mountfort about 1686–1687, and, about two years after his death in 1692, Jack Verbruggen — both accomplished actors. She thus appears on the bills under three different names. Mrs. Percival (as she was at first) was the original Belinda in *The Old Bachelor*, Lady Froth in *The Double Dealer*, and Charlotte Weldon in Southerne's *Oroonoko*. Cibber devotes several pages to eulogy of her versatile talents.

Another recruit of some note was Mrs. Butler, who, says Cibber, "prov'd not only a good Actress, but was allow'd in those Days to sing and dance to great Perfection." By the time Cibber joined the company she had won an important place, but in 1692 she was persuaded by Joseph Ashbury to leave the parsimonious patentees and go over to the Dublin stage.

For a short time the Duke's house also enjoyed the services of Jo Haynes, who had come to the Theatre Royal from the Nursery in 1668, and was now most justly kicked off that stage by Hart, after the burning of Drury Lane, for a piece of disloyal buffoonery which is described in his notorious *Life*. Jo's accomplishments were, however, too valuable to be dispensed with, and it was not long before he was received again at the Theatre Royal. Till his death in 1701 Haynes was one of the most popular of the low comedians, though he was less notable as an actor than as a speaker of prologues and epilogues.

The King's Company opened its new house on March 26, 1674. The best of the new writers, William Wycherley, had produced the first of his four comedies at the Theatre Royal before the fire. His second, *The Gentleman Dancing-Master*, was acted at Dorset Garden in 1672. Shortly after the King's Company reopened at Drury Lane, his masterpiece, *The Country Wife*, was acted there, and Mr. Horner and his china became the topic of the *beau monde*. Two years later *The Plain Dealer* again provided the Theatre Royal with one of its strongest pieces.

The second Drury Lane theatre was built on the site of the first, that is, between Drury Lane and Brydges Street. For the opening Dryden furnished the prologue, which scoffs at the operatic activities of the other and larger house in Dorset Garden. During the previous year Elkanah Settle's *The Empress of Morocco* had been published with views of that theatre; and now Dryden, collaborating with Shadwell and Crowne, took a fling at it with *Notes and Observations on the Empress of Morocco; or Some few Erratas to be printed instead of the Sculptures with the second edition of that Play*.

It appears that, in order to maintain themselves on their too spacious stage and against the competition of the Theatre Royal, the Duke's company had decided to stake everything on opera. Throughout the seventeenth century this hybrid art had been growing in favor on the Continent. The first public opera-house was built in Venice in 1637; Italian opera was introduced into France in 1645.[70] Its growing importance in England directly affected not only the staging but the current texts of Shakespeare.

Dryden defines an opera as "a poetical tale, or fiction, represented by vocal or instrumental music, adorned with scenes, machines, and dancing." But actually the type was less definite, and in common usage included what we would call spectacle and extravaganza. It consisted of spoken dialogue, songs, dances, and mechanical effects — the last being quite as important as the music in turning a play into an opera. D'Avenant's version of *Macbeth*, for instance, was operatic, since not only were new songs and dances provided for the witches, but those weird sisters frisked about in the air on slack wires and trapezes. Music, dancing, elaborate scenery, and mechanical *tours-de-force* were the four essentials of Restoration opera. Not long after the Restoration, operatic embellishments were being used to enhance the charms of English drama, but it took some time for the opera as a distinct art-form to make its way across the channel.

It is important to remember that pictorial splendor came to be demanded by the Restoration audience. Thus when, during the season of 1691–1692, *A Midsummer Night's Dream* was made into an opera, its scenic lavishness was even more celebrated than the music Purcell wrote for it. In its original form (or something like it) this charming comedy had failed to please upon its first revival by the Theatre Royal. As *The Fairy Queen* it was thirty years later a notable success. The new features which made it so will be described in Part Two. The Restoration opera might, on the other hand, be the bastard offspring of tragedy. The heroic style readily lent itself to the further artificiality of this form.

The most notorious of the Shakespeare adaptations was, however, another comedy made operatic—*The Tempest*, produced at Dorset Garden in April, 1674. It was such a colossal success that it supplanted for many years both Shakespeare's original play, and the D'Avenant–Dryden adaptation, of which it is almost entirely composed. The new features were added by Shadwell, whose version has been reprinted ever since, instead of the comedy, in Dryden's works.[71]

Downes is our authority for attributing this operatic version of *The Tempest* to Thomas Shadwell.[72]

> The Year after in 1763.[73] The Tempest, or the Inchanted Island, made into an Opera by Mr. Shadwell, having all New in it; as Scenes, Machines; particularly, one Scene Painted with Myriads of Ariel Spirits; and another flying away, with a Table Furnisht out with Fruits, Sweet meats, and all sorts of Viands; just when Duke Trinculo and his Companions' were going to Dinner; all was things perform'd in it so Admirably well, that not any succeeding Opera got more Money.[74]

Shadwell's opera probably appeared about April 30, 1674. This date is established by Mr. William J. Lawrence, on the following grounds. A "Prologue and Epilogue to the Tempest" among the Egerton MSS[75] in the British Museum appears to be the work of Shadwell. Mr. Lawrence makes it clear that the two pieces are a rejoinder to Dryden's prologue and epilogue for the opening of the new Theatre Royal, March 26, 1674. Mr. Lawrence's contention is strengthened by an entry in the Lord Chamberlain's accounts for May 16, 1674:

> It is his Majesty's pleasure that Mr. Turner and Mr. Hart, or any other men or boys belonging to his Majesty's Chappell Royall that sing, in ye Tempest at his Royall Highnesse Theatre, doe remaine in towne all the week (dureing his Majesty's absence from Whitehall) to perform that service, onely Saturdayes to repaire to Windsor, and to returne to London on Mundayes if there be occasion for them.[76]

Piqued by the success of *The Tempest* on their rivals' stage, the Theatre Royal employed the hog Duffett, as Furnivall calls him,[77] to burlesque it. His piece was written, Langbaine tells us, "on purpose to draw Company from the other Theatre, where there was great resort about that time, to see that reviv'd Comedy, call'd, *The Tempest.*" [78]

Duffett's travesty has, as far as I know, only one admirer, and I must refer the curious reader to Mr. Summers's reprint and eulogistic introduction. Though the piece is in part satirical of the absurdities of the D'Avenant–Dryden–Shadwell version, Duffett also exercised his talent for throwing dirt at Shakespeare. *The Mock Tempest* not only turns the enchanted isle into Bridewell Jail, and Prospero into its head turnkey, but goes out of its way to burlesque passages in *Othello*, *Julius Caesar*, *Macbeth*, and *Hamlet.*[79] "The powdering-tub of infamy" (delicately mentioned throughout the piece) is the fittest receptacle for this witless piece of nastiness.

As the seventies wore on, the "old plays" of Shakespeare, Jonson, and Fletcher were increasingly rivalled at both houses by the work of the new authors. In the year following the opening of the second Drury Lane, Dryden produced there *Aureng-Zebe*, the last and most reasonable of his heroic plays. Lee's *Sophonisba* was also acted in that year; his *Nero* had been produced there the year before.

In the meantime a new star had appeared in the galaxy of Dorset Garden authors: Otway's first play, *Alcibiades*, was produced there in 1675. The year after, his *Don Carlos* was first acted; it proved successful for many years. Also in 1676, the masterpiece of Etherege, *The Man of Mode, or Sir Fopling Flutter*, was produced at Dorset Garden. In 1677 Lee's *The Rival Queens, or The Death of Alexander the Great*, provided Hart with one of his most famous parts, while at the Duke's house Otway's *Titus and Berenice* failed to do as well for Betterton. Otway's adaptation from Molière, *The Cheats of*

Scapin, proved successful, however, and held the stage for a century.[80] It was written for performance with *Titus and Berenice*, which has but three acts. In the same year Sedley's *Antony and Cleopatra*, an independent version, was acted at Dorset Garden, at least as early as February 12.[81] This was the last of the heroic plays in couplets.[82]

About this time the Duke's house was strengthened by the accession of several young men, one of whom became an actor of the first rank. This was William Mountfort, whose career as a regular player began about 1678. He had, however, been a member of the company as a boy. Downes says that by 1682 he had "grown to the maturity of a good actor." By 1690, when Cibber entered, Mountfort, now married to Miss Percival, was one of the leading players; Cibber calls him "In Tragedy, . . . the most affecting Lover within my Memory." He was Hart's successor in the title rôle of Lee's *Alexander the Great*, which he acted with distinction till his death, when Betterton assumed it. As a comedian, especially in foppish parts, Cibber owned him his model. Downes declares that as Sir Courtly Nice none but Cibber ever equalled him.

The King's Company was also recruited about this time. A newcomer of importance was the notorious Cardell ("Scum") Goodman, whose career extended from about 1677 to 1688. Among his best parts were Julius Caesar, Alexander, Alexas in *All for Love*, and Valentinian in Rochester's adaptation of Fletcher's play.[83] Scum's boon companion, Griffin, Downes tells us, joined the Theatre Royal "after they had begun at Drury Lane." Lowe states that his name does not appear till 1674, when he acted Varnish in *The Plain Dealer*. After 1688 there is no record of his acting till 1701, when he reappears at Drury Lane as Captain Griffin. He retired about 1708.[84]

The year 1678 was one of great importance to the drama. In the first place, Thomas Rymer published his *Tragedies of the Last Age*, a slashing attack on the Elizabethans, that must have given aid and comfort to the adapters who were about to lay violent hands on Shakespeare's texts. At any rate there ensued an epidemic of alteration, no fewer than eleven of the plays being newly set forth during the four years which followed.

The first of these was Dryden's famous imitation of *Antony and Cleopatra*, styled by him *All for Love, or The World Well Lost*. It was produced at Drury Lane with great success during the winter of 1677–1678 (probably in December or January) with Hart as Antony; Mohun, Ventidius; Clarke, Dolabella; Goodman, Alexas; Griffin, Serapion; Coyash, Priest; Mrs. Boutell, Cleopatra; Mrs. Corey, Octavia. In this play, written professedly in imitation of Shakespeare's style, Dryden abandoned the use of rhyme for the drama, and the vogue of the heroic play — of its composition, that is — was over.

Four years later, upon the union of the patent companies, the rôle of Antony passed into Betterton's repertory. The most notable cast on record is given by Downes near the end of his chronology:

> Note, From Candlemas 1704, to the 23d, of April 1706. There were 4 Plays commanded to be Acted at Court at St. Jame's, by the Actors of both Houses, viz. First, All for Love: Mr. Betterton, Acting Marc. Antony; Mr. Vantbrugg, Ventidius; Mr. Wilks, Dolabella; Mr. Booth, Alexas the Eunuch; Mrs. Barry, Cleopatra; Mrs. Bracegirdle, Octavia: All the other Parts being exactly done, and the Court very well pleas'd.[85]

The year 1678 saw also Edward Ravenscroft's alteration of *Titus Andronicus* acted at Drury Lane;[86] while Dorset Garden took a hand in the game with Shadwell's *Timon of Athens*, perhaps the least objectionable of all the Restoration tamperings. Shakespeare's youthful tragedy-of-blood does not appear to have been acted on the Restoration stage until Ravenscroft took it in hand. The first edition of the adaptation (1687) fails to give us the names of the actors. Genest notes performances (presumably of Ravenscroft's version) at Drury Lane in 1704. And Professor Odell observes that, long after the Restoration, Aaron was one of the favorite rôles of Quin.[87]

The Shadwell *Timon* also held the stage for many years; it ran through about a dozen editions. Unmindful of his success with *The Tempest*, Shadwell failed to introduce operatic features, but this defect was afterwards remedied, as is attested by the following lines from the epilogue to Granville's *The Jew of Venice:*

> How was the Scene forlorn, and how despis'd,
> When Tymon, without Musick, moraliz'd?
> Shakespears sublime in vain entic'd the Throng,
> Without the Charm of Purcel's Syren Song.[88]

In 1699 the Langbaine–Gildon *Lives and Characters* asserts that Shadwell's *Timon* had been "for a few Years past, as often acted at the Theatre Royal, as any Tragedy I know." [89] Genest notes numerous performances in the first decade of the eighteenth century; it was acted at the Theatre Royal in Drury Lane, and by the seceding actors at Little Lincoln's Inn Fields and the Haymarket.

The year after *All for Love*, *Titus Andronicus*, and *Timon of Athens*, Dryden's *Troilus and Cressida*, the last of his alterations of Shakespeare, was staged at Dorset Garden, "Glorious John" having gone over to that theatre with *The Kind Keeper, or Mr. Limberham*, in 1678, and *Oedipus* earlier in 1679. The cast of characters (given in the first edition, 1679) was as follows: Hector, Smith; Troilus, Betterton; Priam, Percival; Aeneas, Joseph Williams; Pandarus, Leigh; Calchas, Percival; Agamemnon, Gillow; Ulysses, Harris; Achilles, David Williams; Ajax, Bright; Nestor, Norris; Diomedes, Crosby; Patroclus, Boman; Menelaus, Richards; Thersites, Underhill; Cressida, Mrs. Mary Lee; Andromache, Mrs. Betterton. The prologue "Representing the Ghost of Shakespear" was spoken by Betterton himself. Downes does not describe the production, merely listing it as one of several new plays that met with indifferent success.[90] It was, however, occasionally acted throughout the period we are concerned with; Genest notes a performance on June 2, 1709. Betterton had surrendered the leading rôle to Wilks and played Thersites. Other performers were: Powell, Hector; Booth, Achilles; Mills, Agamemnon; Keen, Ajax; Thurmond, Ulysses; Estcourt, Pandarus; Mrs. Bradshaw, Cressida; Mrs. Rogers, Andromache.[91]

Like Dryden, Lee and Otway were both at this time writing for Dorset Garden. In 1680 the *Caesar Borgia* of the former,[92] and the latter's great tragedy, *The Orphan*, which held the stage till the middle of the nineteenth century, were both produced. As Monimia in *The Orphan* the great Mrs. Barry came into her own, and in the same production Mrs. Bracegirdle appeared as the Page of Polydore.

The beautiful Anne Bracegirdle (*c.* 1663–1748) became second only to Mrs. Barry. It was said that when she acted half the audience were in love with her. Congreve's unrequited passion was well known; it had this happy issue, that it inspired the series of brilliant women he created for her, among them the incomparable Millamant. Downes assures us that, though John Crowne's *Justice Busy* was not a success, "Mrs. Bracegirdle, by a Potent and Magnetick Charm in performing a Song in 't, caus'd the Stones of the Streets to fly in the Men's Faces."

Her most important "creations" were, besides Millamant, Araminta in *The Old Bachelor*, Angelica in *Love for Love*, Almeria in *The Mourning Bride*, Belinda in Vanbrugh's *The Provoked Wife*, Selina in Rowe's *Tamerlane*, and Lavinia in his *The Fair Penitent*. Her chief Shakespearean impersonations were Isabella, Portia, Desdemona, Ophelia, Cordelia, and Mrs. Ford. In person she was a striking brunette. She was the successor of Nell Gwyn and Moll Davis in breeches parts, yet she remained, as Tony Aston puts it, the Diana of the Stage.

Also in 1680, Lee's *Theodosius, or The Force of Love*, which held the stage for a hundred years, was produced at Dorset Garden, as were the same author's *Junius Brutus* and Dryden's *The Spanish Friar*. *The History and Fall of Caius Marius*, Otway's grotesque adaptation of *Romeo and Juliet*, had also been acted there during the season of 1679–1680, probably in the fall. Betterton had the title rôle, and Smith, Marius Junior (Romeo). The most famous part was the Nurse as played by James Nokes, whence his sobriquet, as in the Epilogue (spoken by Mrs. Barry):

> And now for you who here come wrapt in Cloaks,
> Only for love of Underhill and Nurse Nokes.

Bullock and Norris both appeared in the rôle during the early years of the eighteenth century. Other performers in the original production were Williams, Sylla; Percival, Granius; Gillow, Metullus; Williams, Pompeius; Jevon, Cinna; Underhill, Sulpitius (Mercutio); Mrs. Barry, Lavinia (Juliet). The most distinguished cast in the long history of this adaptation was that noted by Genest for Wilks's benefit at the Haymarket on February 18, 1707. It included Betterton as Marius, Sr.; Wilks, Marius, Jr.; Booth, Granius; Johnson, Sulpitius; Cibber and Norris, Citizens; Mrs. Bracegirdle, Lavinia; Bullock, Nurse.[93]

The popularity of this adaptation banished *Romeo and Juliet* from the London stage till 1744, when Theophilus Cibber produced a less objectionable version of Shakespeare's play. Even after that, Otway's dénouement (the waking of the heroine before her lover's death) was retained by both Theophilus Cibber and Garrick, and survived till well into the nineteenth century.[94]

And now, while mutes restrain the stringed choir and the brasses are hushed, let the reedy utterance of the oboes announce a new theme. The unwitting clown of the piece is about to enter. He will prove it a true tragi-comedy: in the very act of slaying the sublime he will compel us to look on with laughter.

The relative chronology of Nahum Tate's murderous attempts to improve Shakespeare is uncertain. Probably the first to be produced, though the second composed, was his *Richard II*. This was one of several Shakespeare adaptations inspired by the political troubles subsequent to the Popish Plot. The years 1680–1682 (when all three of Tate's versions appeared) were dangerous ones. On November 24, 1681, the Grand Jury received the bill of indictment against Shaftesbury and returned the verdict *Ignoramus*. Only a week earlier Dryden had published *Part I* of *Absalom and Achitophel*. And soon after came *The Medal*, to satirize the Whiggish felicitations on the Earl's release from custody.

No wonder that in those troublous times the government looked with little favor on a play in which legitimate succession is set aside; the brothers Stuart doubtless made the same personal application as Queen Elizabeth. The warrant for suppression is dated December 14, 1680, which appears to fix the date of production two days before, since Tate complains in his preface that the play ran but two days. In a last desperate attempt to avert the disaster, he changed his characters' names and rechristened his version *The Sicilian Usurper*. It was in this form that the play had its short life on the stage. But the changes were of no avail, and in fact served only to make the play less interesting to its audiences. Apparently it was never revived.

But if Tate's *amour propre* was wounded at Drury Lane, it was immensely gratified a few months later at Dorset Garden. Early in 1681 appeared his astounding adaptation of *King Lear*, one of the longest-lived of all the Restoration versions. The first edition (Quarto, 1681) gives the following cast: Betterton, Lear; Gillow, Gloster; Wiltshire, Kent; Smith, Edgar; Williams, Bastard; Norris, Cornwall; Bowman, Albany; Jevon, Gentleman-Usher; Mrs. Shadwell, Goneril; Lady Slingsby, Regan; Mrs. Barry, Cordelia.

Genest lists many performances in the first decade of the eighteenth century. The title rôle was played at Drury Lane during Rich's régime by Mills and Powell. Betterton continued to play the part till the end of his career; Genest lists performances by him in 1706, 1708, 1709, and February, 1710. Cordelia was variously played at this time by Mrs. Bracegirdle and Mrs. Rogers; Edgar was acted by Verbruggen, and after his death by Wilks; Edmund became one of Mills's chief parts; and Gloster was one of Cibber's. After Betterton's death Barton Booth succeeded him in the title rôle. Still later this became one of Garrick's most celebrated parts. The reader has noted, of course, the excision of the Fool. This fascinating character was not restored till 1838.[95]

Tate had learned his lesson with *Richard II*. His third and final meddling with Shakespeare was inspired by contemporary politics, but he stuck to ancient history in selecting *Coriolanus* as his hero. *The Ingratitude of a Commonwealth* appeared at Drury Lane during the winter of 1681–1682. It is not mentioned by Downes, and probably died a natural death in extreme infancy. The first edition was printed in 1682, without a cast of characters.

Shortly before Tate commenced his Shakespearean labors, political employment had been found at Dorset Garden for still another of Shakespeare's plays. John Crowne's two adaptations of *Henry VI* belong to the series of "loyal" dramas designed to horrify the public by depicting the dire consequence of factional conflict. *The Misery of Civil War*, though it may have been written after *Henry the Sixth, the First Part*, was almost certainly performed earlier, apparently in the late winter or early spring of 1680. *The First Part* was also staged at Dorset Garden during the following year.

Quarto 1680 of *The Misery* gives the following cast: Williams as King Henry VI; Smith, Edward IV; Bowman, Clarence; Gillow, Richard of Gloucester; Betterton, Warwick; Percival, Old Clifford; Wiltshire, Young Clifford; Mrs. Leigh, Queen Margaret; Mrs. Betterton, Lady Grey; Mrs. Currer, Lady Elianor Butler [a new character, one of Edward's mistresses]. *The First Part* was printed in 1681. As in *The Misery*, Williams was the King Henry. Betterton played Duke Humphrey; and his wife, the Duchess. Harris was the Cardinal; and Lady Slingsby (formerly Mrs. Lee), Margaret. Evidence is wanting to inform us concerning the reception these pieces encountered. It is not likely that they had much success.

The union of 1682 put a stop for twenty years to this orgy of Shakespeare alteration. But before it was consummated one more version was produced, at Drury Lane. The author was none other than Tom D'Urfey; the play was *Cymbeline*, under a new title, *The Injured Princess*. We have no record of Restoration performances of Shakespeare's play before 1702, except in this version.

Whether D'Urfey's play was put on before or after the union of the two houses is a pretty question. Professor Odell thinks after.[96] The stage direction at the beginning of Act II specifies: "Enter behind Cymbeline, Queen, a Purse, Pisanio, Doctor and Guards, a Viol, Mrs. Holten, Sue." The inclusion of an actress's name in a stage direction is a not uncommon slip. Mr. Odell wishes to identify Mrs. Holten (who probably played the small part of Aurelia, the Queen's attendant) with the Mrs. Holden whose celebrated blunder in the part of "Count Paris's Wife" in D'Avenant's production of *Romeo and Juliet* has been referred to earlier in this work. He suggests that since the law forbade actors to jump from one company to the other, Mrs. Holden, a member of the old company of D'Avenant, must have acted in *The Injured Princess* after the reunion. Against this theory are the facts

(1) that the law did not forbid actors to transfer with the consent of the governors, (2) that the law as it stood was frequently not enforced, (3) that Downes, who describes with great detail the season which followed the union, says nothing of *The Injured Princess*, and (4) that the play was entered for publication in May.[97] I am inclined therefore to agree with Genest that the play was probably acted during the last days of the separate existence of Killigrew's company.[98] Moreover, the statement is made in the epilogue that the play "was writ nine years ago"; it may therefore have been acted before 1682. The Quarto fails to give the cast. As far as is known, this adaptation did not hold the stage.

Meanwhile, there were a number of important productions at Dorset Garden. John Banks's *Anna Bullen* (not an alteration of Shakespeare) was acted there before the union. So was Otway's masterpiece, *Venice Preserved*, with Betterton as Jaffier, Smith as Pierre, and Mrs. Barry as Belvidera. So was Ravenscroft's successful farce, *The London Cuckolds*, annually revived for a century on Lord Mayor's Day.

During these last few years, the reader will have noticed, the best of the new authors have gravitated toward the Duke's house. The chiefs of the rival company were past the prime of life, and their younger competitors doubtless presented a superior array of talent. Negotiations were now begun with a view to uniting the two houses.

Notes to Chapter III

1. "Mrs." was still used of the unmarried, "Miss" being reserved for young girls and kept women.
2. Cibber, i, 133.
3. Reprinted by Fitzgerald, *New History of the English Stage*, i, 77–80.
4. Reprinted by Fitzgerald, i, 73–77; and by Lowe, Cibber, vol. i, pp. liii–lxi.
5. Professor Nicoll (*Restoration Drama*, p. 277, n. 2) believes that Jolly's company was acting at Salisbury Court about this time; but this view flies in the face of the Lord Chamberlain's order of Nov. 13, 1661 (L. C. 5/137, p. 333, cited by Mr. Nicoll), addressed to Jolly at the Cockpit. The order of Nov. 26 shows pretty clearly that the quarrel between Beeston and Jolly arose because Jolly had *refused* to act at Salisbury Court.
6. Cibber is doubtless hitting at his colleague, Wilks.
7. Cibber, i, 100 f.
8. *Ibid.*, ii, 300 f.
9. Downes, p. 21.
10. All my references to any of these plays are to performances not later than 1710.
11. Cibber, i, 301.
12. Downes, p. 23.
13. William Winter (*Shakespeare on the Stage*, Second Series, p. 15) gives 1668, which *was* the date, but Old Style.
14. Downes, p. 26.
15. Odell, i, 27.
16. Summers, *Shakespeare Adaptations* (1922), p. xxxv n. The same suggestion had already been made by F. W. Kilbourne, *Alterations and Adaptations of Shakespeare* (1906), p. 128.
17. Downes, p. 26.
18. Hist. MSS Com., 3: 266.
19. Downes, ed. 1789, p. 36.
20. Garrick did not dare to restore the Fool; not till Macready's production in 1838 did he reappear.
21. Downes, ed. Knight, p. 24. Dr. Sprague sends me a reference to this play in a letter of Mrs. Katharine Philips, Jan. 22, 1664 (cited by Julia G. Longe, *Martha Lady Giffard*, p. 39): "They say Harry the 8th and some later ones are little better than puppet plays and will therefore be likely to please the citizens' wives."
22. Lowe, *Betterton*, p. 90. This view is shared by Frederick Hawkins in his "*Henry VIII* on the Stage" (*English Illustrated Magazine*, ix, 291–298; see p. 293). There are two references in *The Rehearsal* (II, v, and V, i) but neither points to an actual adaptation.
23. Summers, *Shakespeare Adaptations*, p. xxxvii.
24. Kilbourne, *Alterations and Adaptations of Shakespeare*, p. 112.
25. Which Dr. Sprague gives me. (*Shakspere Allusion Book*, ii, 321.)

26. Genest, ii, 365.
27. *Ibid.*, ii, 399.
28. *Ibid.*, ii, 413.
29. Cf. Langbaine, *An Account of the English Dramatick Poets* (1691), p. 457; Langbaine–Gildon, *The Lives and Characters of the English Dramatick Poets* (*c.* 1699), p. 127.
30. My observations on the Restoration *Macbeth* originally appeared in *Publications of the Modern Language Association of America*, xl, 619–644 (Sept., 1925).
31. Mr. William Jaggard describes (*Shakespeare Bibliography*, p. 676), as an imitation of *Macbeth*, an anonymous play published in 1662. It is the first in a collection entitled "Gratiae Theatrales, or A choice Ternary of English Plays, Composed upon especial occasions by several ingenious persons; viz. Thorny-Abbey, or The London-Maid; a Tragedy by T. W. The Marriage-Broker, or The Pander, a Comedy; by M. W. *M. A.* Grim the Collier of Croydon, or The Devil and his Dame; with the Devil and St. Dunstan: a Comedy, by I. T. Never before published: but now printed at the request of sundry ingenious friends. London, Printed by R. D. and are to be sold at the sign of the Black Bear in S. Paul's Church-yard. 1662." Langbaine (*Momus Triumphans*, p. 28) lists these plays but gets his notes mixed. His comment on *The Marriage-Broker* obviously belongs to *Thorny-Abbey*. Some prefatory verses by a eulogistic friend refer to the plays as

    "unposted yet, nor with applause
    Or acted here or there. . . .
    Nor need you doubt, in this our Comick Age,
    Welcome acceptance for them from the Stage . . .
    This I'le dare to foretell, although no Seer,
    That Thorny-Abbey will out-date King Lear."

    There is no evidence that *Thorny-Abbey* was ever acted, and almost as little warrant for calling it an imitation of *Macbeth*. A king is murdered by a noble who is his host, and who is instigated by his wife. The murderer slays the king's pages, as Macbeth kills Duncan's grooms. Yet the motive is not ambition but the necessity of covering up oppression of the people, whose cause the good king has espoused. Moreover, the murder and its consequences are a small part of the play. The chief interest lies in the seduction of old Thorny's daughter by the king's brother, who afterwards succeeds to the throne and marries her.
32. Adams, *Dram. Rec.*, p. 138.
33. It was entered in the *Term Catalogue* for July, 1674 (Arber's ed., i, 179).
34. Downes, p. 33.
35. Genest, i, 139.
36. Professor Odell doubts this because the publication of the play after its production at Dorset Garden suggests that much of the machinery may have been added at that time for the larger stage. (Odell, i, 28.)

But the publication (in 1674) was not directly after the performance. As I shall show, it was probably occasioned by the appearance of an unauthorized Quarto in 1673. It is likely enough that after the removal of the Duke's company to Dorset Garden the mechanical features of their performance of *Macbeth* were further elaborated; the state of the text, however, is in my opinion quite another matter.

37. Wheatley (Pepys's *Diary*, iv, 264, n. 1) assumes this to be D'Avenant's version.
38. The other entries throw no light on the question.
39. This is the conclusion of William Archer. See his "*Macbeth* on the Stage," *English Illustrated Magazine*, vi, 234 (Dec., 1888).
40. This was Nathaniel Lee, the dramatist, whose ill success as an actor, as well as that of Otway and of Downes himself, the old prompter describes with gusto (p. 34).
41. Waldron's note in the 1789 ed. of Downes's *Roscius Anglicanus*, p. 43. Mr. Archer justifies the bifurcation of Banquo, in the following terms: "Hamlet's father naturally appeared to his son 'in his habit as he lived,' but Banquo shaking his gory locks at Macbeth should certainly be repulsive rather than 'majestical.' We should be shown the horrid vision of his victim as it appears to the murderer's heated imagination. The elegant Smith probably declined to 'bedabble his face with gore.'" "*Macbeth* on the Stage," *Eng. Ill. Mag.*, vi, 234.
42. Cibber, i, 161 f.
43. We know more about performances at this time than earlier because they were often advertised in the *Daily Courant*.
44. In D'Avenant's version Lennox is a more important part than in the original.
45. Genest, ii, 394.
46. *Ibid.*, 447.
47. It was not so designated in its own time, though it was sometimes called "the theatre *in* Drury Lane."
48. See Pepys, May 7 and 8, 1663. Several historians have accepted as genuine a playbill which appears to confirm the old prompter's date. It advertises that "By his Majesty's Company of Comedians, At the New Theatre in Drury Lane, This day being Thursday, April 8, 1663, will be acted a Comedy called The Humorous Lieutenant." Lowe has pointed out that the date as given by Downes and this playbill contradicts itself, "for April 8, 1663, was not Thursday in Easter Week, and in point of fact was not a Thursday at all, but a Wednesday; which," adds Lowe, "I am afraid, stamps the play-bill . . . as a not very astute forgery." (Lowe, *Betterton*, pp. 100 f.) For a full statement of the case against the playbill see *Notes and Queries*, 1st ser., x, 99, 100. For a copy of the bill itself see J. P. Collier's MS. History of the Restoration Stage (Theatre Collection of Harvard University), Final Draft, p. 62, or the extra-illustrated copy of Doran's *Their Majesties Servants*, p. 60, also in the Theatre Collection.
49. Among her chief rôles were Celia in *Volpone*, Evadne in *The Maid's Tragedy*, Olivia in *The Plain Dealer*, and a number of Dryden's

heroines — Almeria in *The Indian Emperour*, the Queen of Sicily in *Secret Love*, Berenice in *Tyrannick Love*, Lyndaraxa in *The Conquest of Granada*, and Nourmahal in *Aureng-Zebe*.

50. Doran, *Their Majesties' Servants*, ed. Lowe, i, 81.
51. Downes, p. 2. For comment on this list see Knight's preface, p. xxiii.
52. Dr. Arthur C. Sprague (*Beaumont and Fletcher on the Restoration Stage*, p. 77) cites a letter from Lord Granville to Sir William Leveson dated May 5, 1688 (Hist. MSS Com., 5 [part i]: 198), which appears to establish the identity of the Mrs. Boutell of 1697 with this actress.
53. Adams, *Dram. Rec.*, p. 138. The regular fee was £1 for a revived play and £2 for a new one.
54. See *Diary*, Dec. 10 and 22, 1663.
55. Where no authority is hereafter cited for the date of production of a play, the reader may assume Genest. I have also made extensive use of Professor Nicoll's invaluable "Hand-list of Restoration Plays" in his *Restoration Drama*.
56. See A. C. Sprague, *Beaumont and Fletcher on the Restoration Stage*, pp. 28, 29, and 129–137.
57. Downes, p. 33.
58. Nicoll, *Restoration Drama*, pp. 308, 309.
59. Hippolito and Dorinda survived till Macready's production on Oct. 13, 1838. Summers, *Shakespeare Adaptations*, p. lvii.
60. This we may infer from Pepys's entry of May 11, 1668, when he got Harris to repeat the words of the Echo song.
61. Mr. Summers refers to "An Elegy Upon . . . Mr. Edward Angell," reprinted in *A Little Ark*, pp. 38, 39:

    " Who shall play Stephano now? your Tempest's gone
    To raise new Storms i' th' hearts of every one."

    His successor in the part was Estcourt.
62. Underhill was nicknamed "Prince Trincalo." He played the part at Drury Lane for his benefit on May 12, 1710. Genest, ii, 438.
63. There is a gross reference in the prologue to the assumption by a woman of one of the male rôles. There can be little doubt that the indecencies of the D'Avenant–Dryden version had much to do with its success. Hippolito was played at Drury Lane on Jan. 1, 1707, by Mrs. Mountfort. Genest ii, 356.
64. Summers, pp. xlviii f.
65. Nicoll, *Restoration Drama*, pp. 314–316.
66. It must not be supposed that the composition of heroic plays immediately ceased. See Allardyce Nicoll, "The Origin and Types of Heroic Tragedy," *Anglia*, xliv (1920), 325–336.
67. Hist. MSS Com., 2: 22.
68. *Ibid.*, 13 (Appendix, part vi): 270.
69. *Ibid.*, Egmont MSS, ii, 24.
70. Lily B. Campbell, *Scenes and Machines*, p. 217.

71. This curious fact was discovered independently by Mr. W. J. Lawrence (i, 195 f.) and Sir Ernest Clarke (*Athenaeum*, Aug. 25, 1906). Shadwell's changes are not, however, extensive.
72. His statement is confirmed by the publication in 1680, in part ii of Pietro Reggio's Songs, of the new lyric at the end of Act II, beginning "Arise ye subterranean winds," under the title of "A Song in the Tempest. The Words by Mr. Shadwell." See Lawrence, i, 199.
73. Actually 1674. For the date see Lawrence, i, 195 f.
74. Downes, pp. 34 f.
75. No. 2623.
76. Cited by Mr. Lawrence from H. C. de Lafontaine, *The King's Musick*, p. 271. Lawrence, i, 203, 204.
77. *New Shaks. Soc. Papers*, Fourth Series, no. 3, p. 242.
78. *Lives and Characters*, p. 48.
79. See Mr. Summers's reprint, *Shakespeare Adaptations*, pp. 114, 119, 131, 169.
80. Molière was translated, adapted, and stolen over and over again by the Restoration playwrights, usually without acknowledgment.
81. Nicoll, *Dryden as an Adapter of Shakespeare*, p. 34.
82. *Cambridge History of English Literature*, viii, 139.
83. The author of the *D. N. B.* article on Goodman asserts that Cibber praised this actor and predicted his success. It was, of course, the youthful Colley who received the encouragement of Goodman, by that time retired from the stage but fond of dropping in at rehearsals.
84. Cibber, i, 83, n. 1.
85. Downes, pp. 46, 47.
86. Genest, i, 232; Odell, i, 44. Professor Nicoll (*Restoration Drama*, p. 370) says *c.* Dec., 1686. The play was not printed till 1687, and then without a cast of characters; but Downes (p. 9) lists *Titus Andronicus* among the old stock plays of the Theatre Royal from 1663 to the union in 1682, and we have no record of the performance of the play during the Restoration period except in Ravenscroft's version. Moreover, in his "Address to the Reader" Ravenscroft says it appeared at the time of the Popish plot.
87. Odell, i, 46.
88. Dr. Borgman thinks that Purcell's music was probably composed, not for the original production, but some time between 1690 and 1695. A. S. Borgman, *The Dramatic Works of Thomas Shadwell*, Harvard dissertation (1919), unprinted, p. 173.
89. Langbaine–Gildon, *Lives and Characters* (1699), p. 129.
90. Downes, p. 41.
91. Genest, ii, 420.
92. *Ibid.*, i, 277 f.; Nettleton, *English Drama of the Restoration and the Eighteenth Century*, p. 98. Nicoll (*Restoration Drama*, p. 367) says *c.* Sept., 1679, but again fails to give his evidence.
93. Genest, ii, 365.

94. Odell, i, 51 f. Thorndike (*Tragedy*, p. 270 n.) notes that Ward (*Hist. Eng. Dram. Lit.*, iii, 415) is in error in crediting public taste with condemnation of Otway's play.
95. Odell, i, 54, though Wheatley says Elliston revived Shakespeare's play at Drury Lane in 1820 (*Library*, Third Series, iv, 256).
96. Odell, i, 67 f.
97. *Term Catalogue* (ed. Arber), i, 485.
98. Genest, i, 331.

CHAPTER IV

UNION, SECESSION, AND REUNION

From the Union of the Two Patent Companies to the Accession of the First Drury Lane Triumvirate. (November 16, 1682–November 6, 1710.)

THE union was engineered by the Duke's company and was in fact an absorption by it of the Theatre Royal. Betterton and his colleagues now had twenty years of experience behind them. They were in the prime of life; the great actors of the other house were past it, and the public was following the younger men. On October 14, 1682, Hart and Kynaston signed an agreement with Dr. Charles D'Avenant, Thomas Betterton, and William Smith to leave the Theatre Royal and retire on a pension. Mohun actually entered the Dorset Garden company, but probably did not long continue playing. Harris seems to have left the stage before the union. Lacy had died the year before. Kynaston acted for Betterton till about the year 1699. The union has its shady side; there may have been treachery at the Theatre Royal. But, willingly or unwillingly, the patentees joined their rights and the actors their talents. Articles were signed on May 14, 1682.[1]

The united company opened at Drury Lane on November 16, 1682, as the King's Company. Dorset Garden was for some years occasionally used for opera and for the production of the more blatant spectacles. By the turn of the century it had degenerated to an arena for acrobats and animals. It was pulled down in 1709. Killigrew[2] and Hart died in 1683, Mohun in the following year, and their royal patron on February 6, 1685. In the same year as Charles, Otway died, and Etherege began his exile at Ratisbon. Crowne was perhaps the most active of the popular dramatists at this time. The best of his plays, *Sir Courtly Nice*, was produced at Drury Lane in that year; it long held the stage.

But for some years after the union of 1682 there was little important production of new pieces. There now lay available to Betterton an excellent stock of plays that had been the property of the original King's Company, and he turned eagerly to the old rôles of Hart. This accounts for the sudden cessation of tampering with Shakespeare, as well as for the complaints of the dramatists that they find it harder to induce Betterton to stage their works.

With the retirement and death of the veterans of the pre-Wars stage, Betterton was without a competitor for the first place in his profession. *Julius Caesar* was revived in 1683 or 1684, Betterton taking Hart's old part, Brutus. So was *Othello;* the Moor must have been singularly adapted to his genius. Downes gives a list of "old plays" revived at this time by the "mixt company": Fletcher's *Rule a Wife and Have a Wife*, *The Scornful Lady*, *The Beggar's Bush*, *The Double Marriage*, *The Humorous Lieutenant*, and *Rollo;* Wycherley's *The Plain Dealer;* Dryden's *An Evening's Love, or The Mock Astrologer;* Brome's *The Jovial Crew;* Jonson's *Bartholomew Fair;* and Shakespeare's *The Moor of Venice*. As Downes adds, these were acted "withdiversothers," among them *Julius Caesar* and *Henry IV*, probably only *Part I*. Betterton played Hotspur, as we learn from Colley Cibber; in his old age he abandoned that part for Falstaff.

In June, 1685, Dryden's opera, *Albion and Albanius*, was produced. In the preface to the printed text the author compliments Betterton on his staging of the piece; his remarks indicate that at this time the great actor controlled the expenditure for mounting plays and operas. That he was obliged, either by the taste of the court or by the failure of the legitimate drama to fill his house, to divert a portion of his energies from the producing of plays to the introduction of opera is evident from the letters of Lord Preston, the English Ambassador to France. In the summer of 1683 Betterton was in Paris, endeavoring to induce the French opera to give a season in London. Lord Preston writes on August 25 to the Earl of Sunderland:

I have received the honour of your lordship's by Mr. Betterton with his Majesty's commands to me to assist him in treating with some persons capable of representing an opera in England, which I have obeyed as far as it was possible to do it, and Mr. Betterton hath by this post given a full account to Mr. Bridgman of what hath passed, to which I must refer your lordship. By the last post I also received another letter of the 9th instant from your lordship, in which you were pleased to intimate that his Majesty would have me treat again with the Italian players, if by reason of this Queen's death those divertisements cease for this winter here. I am very ready to obey his Majesty in it, but I must acquaint you that all those things are begun again. The comedians acted on Sunday last, and the Italian players on Monday, and to-morrow or the next day the opera will be represented again, so that I believe it will be difficult to persuade these people to leave this place this winter. Your lordship will be pleased to acquaint his Majesty with this, and by the next post to let me know if it be his pleasure that I should treat with them. I shall in the mean time at a distance take care to have them sounded without engaging with them.[3]

In a letter from Paris to the Duke of York on September 22 of the same year Lord Preston recommends one Grahme, and asks the Duke "to speak a good word for him to the King."

Mr. Betterton coming hither some weeks since by his Majesty's command, to endeavour to carry over the Opera, and finding that impracticable, did treat with Monsr. Grahme to go over with him to endeavour to represent something at least like an Opera in England for his Majesty's diversion.

But if the foreign singers were soon to be competitors for the favor of English audiences, there were constant accessions to the ranks of the native actors. George Powell now joined the company; he became, after the secession of 1695, its chief actor.

In 1688 Shadwell's excellent comedy, *The Squire of Alsatia*, was produced, and the year after, his amusing *Bury Fair*, with Betterton and Mountfort as Bellamy and Wildish. Shadwell, now in process of restoration to the decent eminence from which Dryden so brutally dislodged him, was perhaps the most successful of the major dramatists at this time. A letter from Peregrine Bertie to the Countess of Rutland on May 12, 1688, mentions the former of these plays:

> We have had since my last another new play, a comedy writ by Shadwell, called the *Esquire of Alsatia*. It has been acted nine days successively, and on the third day the poet got 16 *l.* more than any other poet ever did.[4]

Other active dramatists during these years were Crowne, Settle, Mrs. Behn, and, of course, Dryden, whose *Don Sebastian* was acted during the season of 1689–1690.

In the meantime the Revolution intervened, but this event hardly influenced the drama at first, except to bring Whig sentiments to the fore.[5] The drama was still distinctly a court affair, though William himself took little interest in it.

In 1690 Dryden's last comedy, *Amphitryon*, was acted, and young Colley Cibber joined the company. In the following year Thomas Dogget, who was to become the leading comedian and, with Cibber and Wilks, manager for a time of the company, began acting at Drury Lane. His first appearance was as Nincompoop in D'Urfey's *Love for Money*. Ben in *Love for Love*, which he created, was the most famous of his rôles. In Shakespeare he was most celebrated as the Shylock of Granville's adaptation, *The Jew of Venice*. Other important rôles were the First Gravedigger, Dapper in *The Alchemist*, and Tom Thimble in *The Rehearsal*. Dogget was the financial genius of the triumvirate that took over the management of Drury Lane in 1710. Three years later, when they were ordered to admit Barton Booth to partnership, he withdrew, though he acted occasionally for several years thereafter. Cibber tells us that the principal actors when he himself joined the company were Messrs. Betterton, Mountfort, Kynaston, Sandford, Nokes, Underhill, and Leigh, and Mmes. Betterton, Barry, [Elizabeth] Leigh, Butler, Mountfort, and Bracegirdle.

In the spring of 1691 a lawyer named Christopher Rich bought out the D'Avenant interest in the patent, and, though this was only slightly more than one sixth of the whole, he managed to control the business for a number of years. In 1691, also, came from Ireland to Drury Lane the fine actor, Robert Wilks. Betterton thought highly of him, but Rich refused him an adequate salary and he returned to his native land. It was at this time that Mrs. Butler also forsook the London stage.

In the MSS of the House of Lords there are several references to an enforced suspension of the company during December of this year. The episode is not without interest, as evidence of the high-handed methods of the nobility in dealing with the theatres. The suspension was ordered on Lord Longueville's complaint that he had been assaulted by the soldiers on guard at the Drury Lane house. Apparently a party of aristocrats tried to enter without the formality of tickets (one of them tossed a guinea to the sentry). A scuffle ensued. The Lords examined the members of the Guard, reprimanded their commander, jailed the sergeant and the sentry, requested the King to stop the use of soldiers at the playhouse (which was done), and then, and not till then, granted the petition of the patentees for the removal of the suspension.[6]

The year 1692 saw several events of importance to the stage. The comedians Anthony Leigh and James Nokes, and the dramatists Thomas Shadwell and Nathaniel Lee, all died in this year. Mountfort was killed by one Captain Hill, a scoundrel who had attempted to abduct Mrs. Bracegirdle, now the second woman of the company. Mountfort was believed, but apparently without just cause, to be her successful lover. About two years later his widow married Jack Verbruggen, an important actor, and by that time second only to Betterton himself.[7]

This year is also notable for the production of *The Fairy Queen*, the only alteration of Shakespeare perpetrated between the close of the epidemic of 1678–1682 and the turn of the century. This piece consists of a selection of scenes from *A Midsummer Night's Dream*, embellished with scenery and a great deal of dancing, the whole set to music by Purcell. For this production the Dorset Garden theatre was used. The Quarto (1692) does not give the cast.[8]

That this opera had some success is evident from the appearance of another edition in 1693 with additional songs,[9] and from Downes's description:

> The Fairy Queen, made into an Opera, from a Comedy of Mr. Shakespears: This in Ornaments was Superior to the other Two [*King Arthur* and *The Prophetess*]; especially in Cloaths, for all the Singers and Dancers, Scenes, Machines and Decorations, all most profusely set off; and excellently perform'd, chiefly the Instrumental and Vocal part Compos'd by the said Mr. Purcel, and Dances by Mr. Priest. The Court and Town were wonderfully satisfy'd with it; but the Expences in setting it out being so great, the Company got very little by it.[10]

The united company lasted for thirteen years. Since *The Fairy Queen* was its only new alteration of Shakespeare, we need not attempt to describe in detail its further activities, or to trace the various steps in the quarrel between the actors and Rich, their manager, which led in 1695 to the secession of Betterton and his principal colleagues.[11] Dorset, the Lord Chamberlain, was the actors' friend at court, and King William favored their cause, legal opinion holding that no royal patent could tie the hands of a later monarch. While the dispute was in progress Queen Mary died (December 28, 1694), and plays were suspended till the following April.

The patentees recognized the inevitability of secession and hastened to secure the actors that were left to them. Powell,

Verbruggen, and Cibber all received increases in salary. The patent company was, however, so decimated that new recruits had to be sought. Benjamin Johnson and William Bullock now joined. They were excellent actors. The former had a long career; he died in August, 1742, in his seventy-seventh year, having retired from the stage but two or three months before. He was proud of his name, and was successful in the Jonsonian comedy, among other rôles as Morose, Corbaccio, Waspe, and Ananias. Among his Shakespearean parts were the First Gravedigger, Shallow, Caliban, and (in Macklin's famous revival of *The Merchant* in 1741) Old Gobbo. On the retirement of Dogget he became the leading low comedian. Bullock was very popular. Gildon pronounces him "the best comedian that has trod the Stage since Nokes and Lee." [12] He remained on the stage at least till 1739.

Cibber continues:

> Forces being thus raised, and the War declared on both Sides, Betterton and his Chiefs had the Honour of an Audience of the King, who consider'd them as the only Subjects whom he had not yet deliver'd from arbitrary Power, and graciously dismiss'd them with an Assurance of Relief and Support — Accordingly a select number of them were impower'd by his Royal Licence to act in a separate Theatre for themselves. This great Point being obtain'd, many People of Quality came into a voluntary Subscription of twenty, and some of forty Guineas a-piece, for erecting a Theatre within the Walls of the Tennis-Court in Lincoln-Inn Fields.

The time required for fitting it up enabled the patentees to begin first. They reopened Drury Lane on April 4 with Mrs. Behn's *Abdelazer, or The Moor's Revenge*. There was a good house the first day, but the "next Day's Audience sunk to nothing."

On April 30, 1695, "the New Theatre in Lincoln's Inn Fields" opened with a tremendous hit, Congreve's *Love for Love*, which ran for thirteen days. Cibber declares that "they had seldom occasion to act any other Play 'till the End of the

Season." The new house stood in what was afterwards called Portugal Street (parallel with Portugal Row — the site of D'Avenant's old Lincoln's Inn Fields house — and farther south); the theatre was sometimes described as in Little Lincoln's Inn Fields.[13]

The leading members of the new association were Betterton, Mrs. Barry, Mrs. Bracegirdle, Bowman, Williams,[14] Underhill, and Dogget. Sandford and Smith (who had been prevailed on to return to the stage after a temporary retirement) preferred to take salaries rather than shares, for their names do not appear in the license. That this was the case with Sandford, and therefore assumably with Smith, we are assured by one of Tony Aston's anecdotes.[15]

At first the seceding company prospered. Even, says Cibber, when their affairs were declining, they stood much higher in the public estimation than their rivals. Shakespearean representation in particular, he declares, was inferior at Drury Lane. Powell was rashly eager to display himself in Betterton's rôles, and the effect was not happy. But dissensions ensued at Little Lincoln's Inn Fields. The tragedians took a superior tone with the comedians, as if differences in mimic rank on the stage extended to the realities of actual life; while the comedians resented the mounting costs of the trappings required for tragedy, and insisted on the superior merits of comedy, which Dogget held to be aesthetically superior, being closer to nature. Finally, in November, 1700, the Lord Chamberlain ordered Betterton to take supreme command.

Moreover, the younger actors at Drury Lane gradually improved. The newest of the dramatists, Sir John Vanbrugh, elected to give them most of his work, which proved a considerable factor in the success of the patent theatre. The year 1696 brought a smashing hit, Southerne's *Oroonoko*, based on Mrs. Behn's famous novel. Powell had been cast for the title rôle, but the Lord Chamberlain, whose authority over the stages was practically unlimited, ordered it given to Verbruggen, a less polished but more rugged actor, whose performance found great favor with the public. In the same year was acted the first of two successful plays with fop parts, in which Cibber, now an actor of consequence, leaped into actual fame. This was his own *Love's Last Shift*, which was followed during the season of 1696–1697 by Vanbrugh's sequel to it, *The Relapse*. Lord Foppington in the latter play became one of Cibber's most celebrated vehicles. Against these successes the only novelties the Bettertonians could offer were Vanbrugh's masterpiece, *The Provoked Wife*, with their leader as Sir John Brute, and Congreve's sole essay in tragedy, *The Mourning Bride*, both acted in 1697.

In the preceding year John Mills had joined the seceding actors. He was a valuable recruit and had a long career, spending nearly thirty years, after the reunion, on the stage of Drury Lane. Among his important rôles were Macbeth, Corvino in *Volpone*, Ventidius in *All for Love*, Winlove in Lacy's *Sauny the Scot*, and Pierre in Otway's *Venice Preserved*. He died in 1736.

In 1698 appeared Jeremy Collier's notorious onslaught on the theatres, *A Short View of the Immorality and Profaneness of the English Stage*. Into the details of the long-winded controversy which followed we cannot go. Collier was not a voice crying in the wilderness; he vocalized what many Englishmen had been thinking. Yet the result of his fulminations is doubtful. "The pages of Genest, a much surer guide than tradition or desire," says the *Cambridge History*, "make evident the complete failure of Collier's attack. Dryden, Shadwell, Aphra Behn and D'Urfey, Ravenscroft and Wycherley were still triumphant." [16] True enough, as regards performance. But the new plays of the younger dramatists, Cibber and Farquhar, show some consciousness of Collier's strictures. Lowe, indeed, attributes directly to Collier's ferocity the lack of new plays of merit for the next two or three years, about the only exceptions being those of Farquhar.[17] Perhaps this dearth was to some extent responsible for the next outburst of Shakespeare alteration, which began in the season which saw the turn of the century.

About this time Kynaston, Sandford, and Williams seem to have left the stage. Smith had died shortly after the opening at Little Lincoln's Inn Fields. On the other hand, Drury Lane was greatly strengthened by the engagement of Mrs. Oldfield and Robert Wilks. The former slowly made her way to the first rank of the profession. Wilks, already an accomplished actor, speedily surpassed Powell in public favor. Upon Betterton's death Wilks succeeded to his principal comic rôles and a number of his tragic ones, including *Hamlet*.

The season of 1699–1700 found neither company enjoying prosperity. There was ruthless competition between them, and a running fire of recrimination was kept up in the prologues and epilogues at both houses. Dryden died on May 1, 1700; some of his last writing was of this nature in the service of the Bettertonian troupe.

Once again we find an epidemic of Shakespeare alteration coëxistent with the bitter rivalry of theatres and with desperate efforts to attract the public by opera. Downes tell us that

> Mr. Betterton to gratify the desires and Fancies of the Nobility and Gentry; procur'd from Abroad the best Dances and Singers, as, Monsieur L'Abbe, Madam Sublini, Monsieur Balon, Margarita Delpine, Maria Gallia and divers others; who being Exorbitantly Expensive, produc'd small Profit to him and his Company, but vast Gain to themselves; Madam Delpine since her Arrival in England, by Modest Computation; having got by the Stage and Gentry, above 10000 Guineas.

Betterton's *Henry IV* and Gildon's *Measure for Measure* were acted during the season of 1699–1700. Both were produced at Little Lincoln's Inn Fields, and both were printed in quarto in 1700.

We have noticed that, after the union of 1682 had placed *Henry IV* at Betterton's disposal, the great actor had played Hotspur. As he grew older, that impetuous character probably became less suited to him; perhaps the play had been shelved for several seasons when he determined to revive it, and, accepting the inevitable, to seek favor in that magnificent retreat of elderly comedians, the easy-going rôle of Falstaff. As far as we know, only *Part One* was produced by Betterton. His text is not an adaptation but an unobjectionable acting version with cuts. It was produced in midwinter, as is evident from a letter written by Villiers Bathurst to Dr. Arthur Charlett, Master of University College, dated Bond Street, January 28, 1699/1700:

> The Wits of all qualities have lately entertained themselves with a revived humour of Sir John Falstaff in Henry the Fourth, which has drawn all the town, more than any new play that has bin produced of late; which shews that Shakespeare's wit will always last: and the criticks allow that Mr. Betterton has hitt the humour of Falstaff better than any that have aimed at it before.[18]

Betterton acted Falstaff throughout the remainder of his career. Genest notes performances on November 9, 1704,[19] at Little Lincoln's Inn Fields; on October 26, 1706, at the Haymarket (Verbruggen, Hotspur; Wilks, Prince Hal; Keen, King; Booth, Vernon); on November 19, 1707, at the Haymarket (Booth, Hotspur; Cibber, Worcester); and on October 28, 1708, by the reunited company at Drury Lane (Powell, Hotspur; Keen, King Henry; Wilks, Prince Hal; Cibber, Glendower; Johnson and Bullock, Carriers; Mrs. Bradshaw, Lady Hotspur; Mrs. Powell, Hostess).[20]

Gildon's operatic adaptation of *Measure for Measure* was, on the contrary, a comparative failure, though Mrs. Willis and Mrs. Porter thought enough of it to choose it for their joint benefit at the Haymarket on April 26, 1706.[21] The original cast included Betterton, Angelo; Verbruggen (at the moment a renegade from Drury Lane), Claudio; Arnold, the Duke; Berry, Escalus; Baile, Lucio; Pack, Balthazar; Freeman, Provost; Mrs. Bracegirdle, Isabella; Mrs. Bowman, Julietta; Mrs. Prince, Mariana. A reference to Falstaff in the epilogue indicates that the play was produced after the Bettertonian *Henry IV*.

Probably not long after, appeared at the other house the longest-lived of all the alterations of Shakespeare's plays, the *Richard III* of Cibber, which has never been quite driven off the stage. It was launched on its long career at Drury Lane in 1700, Cibber himself playing Richard. Wilks acted Henry VI; Powell, Buckingham; Mills, Stanley; Simpson, Norfolk; Kent, Ratcliff; Thomas, Catesby; Evans, Richmond; Fairbank, Oxford; Mrs. Knight, Elizabeth; Mrs. Rogers, Anne; Mrs. Powell, Duchess of York; Mrs. Allison, Prince of Wales; Miss Chock, Duke of York. Apparently this play had not been acted before on the Restoration stage, though Betterton had appeared as Richard in an independent play, Caryl's *The English Princess*.[22]

In his *Apology* Cibber offers some observations on his version and its reception by the public. His enemies derided his acting of the title rôle, as, for instance, in *The Laureate:*

> This same Mender of Shakespear chose the principal Part, viz. the King, for himself; and accordingly being invested with the purple Robe, he screamed thro' four Acts without Dignity or Decency. The Audience ill-pleas'd with the Farce, accompany'd him with a smile of Contempt, but in the fifth Act, he degenerated all at once into Sir Novelty; and when in the Heat of the Battle at Bosworth Field, the King is dismounted, our Comic-Tragedian came on the Stage, really breathless, and in a seeming Panick, screaming out this line thus — *A Harse, a Harse, my Kingdom for a Harse.* This highly delighted some, and disgusted others of his Auditors; and when he was kill'd by Richmond, one might plainly perceive that the good People were not better pleas'd that so execrable a Tyrant was destroy'd, than that so execrable an Actor was silent.[23]

The original production was acted without the first act, which the Master of the Revels, Charles Killigrew, would not allow. Of this arbitrary procedure Cibber complains bitterly in his *Apology*.

This extraordinary Stroke of a *Sic volo* occasion'd my applying to him for the small Indulgence of a Speech or two, that the other four Acts might limp on with a little less Absurdity! no! he had not leisure to consider what might be separately inoffensive. He had an Objection to the whole Act, and the Reason he gave for it was, that the Distresses of King Henry the Sixth, who is kill'd by Richard in the first Act, would put weak People too much in mind of King James then living in France; a notable Proof of his Zeal for the Government! Those who have read either the Play or the History, I dare say will think he strain'd hard for the Parallel. In a Word, we were forc'd, for some few Years, to let the Play take its Fate with only four Acts divided into five; by the Loss of so considerable a Limb, may one not modestly suppose it was robbed of at least a fifth Part of that Favour it afterwards met with? For tho' this first Act was at last recovered, and made the Play whole again, yet the Relief came too late to repay me for the Pains I had taken in it.

Despite the long vogue of the piece, it did not immediately hit the public fancy. For his third day (when the author regularly received the proceeds) Cibber had less than £5![24] The lucky author-actor lived to see it played over and over again.[25]

But the most important production of 1700 had nothing to do with Shakespeare. That year saw the original performance in Lincoln's Inn Fields of Congreve's masterpiece, *The Way of the World*. Betterton played Fainall, leaving Mirabell to Verbruggen. Mrs. Bracegirdle acted Millamant, and Mrs. Barry, Mrs. Marwood. The reason for the play's failure to please is set forth in a letter of March 12, 1700,[26] to Arthur Kay from Lady Marow, who, with a sagacity not always found in an amateur critic, puts her finger on the precise weak spot in the play and indeed in the school of which it is the great example: "'The way of the World,' Congreve's new play, doth not answer expectation, there being no plot in it but many witty things to ridicule the Chocolate House, and the fantastical part of the world." The criticism is just: the plot is extremely difficult to follow.

The seceding actors were joined during 1700 by Barton Booth (1681–1733), who was destined to become Betterton's successor in most of the great tragic rôles. His colleagues were slow to acknowledge his merit; not till his performance of Addison's *Cato* in 1713 did he take his rightful place. He was then, by royal command, admitted into the management, from which the jealousy of Wilks, who, in the assignment of parts, had favored Mills at Booth's expense, had hitherto excluded him. Unlike some of his theatrical associates, Booth was a gentleman and, if not a scholar, at least a cultivated person. His love of Shakespeare and of Milton (he could repeat from memory long passages of *Paradise Lost*) stamps him as a man of taste.

In 1701 Jo Haynes died. In the same year Dogget (who had seceded from the seceders) returned to Betterton and acted Shylock in Granville's *The Jew of Venice*. Betterton played Bassanio; Mrs. Bracegirdle, Portia; Verbruggen, Antonio; Booth, Gratiano; Bailey, Lorenzo; Harris, the Duke; Mrs. Bowman, Nerissa; Mrs. Porter, Jessica. This adaptation lasted till 1741, when Macklin restored "the Jew that Shakespeare drew."

Another production of Shakespeare at Little Lincoln's Inn Fields came the following year (1702), when *Cymbeline* was performed. Facts are lacking concerning this revival; how many of D'Urfey's alterations were retained we have no means of knowing.

Also in 1702, but at Drury Lane, Dennis's *The Comical Gallant* was staged. The eminent critic's vulgarization of *The Merry Wives* was printed in the same year, but without a list of the actors. Genest thinks that the Falstaff was Powell.

ROBERT WILKS

ANNE BRACEGIRDLE

CAVE UNDERHILL AS OBADIAH

BARTON BOOTH

It is evident from the preface that the piece was a flat failure.

The last Shakespeare alteration for many years was staged at Little Lincoln's Inn Fields in 1703. This was a stupid version of *Twelfth Night*, by Charles Burnaby, entitled *Love Betray'd, or The Agreable Disappointment.* The Quarto printed the same year gives the following cast: Verbruggen, Moreno; Powell, (temporarily a rebel against Rich) Drances; Booth, Sebastian; Dogget, Taquilet; Fieldhouse, Rodoregue; Pack, Pedro; Mrs. Bracegirdle, Vilaretta; Mrs. Prince, Caesario; Mrs. Leigh, Dromia; Mrs. Lawson, Lawra. Genest records another performance, a benefit revival, at the same theatre on March 1, 1705,[27] but the play seems to have had but moderate success.

The period of tampering with Shakespeare which now closes would thus be inconsiderable in comparison with that of 1678–1682, were it not that it launched Granville's *Jew* and Cibber's *Richard* on their careers. Before mid-century the tide was turning. Addison's was but one of several voices raised to protest against the mangling of the plays. It remains for me only to mention a few matters of subsequent stage history.

The début of the celebrated Irish comedian, Estcourt, calls for notice because of his activity in Shakespearean parts. His first appearance in London was on October 18, 1703, as Dominique in Dryden's *The Spanish Friar.* He retired from the stage about 1712 and opened the Bumper Tavern in Covent Garden. Among his chief rôles were Falstaff and the First Gravedigger, Bayes in *The Rehearsal*, Crack in *Sir Courtly Nice*, Captain Bluff in *The Old Bachelor*, and Sergeant Kite in *The Recruiting Officer*, which he created.

Early in 1705 Betterton assigned his interests to Vanbrugh and Congreve, who proposed to build a larger and more suitable theatre for Betterton and his company, and to that end invited subscriptions. Congreve soon withdrew; but thirty persons of quality paid £100 each, in return for which they were to have free admission for life. On March 31 the last performance was given at Little Lincoln's Inn Fields.[28] The new house, the Haymarket, opened on April 9, 1705, with *The Triumphs of Love* "set to Italian music." The venture was a failure, partly because the new foreign singers did not please, partly because Vanbrugh had built on too grand a scale and when legitimate plays were performed the actors could not be heard.[29]

For several years there had been talk of reuniting the companies, but Rich would not hear of it. In the summer of 1706 Vanbrugh gave up hope at the Haymarket, and leased that house to Owen Swiney, a factotum of Rich's, who allowed him to engage nearly all his best actors while he himself devoted the season of 1706–1707 at Drury Lane to opera. Accordingly, the Bettertonians at the Haymarket were joined by Wilks, Mills, Keen, Johnson, Bullock, Mrs. Oldfield, and Mrs. Rogers; only Cibber, Powell, Pinkethman, and (probably) Estcourt remaining at Drury Lane.

The recruited Haymarket company opened on October 15, 1706, and speedily became so successful that Swiney actually began to pay his actors' salaries. He next induced Cibber to join him, broke with Rich, and in about a month was able to wipe out his indebtedness to the magnate of Drury Lane.

From then on, Rich played a losing game, and in 1707 the union was forced upon him. The edict was issued on December 31, at the instance of Colonel Henry Brett, to whom his friend, Sir Thomas Skipwith, had jocosely (as he afterwards maintained) assigned his considerable share in the Drury Lane patent. By its terms the companies were united and the theatres were separated. The time was, in fact, ripe for an independent opera. The Neapolitan mezzo-soprano, Nicolini (Nicolo Grunaldi), had just arrived in England and was at once engaged. No. 115 of the *Tatler* (January 3, 1710) is loud in his praise. Like Chaliapin to-day, he was renowned as a better actor than the actors themselves. Swiney accepted the directorship of opera at the Haymarket, and all the actors were ordered to assemble at Drury Lane as "her Majesty's only Company of Comedians." [30] On January 6, 1708, the Lord Chamberlain ordered that no actors should be employed at Drury Lane who were not her Majesty's servants. Four days later the company at the Haymarket gave their final performance there. The occasion was Wilks's benefit, and the play was *Macbeth*.

On January 15, 1708, the united company opened at Drury Lane in *Hamlet* with Wilks as the Prince. The season proved successful, and Skipwith naturally repented the transfer of his share to Brett. He finally brought suit, alleging that the assignment was in trust. Brett withdrew in disgust from active participation in the enterprise, constituting (in an indenture dated March 31, 1708) Wilks, Estcourt, and Cibber his deputies.[31] After Skipwith's death Brett assigned the share to the former's son.

Now the old actors begin rapidly to drop out. By April 26, 1708, Verbruggen had died, for on that date a benefit was held for his "young orphan child." In June, at the end of the season, Mrs. Barry retired, though she acted again at the Haymarket during the season of 1709–1710. On February 5, 1709, Betterton created a part for the last time; it was Virginius in Dennis's tragedy of *Appius and Virginia*. On April 7 was held his most famous benefit. The play selected was *Love for Love*. Mrs. Barry and Mrs. Bracegirdle returned to the stage to act Mrs. Frail and Angelica; and Dogget, though no longer a member of the company, came back to play Ben for his old chief.

In the meantime a quarrel, which led eventually to Rich's downfall, was brewing over this very matter of benefits, which, having come to be more profitable than salaries, were always a matter of stipulation when the actors were engaged. Rich refused to keep the oral agreements he had made upon the return of the actors from the Haymarket, and they appealed to the Lord Chamberlain for redress. The manager remaining obdurate, that official closed Drury Lane on June 4, 1709.

Swiney, at the Haymarket, was then allowed to form a new company. Wilks, Dogget, and Cibber became sharers, and practically all the other actors of importance walked out of the patent theatre with them. Mrs. Oldfield, now the leading woman, had been nominated among the sharers, but upon Dogget's objection on the ground of her sex she was asked to name her own figure. Betterton doubtless preferred a salary to managerial cares. Mrs. Barry and Mrs. Bracegirdle had retired. The only other actor who could have claimed a share in the direction was Barton Booth. Cibber says he was too young, but Lowe thinks it was Wilks's favoritism to Mills in the assignment of parts that made Booth elect to remain at Drury Lane.[32] Rich still hoped to reopen that house and kept a company together, headed by Booth and Powell.

During the summer the seceding actors remodelled the Haymarket, to some extent improving its acoustics, and on September 15, 1709, began acting there. Five days later, Betterton played *Hamlet* for the last time. He was then nearly seventy-four years old; yet Steele, in a passage already cited, applauded the youthfulness of his performance.

Cibber informs us that the business of the independents was injured during the season of 1709–1710 by the long trial of Dr. Sacheverell,—it lasted over three weeks and drew their aristocratic clientèle to Westminster Hall,—and by the success of a new play performed at Drury Lane by a new company.

Rich had gone over the Lord Chamberlain's head in an effort to secure revocation of the order against him; but in vain. Besides Rich, the patentees who joined in petitioning the Queen at this time were Charles Killigrew, Dr. Charles

D'Avenant, Sir Thomas Skipwith, Bart., William Collier, Lord Guildford, Lord Harvey, Ann Shadwell, widow, and about eleven other persons. Rich's actors also petitioned; the only names of importance are those of Barton Booth, Theophilus Keen, and George Powell. On September 6, 1709, Rich advertised a performance of *The Recruiting Officer*, but, as Genest observes, there is every reason to believe it was not given.

The next move was made by the William Collier whose name appears as one of the patentees petitioning. He was a lawyer, M. P. for Truro, and a convivial favorite. For one or more of these reasons he apparently had no difficulty in securing a license to perform plays. His problem then became how to get possession of Drury Lane. There Rich was still entrenched, for by the terms of his tenancy he was obliged to pay rent only when plays were acted. Collier secured a lease by the simple process of offering to pay a higher rent, and then, "by the assistance of a rabble," stormed and occupied the theatre itself. Rich, however, had got wind of the attack and succeeded in making off with everything movable except a few old scenes. The *Tatler* for November 26, 1709, gives an account of this somewhat hilarious episode. All Rich's remaining actors went over to Collier. The next evening, November 23, 1709, they reopened Drury Lane with *Aureng-Zebe*.

The play which, along with the trial of Sacheverell, gave concern to the other (the independent) company was Charles Shadwell's *The Fair Quaker of Deal*, produced at Drury Lane on February 5, 1710. But after the trial was over, and Shadwell's play had run its course, the tide, Cibber tells us, began to turn in favor of the troupe at the Haymarket. At last Collier proposed to exchange theatres, equipment, and companies with Swiney, who accepted the offer.

Meanwhile Betterton had acted for the last time. He appeared at the Haymarket on April 13, 1710, for his benefit, as Melantius in *The Maid's Tragedy*. Enfeebled by a severe attack of the gout, he would not disappoint his audience, and played with one foot in a slipper. The exertion killed him; he died on April 28, and on May 2 he was buried in Westminster Abbey. In the course of the next month the oldest of his colleagues, Cave Underhill, made his final appearance.

On November 6, 1710, a license to use the Drury Lane theatre was issued to Swiney, Wilks, Cibber, and Dogget. From then on "the Comedians were in Possession of Drury-Lane from whence," declares Cibber, "during my time upon the Stage they never departed." [33]

Notes to Chapter IV

1. These are given by Fitzgerald, i, 154–158.
2. His son Charles had already succeeded to the patent and had also been appointed (1677) Master of the Revels.
3. Hist. MSS Com., 7: 288.
4. *Ibid.*, 12 (Appendix, part v): 119.
5. In a private letter of June 10, 1693, a curious episode is narrated which perhaps indicates some recalcitrancy on the part of the players: "A woman of the play-house, being heard to sing a beastly lampoon on the Queene, an officer was sent to seize her, and in her lodgings were found several of the libells, and one of her own handwriting. She was . . . tryed, and sentenced to be exposed on the pillory at 3 severall places." (Hist. MSS Com., 5: 384.)
6. *Ibid.*, 13 (Appendix, part v): 464 f.
7. Verbruggen's career began about 1688. *The Laureate* (p. 58) rebukes Cibber because "he hardly ever mentions Mr. Verbruggen, who was in many Characters an excellent Actor." (Cibber, i, 157, n. 2.) Among his more important rôles were Edgar in Tate's *Lear*, Cassius, Hotspur, Horatio, Oroonoko in Southerne's play, Ventidius in Dryden's *All for Love*, Pierre in Otway's *Venice Preserved*, Mirabell in Congreve's *The Way of the World*, and, above all, Alexander in Lee's *The Rival Queens*.
8. The "book" has been attributed to Settle. See the communication of Professor Nicoll, in *London Times Lit. Sup.*, March 15, 1923, p. 180.
9. Thus Jaggard, p. 409. But Miss Bartlett (*Mr. William Shakespeare*, p. 78) distinguishes two series of the first edition, and states that a second edition also appeared in 1692, "containing an extra scene in Act I." The British Museum copy of the second edition is, however, dated 1693.
10. Downes, pp. 42, 43.
11. For the whole affair see Cibber, i, 187 f.
12. Charles Gildon, *Comparison between the Two Stages*, p. 199. Mr. G. Thorn-Drury rejects Malone's ascription of this work to Gildon. (*Rev. of Eng. Studies*, i, 96.)
13. Cunningham–Wheatley (*London Past and Present*, ii, 397) state that it was on the site of the first Duke's theatre in Lincoln's Inn Fields, originally occupied by Lisle's tennis court, which had again been devoted to that sport after the removal to Dorset Garden in 1671, and was now, for the second time, fitted up as a theatre. Professor Kittredge, to whom I am indebted for the location of the new theatre in Portugal *Street*, points out that Aubrey makes it clear that, after D'Avenant's old Lincoln's Inn Fields theatre was abandoned in favor of Dorset Garden, the building was again used as a tennis court: "It is now a Tennis court again, upon the building of the duke's house in Dorset garden." (Aubrey, *Brief Lives*, ed. Clark, i, 208.) That the site was Portugal Street we learn from Strype's Stow (ed. 1720), vol. ii,

bk. 4, p. 119, where Rich's later Lincoln's Inn Fields theatre (the third theatrical enterprise there) is described as "On the Back side of Portugal Row."

14. Williams and Mrs. Verbruggen speedily returned to Drury Lane. See Genest, ii, 64; Cibber, i, 201. The latter declares that they were "of more Importance than any of those to whose Assistance they came." The reason for their desertion of the seceding actors Cibber explains as "upon a too nice (not to say severe) Punctilio; in not allowing them to be equal Sharers with the rest." According to Cibber neither actually appeared at Little Lincoln's Inn Fields. The following lines in the prologue of the opening play, Congreve's *Love for Love*, presumably refer to these two players:

   "Forbear your Wonder, and the Fault forgive,
   If in our larger Family we grieve
   One falling Adam, and one tempted Eve."

15. See Cibber, ii, 306 f.
16. *Camb. Hist. Eng. Lit.*, viii, 168.
17. Lowe, *Betterton*, p. 162.
18. Cited by G. Thorn-Drury, *More Seventeenth Century Allusions to Shakespeare*, p. 48.
19. I have not attempted to give complete lists of performances between 1700 and 1710. The best collections are in Genest, ii, and Nicoll, *Early Eighteenth Century Drama*.
20. This performance was probably not given. See Genest, ii, 409.
21. *Ibid.*, 351.
22. And, as Dr. Sprague reminds me, the *Covent Garden Drollery* contains a "Prologue to *Richard the third*." (*Shakspere Allusion Book*, ii, 103, 104.) The existence of this composition is not, of course, admissible as evidence that the play was ever acted. Furnivall makes no such claim, though he dates the piece (with little warrant) in 1661.
23. *The Laureate*, p. 35, cited by Lowe, Cibber, i, 140 n.
24. Cibber, "To the Reader," *Ximena* (1719). Cited by Sprague, *Mod. Lang. Notes*, xlii, 31, n. 8 (Jan., 1927).
25. See Nicoll, *Early Eighteenth Century Drama*, p. 307, for a long list of performances.
26. Hist. MSS Com., 15 (Appendix, part i) (Dartmouth MSS, iii): 145.
27. Genest, ii, 291, 329.
28. *Ibid.*, 329. The company seems, however, to have begun the season 1705–1706 there. See *Ibid.*, 342, 343. Collier (MS. Hist. Rest. Stage, Final Draft, p. 366) suggests that perhaps minor alterations at the Haymarket lacked completion. The company had returned to the Haymarket by Oct. 30.
29. Cf. Cibber, i, 325; Downes, p. 48.
30. Cibber, ii, 48 f.; Genest, ii, 385 f. Fitzgerald (i, 258, 259) gives substantially the terms of the edict of Dec. 31, 1707.
31. Genest, ii, 405 f.; Cibber, ii, 56, n. The indenture is reprinted by Fitzgerald, ii, 443–446.

32. Cibber, ii, 70, n. 2. Cf. his hint that Mills's chief recommendation was his friendship with Wilks, who "rather chose him for his second in many Plays, than an Actor of perhaps greater Skill that was not so laboriously diligent" (i, 260).

33. Collier soon repented his election of opera and contrived the ousting of Swiney, who was forced, after another season as impressario at the Haymarket, to flee from his debts and sojourn for twenty years abroad. The actor-managers bought off Collier from meddling with them; he was finally evicted in favor of Steele upon the accession of George I. Dogget soon retired, and Booth was admitted to a share in the management with Wilks and Cibber. This arrangement lasted for twenty years. Rich continued to scheme; his project was to rebuild in Lincoln's Inn Fields the theatre occupied by the Bettertonians, 1695–1705. He died before his plan was realized, but his son revived the patent there in 1714. See Cibber, ii, 78 f.

PART II

THE RESTORATION TEXTS

CHAPTER V

D'AVENANT'S ADAPTATIONS

1. The Law against Lovers

OF D'Avenant's three adaptations of Shakespeare, *Macbeth*, as we have seen, was the earliest to be produced. It is also the least altered. I defer consideration of it, however, because Sir William's revising hand will be much plainer to the reader if he examines the other adaptations first. These are unquestionably D'Avenant's; I hope to show that the hand is the same in all three.

As Elze remarks, D'Avenant's dramatic intentions were very different from Shakespeare's. The Caroline Laureate anticipates the younger Dumas in aiming at pomp, virtue and refinement. The Frenchman was the bastard son of the great exemplar of the cloak-and-sword formula, while Sir William is said to have encouraged the tale that his paternity was also highly romantic. Whether or not it was in their blood, neither was kept from the extravagances of melodrama by the passion for reform.

Yet in contrast with most of his weightier contemporaries, and especially with his successor to the laurel, D'Avenant might almost be called a prude. He took quite seriously the injunction of the royal patent to purge the old plays of scurrility. But he was a very conscious artist, too; and we shall find him making many changes in Shakespeare's structure and text, sometimes from subservience to the rules of drama as expounded by the French neo-classicists and their English followers, sometimes for the mere sake of modernizing, sometimes apparently out of sheer delight in tampering. He used to say that he thought he wrote with the very spirit of Shake-

CHAPTER V

D'AVENANT'S ADAPTATIONS

1. The Law against Lovers

OF D'Avenant's three adaptations of Shakespeare, *Hamlet*, as we have seen, was the earliest to be produced. It is also the least altered. I defer consideration of it, however, because Sir William's revising hand will be much plainer to the reader if he examines the other adaptations first. These are unquestionably D'Avenant's; I hope to show that the hand is the same in all three.

As Elze remarks,[1] D'Avenant's dramatic intentions were very different from Shakespeare's. The Caroline Laureate anticipates the younger Dumas in claiming to promote virtue and refinement. The Frenchman was the bastard son of the great exemplar of the cloak and sword formula, while Sir William is said to have encouraged the yarn that his paternity was also highly romantic. Whether or not it was in their blood, neither was kept from the extravagances of melodrama by his predilection for reform.

Yet in contrast with most of his writing contemporaries, and especially with his successor to the laurel, D'Avenant might almost be called a prude. He took quite seriously the injunction of the royal patent to purge the old plays of scurrility. But he was a very conscious artist, too; and we shall find him making many changes in Shakespeare's structure and text, sometimes from subservience to the rules of drama as expounded by the French neo-classical critics and their English followers, sometimes for the mere sake of modernizing, sometimes apparently out of sheer delight in tampering. He used to say that he thought he wrote with the very spirit of Shakespeare. Though this extravagance was uttered in his cups, it illuminates his willingness to "improve" what he liked to regard as a paternal legacy.

The Law against Lovers occupies pages 272–329 of the second part of the posthumous folio of D'Avenant's works (1673). "The Names of the Persons" are as follows:

The Duke of Savoy.	Provost.
Lord Angelo, his Deputy.	Fryer Thomas.
Benedict, Brother to Angelo.	Bernardine, a Prisoner.
Lucio } His Friends.	Jaylor.
Balthazar }	Fool.
Eschalus, a Counsellor.	Hangman.
Claudio, in love with Julietta.	Pages.

Beatrice, a great Heiress.
Isabella, Sister to Claudio.
Julietta, Mistress to Claudio.
Viola, Sister to Beatrice; very young.
Francisca, a Nun.

Scene: Turin.

The play, then, is based in the main on *Measure for Measure*, with the importation of Benedick, Beatrice, and the singing Balthasar from *Much Ado about Nothing*.

The action proceeds as follows:[2]

ACT I

As in *Measure for Measure*, Angelo is commissioned deputy. Upon the Duke's departure Angelo and Eschalus retire for conference. Then enter Beatrice, Julietta, Viola, and Balthazar, who maintain the dialogue of *Much Ado about Nothing*, I, i, concerning Benedick. Viola, though "very young," is ungracious enough to rob her elder sister of that tart reply to the observation, "Madam, the Gentleman is not in your Books." It is not Beatrice who answers, but

Viol[*a*]. If he were, I have heard my Sister say
She would burn her Study.

SIR WILLIAM D'AVENANT

Balt[*hazar*]. Small Mistress, have you learnt that in your Primer?
This, Madam, is your pretty Bud of wit.
Viol. A Bud that has some prickles, Sir. Take heed; You cannot gather me.

Decidedly, this young person can take care of herself.

Throughout the scene Julietta takes Leonato's lines. Benedick now arrives. Lucio, whose character is considerably "elevated," informs him of the new government and its determination to enforce the law against (illicit) lovers.[3] Beatrice and the other ladies have been hiding behind the hangings; they now reappear, and the verbal skirmish of *Much Ado*, I, i, 116–143, ensues. Next the Provost comes in, with Claudio under arrest. Thus we lose *Measure for Measure*, I, ii, 1–119, though the real structure of the play is not altered, since the exposition provided in these lines by the fantastic Lucio, the two walking gentlemen, and Mrs. Overdone has already been supplied by the (relatively) sober Lucio. Mrs. Overdone, indeed, does not appear at all; and this, as Elze observes, seriously injures the motivation of Angelo's revival of the old law. Claudio now informs Lucio of his plight and begs him to seek Isabella. Next comes *Measure for Measure*, I, iii, the Duke and Friar Thomas. Finally, we have *Measure for Measure*, I, iv, Lucio and Balthazar finding Isabella at the nunnery. The acts of *The Law against Lovers* are not divided into scenes. There are no scenic directions.

ACT II

Benedick attempts vainly to induce his brother not to execute Claudio; this is *M. for M.*, II, i, Benedick taking the lines of Escalus, who later appears and is ordered by Angelo to broach to Benedick the subject of marriage; this is essentially *Much Ado*, I, i, 159 f., though the scene is greatly reduced in length and most of the speeches are altered nearly out of recognition. Some of Benedick's best lines (*e. g.*, in the speech beginning *Much Ado*, I, i, 232, "That a woman conceiued me, I thanke her") are given, in mangled form, to Balthazar, who comes in with Lucio. The latter's part is also "fattened" at Benedick's expense, *e.g.:*

> If I ever marry, let mine eyes be
> Pickt out with the Pen of a Ballad-maker,
> And hang me up at the door of a Brothel,
> For the Sign of blind Cupid.

Another encounter between Benedick and Beatrice follows immediately; the first shot is:

> I wonder you will still be talking, Benedick;
> No body marks you,

for which D'Avenant went back to *Much Ado*, I, i, 114, 115. Here also is introduced Beatrice's description of the ideal husband (*Much Ado*, II, i, 9 f.); but nearly all the speeches in this scene are D'Avenant's own. Next follow the interviews between Angelo and the Provost, and between Angelo and Isabella. This is *M. for M.*, II, ii; we lose scene i, of course, and therefore the fun provided by Elbow, Froth, and Pompey. We then see the prison, and hear the disguised Duke's colloquy with Julietta (*M. for M.*, II, iii). Lucio and Balthazar visit Claudio. Angelo ends the act with his speech, *M. for M.*, II, iv, 19–30.

ACT III

The third act begins with Angelo's offer to Isabella (*M. for M.*, II, iv, 31 f.). Then Benedick and Beatrice meet for an exchange of feeble witticisms, mostly pure D'Avenant. She bids him steal his brother's signet, with which they can secure the lovers' liberty. "This," Benedick easily replies,

> is but betraying an ill Brother,
> For a good purpose; I'll do't if I can.

Follows a little tiff — who is to employ the signet when once it is stolen?

Next comes Viola (Pepys's "little girl") to sing a song lamenting the fatal law. Lucio and Balthazar appear and inform Beatrice that Benedick wrote the verses, and that in very truth he loves her. Beatrice, however, flirts with Lucio. This scene is almost wholly D'Avenant's.

Next follows an abridgment of *M. for M.*, III, i. But, though he is given a mangled version of the great outburst on death, Claudio does not ask his sister to save him; on the contrary, he resigns himself and commends Julietta to Isabella's care. As in Shakespeare, the disguised Duke overhears their farewell and interposes. In Shakespeare he tells them that Angelo never meant corruption; but in D'Avenant he asks their silence concerning it, since Angelo will answer accusation by asserting that he meant only to make trial of Isabella's virtue.

In the next scene, Benedick brings Beatrice the pardon, in the forging of which Eschalus has joined. Viola closes the act with a visit to Julietta.

ACT VI

Lucio assures Benedick that his wooing of Beatrice was feigned. She appears and advises dissembling their plot by merrymaking; this affords a lame excuse for Viola to pop in "dancing a Saraband awhile with Castanietos." The Provost and Lucio come in with the "Fool" (Pompey) "in a Shackle," and we are treated to a mangled version of *M. for M.*, III, ii. The disguised Duke informs Lucio that shortly after the pardon an order was received at the prison for Claudio's execution, which, however, Friar Thomas had been able to postpone till the following day.

Next comes a much-abridged version of Lucio's slandering of the Duke. It is followed by one of D'Avenant's original scenes, between Isabella and Julietta, who would have her yield to Angelo. Isabella retorts by proposing acceptance, Julietta to keep the assignation in her stead. Julietta refuses.

This is the only reference to such substitution, the Mariana story being entirely omitted by D'Avenant. After this comes another Benedick–Beatrice scene, the lady urging her lover to force Claudio's release. This is followed by *M. for M.*, IV, ii, greatly altered and cut down. After the Fool has agreed to help the hangman, and the warrant has arrived, comes the scene (curtailed) in which Bernardine reveals his callousness (*M. for M.*, IV, iii).

Then follows a scene between Claudio and the Fool. The latter is bribed to take a page's clothes to Julietta. An officer of the guards has agreed to secure clear passage for one of the lovers, but not for both. If Julietta does not escape she must suffer the ignominy of public penance; rather than that, Claudio will remain and die. As the Fool goes out, Julietta's maid arrives with a letter. The Provost's wife, it seems, has agreed to allow Claudio to escape from Julietta's window, but will not consent that she too shall go, though if it becomes known that Julietta has been concerned in Claudio's escape she must die.

The next scene is again between Angelo and Isabella. This is D'Avenant's own; it is in rhyme. Isabella pleads again, and again Angelo urges compliance. He even attempts to corrupt her with jewels. Then, like a bolt from the blue, comes new motivation, and the intensely dramatic situation which Shakespeare created is shattered.

> Forgive me, who till now, thought I should find
> Too many of your beauteous Sex too kind.

Angelo has only been testing her virtue, and never meant to take Claudio's life! Isabella is not greatly impressed by this *volte-face;* nor is it any more convincing to the reader. Angelo is left in despair:

> Break heart! farewel the cruel and the just!
> Fools seek belief, where they have bred distrust:
> Because she doubts my virtue I must die;
> Who did with vitious arts her virtue try.

ACT V

Act V opens with an operatic feature — a quartet number beginning "Our Ruler has got the vertigo of State"; this is rendered by Beatrice, Viola, Benedick, and Lucio. After this harmonious prelude to a revolution, Benedick puts himself at the head of the troops, and the fight is on. The next scene is at the prison. The disguised Duke has complete ascendancy over the Provost, whom he advises to offer a parley from the battlements. Benedick demands the prisoners, and is refused. The following scene is with the ladies, who await news of the fighting. Balthazar brings it: Benedick has cut Angelo's forces to pieces, but upon assaulting the prison again was met by the Provost, who showed him Claudio's head. The Duke threw off his disguise; and now both Angelo and Benedick are in prison. One of the most dramatic moments of Shakespeare's play, when the bragging Lucio pulls off the supposed Friar's hood, is thus in D'Avenant's version only narrated.

Beatrice now appears before the Duke to plead for Benedick, and then we see Angelo in jail. Informed by the Provost of Claudio's execution, he offers to give his whole estate to Julietta, but Eschalus appears and announces that the Duke has awarded it to Isabella. The latter comes to see Angelo in eclipse; but she refuses to accept his wealth. Claudio and Julietta now come in, to the surprise and joy of Angelo and of Benedick, who arrives to explain that the executed man was Bernardine. Beatrice is the next arrival; she brings Benedick's pardon. Finally the Duke appears and forgives all hands; he announces that not a life has been lost; as in *Measure for Measure*, even Bernardine is whole. The union of Claudio and Julietta is approved by the Duke, who also bestows Beatrice on Benedick, and, queerly enough, Isabella on Angelo. The fifth act, as the reader will have observed, is almost entirely D'Avenant's own.

In general, the most serious omission is that of the Mariana story.[4] We can ill spare, too, the cheerful presence of Pompey, Froth, and Elbow. All that is left of their scenes is the Fool's colloquy with the hangman. Lucio is grievously "elevated." Isabella is not treated so badly as the other important characters, but Angelo, one of the most interesting of Shakespeare's analytical portraits, becomes simply impossible. Apparently we are to believe in the rectitude of his intentions. The Duke's character is not much altered.

As for plot, there is a certain ingenuity to the weaving in of Benedick and Beatrice, whose characters are left substantially intact, though their wit suffers severely. The handling of the dénouement, the Duke's reappearance, is atrocious. Indeed, the whole fifth act shows inability to bring together into one situation the various threads left at loose ends earlier in the play. Thus the act is both protracted and episodic.

So far I have offered no remarks concerning the alteration of Shakespeare's language; but I hope the extracts already quoted have duly impressed the reader. Let us now examine a few cases of direct alteration of the Shakespearean line. I first quote, in each case, the text as it appears in *The Law against Lovers*, and then the Shakespearean original. Lines from *Measure for Measure* are quoted from the *National Shakespeare* facsimile of the First Folio, with which the text (excerpt or MS.) used by the actors must have agreed, since no Quartos of this play were printed. My references to act, scene, and line in *Measure for Measure* are numbered to agree with Neilson's Cambridge edition of Shakespeare's works. In the case of *Much Ado about Nothing*, references and text are according to the New Variorum edition of Dr. Furness. There was one Quarto edition of the latter play; since the Folios derive from it, I have not attempted to discover which edition D'Avenant used.

In dealing with many of the verbal alterations made by

D'Avenant in this and other plays, it is easier to condemn than to explain. The adapter felt no restraint — of that we may be certain. Thus, while we can account for many of the changes, there are others that appear to be arbitrary. Textual emendation, as the horde of later commentators discovered, is not the least fascinating of indoor sports; but if one finds it agreeable, or even thrilling, one may find also that to be too busy is some danger. The Restoration adapter was not trying to *restore* his text, the professed aim of the long line of later tamperers, but to *improve* it. From changing a phrase in order to make its meaning clearer, to changing it because one thinks of a better phrase, is an easy step. D'Avenant took it with complete aplomb.

He regarded Shakespeare, I imagine, almost with affection; but he was the victim of his age. The cocksureness of the Restoration intelligentsia is almost incredible. The England of Elizabeth seemed barbarous to the England of Charles II, though less than sixty years had elapsed between the great queen's death and the accession of that graceless king. In the presence of the masterpieces of the old drama, the Restoration critics (all but Rymer) experienced a certain awe; they recognized vaguely a grandeur that was not characteristic of their own art. Dryden wrote:

> Our age was cultivated thus at length,
> But what we gain'd in skill we lost in strength.
> Our builders were with want of genius curst;
> The second temple was not like the first.[5]

The Restoration temples were constructed, supposedly, according to the French rules for classical architecture; squared by these, the Elizabethan monuments were seen to be abounding in errors. Thus the critic and adapter of Shakespeare in the later seventeenth century, though he might sincerely enough protest his admiration for the whole, found, when he actually came to consider details, so many faults crying for correction, that while he eulogized in general he had little but condemnation in particular. He was willing to concede greatness of soul to Shakespeare, but neither a civilized taste nor a competent craftsmanship.

That this was D'Avenant's view is shown by the character of his alterations. As good an illustration as any, of the general nature of D'Avenant's methods, is the great outburst of Claudio on death (*M. for M.*, III, i, 118–132). This appears in *The Law against Lovers* as follows:

> Oh Sister, 'tis to go we know not whither.
> We lye in silent darkness, and we rot;
> Where long our motion is not stopt; for though
> In Graves none walk upright (proudly to face
> The Stars) yet there we move again, when our
> Corruption makes those worms in whom we crawl.
> Perhaps the Spirit (which is future life)
> Dwells Salamander-like, unharm'd in fire:
> Or else with wand'ring winds is blown about
> The world. But if condemn'd like those
> Whom our incertain thought imagines howling;
> Than the most loath'd and the most weary life
> Which Age, or Ache, want, or imprisonment
> Can lay on Nature, is a Paradise
> To what we fear of death.

For:

> I, but to die, and go we know not where,
> To lie in cold obstruction, and to rot,
> This sensible warme motion, to become
> A kneaded clod; And the delighted spirit
> To bath in fierie floods or to recide
> In thrilling Region of thicke-ribbed Ice,
> To be imprison'd in the viewlesse windes
> And blowne with restlesse violence round about
> The pendant world: or to be worse then worst
> Of those, that lawlesse and incertaine thought,
> Imagine howling, 'tis too horrible.
> The weariest, and most loathed worldly life
> That Age, Ache, periury, and imprisonment
> Can lay on nature, is a Paradise
> To what we feare of death.

D'Avenant often condenses Shakespeare's long speeches. Claudio's explanation of his plight (*M. for M.*, I, ii, 160–175) is a good example of this sort of alteration:

> 'Tis so;
> And the new Deputy
> Awakens all the enroll'd penalties,
> Which have been Nineteen years unread, and makes
> Me feel the long neglected punishment,
> By such a Law, as three days after
> Arrest, requires the forfeit of my head.

For:

> Vnhappely, euen so.
> And the new Deputie, now for the Duke,
> Whether it be the fault and glimpse of newnes,
> Or whether that the body publique, be
> A horse whereon the Gouernor doth ride,
> Who newly in the Seate, that it may know
> He can command: lets it strait feele the spur:
> Whether the Tirranny be in his place,
> Or in his Eminence that fills it vp,
> I stagger in: But this new Gouernor
> Awakes me all the inrolled penalties
> Which haue (like vn-scowr'd Armor) hung by th' wall
> So long, that nineteene Zodiacks haue gone round,
> And none of them beene worne; and for a name
> Now puts the drowsie and neglected Act
> Freshly on me: 'tis surely for a name.

These changes take the force and color out of the speech; on the other hand, it is simpler and clearer, as well as briefer.

Still another type of alteration ensues from D'Avenant's attempts to trim Shakespeare's prose into blank verse. The results, as metre, are usually unhappy, but they are not worse than many of D'Avenant's original lines. The following verses (*Much Ado*, I, i, 63–70) are D'Avenant's substitute for the lively prose of Beatrice:

> In our last encounter
> Four of his five wits did go halting off;
> And now the whole man is govern'd by one.

I pray, Sir, who's his Companion now? for he was wont,
Every Month to have a new sworn Brother.

For:

In our last conflict, foure of his fiue wits went halting off, and now is the whole man gouern'd with one: so that if hee haue wit enough to keepe himselfe warme, let him beare it for a difference betweene himselfe and his horse: For it is all the wealth that he hath left, to be knowne a reasonable creature. Who is his companion now? He hath euery month a new sworne brother.

Many minor changes seem due to an inordinate passion for the adjective, and a certain pride in its dexterous use. Thus D'Avenant writes (*M. for M.*, III, i, 84 and 86, 87):

"I'll welcome darkness as a *shining* Bride"

and

"there my Fathers Grave
Utter'd a *chearful* voice."

For:

"I will encounter darknesse as a bride"

and

"there my fathers graue
Did vtter forth a voice."

Many of D'Avenant's superfluous adjectives are, however, due to metrical exigencies.

Some of the alterations represent merely an attempt to modernize (*M. for M.*, III, i, 88, 89):

"You are too noble to conserve a life
By wretched remedies."

For:

"In base appliances."

Other changes seem intended to clarify Shakespeare's meaning. Examples:

M. for M., II, ii, 114:

"We nothing should but Thunder hear."

For:

"Nothing but Thunder."

Ibid., III, i, 67–70:

"*Claud.* Perpetual durance?
Isab. 'Tis worse than close restraint, and painful too
Beyond all tortures which afflict the body;
For 'tis a Rack invented for the mind."

For:

"*Cla.* Perpetuall durance?
Isa. I iust, perpetuall durance, a restraint
Through all the worlds vastiditie you had
To a determin'd scope."

This is an excellent example of D'Avenant's unwillingness to leave anything to his audience. That Isabella intends the mental anguish which she thinks her yielding to Angelo would cause her brother is evident from Shakespeare's lines, and, as spoken by any competent actress to an audience which has already heard Angelo's infamous proposal, ought not to be capable of misconstruction. Did D'Avenant distrust his audience, or his players? I think, neither. D'Avenant, though he lisped in numbers, appears to have been blessed with an uncommonly matter-of-fact temperament, and a distinctly literal mind. He objected to the profuse hand with which Shakespeare laid on his "colours of rhethoryke." And so we often find him toning down soaring flights of fancy, literalizing figurative expression, and consequently throwing away everything that made a line splendid. This process of chastening the wild, untutored phrases of his source accounts for another group of D'Avenant's alterations. It is closely related, of course, to D'Avenant's devotion to clearness at any cost.

M. for M., I, iii, 2, 3:

"Lov's too tender to dwell in my cold bosom."

For:

"Beleeue not that the dribling dart of Loue
Can pierce a compleat bosome."

Ibid., I, iii, 29:

"and froward liberty,
Does Justice strike."

For:

"And libertie, plucks Iustice by the nose."

M for M., II, ii, 10–12:

"Under your good correction, I have seen
When, after execution, *the wise Judge*
Has his rash doom repented."

For:

"Iudgement hath
Repented ore his doome."

Ibid., II, iv, 111, 112:

"Ignoble ransom, no proportion bears
To pardon freely given."

For:

"Ignomie in ransome, and free pardon
Are of two houses."

Ibid, IV, iii, 68:

"He is unfit to live or dye."

For:

"Vnfit to liue, or die: oh grauell heart."

D'Avenant's prudery was chiefly aroused by verbal grossness; the *double entendre* was not ungrateful to the Restoration Laureate, but, unlike many of the other writing gentlemen, he avoids indecent words. Unfortunately, he often excises not merely the indecent but the coarsely accurate. The following examples show his squeamishness:

M. for M., I, ii, 143:

"I believe 'tis that which the precise call Incontinence."

For:

"Lecherie?"

Ibid., II, iv, 161:

"Yield to my passion."

For:

"Fit thy consent to my sharpe appetite."

Ibid., III, i, 98:

"if I would Heaven
(Which never injur'd us) fouly offend?"

For:

"If I would yeeld him my virginitie."

Finally, there are traces of subservience to the rules of the neo-classicists. An amusing example of the power of decorum occurs in the following passage:

M. for M., III, i, 104–106:

"O, were it but my life,
I would for your deliverance throw it down,
Most frankly, *Claudio*."

For:

"I'de throw it downe for your deliuerance
As frankely as a pin." [6]

Pins are vulgar, and whether thrown down or picked up are not in the least "elevated." I must ask the reader to remember this one of Isabella's with some particularity, for we shall find a good reason for picking it up again later in this chapter.

To the other canons of the French school [7] D'Avenant is on the whole subservient. The fundamental doctrine of the unities is well enough observed, though the lapse of time probably exceeds the strict limitation. The action is all at Turin, and, as we have seen, the plot is unified with some skill. To the present writer, the play seems to be distinctly a comedy, not a tragi-comedy, as it is usually described; the critical rule which specifies the separation of the two kinds is pretty well observed. Violence is avoided; there is plenty of fighting, but it is not of a sanguinary character, and it all happens off stage. Poetic justice is not forgotten; the good intentions gratuitously supplied to Angelo by D'Avenant warrant, of course, his fortunate conclusion in Isabella's arms.

But in spite of the rules, the audience seems to have voted the play a dull thing, and not even the spirited jigging of the flapperish Viola was able to save it. Forty years afterwards Charles Gildon made another adaptation of *Measure for Measure*, which we shall consider in due course. Neither the original of that play nor *Much Ado about Nothing* was acted at all during the Restoration.

2. Macbeth

The true relation of the first two separate editions of *Macbeth* has been correctly stated by several scholars. Furness, in 1873, makes the distinction clearly. But since a number of more recent writers have confused the two texts and still others appear to be uncertain, it seems worth while to elaborate at this point in order to settle the question once for all.[8]

D'Avenant's version of *Macbeth* was first printed in 1674, not in 1673, as is asserted by the latest handler of Shakespeare alterations, Mr. Montague Summers,[9] who with some justice warns his readers against the "blunders and absurdities" of Maidment and Logan's critical preface to it in the fifth volume of their edition of D'Avenant's plays. Mr. Summers follows Mr. William J. Lawrence, who appears to have misread one of Dr. Furness's notes. Mr. Lawrence writes:

> No copy of the D'Avenant *Macbeth* was issued until 1673, early in the spring of which year W. Cadman published his anonymous quarto (Quarto 1). A little better than a year later, P. Chetwin printed another version, "with all the alterations, amendments, additions and new songs. As it is now acted at the Duke's theatre."[10] (Quarto 2). Beyond some transpositions of the scenes and some alterations in the sequence of the "business," Quarto 2 does not differ very materially from its immediate predecessor. For the variations see Furness, *Variorum Shakespeare*, vii. (1873), introduction. In the same volume will be found the text of Quarto 2. My impression is that the discrepancies between the two arose from the fact that Cadman, in his haste to take advantage of the ornate revival at Dorset Gardens in 1673, derived his text from a copy of D'Avenant's first version of the tragedy, and that Quarto 2 represents the maturer revisal.[11]

Leaving for the moment Mr. Lawrence's conclusion, let us examine his facts. Quarto 2, he asserts, is not very different from Quarto 1. The latter edition I have not seen, though I have examined with care its variant readings as recorded by Dr. Furness.[12] I might hesitate therefore to controvert Mr. Lawrence's remarks if it were not that he refers to Furness as his own authority. Now Dr. Furness, so far from asserting the *similarity* of the two Quartos, lays stress on their *difference:*

In 1673 [he writes] there appeared "Macbeth: A Tragedy. Acted At the Dukes-Theatre." This has hitherto been cited as D'Avenant's Version, even by the very accurate Cambridge Editors, and in sooth it may be that it is, but it is very different from the D'Avenant's Version published in the following year, to which almost uniformly all references apply, and not to this edition of 1673. *The only points of identity between the two* [my italics] are to be found in the Witch-scenes, and there they are not uniformly alike, nor are the Songs introduced in the same scenes at the same places; and of the Song "Black Spirits and white," &c., only the first two words are given. In other respects the edition of 1673 is a reprint of the First Folio. . . . As a general rule . . . the readings of F 1 [in Furness's textual notes] include the edition of D'Avenant of 1673.[13]

Dr. Furness next expresses regret that he has not more clearly distinguished the two versions by giving the earlier some other title in his citations; "Betterton's," he suggests, but why he does not specify. Certainly the suggestion is misleading. He continues:

It is a mere suspicion of mine that the success which attended the representation of this earlier version induced the Poet Laureate in the following year to "amend" it still more, and prefix an "Argument" which, by the way, he took word for word from Heylin's *Cosmography*.

Unfortunately for this theory, the Quartos are dated 1673 and 1674, while D'Avenant died in 1668.

Dr. Furness returns to the differences between Quarto 1 and the First Folio. I quote in full:

The first divergence from the First Folio in Betterton's version (if I may be permitted so to term it for the nonce, to avoid repetition and confusion)[14] occurs at the end of the Second Scene in the Second Act, where the Witches enter and "sing" the song found in D'Avenant's Version[15] (see p. 324[16] [519[17]]), beginning "Speak, Sister, is the Deed done?" &c., down to "What then, when Monarch's perish, should we do?"[18]

At the end of the next scene [19] occurs the second divergence, consisting of the Witches' Song (see p. 325 [20] [519 [21]]), beginning "Let's have a Dance upon the Heath," &c., down to "We Dance to the Ecchoes of our Feet," as it is in D'Avenant's version, except that "the chirping Cricket" is changed into the "chirping Critick." [22]

The third and last addition, which is not wholly unauthorized, since it is indicated in the Folios, is to be found at III, v, 33. Here the extract from Middleton (see pp. 337 [23] [376 [24]] and 401 [23] [525 [24]]) is given: "Come away Heccat, Heccat, Oh, come away," &c., down to "Nor Cannons Throats our height can reach." [25] As I have before said, with these three exceptions, Betterton's version [*i. e.*, the Quarto of 1673] is a more or less accurate reprint of the First Folio.[26]

Since to this plain statement Mr. Lawrence refers as his authority, it is evident that his assertion that the Quartos of 1673 and 1674 are in virtual agreement is one of his very rare slips.

Dr. Furness continues with a list of "some of the most noteworthy discrepancies" between Q 1673 and F 1, selected from the first Act.[27] He lists the following passages:

I, vi, 35:	"to count." For: "in compt."
I, vii, 11:	"*Commands* th' Ingredience." For: "Commends."
I, vii, 17:	"First, I am." For: "First, as I am."
I, vii, 26:	"Heavens Cherubim." For: "Heauen's Cherubin."
I, vii, 60:	"Be *much more* the Man." For: "so much more."
I, vii, 81:	"What not upon." For: "What not put vpon."
I, vii, 88:	"their Daggers." For: "their very Daggers."

The following variant readings in the remaining acts are recorded in Furness's textual notes: [28]

II, i, 64:	"now witchcraft." For: "Witchcraft." Q 1674: "now witchcraft."
II, ii, 48:	"rips."
For:	"Sleepe that *knits* vp the rauel'd Sleeue of Care."
Q 1674:	"Sleep, that locks up the senses from their care."
II, ii, 79:	"Green one red."
For:	"Making the *Greene one*, *Red*."
Q 1674:	"and turn the green into a red."

II, ii, 94: "this." For: "Wake Duncan with *thy* knocking." Q 1674: "this."

II, iii, 8: "come in, time." For: "Come in time." Q 1674 cuts the drunken porter.

II, iii, 21: "Bone-fire." For: "Bonfire."

II, iii, 135, 136: "Out-ran."
For: "Th' expedition of my violent Loue
Out-run the pawser, Reason."
Q 1674: "*Out-ran* my pausing reason."

II, iv, 4: "I've." For: "I *haue* seene." Q 1674: "I've."

II, iv, 5, 6: "stifled."
For: "but this sore Night
Hath *trifled* former knowings."
Q 1674: "but this one night
Has made [t]hat knowledge void."

III, i, 68: "Caesar's." For: "Caesar." Q 1674 cuts the reference to Antony and Caesar.

III, iv, 51: "May it." For: "May't." Q 1674: "May it."

III, iv, 58: "company." For: "Company?" Q 1674: "Company?"

III, vi, 6: "born." For: "Things haue bin strangely *borne*." Q 1674: "carry'd."

III, vi, 20: "born." For: "borne." Q 1674: "born."

IV, i, 29, 30: "Silver'd."
For: "Slippes of Yew,
Sliuer'd in the Moones Ecclipse."
Q 1674: "Pluckt when the Moon was in Eclips."

IV, i, 136: "Gold bound-brow." For: "Gold-bound-brow."

IV, iii, 255: "see." For: "Did you *say* All?" Q 1674: "say."

V, i, 27: "is." For: "their sense *are* shut." Q 1674: "is."

V, iii, 26: "chear." For: "cheere."

V, viii, 3: "while." For: "whiles." Q 1674 cuts this line.

The variations of Quarto 1673 from the First Folio we thus find to be inconsiderable. Both Dr. Furness and Mr. Lawrence are wrong, the latter in asserting the similarity of the two

Quartos, the former in suggesting that D'Avenant made some additional alterations in 1674, being emboldened by the success of the version of the previous year.

In lieu of their conclusions I can offer only a conjecture, which has, however, this warrant, that it is compatible with the textual condition of both Quartos. Soon after the gorgeous revival of D'Avenant's *Macbeth* at Dorset Garden (1672–1673), a publisher apparently decided to reprint Shakespeare's original play as found in the First Folio, and thus take advantage of its renewed popularity. He included, perhaps without authority, three additions (carefully distinguished by Furness), which may have been taken down in the theatre, but which had probably got attached to the play long before D'Avenant began tampering with it. The proprietors of D'Avenant's version, unwilling to allow this text to circulate under the name of their recent theatrical success and to reap the publishing profits thereof, gave the D'Avenant text to the printer. This, the text of Quarto 1674, must have been written at least before 1668, when D'Avenant died, and probably before 1663–1664, when it appears to have been produced at Lincoln's Inn Fields.

The Quarto of 1673, accordingly, as Furness distinctly states, is not an alteration but a reprint of the First Folio, with the addition of three songs and with a few of those minor changes inevitable in every such reprint. Though published before the Quarto of 1674, it was undertaken by the printer long after that version had been prepared. It is in fact not improbable that Quarto 1673 represents the play as it was acted even before the Wars; for Shakespeare's text appears to have been tampered with before its original publication in the First Folio.

The Quarto of 1674, on the other hand, is D'Avenant's version of *Macbeth*, probably written, or at any rate overhauled, *c.* 1663–1664. It was not included in the posthumous D'Avenant folio of 1673 for the same reason that denied inclusion to

D'Avenant's version of *Hamlet*. Compared with *The Law against Lovers*, which was included, both the *Hamlet* and the *Macbeth* are chiefly distinguished by verbal alteration and cutting. The editor felt (as very likely D'Avenant himself did) that *The Law against Lovers*, though based on two of Shakespeare's plays, was really a new play, while the *Hamlet* and the *Macbeth* were still Shakespeare's.[29]

The *Macbeth* Quarto of 1674 was reprinted in 1687,[30] 1689, 1695, and 1710. I have not collated these texts. I have, however, examined those of 1687, 1695, and 1710 with sufficient care to be sure that they represent D'Avenant's version. They appear to be faithful reprints of Quarto 1674.

Let us now turn to that text and examine the changes introduced by William D'Avenant in order to "reform and make fit" the *Macbeth* of William Shakespeare.

ACT I

The first act is not much altered structurally, but, as will be apparent from a glance at the verbal "improvements" I shall cite, the text is badly garbled. The Bleeding Sergeant (I, ii) becomes Seyton; Macduff takes over Ross (I, ii and iii); Angus is excised, though his name appears among the dramatis personae. Angus's speech, I, iii, 110–113, is cut; but I, iii, 121–129, is given to Macduff. The evil thought of Macbeth is expressed more definitely as early as scene iii. At the end of scene iv, in the Prince of Cumberland aside, D'Avenant inserts another couplet before the final one, which he alters considerably:

> The strange Idea of a bloudy act
> Does into doubt all my resolves distract.
> My eye shall at my hand connive, the Sun
> Himself should wink when such a deed is done.

Professor Kittredge calls my attention to the source of the first of these couplets; it is *Macbeth*, I, iii, 155–157:

My Thought, whose Murther yet is but fantasticall,
Shakes so my single state of Man,
That Function is smother'd in surmise.

Such structural alterations as appear in this play are due principally to D'Avenant's passion for balance in characterization. This obsession is a natural consequence of the systematic creation of typical rather than complex characters. Shakespeare's faculty of viewing whole not only life in general but the isolated personality was simply beyond the horizon of the critics from whom the dramatists of the Restoration derived their standards. It is not permissible, Dryden declares, to set up a character as composed of mighty opposites:

> When a Poet has given the Dignity of a King to one of his persons, in all his actions and speeches, that person must discover Majesty, Magnanimity, and jealousy of power; because these are sutable to the general manners of a King. . . . When Virgil had once given the name of Pious to Aeneas, he was bound to show him such, in all his words and actions through the whole Poem. . . . A character . . . is a composition of qualities which are not contrary to one another in the same person: thus the same man may be liberal and valiant, but not liberal and covetous.[31]

The principle thus unqualifiedly laid down leads eventually to the personification of dominant characteristics. It comes, in fact, pretty close to the humours theory of Ben Jonson, and I for one am convinced that his methods influenced Restoration tragedy as well as comedy. Dryden, for instance, examining the merits of Shakespeare, Fletcher, and Jonson, awards the palm for characterization to the last, on account of the "consistency" of his persons — even the minor ones. This significant opinion, as well as the last passage quoted, is to be found, not in a treatise on comedy, but in Dryden's preface to his alteration of *Troilus and Cressida*, which contains a formal essay on the *Grounds of Criticism in Tragedy*.

D'Avenant never went so far as Dryden, who worked in Shakespeare revision with a freer hand than did his predecessor; but the older Laureate was powerfully influenced by this canon of consistency. Once you surrender to it, composition becomes largely a matter of antithesis: if A stands for Pride, let B represent Humility; if A incarnates pure Malignity, B shall broadcast Benevolence. Thus in *Macbeth* D'Avenant saw the hero's Lady as a symbol of wicked ambition. Very well, then, let us have a good woman, quite unscorched by any spark of self-interest, and available to lecture the other characters and the audience on the cinerary consequences of worldly hope. And since Shakespeare proposes an unobjectionable figure in Lady Macduff, D'Avenant selects her to be all that Lady Macbeth is not. In his hands she become a most sanctified dame, and a much more important character than Shakespeare had made her.

This pious matron's first opportunity comes in I, v, in a scene of 37 lines which precedes the reading of Macbeth's letter.[32] The notorious *love and honour* (or more accurately, love *or* honour) motive appears in all its glory in her first speech. Soon, in response to Lady Macbeth's martial enthusiasm, Macduff's domestic angel begins her lecture:

> The world mistakes the glories gain'd in war,
> Thinking their Lustre true: alas, they are
> But Comets, Vapours! by some men exhal'd
> From others bloud, and kindl'd in the Region
> Of popular applause, in which they live
> A-while; then vanish: and the very breath
> Which first inflam'd them, blows them out agen.

Having thus impressed us with her insusceptibility to ambitious temptings she retires, Lady Macbeth breaks into the letter, and the action proceeds as in Shakespeare's play, though the diction is horribly mutilated.

ACT II

The sleepy Porter is contemptuously ejected from his station in this act. The scene is replaced by the following awkward lines:

Enter Lenox and Macbeth's Servant.

Lenox. You sleep soundly, that so much knocking
Could not wake you.
Serv. Labour by day causes rest by night.
Enter Macduff.[33]

In II, iv, the Old Man's lines are reduced and bestowed on Seyton. As in the original, Macduff announces his departure for Fife.

The next scene is D'Avenant's own. Once more we see the heath, where "Lady Macduff, Maid, and Servant" await their lord. "Here," says the Servant,

He order'd me to attend him with the Chariot.

The children are not presented:

They are securely sleeping in the Chariot.

Macduff arrives. It soon appears that he has chosen an uncanny spot for the rendezvous: the witches (four of them) bounce in and present the "divertisement" which Mr. Pepys found not only entertaining but appropriate. Their lyrics have already been quoted. The Thane of Fife sourly pronounces their first selection "an hellish Song," but stays for the encore. After that the Witches dance. Macduff is next treated to a triple-barrelled prophecy in the manner of those addressed to Macbeth and Banquo:

1 Witch. Saving thy bloud will cause it to be shed;
2 Witch. He'll bleed by thee, by whom thou first hast bled.
3 Witch. Thy wife shall shunning danger, dangers find,
And fatal be, to whom she most is kind.

Then the Witches vanish, and after a brief lecture by Lady Macduff on the folly of believing these "Messengers of Darkness," the doomed family troops off to the waiting chariot.

ACT III

D'Avenant was not inclined to trust his audience to take any save the broadest of hints. A good instance of his little faith occurs in III, i, after Banquo has departed on his fatal ride, and the courtiers have been dismissed. Macbeth thereupon reveals his intentions unmistakably:

> Macduff departed frowningly, perhaps
> He is grown jealous; he and Banquo must
> Embrace the same fate.

Immediately after the interview with the murderers comes another of D'Avenant's original Macduff scenes, neatly versified in rhyming couplets. The Thane has made up his mind:

> It must be so. Great Duncan's bloudy death
> Can have no other Author but Macbeth.
> His Dagger now is to a Scepter grown;
> From Duncan's Grave he has deriv'd his Throne.

Lady Macduff, in her character of good counselor, never lets an opportunity slip:

> Ambition urg'd him to that bloudy deed:
> May you be never by Ambition led:
> Forbid it Heav'n, that in revenge you shou'd
> Follow a Copy that is writ in bloud.[34]

Macduff feels bound to avenge the murdered King, but his wife would leave all to Heaven. The Thane longs to rescue his country from "the bloudy Tyrants violence." She has her answer pat:

> I am affraid you have some other end,
> Than meerly Scotland's freedom to defend.
> You'd raise your self, whilst you wou'd him dethrone;
> And shake his Greatness, to confirm your own.

Macduff replies that it would be no usurpation to assume the sceptre for the nation's good. But his Lady stands firm against ambition in any form. She is, in fact, a thoroughgoing Restoration loyalist.

The action then proceeds as in the original till the scene of Banquo's assassination, in which the conference of the murderers before the deed is greatly reduced; the Third Murderer's appearance is not accounted for. Banquo is pursued and killed off stage. After the banquet, a short scene in couplets shows Macduff's leave-taking. Next comes the expository interview between Lennox and a Lord — in D'Avenant's version, Seyton (III, vi). The act closes with III, v. Hecate's long harangue to the Witches is greatly reduced, in order to make room for the song, "Come away, Heccate, Heccate! Oh come away," and her flight with the Witches on a "machine." The text is taken, with a few slight alterations, from Middleton's *The Witch*, III, iii, 39–74.[35]

ACT IV

The first scene opens, as in the original, with the brewing of the hellish broth; this is enriched by still another excerpt from Middleton's play (V, ii, 60–78). There are new and spicier ingredients: "Of Scuttle Fish the vomit black," and instead of a tiger's, a "fat Dutchman's Chawdron," an inelegant but eminently topical reference to England's chief competitor at sea. Then Hecate appears, and the song mentioned in the First Folio as "Blacke Spirits, &c." is sung by the Witches. How much of this Middletonian embellishment had been in use before D'Avenant's time is problematical. The text, according to the Quarto of 1674, is as follows:

Musick and Song.

Hec. Black Spirits, and white,
Red Spirits and gray;
Mingle, mingle, mingle,
You that mingle may.
1 Witch. Tiffin, Tiffin, keep it stiff in,
Fire drake Puckey, make it luckey:
Lyer Robin, you must bob in.
Chor. A round, a round, about, about,
All ill come running in, all good keep out.

1.	Here's the blood of a Bat!
Hec.	O put in that, put in that.
2.	Here's Lizards brain,
Hec.	Put in a grain.
1.	Here's Juice of Toad, here's oyl of Adder
	That will make the Charm grow madder.
2.	Put in all these, 'twill raise the stanch;
Hec.	Nay here's three ownces of a red-hair'd Wench.
Chor.	A round, a round, &c.

When Macbeth arrives he demands:

What Destinie's appointed for my Fate?

He is answered by Hecate, for the apparitions do not appear. This omission is puzzling — they afford an obvious chance for the display of mechanical ingenuity. The "shaddow of eight Kings, and Banquo's Ghost after them" is, however, presented. It is Seyton, not Lennox, who comes in with the news of Macduff's flight. This change is made to enable Lennox, whose part is distinctly "fattened," to take the place of Ross in the next scene as the friend of Lady Macduff. Seyton then comes in as the messenger.[36] This scene ends with the warning, since the murderers do not appear. Their excision may be due to the theoretical objection to scenes of violence, or to a desire to make room for new material.

Next comes the interview, greatly reduced, between Malcolm and Macduff. It takes place, not in England, but

In these close shades of Birnam Wood.[37]

It is broken, after the reference to Edward's success in touching, by an original scene in halting blank verse between Macbeth and Seyton. This is perhaps the most ludicrous of D'Avenant's structural changes in this play; for we see the grim Macbeth hesitating in the conventional manner between love and honour. His army needs his presence, but his Lady is indisposed. And so:

Macb. The Spur of my Ambition prompts me to go
And make my Kingdom safe, but Love which softens me
To pity her in her distress, curbs my Resolves.
. . . .
Yet why should Love since confin'd, desire
To controul Ambition, for whose spreading hopes
The world's too narrow, It shall not; Great Fires
Put out the Less; Seaton go bid my Grooms
Make ready; Ile not delay my going.
Seat. I go.
Macb. Stay Seaton, stay, Compassion calls me back.
Seaton. He looks and moves disorderly.
Macb. I'le not go yet.
Seat. Well Sir . . . [*Exit Seat.*]

And now Lady Macbeth comes in, not yet sleep-walking, but so broken by remorse that she heaps reproaches on her husband for having committed the initial crime. Her first words are: "Duncan is dead." She thinks his ghost pursues her. Taking his cue from Shakespeare's great banquet scene, D'Avenant makes her see the ghost, though the stage directions do not indicate that it was actually brought on at this point. Macbeth assures her:

It cannot be My Dear,
Your Fears have misinform'd your eyes.
Lady Mb. See there; Believe your own.
Why do you follow Me? I did not do it.
Macb. Methinks there's nothing.
Lady Mb. If you have Valour force him hence.
Hold, hold, he's gone. Now you look strangely.
Macb. 'Tis the strange error of your Eyes.
Lady Mb. But the strange error of my Eyes
Proceeds from the strange Action of your Hands.

Let him resign, she urges, his "ill gain'd Crown." He reminds her that she incited him to the crime. But her reply is unanswerable:

You were a Man.
And by the Charter of your Sex you shou'd
Have govern'd me.

Against the counsel of the Witches she warns him earnestly. Now the Ghost actually appears, and the distracted woman raves. Macbeth finally summons her attendants to lead her off, and then offers the following diagnosis and prescription:

> She does from Duncons death to sickness grieve,
> And shall from Malcolms death her health receive.
> When by a Viper bitten, nothing's good
> To cure the venom but a Vipers blood.

On this homeopathic principle the scene ends. One must confess that from theatrical point of view it is highly effective.

Finally, we return to Birnam Wood. Lennox is still in the shoes of Ross and brings the terrible news from Fife.

ACT V

The sleep-walking scene is reduced to 36 lines from 81. The witnesses are Seyton and a lady; both Doctors are omitted from D'Avenant's version.

Scene ii shows us, instead of the rebellious thanes, Donalbain and "Flean" met by Lennox. The scene is brief, original, and writ in most villainous blank verse.[38]

And now follows V, iii, but this Macbeth is not Shakespeare's. Vanished is that fierce contumely which reveals the extremity of his bewildered spirit: we get instead such insipidities as

> Now Friend, what means thy change of Countenance?

For:

> The diuell damne thee blacke, thou cream-fac'd Loone:
> Where got'st thou that Goose-looke.

It is when considering such passages as this and the one following that the modern admirer of Shakespeare's poetry finds it difficult to remain judicial:

V, iii, 24–34:

> Take thy Face hence.
> He has Infected me with Fear

I am sure to die by none of Woman morn.
And yet the English Drums beat an Alarm,
As fatal to my Life as are the Crokes
Of Ravens, when they flutter about the Windows
Of departing men.
My Hopes are great, and yet me-thinks I fear
My Subjects cry out Curses on my Name,
Which like a North-wind seems to blast my Hopes.

This twaddle, we must suppose, was turned off by the Laureate with the greatest satisfaction, in the firm belief that he was writing "with the very spirit of Shakespeare." His creaking lines replace:

Take thy face hence. Seyton, I am sick at hart,
When I behold: Seyton, I say, this push
Will cheere me euer, or dis-eate me now.
I have liu'd long enough: my way of life
Is falne into the Seare, the yellow Leafe,
And that which should accompany Old-Age,
As Honor, Loue, Obedience, Troopes of Friends,
I must not looke to haue: but in their steed,
Curses, not lowd but deepe, Mouth-honor, breath
Which the poore heart would faine deny, and dare not.

Since the Doctor is excised, we lose the great passage beginning,

Can'st thou not Minister to a minde diseas'd . . . ?

In an aside Seyton announces his intention of deserting, and the scene ends. It is followed by a scene largely original with D'Avenant, showing the united forces under "Seymor," and including the order to hew the boughs.

The great fifth scene is, like the third, hopelessly garbled, as witness the speech in which Macbeth's numbed mind reacts, or fails to react, to the news of his wife's death — surely one of the most profoundly tragic sentences ever composed for an actor's lips. It appears thus transmuted in D'Avenant's version:

She should have Di'd hereafter,
I brought Her here, to see my Victines,[39] not to Die.
To Morrow, to Morrow, and to Morrow,
Creeps in a stealing pace from Day to Day,
To the last Minute of Recorded Time:
And all our Yesterdays have lighted Fools
To their Eternal Homes: Out, out that Candle . . . etc.

From this point on the text is left unchanged, but the havoc already made is unforgivable.

The final scene is no less objectionable. Lennox assumes the rôle of Young Siward, and his death; but his lines are D'Avenant's. Macbeth falls on stage, and dies with a moral on his lips:

Farewell vain World, and what's most vain in it, Ambition.

For obvious reasons Macduff presents the new sovereign with, not his enemy's head, but his sword.

Several of the stage directions in the Quarto of 1674 indicate the "operatic" (that is, mechanical) nature of the performances of this adaptation.

I, i, 15: "[Ex. flying."
I, iii, 2: "Enter three Witches flying."
III, iv, 92: "[the Ghost descends."
III, iv, 116: "[the Ghost of Banq. rises at his feet."
III, v, 40: "[Machine descends." [For the flight of the Witches.]
IV, i, 155: "[Musick. The Witches Dance and Vanish. The Cave sinks."

The verbal changes made by D'Avenant are on the whole very like those in *The Law against Lovers* and in his version of *Hamlet*. The categories I suggest are in many cases not especially accurate, for some alterations belong to more than one type, and in many cases a guess at the motive rather than an appraisal of the result is responsible for my classification. I give, of course, only samples.

Some changes owe their existence to D'Avenant's desire to modernize his text.[40] Example:

I, iii, 87: "what seem'd Corporeal."
For: "and what seem'd corporall."

Other revisions appear to be attempts to correct Shakespeare's grammar. Others are rhetorical improvements; for instance, the historical present seems to have been objectionable to D'Avenant. Examples:

I, ii, 59: "Whence *com'st* thou, worthy Thane?"
For: "cam'st."

I, iii, 9: "the rump-fed Ronyon *cry'd*."
For: "cryes."

I, iii, 55: "who."
For: "that."

I, iii, 167: "*Patience and time run* through the roughest day."
For: "Time, and the Houre, runs."

Metrical improvements are aimed at in many of D'Avenant's changes. Too much importance should not, however, be attached to these, for they are often ignored both in altered and in original lines. Examples:

I, i, 14: "To us fair weather's foul, and foul is fair!"
For: "faire is foule, and foule is faire."

I, ii, 75: "Until at Colems-Inch he had disburs'd."
For: "Till he disbursed, at Saint Colmes ynch."

There are numerous changes like this, as a consequence of the weakening of the suffix of the past participle.

The great principle of decorum, D'Avenant found, clashed with several passages in Shakespeare's *Macbeth*.

I, v, 47, 48: "Empty my Nature of humanity,
And fill it up with cruelty."
For: "And fill me from the Crowne to the Toe, top-full
Of direst Crueltie."

I, v, 57: "steel." For "Knife." Cf. I, vii, 20: "sword" for "knife."

I, vii, 51, 52: "You dare not venture on the thing you wish:
But still wou'd be in tame expectance of it."

For: "Letting I dare not, wait vpon I would,
Like the poore Cat i' th' Addage."

We have already noticed D'Avenant's irritating practice of literalizing Shakespeare's figures of speech. This trick has the same effect on the reader as explaining the point of a joke. The worst case I have met occurs in *Macbeth:*

II, iii, 85, 86: "Approach the Chamber, and behold a sight
Enough to turn spectators into stone."

For: "Approch the Chamber, and destroy your sight
With a new Gorgon."

But by far the largest number of D'Avenant's explicable alterations are due, apparently, to his zeal in elucidation. Shakespeare's text seemed full of obscurities in language and thought, and for the sake of making it transparent to the audience at Lincoln's Inn Fields the Laureate was willing to sacrifice metre, imagination, or anything else. Examples:

I, ii, 5–7: "if we may guess
His message by his looks, He can relate the
Issue of the Battle!"

For: "he can report,
As seemeth by his plight, of the Reuolt
The newest state."

I, ii, 78: "Our *confidence*." For: "Bosome interest."

I, iii, 62: "With which he seems surpriz'd."
For: "That he seemes wrapt withall."

I, iii, 65, 66: "who neither beg your favour,
Nor fear your hate."

For: "who neyther begge, nor feare
Your fauors, nor your hate."

I, iii, 135–137: "If all be true,
You have a Title to a Crown, as well
As to the Thane of Cawdor."

For: "That trusted home,
Might yet enkindle you vnto the Crowne,
Besides the Thane of Cawdor."

I, iii, 170, 171: "I was reflecting upon past transactions."
For: "Giue me your fauour:
My dull Braine was wrought with things forgotten."

I, v, 50: "no relapses into mercy."
For: "no compunctious visitings of Nature."

II, iii, 141–143: "who could then refrain,
That had an heart to love; and in that heart
Courage to *manifest his affection.*"
For: "make's loue knowne?"

II, iv, 6: "Has made that knowledge void."
For: "Hath trifled former knowings."

III, i, 59: "I am no King till I am safely so."
For: "To be thus, is nothing, but to be safely thus."

III, ii, 47: "But they are not Immortal."
For: "But in them, Natures Coppie's not eterne."

These examples might be greatly multiplied. Acts IV and V are, however, more D'Avenant's own than the first three, and I have not thought it worth while to make further citations under this head.

Not a few of D'Avenant's verbal changes defy, for me at least, reasonable classification except as wanton tampering. Perhaps the example which follows may serve as well as any to show how unrestricted the improver felt:

III, ii, 25–33: Better be with him
Whom we to gain the Crown, have sent to peace;
Then on the torture of the Mind to lye
In restless Agony. Duncan is dead;
He, after life's short feavor, now sleeps; Well:
Treason has done it's worst; not Steel, nor Poyson,
No Ferreign force, nor yet Domestick Malice
Can touch him further.

For: Better be with the dead,
Whom we, to gayne our peace, haue sent to peace,
Then on the torture of the Minde to lye
In restlesse extasie.
Duncane is in his Graue:
After Lifes fitful Feuer, he sleepes well,[41]
Treason ha's done his worst: nor Steele, nor Poyson,
Mallice domestique, forraine Leuie, nothing,
Can touch him further.

The chorus of disapproval of this outrageous alteration began at least as early as 1674, when Thomas Duffett's *The Empress of Morocco* was printed.[42] This was a burlesque of the very successful *The Empress of Morocco* by Elkanah Settle, which had been produced shortly before at Dorset Garden. The Theatre Royal thereupon employed Duffett to ridicule their rivals' success, as at about the same time they used his *Mock Tempest* to satirize the D'Avenant–Dryden–Shadwell opera. Though his game was Settle, he could not resist a shot at the great Elizabethan.[43] To his *Empress* is appended:

An Epilogue spoken by Witches, after the mode of Macbeth. [Title page:] Epilogue. Being a new Fancy after the old, and most surprising way of Macbeth, Perform'd with new and costly machines, Which were invented and managed by the most ingenious Operator Mr. Henry Wright. P. G. Q. London, Printed in the Year 1674.

There is a sort of wit in the cast of characters; it includes: Hecate, Mr. Powel; 1 Witch, Mr. Harris; 2 Witch, Mr. Adams; 3 Witch, Mr. Lyddal; Thunder, Mr. Goodman; Lightning, Mr. Kew; Spirits, Cats, and Musicians. The *Epilogue* begins:

The most renowned and melodious Song of John Dory, being heard as it were in the Air sung in parts by Spirits, to raise the expectation, and charm the audience with thoughts sublime, and worthy of that Heroick Scene which follows. The Scene opens. Thunder and lightning is discover'd, not behind Painted Tiffany to blind and amuse the Senses, but openly, by the most excellent way of Mustard-bowl, and Salt-Peter. Three Witches fly over the Pit Riding upon Beesomes. Heccate descends over the Stage in a

Glorious Charriot, adorn'd with Pictures of Hell and Devils, and made of a large Wicker Basket.

Then follows a burlesque of Hecate's reproaches and instructions to the Witches, with parodies of their songs, which, to borrow the trusty formula of John Genest, must not be quoted here.

But, "being in the nature of an opera," the D'Avenant *Macbeth* delighted the public, and remained, as we have noticed, a stock piece with Betterton throughout the remainder of his career. Not, in fact, till Shakespeare's play was revived by David Garrick in 1744 did D'Avenant's version relinquish its usurped place in the repertory.[44]

It can scarcely be denied that some of D'Avenant's interpolations are theatrically effective. Among these are the appearance of Duncan's Ghost to Lady Macbeth, and her accusation of her husband. I have little doubt that as acted by Mr. and Mrs. Betterton this scene was more than merely theatrically effective. Indeed, what makes D'Avenant's version contemptible is not so much the structural alteration, unhappy as a great deal of it is. In the first place, the Witches lose their mysterious flavor — they become vaudevillians. They sing, they dance, and, above all, they cavort on the "machines." The delight of the Restoration in these contraptions seems to us childish enough — till we think of our own theatre, where material accessories have come to dominate the stage even more than in D'Avenant's time, though now our mechanics sometimes achieve a pictorial prettiness which the Restoration producer only dreamed of.

The other depressing thing about D'Avenant's version is the ruin of some of Shakespeare's finest poetry. In spite of its apparent incompleteness and general appearance of having been tampered with, the Shakespearean *Macbeth* has several scenes which for tragic oppressiveness have seldom been equalled in all the literature of the drama. This overpowering intensity of despair comes, not from the unforgettable fact of a terrible or hideous situation (as it frequently does in Greek tragedy), but from the sheer weight of the phrasing. Macbeth is past the breaking-point in the fifth act, though in the second and third he is repeatedly near it — and knows it. He does not break, but he bends to the burden of horror that is crushing him; and his momentary collapses are made vocal by Shakespeare in those frantic outbursts like the great passage on sleep, when to the mind of the guilty thane comes the awful conviction that his crime is to isolate him.

In the last act, breaking is no longer possible; unlike his wife, King Macbeth cannot find surcease in madness or in death. She snaps under the strain; he crumbles. And the utter bleakness and blankness of his despair are, again, phrased perfectly. Sound and disordered sense combine to reveal a man dying daily, and out of the world long before his battered harness yields to the avenging sword. Of these great periods D'Avenant ruins line after line. Now smoothing the excited, tumbling verbiage into decorous decasyllabics, now sacrificing even smoothness to matter-of-factness, he trims and clips with complete assurance, only pausing now and then to let his own fancy, such as it is, soar to bombastic heights and swoop to bathetic vales with equal facility and equally disastrous consequences to the necessary question of the play.

By far the largest number of his verbal changes appears to be attributable to his passion for perspicuity. This, rather than subservience to the critical canons, seems to animate him chiefly. The canons, however, are not without their influence. A certain deference to the unities of place and time may be inferred from D'Avenant's removal to Birnam Wood of the conference between Malcolm and Macduff. Yet, as in Shakespeare, the action is now at Forres, now at Inverness, now at Fife. Strict separation dictated the excision of the Porter, yet it allowed the aërial gyrations of the Witches, which must have been comic in effect, though perhaps not in intention. The rules were supposed to prohibit scenes of violence, yet Macbeth is killed on stage. This precept, indeed, never appealed to English audiences, and was rejected by many English critics. It remains the great barrier to British and American appreciation of the classical tragedy of France. Our blindness to the often dazzling brilliance of this drama is a deplorable failing which Mr. John Masefield has lately been endeavoring to correct.

Contemptible as this version of Macbeth assuredly is, it is far less outrageous than some of the alterations which followed it — those of Nahum Tate, for example. D'Avenant rarely penned absolutely idiotic lines, as Tate often did; yet when we compare with its source the result of his efforts to refine and improve, he seems puny and impertinent. How this Laureate, whose technique could change "After Lifes fitful Feuer, he sleepes well" into "He, after life's short feavor, now sleeps: Well," ever managed to achieve "The lark now leaves his watery nest,"[45] one of the finest aubades in English, is a question which I confess still troubles me.

3. Hamlet

The Restoration version of *Hamlet* was not printed till 1676, later, that is, than the texts of D'Avenant's two other adaptations. But, as we have seen, it was the first to be acted. That the condition of the text has escaped the attention of previous writers is a curious fact; there has even been praise of D'Avenant's delicacy in leaving this masterpiece undefiled.[46]

The Quarto of 1676 was reprinted in 1683, 1695, and 1703.[47] The last pre-Wars edition was in 1637. Dr. Furness states that he was unable to procure a copy of this edition (Quarto 6). "The lack of this Quarto," he continues, "is the less to be regretted, since to judge by the Textual Notes of the Cambridge Edition only slight differences are to be perceived between it and my copy of the Quarto of 1676, which was evidently printed from it." Dr. Furness's conclusion that Quarto 6 is the source of Quarto 1676 is correct; but the later text departs widely and is in fact an altered version.

In his interesting brochure, *Dryden as an Adapter of Shakespeare*, Professor Allardyce Nicoll, whose researches have put all students of the drama deeply in his debt, calls for a study of the altered versions of the Restoration and suggests that it might throw light on the true text.[48] In my opinion this hope is unfounded. The source of the Restoration version was not "some quarto unknown to us" or "some MS. prompt-book." As a rule the adapter follows a single text, which can usually (except where there has been more than ordinarily violent adaptation) be readily identified. Most of these sources have, as a matter of fact, long ago been spotted by indefatigable Germans; there is a German doctoral thesis on nearly every one of the Restoration versions.

My own collations point to the general conclusion that until after the publication of the Fourth Folio, and except in the case of plays not printed separately before the Restoration, the source of the adapter is regularly the latest pre-Wars Quarto. I use the term pre-Wars rather than pre-Restoration because the separate editions issued between 1642 and 1660 do not appear to have made their way into the libraries of the theatres; and it was through the actors that the independent texts of the Quartos preserved their independence and their continuity at least up to the publication of the Fourth Folio in 1685. Collation was simply not a practised art in the seventeenth century. And so the Shakespeare Quartos run on, heedless except very rarely of the Folios, and then almost invariably with every appearance of casual coincidence, and repeating, without embarrassment and in edition after edition, absurdities which a glance at any one of the Folios would have cleared up.

The Quartos, in fact, give us the players' text. When a Restoration publisher, impelled by a successful revival or the first appearance of a popular actor in a new rôle, decided to take advantage of renewed public interest in one of Shakespeare's plays, he went presumably to the theatre and secured the actors' latest version. Hence the term, quite accurate, "Players' Quartos." Hence too the unimportance, as sources of Restoration texts, of the Quartos of 1655, issued while the theatres were closed, and for that reason never making their way into their libraries.

That the adapter of *Hamlet* made no attempt to check his readings with the Folios is clear from such passages as these:

I, iii, 76: "For *Love* oft loseth." For: "loan."

II, ii, 534: "Had he the motive, and *that* for passion."
For: "the cue."

There are many similar cases — obviously incorrect readings which reference to the Folios would have shown to be such. For proof of Quarto 6 as the source of Quarto 1676 the reader may consult my "*Hamlet* under the Restoration," already cited.

The *Hamlet* of 1676 *et seq.* was not structurally altered, except for being ruthlessly cut, though not more ruthlessly than our actors cut it now. All the Restoration Quartos of this play carry the following address:

> To the Reader.
> This Play being too long to be conveniently Acted, such Places as might be least prejudicial to the Plot or Sense, are left out upon the Stage: but that we may no way wrong the incomparable Author, are here inserted according to the Original Copy with this Mark "[49]

Nearly all the Fortinbras material is so marked, but not the Fortinbras ending. Voltimand and Cornelius thus drop out entirely. Other passages left out are: Horatio's excursus on omens (I, i). Marcellus's "Christmas" speech. The King's address from the throne on the state of the government. Polonius's advice to Laertes, and the scene with Reynaldo. Hamlet's advice to the players. Polonius's remarks on hypocrisy and the King's comment. Rosencrantz's flattering speech in the oratory. The whole scene in which Hamlet meets the army of Fortinbras. The following passages are greatly reduced: Marcellus's inquiries and Horatio's explanation of the preparations for war. The King's speech of reproof to Hamlet (I, ii). Hamlet's soliloquy, "O that this too too solid flesh would melt." Laertes's advice to Ophelia, and Polonius's advice to Ophelia. Hamlet's dissertation on Danish boozing, and much of his first colloquy with the Ghost. Hamlet's conversation with the First Player, and the latter's recitation. Hamlet's soliloquy, "O what a rogue and peasant slave am I." Hamlet's speech of instruction to Horatio. The first scene of the Mouse-trap. Hamlet's conversation with the Queen, after the Ghost's disappearance (III, iv). The King's speeches of conspiracy with Laertes. In general, the cutting is done with a view to retaining what is dramatic, and lopping off the lyric and sententious passages which have now become elocutionary arias.

These are far from fatal changes. What makes this *Hamlet* an alteration, and reprehensible, is the mutilation of Shakespeare's diction. I shall be bold enough to guess at the reasons for some of the changes; many of them fall into easily recognizable categories. Others, however, baffle conjecture, at least my own. It is significant that verbal changes were made, not only in the lines that were spouted on the stage, but also in the text marked by the editor as there omitted. This is evidence that the exigencies of the theatre do not fully account for the maltreatment of the Shakespearean line in these Restoration stage versions. The editor felt called upon, not merely to adapt the text for the stage, but to improve it in every conceivable way.

Many of the changes in Q 1676 consist of the excision or dilution of oaths and other expressions offensive to piety. Some of these are of little significance, since similar revisions were often made long before the Wars. Yet from their frequency as well as from the fact that the adapter's squeamishness led him to strike out expressions which seem to us innocuous, we can infer that this version was made long before 1676, when it was printed. D'Avenant's patent, remember, solemnly adjured him to purge the plays. The text of 1676 abounds in such revisions as the following: [50]

I, i, 49: "[by heaven] I charge thee, speak." Om. Q 1676.

I, i, 170: "perhaps." For: "for upon my life."

This is a cautious qualification, but one ought not to predict with much assurance whether or not any given spirit will speak, even to a princely son. The metre requires that Horatio should read "p'r'aps," which sounds more like W. S. Gilbert than like Shakespeare.

I, ii, 195: "*Pray* let me hear." For: "For Gods love."

I, v, 106: "O villain, villain, smiling [damned] villain!" Om. Q 1676.

I, v, 122: "As death, my Lord." For: "I by heaven."

II, i, 76: "With what [i' th, name of God]?" Om. Q 1676.

II, ii, 171: "Excellent well." For: "Well, God a mercy."

II, ii, 298, 299: "in apprehension, [how like a God!] the beauty of the World. . . ." Om. Q 1676.

V, i, 246: "Perdition catch thee."
For: "The Divell take thy soule."

Many other examples might be cited.

Two principal aims seem to have governed the editor of this text: he sought to make it clearer and also more elegant. To the Restoration, Shakespeare was frequently both obscure and crude. Many of the changes designed to clarify the text are mere modernizations. For instance:

III, I, 30, 31: "meet / Ophelia here."
For: "here / Affront Ophelia."

III, iv, 118: "And with th' *incorporeal* air do hold discourse?"
For: "incorporall."

V, ii, 140: "Single Rapier." For: "Rapier and dagger."

Of course the next line, Hamlet's comment, had then to be cut: "That's two of his weapons; but well."

Metrical exigencies play some part in the reviser's economy. Sometimes he forces Shakespeare's irregular blank verse into the exact decasyllabic mold. Sometimes he makes a verbal change which compels entire rearrangement. Thus:

I, iv, 5: "[Indeed,] I heard it not: it then draws near the season." Om. Q 1676.

III, ii, 213: "If once I Widow be, and then a Wife."
For: "If once I be a widow, ever I be a wife."

Many changes are due to the weakening of the last syllable of the past participle. Examples:

III, ii, 260: "The Hart ungalled *go* play." Inserted by Q 1676.

(Here the participle was pronounced *ungall'd;* it was usually printed with the apostrophe.)

V, ii, 364, 365: "give order that these Bodies
High on a Stage be *plac'd to publick* view."
For: "placed to the."

I do not, however, emphasize this group of changes. When it suited him, this editor was as willing as anyone to let the metre go hang.

To return to his efforts to achieve greater clearness. One of his methods was to simplify by rearranging inverted word order. Examples:

I, ii, 169: "my good Lord." For: "good my Lord."

I, ii, 207: "They did impart in dreadful secrecie."
For: "In dreadful secrecie impart they did."

III, ii, 352: "yet *you cannot* make it speak."
For: "cannot you."

V, i, 236, 237: "Whose wicked deeds *deprived thee of Thy most ingenuous sense.*"
For: "thy most ingenuous sense Deprived thee of."

V, ii, 14: "*I grop'd* to find out them."
For: "Grop't I."

A not uncommon grammatical change is the elimination of verbal nouns. Examples:

I, v, 186: "May do t' express his Love and *friendship* to you."
For: "friending."

V, ii, 44: "That on the view [and knowing] of these contents." Om. Q 1676.

V, ii, 107, 108: "of very soft society, and great *shew.*"
For: "shewing."

There are many other grammatical changes of various types. Examples:

I, iii, 116: "how *prodigally* the Soul." For: "prodigall."

III, ii, 291: "Your wisdom should shew it self [more] richer." Om. Q 1676.

IV, vii, 4: "That he *who* hath your noble Father slain."
For: "which."

There is a very large number of changes made apparently with the single aim of elucidating the meaning. Examples:

I, ii, 172: "*To be a witness* of your own report."
For: "To make it truster."

II, ii, 105: "Consider." For: "Perpend."

II, ii, 307: "we *met* them on the way." For: "coated."

Let the reader observe that in the interests of perspicuity not even the great soliloquy was immune:

III, i, 84: "And thus the *healthful face* of Resolution."
For: "native hiew."

III, i, 85: "Shews sick and pale with Thought."
For: "Is sicklied ore with the pale cast of thought."

III, ii, 164: "My *working* powers." For: "operant."

IV, v, 196: "Laertes, I must *share in* your grief."
For: "commune with."

IV, vii, 18: "the great love the *people* bear him."
For: "generall gender."

V, ii, 111: "Sir, his definement suffers no *loss* in you."
For: "perdition."

Sometimes these alterations are rendered more excusable by the existence of a real difficulty in Q 6, D'Avenant's source. Examples:

I, i, 93: "as by the same compact."
For: ("covenant"; Fs: "cou'nant"); Q 6: "co-mart."

IV, vii, 14: "*She is so precious* to my life and soul."
For: (Fs: "She's so conjunctive"); Q 6: "She is so conclive."

The changes made in the following passages appear to have been dictated by a desire for greater elegance. Many other examples might be given.

II, i, 79: "his Stockings *loose*." For: "foul'd."

III, i, 77: "To *groan* and sweat under a weary life?"
For: "grunt."

III, iv, 142, 145: "bring me to the Test,
And I the matter will re-word, which madness
Cannot do mother, for love of grace
Lay not. . . ."
For: "Would gambole from. Mother."

IV, v, 80: "*Obscurely* to interr him."
For: "In hugger mugger."

IV, v, 86: "And wants not *whispers* to infect his ear."
For: "buzzers."

IV, v, 120: "That treason *dares not reach at* what it would."
For: "can but peepe to."

IV, vii, 184, 185: "Pull'd the *gentle Maid* from her melodious lay."
For: (Fs: "poor wretch"); Q 6: "poore wench."

V, ii, 15: "*Reach'd* their packet." For: "Finger'd."
V, ii, 65: "*Stept* in between th' election and my hopes."
For: "Popt."

Shakespeare's *Hamlet*, unlike some of the plays written shortly after it, does not abound in wildly figurative flights of fancy. In working with *Macbeth*, which is full of them, D'Avenant is constantly toning them down; any simile or metaphor not immediately transparent is, if not cast out, at least seized upon and literalized. *Hamlet* afforded the Laureate less scope. This version contains, nevertheless, numerous literalizations of figures of speech and much toning down of especially vigorous language. Examples:

I, i, 44: "it *startles* me with fear and wonder."
For: (F 1, 2) "harrowes"; Q 6: "horrowes."
I, ii, 77: "*this Mourning* cloke." For: "my inkie."
I, iii, 46: "*About* my Heart."
For: (Q 2, 3) "as watchman to"; Q 6: "as watchmen to."
III, ii, 76: "Do not it self *discover* in one speech."
For: "unkennell."
V, ii, 243, 244: "Your skill shall like a Star i' th' darkest night *Appear*."
For: "Sticke fiery off indeed."

Many of the changes introduced by the adapter of Q 1676 appear to be simply capricious. Examples:

I, i, 37: "enlighten." For: "illumine."
I, ii, 33: "we *now* despatch." For: "here."
II, i, 77: "as I was *reading* in my Closset."
For: (Warburton) "sewing"; Q 6: "sowing."
III, ii, 312: "O wonderful son that can *thus* astonish a mother!"
For: "so."
IV, vii, 30: "Break not your *steps* for that." For: "sleeps."

In all, I have noted 283 altered passages in this text, without counting those inspired by piety. In view of that fact it can scarcely be maintained that either the theatrical or the general reading public of the Restoration knew Shakespeare's *Hamlet* unaltered.

Hamlet was produced with scenery during the summer of 1661 at the new theatre in Lincoln's Inn Fields. There is no record of its being acted earlier, after the reopening of the theatres in 1660. I have already explained that it was not played while D'Avenant's company was at Salisbury Court, because he preferred to wait till he could stage it to his taste. Accordingly he held it in reserve for the new theatre, and there, after putting on *The Siege of Rhodes*, an "opera," and *The Wits*, a comedy, both of his own composition, he launched the great tragedy, which now represented the mingled genius of himself and his revered predecessor, with whose "very spirit" he is reported to have believed he wrote. These facts are proof enough of D'Avenant's personal interest in this production. Also significant is Downes's statement that D'Avenant coached Betterton in the "business" of the title rôle, having seen it acted before the Wars by Taylor, who was said to have received his instructions from Shakespeare himself.

Now if we did not know that D'Avenant subsequently produced *Macbeth* and *The Law against Lovers*, mangled adaptations of which he was himself the author, we might hesitate to attach his name to this altered *Hamlet*. Fortunately we are certain of his responsibility for the two other plays. In view of his evident solicitude for what good old Downes would designate "the clean and well performance" of this, the most important of all his Shakespearean revivals, is it likely that he would have entrusted the preparation of the text for it to anyone else? That we may add this *Hamlet* to his works seems much more likely. From every point of view D'Avenant is the logical candidate.

Two possible objections suggest themselves, but both are easily answered. Why, it may be asked, if this *Hamlet* is D'Avenant's, was it not printed in the posthumous folio of

1673? For the same reason, we may be confident, that his *Macbeth* was not included. Although much more violently altered than the *Hamlet*, *Macbeth* was considered to be still Shakespeare's play. So was *Hamlet*. *The Law against Lovers*, on the other hand, was as much more altered than *Macbeth* as *Macbeth* was than *Hamlet;* it was considered D'Avenant's play, though it was based on two of Shakespeare's. These facts, indeed, square with our assignment of the version printed in 1676 to a much earlier date, at least in the early sixties.[51] This *Hamlet*, we may presume, reveals D'Avenant's prentice hand as an adapter of Shakespeare. Emboldened by the great success of the production, he was much less tender with his sources in his subsequent adaptations.

The second objection that I anticipate is that this *Hamlet* was not printed till 1676. Does it really represent the version acted in the early sixties? The answer to this is that delayed publication of these alterations is far from uncommon. Lacy's *Sauny the Scot*, for instance, an adaptation of *The Taming of the Shrew*, was acted at least as early as 1667; but it was not printed till 1698. D'Avenant's *Macbeth* was acted at Lincoln's Inn Fields in 1663 or 1664, but it was not published till 1674. Furthermore, there was little printing of Shakespeare in quarto in the sixties. It was during this decade that his reputation was at the lowest ebb it has ever known. As the century drew toward its close his popularity began to recover ground. The frequent reprinting of his chief theatrical successes is in keeping with his growth in favor both with audiences and with the reading public. By the end of the century the tide has much more than turned; and in 1709 Rowe gives us the first critical edition.

But we need not rest our case here. There is nothing external, so far as I know, to connect the name of D'Avenant with this version of *Hamlet*, except the facts I have given, though these concur in pointing in his direction. But there is internal evidence in great plenty. In fact, traces of his hand are so extensive that I can here present only samples of them. I shall merely quote, therefore, from *Macbeth* and from *The Law against Lovers*, a few of the passages which illustrate the same methods of revision as those which we have noticed governing the changes in the Restoration *Hamlet*.[52]

1. Excision of offences against piety.
   Cf. *Macbeth*, I, ii, 58: "Long live the King!" For: "God saue."

2. Modernization.
   Cf. *Macbeth*, I, iii, 87: "what seem'd Corporeal." For: "corporall." [53]

   Cf. *The Law against Lovers*, p. 277 (*Measure for Measure*, I, ii, 134): "An evil Thirst." For: "A thirsty euill."

3. Metrical improvements.
   Cf. *Macbeth*, I, i, 14: "To us fair weather's foul, and foul is fair!" For: "faire is foule and foule is faire."

   Cf. *Macbeth*, I, ii, 75: "Until at Colems-Inch he had disburs'd." For: "Till he disbursed, at Saint Colmes ynch."

4. Grammatical corrections.
   Cf. *Macbeth*, I, ii, 19: "*was* supply'd." For: "is."

   Cf. *Macbeth*, I, ii, 59: "Whence *com'st* thou, worthy Thane?" For: "cam'st."

   Cf. *Macbeth*, I, iii, 55: "who." For: "that."

5. Efforts to achieve greater clearness.
   Cf. *Macbeth*, I, ii, 78: "Our *confidence*." For: "Bosome interest."

   Cf. *Macbeth*, I, iii, 62: "With which he seems surpriz'd." For: "That he seemes wrapt withall."

   Cf. *Macbeth*, I, iii, 101, 102:
   "His wonder and his praises then contend
   Which shall exceed."
   For: "Which should be thine, or his."

   Cf. *Macbeth*, I, iii, 135–137:
   "If all be true,
   You have a Title to a Crown, as well
   As to the Thane of Cawdor."

For: "That trusted home,
Might yet enkindle you vnto the Crowne,
Besides the Thane of Cawdor."

Cf. *Macbeth*, I, iv, 53, 54:
"Now we'll hasten hence
To Enverness: we'll be your guest, Macbeth,
And there contract a greater debt than that
Which I already owe you."

For: "From hence to Envernes,
And binde vs further to you."

Cf. *Macbeth*, I, v, 50: "no relapses into mercy."
For: "no compunctious visitings of Nature."

Cf. *The Law against Lovers*, p. 298 (*Measure for Measure*, III, i, 67–70):

"*Claud*. Perpetual durance?
Isab. 'Tis worse than close restraint, and painful too
Beyond all tortures which afflict the body;
For 'tis a Rack invented for the mind."

For:
"*Cla*. Perpetuall durance?
Isa. I iust, perpetuall durance, a restraint
Through all the worlds vastiditie you had
To a determin'd scope."

6. Attempts at greater elegance.
Cf. *Macbeth*, I, vii, 51, 52:
"You dare not venture on the thing you wish:
But still wou'd be in tame expectance of it."

For: "Letting I dare not, wait vpon I would,
Like the poore Cat i' th' Addage."

Cf. *The Law against Lovers*, p. 279 (*Measure for Measure*, I, iii, 29):
"and froward liberty,
Does Justice strike."

For: "And libertie, plucks Iustice by the nose."

7. Literalization and general toning down.
Cf. *Macbeth*, II, iii, 85, 86:
"Approach the Chamber, and behold a sight
Enough to turn spectators into stone."

For: "Approch the Chamber, and destroy your sight
with a new Gorgon."

Cf. *Macbeth*, I, ii, 61: "where the Norwean Banners
Darkned the Air." For: "flowt the Skie."

Cf. *The Law against Lovers*, p. 279 (*Measure for Measure*,
I, iii, 2, 3): "Lov's too tender to dwell in my cold bosom."
For: "Beleeue not that the dribling dart of Loue
Can pierce a compleat bosome."

Many other passages might be adduced to reënforce each of these groups. I have reserved till last the most striking case of similarity. In *Measure for Measure*, III, i, 104–106, Isabella nobly declares:

> O, were it but my life,
> I'de throw it downe for your deliuerance
> As frankely as a pin,

which becomes in *The Law against Lovers* (p. 298):

> O, were it but my life,
> I would for your deliverance throw it down,
> Most frankly, Claudio.

This amusing evidence of the unpleasantness of pins in the sceptered pall of Tragedy, and consequently of the writer's respect for the principle of decorum, is beautifully matched by an alteration of *Hamlet*, I, iv, 65:

> I do not set my life at a pin's fee,

a superb line for an actor, whatever it may not be for a critic. In the Restoration *Hamlet* this line appears most tamely:

> I do not value my life,

a cadence that might have afforded Betterton, who had to read it, some food for reflection on the advisability of setting up barriers to the Shakespearean ebb and flow. That D'Avenant saw the first pin and indignantly picked it up and out, as incongruous with the elevation of Tragedy, we happen to know. As for the second, if it was not he who refused to "let it lay," then who was it?

Notes to Chapter V

1. Karl Elze, *Essays on Shakespeare* (London, 1874), pp. 346, 347.
2. George Illies (*Das Verhältnis von Davenant's "The Law against Lovers" zu Shakespeare's "Measure for Measure" und "Much Ado about Nothing,"* Halle, 1900) is concerned chiefly with structural alteration and the sources of D'Avenant's text.
3. As Elze observes, Angelo's prejudice against lovers, and the emphasis on the law's being against them rather than aimed merely at unlawful love, are scarcely in keeping with D'Avenant's customary moral vein. *Shakespeare Jahrbuch*, iv, 153; Illies, p. 22.
4. This involves the loss of "Take, oh take those lips away."
5. From the epistle "To Congreve." This passage is sometimes cited in refutation of the charge that Shakespeare was not valued by the Restoration at his true worth. Unfortunately the last line quoted does not end with a full stop but with a colon, and is thus followed:

   "Till you, the best Vitruvius, come at length;
   Our beauties equal, but excel our strength."

   Dryden then goes on to assert Congreve's superiority to Fletcher and Jonson and his equality with Shakespeare.
6. J. D. E. Williams lists numerous changes, in his dissertation on *Sir William Davenant's [Literary] Relation to Shakespeare*, pp. 25–36.
7. For a more systematic examination of the influence of the neo-classical canons than is undertaken in this book see Thomas R. Lounsbury's *Shakespeare as a Dramatic Artist.*
8. I reprint portions of my article, "D'Avenant's *Macbeth* and Shakespeare's," *Publ. Mod. Lang. Ass'n of Am.*, xl, 619–644 (Sept., 1925).
9. Montague Summers, *Shakespeare Adaptations*, pp. xxxv f. Captain Jaggard's great bibliography entertains the same error. (William Jaggard, *Shakespeare Bibliography*, p. 381.)
10. There were at least two issues in 1674, one for P. Chetwin, the other for A. Clark. Whether these contain minor variations I cannot say, not having thought it worth while to collate them carefully. They appear to be identical.
11. W. J. Lawrence, *The Elizabethan Playhouse* [First Series], p. 211, n. 2.
12. I have since examined copies of this Quarto in the British Museum and in the Bodleian.
13. H. H. Furness, New Variorum Ed., vol. ii (revised ed., 1903), pp. vii, viii.
14. He means the Quarto of 1673, that is, Quarto 1.
15. That is, Mr. Lawrence's Quarto 2, of 1674.
16. *Macbeth*, New Var. Ed., 1873.
17. *Ibid.*, revised ed., 1903.
18. The whole song appears as follows in Q 1674, pp. 26, 27:

   "*1 Witch.* Speak, Sister, speak; is the deed done?
   2 Witch. Long ago, long ago:
   Above twelve glasses since have run.

3 Witch. Ill deeds are seldom slow;
Nor single: following crimes on former wait.
The worst of creatures fastest propagate.
Many more murders must this one ensue,
As if in death were propagation too.
2 Witch. He will.
1 Witch. He shall.
3 Witch. He must spill much more bloud;
And become worse, to make his Title good.
1 Witch. Now let's dance.
2 Witch. Agreed.
3 Witch. Agreed.
4 Witch. Agreed.
Chorus. We shou'd rejoyce when good Kings bleed.
When cattel die, about we go,
What then, when Monarchs perish, should we do?"

19. In Q 1673, that is; in Q 1674 it is a few lines farther on in the same scene.
20. *Macbeth*, New Var. Ed., 1873.
21. *Ibid.*, revised ed., 1903.
22. The entire song is as follows (Q 1674, p. 27):

"Let's have a dance upon the Heath;
We gain more life by Duncan's death.
Sometimes like brinded Cats we shew,
Having no musick but our mew.
Sometimes we dance in some old mill,
Upon the hopper, stones, and wheel.
To some old saw, or Bardish Rhime,
Where still the Mill-clack does keep time.
Sometimes about an hollow tree,
A round, a round, a round dance we.
Thither the chirping Cricket comes,
And Beetle, singing drowsie hums.
Sometimes we dance o're Fens and Furs,
To howls of wolves, and barks of curs.
And when with none of those we meet,
We dance to th' ecchoes of our feet.
At the night-Raven's dismal voice,
Whilst others tremble, we rejoyce;
And nimbly, nimbly dance we still
To th' ecchoes from an hollow Hill."

23. *Macbeth*, New Var. Ed., 1873.
24. *Ibid.*, revised ed., 1903. For Furness's 525, read 528, 529.
25. This song is taken, with a dozen verbal alterations, from Middleton's *The Witch* (ed. Bullen, v, 416–418), III, iii, 39–74. It had probably been used in *Macbeth* as early as before the publication of the First Folio. It appears in Q 1674 on pages 44, 45.

26. Furness, New Var. *Ed.* (revised ed.) of *Macbeth*, pp. vii, viii.
27. These are not recorded in Dr. Furness's *textual* notes (1873), since he did not recognize the difference between Q 1673 and Q 1674 until he had made some progress in collation.
28. The text first cited is in each case the reading of Q 1673, and the second is that of F 1, both as given by Furness.
29. H. T. Hall (*Shakspere's Plays: The Separate Editions of, with the Alterations Done by Various Hands*, p. 43) asserts that D'Avenant altered the play in 1672. This was four years after D'Avenant died.
30. Mr. Lawrence doubts the existence of a Quarto of 1687 (*The Elizabethan Playhouse*, I, 212, n. 1), but there is a copy so dated in the Boston Public Library.
31. Dryden, Preface to *Troilus and Cressida*, ed. 1679, sig. a 3 *verso* f.
32. D'Avenant failed to observe that Lady Macbeth is well into the letter when she enters.
33. Weber approves of this excision, which he attributes to D'Avenant's desire to condense the action. Weber here, as elsewhere in his dissertation, forgets the influence of the canons on D'Avenant's methods. The excision of the Porter was directly required by the principle of strict separation. (G. Weber, *Davenant's Macbeth im Verhältnis zu Shakespeare's gleichnamiger Tragödie*, Rostock, 1903, p. 65.)
34. Fairness compels the admission that if we must have couplets this is in excellent vein; at least it is eminently actable.
35. Bullen's ed. of Middleton, v, 416 f. Weber (pp. 64 f.) points out that D'Avenant has shifted this scene with the preceding in order to close the act on these "wunderhübscher Hexengesänge." Shakespeare's ending of the act is undeniably weak — that is, if we are to assume that the Elizabethans knocked off for a cigarette four times during the course of a performance.
36. Kilbourne remarks that it is no wonder Seyton finally rebels against D'Avenant's Macbeth — he has been given so much extra work in this version. (F. W. Kilbourne, *Alterations and Adaptations of Shakespeare*, p. 150.) The Restoration adapters are in fact much more economical than Shakespeare; almost invariably they reduce the number of characters.
37. Williams says the reason for this change is inexplicable, but it seems fairly obvious: D'Avenant here exhibits a certain deference to the unities of time and place. (J. D. E. Williams, *Sir William Davenant's [Literary] Relation to Shakespeare*, p. 45.)
38. Weber (p. 69) observes that the scene is in one respect an improvement: at least the reappearance of the two sons to avenge their murdered sires is justifiable dramatically.
39. Victims, vict'ries (?).
40. In each case, unless the contrary is stated, the text first quoted is that of Q 1674. The words replaced are quoted from the First Folio as given by Furness. Weber (p. 15) concludes that the source of Q 1674 is all but certainly F 1.

41. Lord Morley praised this line as "the most melting and melodious single verse in all the exercises of our English tongue." It seemed otherwise to D'Avenant.
42. "The Empress of Morocco. A Farce. Acted by His Majesties Servants. London . . . 1674."
43. On page 22 there is a silly burlesque of Hamlet's ranting speech to Laertes at Ophelia's grave.
44. See Odell, *Shakespeare from Betterton to Irving*, i, 30.
45. This beautiful lyric has been set to music with notable success by Horatio Parker, *Old English Songs*, op. 47.
46. I reprint portions of my article, "*Hamlet* under the Restoration," *Publ. Mod. Lang Ass'n of Am.*, xxxviii, 770–791 (Dec., 1923).
47. There were two issues of Q 1703; the catchword is the last word in the text on page 1, in one case *Bornardo*, in the other, *Barnardo*. There may have been two issues of Q 1676. The copy I have used, that of the Boston Public Library, differs in many cases from Furness's textual notes. He suspected the existence of two issues because he found the readings of the Cambridge editors frequently at variance with his own copy.
48. Mr. Nicoll reiterates this opinion in "The Rights of Beeston and D'Avenant in Elizabethan Plays," *Review of English Studies*, i, 84–91 (Jan., 1925). See also my criticism in "The Restoration Play Lists," *Ibid.*, i, 443–446 (Oct., 1925), and Mr. Nicoll's note in rejoinder, p. 446.
49. 816 lines and parts of lines were left out on the stage — a substantial reduction. Not all that were omitted are so marked, and some are evidently marked by mistake. See my Harvard dissertation (1923, unpublished), pp. 300–326, for an exhaustive list of these omissions and of the textual variants of Q 1676.
50. Unless the contrary is stated, the text first given is in each case that of Q 1676. Lines are numbered to agree with the New Var. Ed. of Furness. Words replaced or omitted are given according to Q 6.
51. It is, of course, possible that the alterations were not made by D'Avenant till after its first performance. On the other hand they may have been made long before.
52. In each case the text first given is that of D'Avenant's revision, either from the *Macbeth* Quarto of 1674 or *The Law against Lovers* in the 1673 folio of D'Avenant's works. Line references to *Measure for Measure* agree with Neilson's Cambridge ed.; to *Macbeth*, with Furness. Text from the unaltered plays is quoted in the case of *Macbeth* from Furness's reprint of F 1, and of *Measure for Measure* from the *National Shakespeare* facsimile of the same text.
53. This identical change is also made in the *Hamlet* of 1676 (III, iv, 118).

CHAPTER VI

DRYDEN'S ADAPTATIONS

1. The Tempest

A. *The D'Avenant–Dryden Comedy*

THE D'Avenant–Dryden *Tempest* was first printed in 1670 "As it is now Acted at his Highness the Duke of York's Theatre." [1] This was two years after D'Avenant's death. There is a preface by Dryden which gives a brief account of the play's history. Originally composed by Shakespeare, it inspired Fletcher's *The Sea Voyage* and Suckling's *The Goblins*. The material was next taken in hand by D'Avenant, who asked Dryden to collaborate.

Sir William DAvenant, as he was a man of quick and piercing imagination, soon found that somewhat might be added to the Design of Shakespear, of which neither Fletcher nor Suckling had ever thought: and therefore to put the last hand to it, he design'd the Counterpart to Shakespear's Plot, namely that of a Man who had never seen a Woman; that by this means those two Characters of Innocence and Love might the more illustrate and commend each other. This excellent contrivance he was pleas'd to communicate to me, and to desire my assistance in it. I confess that from the very first moment it so pleas'd me, that I never writ any thing with more delight. I must likewise do him that justice to acknowledge, that my writing received daily his amendments, and that is the reason why it is not so faulty, as the rest which I have done without the help or correction of so judicious a friend. The Comical parts of the Saylors were also his invention, and for the most part his writing, as you will easily discover by the style. . . . It had perhaps been easie enough for me to have arrogated more to my self than was my due in the writing of this Play, and to have pass'd by his name with silence in the publication of it, with the same ingratitude which others have us'd to him, whose Writings he hath not

JOHN DRYDEN

only corrected, as he has done this, but has had a greater inspection over them, and sometimes added whole Scenes together, which may as easily be distinguish'd from the rest, as true Gold from counterfeit by the weight.

Since we must decide, if we can, to which of the collaborators the greater share of the blame belongs, the reader should here notice what Dryden actually says D'Avenant did: (1) invented the man who has never seen a woman; (2) corrected what Dryden wrote; (3) invented the comical parts of the sailors, and largely wrote them. This is *all* that Dryden gives D'Avenant credit for. The other new characters, besides Hippolito, "one that never saw Woman, right Heir of the Dukedom of Mantua," must have appealed to D'Avenant's passion for balance, which we have already noticed in his *Macbeth*. Caliban is provided with an unpleasant sister named Sycorax; and Ariel with a sweetheart named Milcha, who obliges at the end of the play with a saraband. Moreover, Prospero has two daughters instead of one, in order that the unexpressed questionings of Miranda may become audible in repeated exchanges of naturalistic confidences between that guileless damsel and her sister Dorinda, and also in order to provide a match for Hippolito.

The plot of the play runs as follows.[2]

ACT I

The opening lines reveal at once a fundamental difference between the methods of Shakespeare and the adapters laureate. The only way to make your audience believe you really have the vasty fields of France within your wooden O is to give them mere glimpses — too brief to reveal discrepancies, yet so vivid and so rapid that the mind is bewildered as in the presence of the events themselves. One of the cleverest of our American motion-picture producers early grasped this principle. In the episode from Mr. David W. Griffith's *Intolerance* entitled "The Fall of Babylon," the producer's task was to simulate on a large scale the operations of ancient warfare. He succeeded because he gave his audience only flashes of his scenes (though these had been constructed with lavish detail) — flashes in which for a moment or two the eye caught impressions of towering walls and tremendous battlements, countless hosts of men and horses, and through the smoke of the burning city the life and death struggle that engrossed it.

Now Shakespeare recognized this principle as clearly as anyone, and his marvellous sense of fact enabled him to succeed where most idealists and all materialists must have failed. The opening scene of *The Tempest* is beyond the resources of Shakespeare's or any other stage; but by glimpses of confusion, momentary rushes of the various groups of characters across the stage, the bawling of orders, terrified questions and excited answers, and at last wild cries of despair, he succeeds in creating, at the very height of the storm, an impression of elemental wildness and human disaster.

In *The Tempest* of D'Avenant–Dryden the storm, like a well-regulated tragedy, has a beginning, a middle, and an end. Instead of a rapid cross-section of the tumult at its climax, we watch the storm beginning after the scene begins. The ship is peacefully at anchor when the mariners predict bad weather. They finally make sail, weigh anchor, and attempt to claw off shore. The guns break loose (off stage, I suppose), and no sooner is she under way than the pumps are manned with six feet of water in the hold. Amid a chaos of contradictory orders the crew attempt to beach the ship, but she strikes a rock on her starboard bow. The altered scene contains 113 lines. Shakespeare's has 72. The former may be more perspicuous; certainly we are not left in any doubt regarding what is happening. Shakespeare does not shout so many orders or tell us that we are headed for the shore, or specify that it is the starboard instead of the port side from which disaster comes.

> *A confused noyse within.*
> Mercy on vs.
> We split, we split, Farewell my wife, and children,
> Farewell brother: we split, we split, we split.

One understands how drowning woe like that can be staged; and how, because it is too brief and too confused to give time to pause and perceive scenic limitations, it can convince.

The second scene of Shakespeare's play is a tedious affair and a striking example of his occasional late failure to measure up to his own previous standard. In the D'Avenant–Dryden comedy it runs along as in the original through I, ii, 375 (Neilson's numbering), though the speeches are greatly reduced. There is little actual alteration of diction. The most surprising thing about the text is that the blank verse is for the most part printed as prose. Of course, all Prospero's references to Miranda as a child are tagged "and Dorinda." Upon Caliban's exit, Prospero also leaves the stage, thus clearing it for Dorinda, who comes to tell the news of the wreck. Miranda informs her there were men in the ship; the opportunity for salty dialogue afforded by the girls' curiosity is fully utilized.

ACT II

Omitting the remainder of I, ii, the first meeting of Miranda with Ferdinand, Act II begins as in Shakespeare's play with Alonzo, who is merely Duke of Savoy, though he is also ducal Usurper of Mantua. Antonio remains Usurper of Milan. Sebastian, Adrian, and Francisco disappear. Gonzalo, shorn of his distinctive character, is of course a noble of Savoy. The comic dialogue which follows his opening speech is omitted (II, i, 10–105). Alonzo and Antonio publicly confess their crimes. Gonzalo's Utopia is excised; likewise the Antonio–Sebastian conspiracy, which has been asserted to be no loss. But Shakespeare's purpose seems to be to contrast the evil of the world with the peacefulness of the isle, as well as to crowd his plot; if so, the conspiracy surely justifies retention.

The gentlemen are not lulled to sleep, but remain awake to hear a "Dialogue within sung in parts." It begins

> Where does proud Ambition dwell?
> In the lowest Rooms of Hell.

The song has two stanzas on this theme. Then: "Enter the two that sung, in the shape of Devils, placing themselves at two corners of the Stage." They summon, in the manner of a modern revue, Pride, Fraud, Rapine, and Murther, who remind the guilty rulers, in general terms, of their hideous crimes. "After which they fall into a round encompassing the Duke, &c. Singing." Then they vanish. The rebuked aristocrats profess repentance and, that duty done, set out to find food.

No sooner are they off stage than Ferdinand enters to the well-remembered tune of "Come unto these yellow sands." A part of the omitted portions of I, ii, 376–407, follows. We can almost forgive the adapters for their ditty on ambition, since they left both Ariel's songs practically untouched. In fact, Ferdinand is brought on solely for these; immediately after "Full Fathoms five" both he and Ariel leave the stage.

The next scene is one of the low comedy patches on which Dryden and D'Avenant plumed themselves. Stephano, who is no longer butler, but none other than ship's captain, sets up as ruler: "for I was Master at Sea, and will be Duke on Land: you Mustacho have been my Mate, and shall be my Vice-Roy." Ventoso, a mariner, objects to this arrangement, but is mollified by appointment as second viceroy. The song, "The Master, the Swabber," etc. (II, ii, 48–56), is introduced at this point with some variations in the personnel. Trincalo (*sic*) who rates as boatswain in the adaptation, now appears, half drunk. Refusing to be a subject, he is proclaimed a rebel. Left alone he meets Caliban, whereupon we return to Shakespeare's dialogue for a few moments (II, ii, 1 f.), though it is both reduced and altered. Trincalo plays Stephano's rôle with Caliban, and this adds two recruits to his rebellion, for the monster is to lead the way to his "lovely Sister, beautiful and bright as the full Moon."

The stage thus cleared, Prospero appears for a bit of somewhat overdue exposition:

> 'Tis not yet fit to let my Daughters know I kept
> The infant Duke of Mantua so near them in this Isle,
> Whose Father dying bequeath'd him to my care,
> Till my false Brother (when he design'd t' usurp
> My Dukedom from me) expos'd him to that fate
> He meant for me. By calculation of his birth
> I saw death threat'ning him, if, till some time were
> Past, he should behold the face of any Woman:
> And now the danger's nigh.

How Prospero had managed to keep this evolution from airy nothing concealed in a local habitation so near his daughters, he fails to tell us. Hippolito is now summoned and solemnly warned against

> Those dangerous enemies of men call'd women.

The terrified youth has hardly departed when Miranda and Dorinda stroll in, looking, not unnaturally, for the Man. Their father warns them to beware; the dialogue is lascivious but witty. It is not difficult to imagine the titters with which the audience of gallants and coquettes, not to mention the "vizards," received such lines as the following:

> *Mir.* But you have told me, Sir, you are a man;
> And yet you are not dreadful.
> *Prosp.* I child! but I am a tame man; old men are tame
> By Nature, but all the danger lies in a wild
> Young man.
> *Dor.* Do they run wild about the Woods?
> *Prosp.* No, they are wild within Doors, in Chambers,
> And in Closets.
> *Dor.* But Father, I would stroak 'em and make 'em gentle,
> Then sure they would not hurt me.

Prospero leaves the girls, commending the really pathological Dorinda to her older but no wiser sister's care. They determine to seek the mysterious yet fascinating creature. Now "The Scene changes, and discovers Hippolito in a Cave walking, his face from the Audience. . . . Enter Miranda and Dorinda peeping." Going by appearances, they decide this must be a tame man. Unfortunately, Prospero is heard calling Miranda. She goes, but her wilful sister stays. Hippolito sees her; the admiration is mutual, but the young people's experiment of clasping hands is ended by Prospero's peremptory shouting for his daughter.

ACT III

The third act begins with Prospero's warning cross-examination of both his daughters. For this we lose the pretty scene of Ferdinand piling logs.[3]

The following scene is Shakespeare's III, iii. The appearance of the gentle spirits is changed. First Ariel sings an encouraging ditty. Then,

Enter eight fat Spirits, with Cornu-Copia in their hands.

Alonz. Are these plump shapes sent to deride our hunger?
Gonz. No, no; it is a Masque of fatten'd Devils, the
Burgo-Masters of the lower Region.
O for a Collop of that large-haunch'd Devil
Who went out last! [4]

But "going to the door," Antonio sees (outside) a well-furnished table, to which the gentlemen promptly adjourn.

The next scene gives Trincalo's meeting with Sycorax; his ardor is immediately cooled, though the hideous creature is most amorous. He has consented, however, to submit to an embrace, when Stephano, Mustacho, and Ventoso, who have run out of food and liquor, appear for a parley. Trincalo claims the island by virtue of his espousal of Sycorax. The others retire to consider a treaty.

Ferdinand, led by the invisible Ariel, now enters for the echo-song which so charmed Mr. Pepys. The scene then changes, and we have Prospero exhibiting Ferdinand to Miranda (I, ii, 408–501). The youth safely disarmed and imprisoned, Prospero summons Hippolito to bear the captive company.

The next scene shows a cave. Hippolito and Ferdinand exchange confidences. The former hears of Miranda — and learns that she and Dorinda are not the only specimens of their sex. The vista enraptures him:

Hip. I will have all of that kind, if there be a hundred of 'em.
Ferd. But noble youth, you know not what you say.
Hip. Sir, they are things I love, I cannot be without 'em:
O, how I rejoyce! More women!

This simple conclusion is naturally unacceptable to Ferdinand, but the young men separate with Hippolito still unconvinced that his plans are impracticable.

ACT IV

The plot now thickens. Prospero bids Miranda urge Ferdinand to be friendly to Hippolito. This she does; but her lover is overcome by jealousy, and concludes, like any Restoration sophisticate, that Miranda resembles "most of her frail Sex."

Why did I think that any Woman could be innocent,
Because she's young? No, no, their Nurses teach them
Change, when with two Nipples they divide their
Liking.

With this novel commentary he rushes out, and Miranda dutifully reports to Prospero.

Hippolito and Dorinda next appear. The enthusiastic youth is still elated by Ferdinand's wonderful news, which unfortunately he passes on to his lady:

As I'm a man, I'le tell you blessed news.
I have heard there are more Women in the World,
As fair as you are too.

Dor. Is this your news? you see it moves not me.
Hip. And I'le have 'em all.

This announcement does not appeal to Dorinda, who makes an indignant exit. Ferdinand now enters and challenges Hippolito, whom he supposes to have obtained Miranda's favor.

The next scene takes us back to Trincalo and his monsters. Stephano and the viceroys sue "for Peace and the Butt";[5] they are to become Trincalo's subjects, and share in the liquor. Caliban entertains with a song, and then all join hands and dance. They are soon thoroughly drunk. Stephano convinces Sycorax that he is the true god, and Trincalo's rule is again in jeopardy. The scene ends in a general fight, Sycorax beating Caliban off the stage, while Trincalo conquers Stephano.

Hippolito and Ferdinand fight to settle the former's pretensions to Miranda. Hippolito falls, apparently dead. Ariel brings in Alonzo and his train. Prospero sentences Ferdinand to death for murder; when Alonzo remonstrates, "he stamps, and many Spirits appear," who drive the courtiers in. Miranda and Dorinda quarrel, and Ariel closes the act with a speech summing up the unpleasantness of the whole situation.

ACT V

Ariel tells Prospero that he has induced the soul of Hippolito to return. The wounded man is then "discovered on a Couch, Dorinda by him." He protests that Ferdinand must not die, and that he himself repents:

the fault
Was only in my blood, for now 'tis gone, I find
I do not love so many.

While Dorinda runs to beg Ferdinand's life of her father, Miranda comes in to cure Hippolito's wound by anointing the sword. His good resolutions go by the board and he regrets his effusion,

for if I had that bloud, I then
Should find a great delight in loving you.

Mir. But, Sir, I am anothers, and your love is given
Already to my Sister.
Hip. Yet I find that if you please I can love still a little.

Ferdinand and Dorinda enter. Hippolito is jealous at seeing them together; Ferdinand is jealous to find him alone with Miranda. But in turn each of the four lovers professes eternal constancy, Hippolito last, and under the compulsion of the others' example.

At this auspicious moment Prospero, Alonzo, and the other gentlemen appear, and the prospective unions are blessed. The adapters make use of the good wishes then expressed, to put a final salvo of suggestive speeches into the mouths of the innocent lovers. The indecency of it all is finally too much for Ferdinand; he intervenes to give Hippolito a harmless, necessary tip:

> you yet are ignorant of your great
> Happiness, but there is somewhat which for
> Your own and fair Dorinda's sake I must instruct
> You in.

Finally Ariel drives in the sailors and the monsters, and Duke Trincalo abdicates. Ariel sings "Where the Bee sucks." Sycorax implores Trincalo to take her with him; she is gently but firmly repulsed. Ariel is ordered to dance. He answers:

> I have a gentle Spirit for my Love,
> Who twice seven years hath waited for my Freedom,
> It shall appear and foot it featly with me.
> Milcha, my Love, thy Ariel calls thee.

She, or "It," comes, and they dance a saraband.

To appraise this wretched stuff in the light of the critical rules would be absurd. One aim and one alone animated its authors: to pander. Starting with the innocence of Miranda in Shakespeare's play, they perceived that comic possibilities lurked there unexploited. Then D'Avenant had the happy thought of making the situation doubly comic by doubling the innocence — more than doubling it, in fact, since an innocent man is more amusing than an innocent woman. Finally, for good measure, a third innocence was thrown in — Dorinda's.

For so much we can perhaps blame D'Avenant in chief; but that Dryden worked out the comedy and wrote it up, there can be little question. As we have seen, D'Avenant was almost a prude where verbal grossness was to be dealt with. Dryden, on the other hand, is one of the loosest of the English dramatists.[6]

Internal evidence is, except on this score, unfortunately meagre. Though it is mangled structurally, such portions of Shakespeare's text as were retained suffered little alteration. The diction of *The Law against Lovers*, *Macbeth*, and *Hamlet* is much more extensively tampered with. There is some minor alteration, such as rearrangement of word order, correction of tenses, substitution of "who" for "that," etc.; but attempts at greater elegance or greater clearness or the toning down of figurative language are inconsiderable. This fact, also, leads to the conclusion that D'Avenant did not actually compose much of the text. As Dryden tells us in his preface, the older man exercised general oversight, invented Hippolito, and largely wrote the comic parts of the sailors. These are practically independent scenes, not based on Shakespeare's text. That this version is, with these exceptions, the work of Dryden, writing on hints given him by D'Avenant, I have little doubt.[7]

The adapters are charged by Hermann Grimm with the theft of certain matter of Calderon's.[8] The latter's romantic drama, *En esta vida todo es verdad y todo mentira* (*c.* 1640), contains situations paralleling those of the naïve lovers in the revised *Tempest*. Grimm finds Dryden's scenes literally[9] in the Spanish play, and his charge has been repeated by Dr. Furness and by Professor Odell. As Mr. Summers points out, however, the treatment of unsophisticated youth by the two dramatists is not in the least parallel, even though a few lines in the two plays afford a fairly close approximation of thought.[10]

But this is not a matter of great importance. Whatever their sources, the adapters ruined Shakespeare's play. On the whole, *The Tempest* of D'Avenant and Dryden may fairly be called the worst, as it was the most successful, of the Restoration alterations prior to 1700. Though they based their plot on Shakespeare's and often used his language, they could not borrow his spirit. Gone is the noble serenity that makes us eager to regard *The Tempest* as Shakespeare's farewell message to the world; in its place we have a licentious farce. Everything that the authors lay their hands on is defiled. The exquisite Miranda is so degraded that, as Professor Lounsbury remarks, "her conversation with her sister Dorinda is the kind that might have gone on between two maids of honor of the court of Charles II."

Prospero's lines are greatly reduced and he becomes little more than a master of cheap ceremonies. His renunciation of his powers is not retained, and "We are such stuff as dreams are made on" is most happily (in these surroundings) omitted. Caliban, too, suffers severely. But let Dryden's great editor speak of him: his "wild and savage character," says Sir Walter Scott, "is sunk into low and vulgar buffoonery." [11]

Scott, like later editors, declares that scenic splendor chiefly accounted for the success of what is really hardly an alteration but a wretched travesty. The opportunity for such magnificence in *The Tempest* is obvious; yet probably of equal importance were the nature of the situation and the opportunity for licentious dialogue. Given a situation which only a romantic delicacy could treat vigorously without indecency, and in charge of that situation an absolute master of genteel smut like John Dryden — and of course the baseless fabric of that cloud-capped vision of Shakespeare's melted into thin air, like the insubstantial pageant we rejoice he made it.

B. *The D'Avenant–Dryden–Shadwell Opera*

A few years later, the D'Avenant–Dryden comedy in its turn suffered a sea-change. There were aërial wires for Ariel and Milcha to frisk about on, a tricksome table that whisked up and down through an eminently "practical" trapdoor, bottles that disappeared undrained by human gullet, a rising sun, and various other mechanical excellencies, not to mention a chorus of devils, ballets of winds and Tritons, and a band of twenty-four violins assisted by harpsicals and theorbos. This paradise of dainty devices was added in 1674 to the D'Avenant–Dryden comedy, which thereby became an "opera." For the reader must remember that the "machines" were almost as important as the music in making an "opera" out of a play.

The new version superseded the D'Avenant–Dryden comedy, of which it is in fact only an alteration. Mr. G. Thorn-Drury [12] is sceptical of Shadwell's hand in the new version, but Downes's explicit statement has not yet been discredited.

Shadwell's changes are not extensive. A few scenes are cut or transposed, and a masque and a new song are added. Here and there the mechanical and musical features are elaborated. The D'Avenant–Dryden comedy had some of these effects, of course; so did the original play by Shakespeare. The part of Milcha is also considerably expanded. These are Shadwell's only changes.

The opera, then, does not differ essentially from the comedy; we can no more accurately describe Shadwell as "writing an opera on the *Tempest*" than we can accuse D'Avenant of writing a tragedy on *Hamlet*. In support of this conclusion, which, in view of recent controversy, I wish I had published four years ago, I submit the following account of the differences between the D'Avenant–Dryden–Shadwell opera and the D'Avenant–Dryden comedy.

The scenery was evidently more elaborate for the opera, which was produced on the large and well-equipped stage of Dorset Garden. The earlier version was conceived and born in the cramped quarters at Lincoln's Inn Fields. In the following synopsis of the opera, I shall give the description of the scenery wherever it is specified.

ACT I

[Scene i.] The Front of the Stage is open'd, and the Band of 24 Violins, with the Harpsicals and Theorbo's which accompany the Voices, are plac'd between the Pit and the Stage. While the Overture is playing, the Curtain rises, and discovers a new Frontispiece, joyn'd to the great Pylasters, on each side of the Stage. This Frontispiece is a noble Arch, supported by large wreathed Columns of the Corinthian Order; the wreathings of the Columns are beautifi'd with Roses wound round them, and several Cupids flying about them. On the Cornice, just over the Capitals, sits on either side a Figure, with a Trumpet in one hand, and a Palm in the other, representing Fame. A little farther on the same Cornice, on each side of a Compass-pediment, lie a Lion and a Unicorn, the Supporters of the Royal Arms of England. In the middle of the Arch are several Angels, holding the Kings Arms, as if they were placing them in the midst of that Compass-pediment. Behind this is the Scene, which represents a thick Cloudy Sky, a very Rocky Coast, and a Tempestuous Sea in perpetual Agitation. This Tempest (suppos'd to be rais'd by Magick) has many dreadful Objects in it, as several Spirits in horrid shapes flying down amongst the Sailers, then rising and crossing in the Air. And when the Ship is sinking, the whole House is darken'd, and a shower of Fire falls upon 'em. This is accompanied with Lightning, and several Claps of Thunder, to the end of the Storm.

[Scene ii.] In the midst of the Shower of Fire the Scene changes. The Cloudy Sky, Rocks, and Sea vanish; and when the Lights return, discover that Beautiful part of the Island, which was the habitation of Prospero; 'Tis compos'd of three Walks of Cypress-trees, each Side-walk leads to a Cave, in one of which Prospero keeps his daughters, in the other Hippolito: The Middle-Walk is of a great depth, and leads to an open part of the Island.

When Prospero commands Ariel to perform yet other tasks, he demurs as in Shakespeare and in D'Avenant–Dryden; but, also as in both, he finally agrees to obey. He suggests, however, that he needs help:

I know that this days business is important, requiring too much toyl for one alone. I have a gentle spirit for my Love, who twice seven years has waited for my freedom: Let it appear, it will assist me much, and we with mutual joy shall entertain each other. This I beseech you grant me.

Prosp. You shall have your desire.

Ariel. That's my noble Master. Milcha!

[*Milcha flies down to his assistance.*

Milc. I am here, my Love.

Ariel. Thou art free! welcome, my dear! what shall we do? . . .

[*They both fly up and cross in the air.*

Milcha, who first appeared at the end of the earlier version and then only as a dancer, now turns out to be an accomplished singer as well.

ACT II

[Scene i.] The Scene changes to the wilder part of the Island, 'tis compos'd of divers sorts of Trees, and barren places, with a prospect of the Sea at a great distance.

The old opening scene, of the repentant rulers and the admonitory duet, is transferred to the end of the act. Instead, we begin with the low comedy of the sailors. At the conclusion of Trincalo's interview with Caliban the scene changes to "Cypress Trees and Cave" for Prospero's exposition, and his warning to Hippolito. "The scene continues" for the meeting of the young innocents. The third scene shows "A wild Island." This is the opening scene of Act II in the D'Avenant–Dryden comedy, gorgeously expanded. After the musical prelude, "The Stage opens in several places," quite terrifying the rulers and their train. The first stanza of the admonition to tyrants is sung under the stage, but when the chorus gets under way the devils rise as they sing. After the little pageant of Pride, Fraud, Rapine, and Murder, the devils vanish. The gentlemen are about to depart when, "as they are going out, a Devil rises just before them, at which they start, and are frighted." "O Heavens!" says Alonzo: "yet more Apparitions." A devil then contributes a song beginning,

> Arise, arise! ye subterranean winds,
> More to disturb their guilty minds.

Sure enough, at the end of his solo, "Two Winds rise, Ten more enter and dance: At the end of the Dance, Three winds sink, the rest drive *Alon. Anto. Gonz.* off. Act Ends."

ACT III

This act begins with Ariel's song, "Come unto these yellow sands." "Full fathom five" is turned over to Milcha. Both lyrics are transferred from early in Act II of the D'Avenant–Dryden version. Scene ii is the first scene of the earlier version's Act III—Prospero's renewed warnings to his daughters. Scene iii follows as in D'Avenant–Dryden but with a new mechanical feat. Instead of the masque of "fat spirits," a "Dance of fantastick Spirits, after the Dance, a Table furnish'd with Meat and Fruit is brought in by two Spirits." But as the gentlemen are about to satisfy their hunger: "Two Spirits descend, and flie away with the Table." Then follow, as in the comedy, Trincalo's scene with the monsters, Ariel's duet with Ferdinand, Prospero's exhibition of the youth to Miranda, and the Hippolito–Ferdinand cave scene.

ACT IV

This act runs as in the comedy. A piece of mechanical trickery is thrown in for good measure during the drunken revels of the sailors:

> A Table rises, and four Spirits with Wine and Meat enter, placing it, as they dance, on the Table: The Dance ended, the Bottles vanish, and the Table sinks agen.

Unimpeachable evidence, this, that the Dorset Garden disappearing table was what is vulgarly known as "sure-fire."

ACT V

Until the very close, the last act of the opera follows the comedy. Then, instead of Ariel's song and dance, Prospero offers to entertain all hands by means of his magic art.

"Scene changes to the Rocks, with the Arch of Rocks, and calm Sea. Musick playing on the Rocks." At the command of Prospero, "Neptune, Amphitrite, Oceanus and Tethys appear in a Chariot drawn with Sea-horses; on each side of the Chariot, Sea-gods and Goddesses, Tritons and Nereides." As Alonzo justly remarks, "This *is* prodigious." Now ensues a perfect orgy of solos, duets, dances, and appearances. Winds fly up and fly down. One striking detail is thus prescribed:

Chorus. {
Sound a Calm.
Sound a Calm.
Sound a Calm.
a Calm.
Sound a Calm.

Here the Trytons, at every repeat of *Sound a Calm*, changing their Figure and Postures, seem to sound their wreathed Trumpets made of Shells.

Next comes "A Symphony of Musick, like Trumpets, to which four Trytons Dance." This is followed by a quartet and chorus, and then, the appetite for Tritons still unappeased, a dance of twelve Tritons.

Ariel, however, has all along been waiting in the wings for his chance. And when the "Scene changes to the Rising Sun, and a number of Aerial Spirits in the Air, Ariel flying from the Sun, advances towards the Pit." Dangling from a wire, we may suppose, he sings "Where the Bee sucks," joined by the ensemble (though the delicacy of these lines seems ill adapted to the exigencies of a Grand Finale by the Entire Company), and still "hovering in the Air" makes his adieu to Prospero.

That this version with its wires, springs, and pulleys is yet another step away from Shakespeare's play cannot, of course, be denied. But it is none the less the same old D'Avenant–Dryden comedy, though cut in places and embellished in others. This fact, it seems to me, sufficiently accounts for the inclusion of the text in Dryden's works.

The comedy was first acted, as we have seen, in 1667, and was printed in quarto in 1670. Mr. Montague Summers states that it has been reprinted only once (in the folio Dryden, Tonson, 1701) before its appearance in his own *Shakespeare Adaptations* (1922). All the other editions, beginning with the Quarto of 1674, give the text of the Shadwell opera, though till Mr. Lawrence's and Sir Ernest Clarke's articles all the editors supposed them to be reprints of the D'Avenant–Dryden comedy. Following the first printing of Shadwell's operatic version in 1674, it was reprinted in 1676 (two issues), 1690, and 1695 (all of which editions I have examined), and, according to Jaggard, in 1701, 1710, and subsequently. It is noteworthy that the publishers of the Shadwell opera did not regard it as a new work, for they retained in all the editions I have seen the prologue and epilogue of the D'Avenant–Dryden comedy.

The success of this D'Avenant–Dryden–Shadwell version was, as Downes observes, very great. There are several contemporary references, the tone of which indicates that everyone was familiar with it. *The Rehearsal* has a scoffing allusion to the "fat spirits" who cavort for Alonzo and his retinue. An anonymous poem published in 1679 contains the couplet:

> Such noise, such stink, such smoke there was, you'd swear
> "The tempest" surely had been acted there.[13]

Mr. Summers quotes, from Tom D'Urfey's *The Marriage Hater Match'd*, produced at the Theatre Royal early in January, 1692, the following reference:

Lord Brainless. A player, ha ha ha, why now you Rave, Madam, — Darewel, thou canst witness the contrary of that, thou toldst me her Breeding was such, that she had been familiar with Kings and Queens.

Darewell. Ay my Lord in the Play-house, I told ye she was a High Flyer too, that is, I have seen her upon a Machine in the *Tempest.*

2. All for Love, or The World well Lost

It is possible in our own time for a dramatist to write "Better than Shakespear" before a play on Cleopatra; Dryden was less inspired, and composed his finest tragedy "in Imitation of Shakespeare's Stile." We do not find it difficult, however, to admire both *Antony and Cleopatra* and *Caesar and Cleopatra*, for, as Mr. Shaw insists, he has something new to say, and every age must rewrite the history of every other. Dryden, on the contrary, was mistakenly attempting to follow a vein that had already been worked to the limit. He gave the thrice-told tale a new form, but had no wiser idea to contribute than the explicit endorsement of his sub-title, *The World well Lost.*

All for Love is hardly an alteration of Shakespeare; for, though its dialogue is full of reminiscences,[14] it is structurally independent and its characterization is entirely different. But, particularly in the last of these respects, its methods are so similar to those employed in Dryden's altered version of *Troilus and Cressida* that we must consider it at this point, though briefly, since critical opinion has handled it extensively, and all students of this period are familiar with it.

The play was first printed in 1678, not long after its production;[15] successive editions appeared in 1696, 1701 (in Dryden's collected works), 1703, 1709, and subsequently. In his preface Dryden directs attention to its agreement with the requirements of poetic justice, since the lovers' passion is unlawful, and to his observation of the unities of time, place, and action "more exactly . . . than, perhaps, the English Theater requires."

> Particularly, the Action is so much one, that it is the only of the kind without Episode, or Under plot; every Scene in the Tragedy conducing to the main design, and every Act concluding with a turn of it.

ACT I

As in Sir Charles Sedley's independent *Antony and Cleopatra*, the play opens after the battle of Actium. Antony is represented conventionally torn between love and honor. The queen's eunuch somewhat paradoxically represents the former concept, while Ventidius, the general, stands for Rome, home, and duty. They confront each other in the first scene; indeed, the play consists largely of their respective attempts to influence Antony. Ventidius, however, is actually two characters: besides his military function he acts as chorus. In the latter rôle he is somewhat depressing, for he persists in commenting bathetically on his hero's emotions, though these are expressed without restraint. He abounds in such pertinent observations as:

> On my Soul,
> 'Tis mournful, wondrous mournful!

and

> How sorrow shakes him!

Antony grieves at the prospect of his downfall. Finally he throws himself on the ground. Ventidius is unwilling to let the spectators grasp this subtlety for themselves. He specifies audibly that "On the ground extends the noble ruin." The noble ruin predicts speedy contraction into a "narrow Urn, Shrunk to a few cold Ashes." But another fate allures him as an alternative:

> Stay, I fancy
> I'm now turn'd wild, a Commoner of Nature;

Of all forsaken, and forsaking all;
Live in a shady Forrest's Sylvan Scene,
Stretch'd at my length beneath some blasted Oke;
I lean my head upon the Mossy Bark,
And look just of a piece, as I grew from it:
My uncomb'd Locks, matted like Mistleto,
Hang o're my hoary Face; a murm'ring Brook
Runs at my foot.

"Methinks," chimes in Ventidius, "I fancy My self there too." Then a reminiscence of *As You Like It* flits across the prostrate emperor's mind:

The *Herd* come *jumping by* me,
And fearless, quench their thirst, while I look on,
And take me for their fellow-*Citizen*.
More of this Image, more; it lulls my thoughts.

Ventidius now abandons his assignment as chorus and resumes general. He reproaches Antony and extracts his promise to take the field. Dryden refers to this dialogue in his preface, declaring that he prefers it "to any thing which I have written in this kind." [16] Though modern critics have concurred in admiring it, the scene is hopelessly sentimental. Ventidius weeps for Antony; whereupon the latter mingles his tears and confesses his shame. The faithful officer then tells him of twelve veteran legions that long for his command. Antony renounces the Serpent of the Nile, and after uttering the outrageous brag that he won Cassius's trenches at Philippi single-handed, he proclaims himself as good as ever, and predicts

that Thou and I,
Like Time and Death, marching before our Troops,
May taste fate to e'm; Mowe e'm out a passage,
And, entring where the foremost Squadrons yield,
Begin the noble Harvest of the Field.

This is almost, if not quite, in the heroic vein of Drawcansir.

ACT II

In the second act, Cleopatra bewails Antony's coolness. Alexas urges her to counteract Ventidius. On her behalf the eunuch presents jewels to the commanders. The wary Ventidius urges his chief not to accept a ruby bracelet which the Queen has sent. Antony sees no harm in it, but finds his fingers too clumsy to tie it. This brings in Cleopatra — that she may fasten it on his arm. Antony reviews her unconventional past, and runs over the necessary exposition concerning Fulvia's rebellion, his marriage to Octavia, and the battle of Actium.

In reply Cleopatra professes her love, shows Antony a handsome offer from Octavius conditional on the betrayal of her lover, and demands to die with him; finally she seizes his hand and begs him to leave her. This is too much for the romantic Roman; and when the Queen requests him to pause a moment that she may breathe her last, her conquest is complete. His reply is reminiscent of a Shakespearean period. We lose in Dryden's play

> He was dispòs'd to mirth, but on the sodaine
> A Romane thought hath strooke him.

But

> Let Rome in Tyber melt, and the wide Arch
> Of the raing'd Empire fall: Heere is my space,

is at this point played over with variations:

> *Ant.* Dye! Rather let me perish: loos'nd Nature
> Leap from its hinges. Sink the props of Heav'n,
> And fall the Skyes to crush the neather World.
> My Eyes, my Soul; my all! —

Of such fustian is a large part of this greatly over-praised tragedy composed. Ventidius's nose is hopelessly out of joint:

> O Women! Women! Women! all the gods
> Have not such pow'r of doing good to Man,
> As you of doing harm.

ACT III

The opening scene shows Antony returning victorious and welcomed by Cleopatra. Dolabella, Antony's *alter ego*, whose budding passion for Cleopatra has driven him from Alexandria, now returns from Caesar's camp. Antony reminds him of his love for the Queen; this affords an excuse for the famous description of her progress down the Nile. Since Dryden thus invites comparison between his style and Shakespeare's, it is no more than fair to take him up.

Ant. Her Gally down the Silver Cydnos row'd,
The Tackling Silk, the Streamers wav'd with Gold,
The gentle Winds were lodg'd in Purple sails:
Her Nymphs, like Nereids, round her Couch, were
plac'd;
Where she, another Sea-born Venus, lay.
Dolla. No more: I would not hear it.
Ant. O, you must!
She lay, and leant her cheek upon her hand,
And cast a look so languishingly sweet,
As if, secure of all beholders hearts,
Neglecting she could take 'em: Boys, like Cupids,
Stood fanning, with their painted wings, the winds
That plaid about her face: but if she smil'd,
A darting glory seem'd to blaze abroad:
That mens desiring eyes were never weary'd;
But hung about the object: to soft Flutes
The Silver Oars kept time; and while they plaid,
The hearing gave new pleasure to the sight;
And both to thought: 'twas Heav'n, or somewhat more;
For she so charm'd all hearts, that gazing crowds
Stood panting on the shore, and wanted breath
To give their welcome voice.[17]

But rarely does Dryden get even so much color into his lines as in this feeble revision. He lacks Shakespeare's sense of fact; the odorous, the atmospheric, are beyond his scope.

Meanwhile, Ventidius has sent for Octavia and her children; another confrontation is staged. The extravagant and wheeling husband yields to his wife's entreaties and the following series of vocatives:

> *Dolla.* Friend!
> *Octav.* Husband!
> *Both Childr.* Father!

Whereupon Antony, something in the style of Falstaff at Herne's oak:

> I am vanquish'd: take me,
> Octavia; take me, Children; share me all.

As the happy family leaves the stage, Alexas comes in, and soon after Cleopatra arrives. Octavia now returns, and the notorious scolding-match ensues. That Dryden had his doubts about it is clear from the preface:

> The French Poets, I confess, are strict Observers of these Punctilio's: They would not, for example, have suffer'd Cleopatra and Octavia to have met; or if they had met, there must only have pass'd betwixt them some cold civilities, but no eagerness of repartée, for fear of offending against the greatness of their Characters, and the modesty of their Sex. This Objection I foresaw, and at the same time contemn'd: for I judg'd it both natural and probable, that Octavia, proud of her new-gain'd Conquest, would search out Cleopatra to triumph over her; and that Cleopatra, thus attacqu'd, was not of a spirit to shun the encounter: and 'tis not unlikely, that two exasperated Rivals should use such Satyre as I have put into their mouths; for after all, though the one were a Roman, and the other a Queen, they were both Women.[18]

ACT IV

Antony dares not meet Cleopatra again; Dolabella is to make his adieux. Everyone has seen the comic device of going repeatedly to the door on an exit and returning again and again for another word. Dryden has the temerity to try it in tragedy. Thrice Antony strides to the portal and thrice he turns and strides back again, with another clause for Dolabella's message. Yet there is genuine feeling in the lines:

Desire her not to hate my memory;

and

Tell her, tho' we shall never meet again,
If I should hear she took another Love,
The news would break my heart.

Here, I suppose, lies the reason for the enthusiasm of many critics for this tragedy. Though it is replete with rant and fustian, there are passages in this play that ring with the simple, direct, and manly style of which John Dryden, when it pleased him, was king. Compared with the tawdry heroics of his colleagues and much of his own dramatic work, such lines as those just quoted seem fresh and genuine.

Dolabella now conceives that Antony's renunciation authorizes his own suit to the Queen. Unfortunately, he says so in a soliloquy which Ventidius overhears. Characters in this play have an obliging way of appearing when their services are needed, without troubling to find a pretext. Into this highly charged situation Cleopatra now walks. Instead of approaching her, Dolabella goes across and talks to the maids, for no apparent reason except that Alexas has a new trick to propose. He advises the Queen to make Antony jealous by "practising" on Dolabella. This idea shocks the simple soul of Cleopatra:

Can I do this? Ah no; my love's so true,
That I can neither hide it where it is,
Nor show it where it is not. Nature meant me
A Wife, a silly harmless household Dove,
Fond without art; and kind without deceit;
But Fortune, that has made a Mistress of me,
Hast [*sic*] thrust me out to the wide World, unfurnish'd
Of falshood to be happy.

Thus, the Serpent of the Nile!

"Force your self," urges Alexas.

I must [Cleopatra acknowledges] attempt it;
But Oh, with what regret!

She goes to Dolabella, who reports Antony as using harsh language of her. Poor Cleopatra finds it impossible to play the game, and "seems more and more concern'd, till she sinks quite down." Dolabella, overcome with remorse, assures her like a gentleman that he has lied like a blackguard. She asks him to beg Antony for an interview; he agrees, if she will give him her hand for a moment. The moment is long enough for Ventidius to show Octavia her rival's disloyalty, as they suppose it to be.

Cleopatra then leaves, and Antony comes. Ventidius reports what he has seen; Antony is so moved that Octavia perceives where his heart really is, breaks with him, and departs. Dolabella and Cleopatra reappear, to meet the reproaches of Antony, whom they are unable to convince of their innocence. The lachrymose weakling Dryden has made the master of one half the world is well exhibited by the speech with which he closes the act:

> Good Heav'n, they weep at parting.
> Must I weep too? that calls 'em innocent.
> I must not weep; and yet I must, to think
> That I must not forgive.—
> Live; but live wretched, 'tis but just you shou'd,
> Who made me so: Live from each others sight:
> Let me not hear you meet: Set all the Earth,
> And all the Seas, betwixt your sunder'd Loves:
> View nothing common but the Sun and Skys:
> Now, all take several ways;
>   And each your own sad fate with mine deplore;
>   That you were false, and I could trust no more.

Why does Dryden's pathos so frequently put the reader in mind of comic situations? Antony's injunction to Cleopatra and Dolabella brings up the vision of another Anthony's invitation to Captain Jack Absolute to get off the earth.

ACT V

The last act begins with Cleopatra's attempted suicide: "She pulls out her Dagger." She is preserved by the usual means — "They hold her." She then proposes what might be called a respiration-strike; she says she will hold her breath and thus "die inward." Her native inability to refrain from conversation is destructive of this method of making a quietus. News comes of Antony's defeat and the desertion of his fleet. Cleopatra goes to seek refuge in her monument.

Antony appears, animated by a spark of his old valor, zealously fanned by Ventidius, and proposes to lead his surviving legionaries in a last attack. But Alexas's false report of the Queen's death [19] strikes him nerveless:

> What shou'd I fight for now? My Queen is dead.
> I was but great for her.

Yet Drawcansir will out:

> 'Tis time the World
> Shou'd have a Lord, and know whom to obey.
> We two have kept its homage in suspence,
> And bent the Globe on whose each side we trod,
> Till it was dinted inwards.

Antony meditates suicide; Ventidius desires to join him, but, in a passage strongly reminiscent of Hamlet and Horatio, Antony will not have it. Ordered to kill his chief, Ventidius stabs himself. This derives, of course, from Eros's heroism in *Antony and Cleopatra*. Antony falls on his sword. Immediately Cleopatra, Charmion, and Iras rush in. The royal lovers are reconciled. Antony's dying speech is good, though the immortal music of "I am dying, Egypt, dying," is not heard.

Cleopatra's death follows at once. It is superbly phrased. Asserting her claim to wifehood, —

> my Nobler Fate
> Shall knit our Spousals with a tie too strong
> For Roman Laws to break, —

she orders the girls to bring the asps.

> Short Ceremony, Friends;
> But yet it must be decent. First, this Laurel
> Shall crown my Hero's Head: he fell not basely,
> Nor left his Shield behind him. Only thou
> Cou'dst triumph o'er thy self; and thou alone
> Wert worthy so to triumph.

Charmion asks why she decks herself with jewels.

> Dull, that thou art! why, 'tis to meet my Love;
> As when I saw him first, on Cydnos bank,
> All sparkling, like a Goddess; so adorn'd,
> I'll find him once again: my second Spousals
> Shall match my first, in Glory. Haste, haste, both,
> And dress the Bride of Antony. . . .
> Now seat me by my Lord. I claim this place;
> For I must conquer Caesar too, like him,
> And win my share o' th' World. . . .
> Reach me the Casket. . . .
> Welcom, thou kind Deceiver!
> Thou best of Thieves; who, with an easie key,
> Dost open life, and, unperceived by us,
> Ev'n steal us from our selves [20] discharging so
> Death's dreadful office, better than him self,
> Touching our limbs so gently into slumber,
> That Death stands by, deceiv'd by his own Image,
> And thinks himself but Sleep. . . .
> Already, Death, I feel thee in my Veins;
> I go with such a will to find my Lord,
> That we shall quickly meet.
> A heavy numness creeps through every limb,
> And now 'tis at my head: my eye-lids fall,
> And my dear Love is vanish'd in a mist.
> Where shall I find him, where? O turn me to him,
> And lay me on his breast.— Caesar, thy worst;
> Now part us, if thou canst.[21]

Lines like these are only to be praised, even though they are almost as far below Shakespeare's as they are above the average of Restoration tragedy. They are, indeed, far above the level of the greater share of *All for Love*. I suspect that it is the close of this play that its eulogists have chiefly in mind; its final impression is certainly that of a first-rate piece of tragic writing. And, as I have tried to show, passages phrased with vigor and simplicity are not rare.

But the moment criticism leaves the question of phrasing, it has another story to tell. There are those who see technical excellence in the play. It seems to me more apparent than real. There is a unity of action, certainly, but it is of the most artificial kind. As a matter of fact, the play is a series of confrontations between Antony and Ventidius, Antony and Alexas, Antony and Cleopatra, Antony and Octavia, Octavia and Cleopatra, etc., etc. One scene does not grow out of another, or out of characterization; the action is essentially arbitrary with the dramatist, not spontaneous with the characters. And the style is rarely good enough to redeem this defect, as it so often is redeemed in Racine.

Characterization (this is the play's most grievous fault) has been dedicated to the great principle of consistency. Antony is the merest sentimentalist; Cleopatra's degradation at Dryden's hands is even more pitiful. Shakespeare's great psychological portrait of the queen and woman is turned to the wall in favor of the puppet of a ruling passion. The complex human being, with her infinite variety, gives place to a lay figure of Woman in Love.

The unity of place is likewise achieved by arbitrary measures; the poet does not even trouble to excuse his characters for appearing so promptly and so pat. They saunter in and saunter out from the four quarters of the Mediterranean world, as if their leisure hours were habitually passed in wandering up and down the streets of Alexandria. Poetic justice is not respected except in the death of the hero and heroine. Violence on the stage is permitted in the deaths of five of the characters. Of comedy, even of ironic comedy, there is none; there is no wishing her joy of the worm.

The influence of the heroic drama is powerful in this play, as it is in Dryden's alteration of *Troilus and Cressida*. The heroics not infrequently pass over into the extreme absurdities of that derided form, yet the passion is rarely wild or indecorous. Even the diction, the best thing in the play, is for the most part smooth and flowing. There is rant in profusion, but the daring homeliness, which makes so many of Shakespeare's metaphors so impressive, is never indulged in. As Professor Saintsbury points out, there is nothing like Cleopatra's

> Peace, peace:
> Dost thou not see my Baby at my breast,
> That suckes the Nurse asleepe?

which, he continues, "no poet save Shakespeare since the foundation of the world, would or could have written." [22]

Judged by what he conceived a tragedy ought to be and by what he tried to accomplish with his source, the author of *All for Love* achieved a remarkable *tour de force*. No one in his senses desires to deny to the great name of Dryden one scruple of the praise that such an accomplishment deserves. But our admiration for its author's genius does not oblige us to like this play or, for more than a moment in the fifth act, to believe in it.

3. Troilus and Cressida, or Truth Found too Late

The year after *All for Love* had demonstrated that Dryden had made in *Aureng-Zebe* his final sacrifice on the altar of the heroic drama, *Troilus and Cressida, or Truth Found too Late*, gave further evidence of Shakespeare's increasing hold upon him. This play, the third and last of his Shakespearean pieces, was published in 1679,[23] and reprinted in 1695, both editions in quarto. It also appears in the Dryden folio of 1701.[24] It is furnished with "A Preface Containing the Grounds of Criticism in Tragedy."

This is one of Dryden's most important critical pronouncements. He begins with a defence of Shakespeare alteration, which he justifies by citing the Athenians' offer of a reward for adaptations of Aeschylus. The difficulties of altering Shakespeare are greater, he points out, because the English language is still in a state of flux, whereas the Greek had attained an exact standard.

Yet it must be allow'd to the present Age, that the tongue in general is so much refin'd since Shakespear's time, that many of his words, and more of his Phrases, are scarce intelligible. And of those which we understand some are ungrammatical, others course; and his whole stile is so pester'd with Figurative expressions, that it is as affected as it is obscure. . . .

The Author seems to have begun it with some fire; the Characters of Pandarus and Thersites, are promising enough; but as if he grew weary of his task, after an Entrance or two, he lets 'em fall: and the later part of the Tragedy is nothing but a confusion of Drums and Trumpets, Excursions and Alarms. The chief persons, who give name to the Tragedy, are left alive: Cressida is false, and is not punish'd. Yet after all, because the Play was Shakespear's, and that there appear'd in some places of it, the admirable Genius of the Author; I undertook to remove that heap of Rubbish, under which many excellent thoughts lay wholly bury'd. Accordingly, I new model'd the Plot; threw out many unnecessary persons; improv'd those Characters which were begun, and left unfinish'd: as Hector, Troilus, Pandarus and Thersites; and added that of Andromache. After this, I made with no small trouble, an Order and Connexion of all the Scenes; removing them from the places where they were inartificially set: and though it was impossible to keep 'em all unbroken, because the Scene must be sometimes in the City, and somtimes in the Camp, yet I have so order'd them that there is a coherence of 'em with one another, and a dependence on the main design: no leaping from Troy to the Grecian Tents, and thence back again in the same Act; but a due proportion of time allow'd for every motion. I need not say that I have refin'd his Language, which before was obsolete; but I am willing to acknowledg, that as I have often drawn his English nearer to our times so I have somtimes conform'd my own to his: & consequently, the Language is not altogether so pure, as it is significant. The Scenes of Pandarus and Cressida, of Troilus and Pandarus, of Andromache with Hector and the Trojans, in the second Act, are wholly New: together with that of Nestor and Ulysses with Thersites; and that of Thersites with Ajax and Achilles. I will not weary my Reader with the Scenes which are added of Pandarus and the Lovers, in the Third; and those of Thersites, which are wholly altered: but I cannot omit the last Scene in it, which is almost half the Act, betwixt Troilus and Hector. The occasion of raising it was hinted to me by Mr. Betterton: the contrivance and working of it was my own. . . .

The beginning Scenes of the fourth Act are either added, or chang'd wholly by me; the middle of it is Shakespear alter'd, and mingled with my own, three or four of the last Scenes are altogether new. And the whole Fifth Act, both the Plot and the Writing are my own Additions.

In the *Essay* itself, Dryden's emphasis on consistency in characterization, and his praise of Jonson as the best exemplar, have already been mentioned in another connection. The reader should note that Dryden treats *Troilus and Cressida* as a tragedy. It is so described in the First Folio, though the only pre-Wars Quarto (1609) styles it a history.

The plot, as amended by Dryden, runs as follows.[25]

ACT I

The action begins with the opening scene of exposition in the Greek camp (I, iii, 1–212). It closes with the description of Achilles's mockery, Æneas not appearing. The long harangues of Ulysses and the others are greatly reduced. It is followed by the first scene between Troilus and Pandarus (I, i, entire). I suppose this shift was made in order that the tragedy might begin with more dignity, and also because Dryden preferred to stake out the general situation and setting before taking up the story of his hero. This scene is not greatly reduced, though some of Troilus's speeches are cut down. Pandarus's lines, on the contrary, are "fattened." They are not exactly naughtier, but there is greater particularity and vulgarity in what he says. After Troilus leaves for battle there is no break in the action; Cressida comes in, soon followed by

Pandarus. Æneas remains on long enough to take the lines of Cressida's servant, though the description of Ajax is omitted. This scene is not otherwise reduced, except that Cressida's wanton speeches are excised. To the Cressida of Chaucer and Shakespeare, Dryden has done exactly what he did to Cleopatra — turned the complex woman into the puppet of a ruling passion.[26] Cressida resembles her original in her sex, her beauty, and her name — and in nothing else.

ACT II

The second act begins with the Trojan council of war (II, ii), passing over I, iii, 213 f., and II, i. The speeches for and against the defence of Helen are greatly reduced both in number and in extent. Cassandra does not appear. After Hector's adoption of Troilus's conclusions, the latter remarks, "I have business," and departs. The others suspect its nature. Hector voices it, in Restoration terms:

> A woman on my life: ev'n so it happens,
> Religion, state affairs, whater'es the theme
> It ends in women still.

Andromache enters hard upon the heels of this observation, but not to entreat her husband to avoid fighting; she is no pacifist, but a bitter-ender. She brings the demand of the valiant infant, Astyanax, for the despatch of a challenge in his name.

Inspired by this precocious valor, Hector determines to fight. His father and brothers attempt to dissuade him, and appeal for support to his wife. But she is all for battle. Whereat Hector:

> Come to my Arms, thou manlier Virtue come;
> Thou better Name than wife! wou'dst thou not blush
> To hug a coward thus? [*Embrace.*
> *Priam.* Yet still I fear!
> *Andro.* There spoke a woman. . . .

Hector's militant lady overbears all opposition, and Æneas is sent off with the challenge. I need hardly remark that this incident is Dryden's own.

The greater part of scene ii is also original with Dryden, who invented an opportunity for writing up the rôle of Pandarus. It is an amplification of the first part of Shakespeare's III, ii. It begins with the Pander's provocative conversation first with Cressida and then with Troilus; the scene ends with his assurance to the former that his mistress is making ready (III, ii, 19–41). Dryden has been charged with writing this scene in order to make his play saltier, but this accusation is hardly just. It is not especially objectionable; certainly it is no worse than several of Shakespeare's, and Dryden may have felt he had a right to more Pandarus at this point, to replace his excision of Pandarus's appearance before Paris and Helen (III, i).

Scene iii takes us back to the Grecian tents, for the first time since the opening scene of Act I. We now have another section of that scene (as it appears in Shakespeare, that is): it consists of Ulysses's plot for setting up Ajax (I, iii, 310 f.). Nestor agrees, but they fear the friendship between Ajax and Achilles. At this point Thersites happens in, and they incite him to sow discord between the champions. Contrary to his Shakespearean custom, Thersites frees his mind in blank verse. This part of the scene is, of course, original with Dryden. It is followed at once by Ajax's entrance and an altered version of II, i, the scene between Thersites, Ajax, Achilles, and Patroclus. Thersites announces Hector's challenge and succeeds in inveigling the men of might into a highly theatrical quarrel, which ends the act.

ACT III

The third act begins, quite unnaturally, with II, iii, of Shakespeare's play; thus it is actually a continuation of the foregoing scene. The reason for its place here is that Dryden is determined to minimize the number of shifts from Troy to the Greek camp. The scene includes the first 71 lines (reduced) of the original, telescoped with III, iii, 241–316, in which Thersites takes off the braggadocio of Ajax. Immediately after Thersites's histrionics we return to II, iii, where we left it, just before the entrance of the leaders (line 72). The rest of the scene follows to the end, though greatly reduced and altered.

Scene ii makes the third shift since the opening of the play. We return to Troy and the meeting of Troilus and Cressida. This is Shakespeare's III, ii, the first part of which we have had already. We now resume the action at line 42 and follow it to the end. Cressida is not much altered in this scene — with one exception. Dryden, having elevated her character, wishes to put the best possible face on her yielding. Accordingly, he inserts several speeches between Pandarus's offer of his name as a by-word, and the final act of his brokerage. The lines are a fair sample of Dryden's broadening of Shakespeare's Pandarus:

Cress. And will you promise that the holy Priest
Shall make us one for ever!

Pand. Priests! marry hang 'em! they make you one! go in, go in, and make your selves one without a priest: I'le have no priests work in my house.

Cress. Ile not consent unless you swear.

Pand. I, do, do, swear; a pretty woman's worth an oath at any time. Keep or break as time shall try; but 'tis good to swear, for the saving of her credit: Hang e'm sweet Rogues they never expect a Man shou'd keep it. Let him but swear, and that's all they care for.

Troil. Heavens prosper me as I devoutly swear,
Never to be but yours.

Pand. Whereupon I will lead you into a chamber: and suppose there be a bed in't; as I fack, I know not: but you'll forgive me, if there be: away, away, you naughty hildings; get ye together, get you together. Ah you wags, do you leer indeed at one another! do the neyes twinkle at him! get you together, get you together.
[*Leads them out.*

Without change of scene then follows the news of Cressida's exchange. This is Shakespeare's IV, i, the interview between Æneas and Diomedes. This ended, the chieftains leave the stage, and Pandarus comes on with a servant and musicians, to serenade the lovers. The song selected is thoroughly optimistic and un-Shakespearean. The lovers appear and the action of Shakespeare's IV, ii, 1–75, follows. The news of the decision to exchange Cressida is brought not by Æneas but by Hector, whose influence over Troilus is supposed to be greater. This interview occupies in Shakespeare's play only sixteen lines and is rather weak, for Troilus, though he may exhibit emotion, certainly gives it no utterance. Dryden seizes upon this moment as one of the most dramatic in the whole story, plays it up for every ounce it is worth, and closes his act on it.[27]

As we have already observed, Dryden does not find it easy to manipulate a well-filled stage, but he shows a good deal of vigor in phrasing spirited confrontations. This scene is a case in point. It is too long—it contains over two hundred and fifty lines—and it is highly theatrical. But it is very effective; on the whole, I think it preferable to the original. Troilus is wild with grief and anger; Hector is cool and tactful. The lover declares his intention of resisting the exchange, and includes his brother in his passionate denunciation of the decision. Hector asserts that he will enforce it, and Troilus madly reproaches him; to Hector his fondness for a traitor's daughter seems unworthy and he bluntly terms her "common." Troilus is enraged and exalts the lady above the chaste Andromache. The brothers are on the point of flying at each other's throats when Hector regains control of himself and starts to walk off. His magnanimity overcomes Troilus, and they are reconciled in a scene that is really affecting. Hector offers to fight for Cressida, but Troilus now sees that he must give her up.

ACT IV

The fourth act picks up the action where the third left it, and we have Shakespeare's IV, ii, 76 f., Cressida's reception of the news. IV, iv, her parting from Troilus, follows immediately. The Greeks do not appear. Instead, Troilus sends Pandarus to delay them and gain another moment for his farewell.

Scene ii makes the fourth shift; we return to the Grecian camp, and the flouting of Achilles (III, iii, 38–79). Ulysses does not, however, tarry; thus we lose his long speeches. Not all of Dryden's omissions are to be discommended; but "Time hath (my Lord) a wallet at his backe" is sadly missed. Shakespeare's scene is resumed at line 216 with Patroclus's speech of reproach, which he prefaces with the charge Ulysses has just made (in the original), that Achilles loves Hector's sister. The action is continued only to line 229, since Thersites's description of Ajax has already been given.

Instead, we pass to the next Grecian scene, the acceptance by Ajax of Hector's challenge — in Shakespeare, IV, v, 1–11. The arrival of Diomedes with Cressida, and her osculatory reception, are naturally omitted, as not in keeping with her elevated character: the scene is resumed with line 64 and Hector's approach. The stage directions for the combat are explicit:

> The Trumpets sound on both sides, while Aeneas and Diomede take their places, as Judges of the Field: The Trojans and Grecians rank themselves on either side. . . . Fight equal at first, then Ajax has Hector at disadvantage: at last Hector closes, Ajax falls on one knee, Hector stands over him but striks not, and Ajax rises. Aeneas throwing his Gantlet betwixt them.

The scene continues to the end as in Shakespeare, though reduced and altered in diction.

The original V, i, follows without a break. This scene is not greatly reduced. As in Shakespeare (V, ii), next comes the interview between Diomedes and Cressida, overheard by

Troilus. The pledge becomes a ring, instead of a scarf; the coquetry of Cressida is not so brazen, and the length of her interview with Diomedes is shortened. Troilus's great outburst on her departure (beginning "To make a recordation to my soule") is reduced to: "Was Cressida here?" Ulysses leaves the despairing lover, and Pandarus appears, gloating over Cressida's sensational success in the camp. He is unable to see why Troilus should be vexed by a little kissing, but the jealous lover heaps reproaches on him and he sadly departs, convinced that mankind is ungrateful. He does not appear again.

The mischievous Thersites now leads Diomedes to Troilus for another of the confrontation scenes in which Dryden specializes. Each is maddened by the other's boasting of the lady's favors; they draw, but Æneas forbids a duel in the dark. The rivals separate, agreeing to meet in battle on the morrow before Calchas's tent.

ACT V

The last act opens with a much-altered version of Shakespeare's V, iii, in which Andromache succeeds in dissuading Hector from battle. But Troilus arrives, and in a scene strongly reminiscent of that between Caesar, Calphurnia, and Decius Brutus,[28] turns the scale by telling his brother that Polixena has urged Achilles to spare him. The champion is now all for slaughter. So is Troilus, in whom the ever-lurking Drawcansir breaks out for a moment:

> And when I breathe, methinks my nostrills hiss!

Cassandra's prophecy of Hector's death (V, iii, 80–87) is given in a rewritten form to Andromache. Pandarus does not appear.

The second scene shifts (for the sixth and last time) to the camp. Agamemnon, Menelaus, Ulysses, Nestor, and Thersites describe the progress of the battle. Their speeches are original with Dryden. Next comes Thersites's encounter with the

Bastard Prince (V, vii, 13 f.). Hector and Troilus then enter "driving in the Greeks," and the former's encounter with Thersites follows (V, iv, 28–38). The Trojans are about to dispatch the satirist when he offers to betray Diomedes. Troilus sets out for Calchas's tent, while Hector goes off to find Achilles. The latter now appears with his Myrmidons, voices a lament for Patroclus, and departs. There is no direction for a change of scene, but we are to suppose ourselves before the tent of Calchas, for Troilus and his troops, guided by Thersites, now appear.

Dryden's distaste for the clergy is apparent throughout the play; Troilus's resentment affords another chance for a fling at the cloth:

> That I shou'd trust the Daughter of a Priest!
> Priesthood, that makes a Merchandise of Heaven!
> Priesthood that sells eve'n to their prayr's and blessings!
> And forces us to pay for our own cousnage!
>
> *Thers.* Nay cheats Heav'n too with entrails and with offals;
> Gives it the garbidge of a Sacrifice
> And keeps the best for private Luxury.
>
> *Troil.* Thou hast deserv'd thy life, for cursing Priests:
> Let me embrace thee; thou art beautifull:
> That back, that nose; those eyes are beautiful:
> Live, thou art honest; for thou hat'st a Priest.

A convenient noise is heard outside, and while Troilus investigates, Cressida and Calchas come in. Her first words show us that, to use the well-worn phrase, "it is all a mistake." "Where is he?" she cries; "I'le be justify'd or dye." Soon Diomedes enters, "retiring before Troilus, and falling as he enters."

> *Troil.* Now beg thy life, or dye.
>
> *Diom.* No: use thy fortune:
> I loath the life, which thou canst give, or take.
>
> *Troil.* Scornst thou my mercy villain!— take thy wish.—
>
> *Cressi.* Hold, hold your hand my Lord, and hear me speak.
>
> *Troilus turns back: in which time Diomede rises: Trojans and Greeks enter, and rank themselves on both sides of their Captains.*

Cressida enrages Troilus by imploring him to spare Diomedes's life. "Hell, and death!" replies the jealous lover. Then Cressida protests her innocence; his rival's death will mean her own captivity. But the caddish Diomedes convinces Troilus of her guilt.

This is an excellent situation and Dryden handles it well, tossing the question of Cressida's infidelity back and forth, yet making it clear that Diomedes lies and that the lady is only to be censured for not having avoided the appearance of evil. Still Troilus will not believe, and to convince him she kills herself, "a stale expedient," as Sir Walter Scott remarks.

However suicide may appeal to us as a syllogism, the scene is well constructed and well written. The heroine, though not the Cressida we knew, speaks and acts with tragic effectiveness, and Diomedes is a capital villain. Of course, Troilus is converted, and the combat is renewed. As the hero triumphs, Achilles brings in the Myrmidons, and Troilus falls on the corpse of Diomedes. "All the Trojans dye upon the place, Troilus last." Dryden's adaptation belongs among the political alterations which were designed to warn the Whiggish faction. As Troilus is slain the Grecian chiefs come in, and the play closes with a topical couplet:

> Then, since from homebred Factions ruine springs,
> Let Subjects learn obedience to their Kings.

In comparison with Shakespeare's inconclusive ending, Dryden's is much more effective, though it is a scene of blood if there ever was one. The Dorset Garden stage was spacious, and to behold it thus paved with weltering corpses must have been a severe dose for the austerer critics. That Dryden spilled so much blood in full view of the house is a fine example of the English contempt for the rule against scenes of violence.

Concerning the play as a whole I venture the opinion that structurally it is superior to Shakespeare's. This conclusion is not based on Dryden's ingenious jig-sawing of the Trojan and Grecian scenes and his dovetailing of them so that he gives us but six shifts between city and camp, while Shakespeare gives us nine; nine changes are no more confusing than six. But at two points Dryden has grasped a situation that Shakespeare failed to grasp, and has exploited it to not only theatric but genuine dramatic advantage. These situations are, first, Troilus's reception of the news that Cressida must leave Troy; and second, the ending of the play. In the hands of a sweet and dignified Cressida, an accomplished tragedian as Troilus, and a coolly insolent stage villain as Diomedes, the final scene must have acted admirably. If I were an actor, I would rather play Dryden's Troilus than Shakespeare's.

Cressida, however, is another story. Like Cleopatra she has lost variety; she is neither a lazar kite nor a natural coquette, but simply Woman in Love. Yet, once granted this conception of her character, Dryden writes well for her. Thersites and Pandarus are not greatly changed; Dryden has merely deepened the lines that Shakespeare drew. He has indeed been charged with making Pandarus talk more bawdy, but the accusation is unjust. He could have done so easily enough. But William Shakespeare was not exactly deficient in that respect; probably Dryden felt that Pandarus's small talk needed no seasoning. After all, one could not have Pandarus without a certain flavor in the dialogue; and we would gladly part with many a more respectable portrait from the great gallery of the world's literature before that confirmed aider and abetter of the blind bow-boy. The Greek chieftains are not so sharply distinguished from each other as in Shakespeare's play; this is the inevitable consequence of rewriting their speeches.

Verbal alteration is frequent, and the condensation or reduction of speeches is too free, even in view of stage exigencies. The following samples of such alteration indicate its nature;

but the reader should remember that many of the speeches have been entirely rewritten, since, in comparison with D'Avenant, for instance, Dryden works with a free hand.

All my line references agree with Neilson's Cambridge Edition; in each case the text first quoted is that of the Quarto of 1679. The source of this edition is not the Quarto of 1609, the only previous separate edition (which I have collated by means of the Griggs facsimile), but the Folios text. Words replaced are accordingly quoted from the *National Shakespeare* reprint of F 1. Dryden's use of the Folio rather than the Quarto, contrary to the general practice of the Restoration adapters, probably indicates that a text copied from the Folios, or perhaps from the text from which F 1 was printed, had superseded the old Quarto of 1609.[29]

There are numerous cases of mere condensation, such as the following:

II, iii, 173–176 (Q 1679, p. 27):
Why he relies on none
But his own will.
For: He doth relye on none,
But carries on the streame of his dispose,
Without obseruance or respect of any,
In will peculiar, and in selfe admission.

Corrections of grammar abound. Examples:

III, iii, 225 (Q 1679, p. 45): "shaken." For: "shooke."

III, iii, 229 (Q 1679, p. 45):
"those wounds heal ill that men *have giv'n* themselves."
For: "do giue."

Many changes are modernizations. Examples:

I, ii, 120 (Q 1679, p. 7): "the *bow* window." For: "compast."

I, iii, 13 (Q 1679, p. 1): "Since." For: "Sith."

III, iii, 294 (Q 1679, p. 26): "Farewell." For: "God buy you."

The following passage is typical of many instances of general simplification:

I, iii, 13–17 (Q 1679, p. 1):

every Action of Recorded Fame
Has with long difficulties been involv'd,
Not Answering that Idea of the thought
Which gave it Birth.

For (Q 1609):

euery action that hath gone before,
Whereof we haue Record, Triall did draw
Bias and thwart, not answering the ayme,
And that vnbodied figure of the thought
That gaue't surmised shape.

A great many changes appear to have been made for the sake of clearness. Examples:

I, iii, 38, 39 (Q 1679, p. 1):

But let the Tempest once inrage that Sea,

For (F 1):

But let the ruffian Boreas once enrage
The gentle Thetis.

II, ii, 192, 193 (Q 1679, p. 11):

For 'tis a cause on which our Trojan honour
And common reputation will depend.

For: For 'tis a cause that hath no meane dependance,
Vpon our ioynt and seuerall dignities.

I have noticed fewer cases of literalization of figurative language than in D'Avenant's alterations; this difference is due in the first place to the fact that Dryden was a great poet, and D'Avenant was not. In the second place, Dryden has so altered the plot of the play that Troilus, into whose mouth Shakespeare put several of those dazzling flights of fancy that almost pass over into bombast, turns his greatest periods not on his love and grief but on his anger against Hector and against Diomedes. Thus Troilus's most vigorous expression comes at points when Dryden is writing originally. We lose, for instance, "To make a recordation to my soule." Yet there are a few cases of literalization and toning down, such as the one following:

I, iii, 142, 143 (Q 1679, p. 2):
The great Achilles whom opinion crowns
The chief of all our Host.
For (F 1): The sinew, and the fore-hand of our Hoste.

There are frequent cases of specific changes due to subservience to decorum and a general desire for greater elegance. Examples:

I, i, 62, 63 (Q 1679, p. 5):
Thou lay'st in every wound her Love has giv'n me
The *Sword* that made it.
For: "Knife."

III, ii, 33 (Q 1679, p. 18):
"and fetches her *breath* so short." For: "winde."

A great many of Dryden's changes seem to be capricious. Examples:

I, i, 15, 16 (Q 1679, p. 4):
"He that will eat of the Roastmeat, must stay for the kindling of the fire."
For: (F 1):
"Hee that will haue a Cake out of the Wheate, must needes tarry the grinding."
Dryden carries out his figure. So we have: "the spitting of the meat" for "the bolting"; "the roasting" for "the leau'[en]ing"; "the taking off the Spitt" for "the Kneading"; "the making of the Sawce" for "the making of the Cake," etc.

I, ii, 245 (Q 1679, p. 8):
"Helenus is a Priest *and keeps a whore; he'll fight for's whore, or he's no true Priest I warrant him.*" Inserted Q 1679.
This gratuitous broadside is due, of course, to Dryden's personal animosity toward the clergy.

I, iii, 312 (Q 1679, p. 18):
"I have conceiv'd an embryo in my brain."
For: "I haue a young conception in my braine."

We should not expect to find Dryden manifesting prudery. The following passage is due to the elevation of Cressida's character, who, as Dryden paints her, would certainly not allow her naughty uncle to talk *too* bawdy in her presence:

IV, ii, 23, 24 (Q 1679, p. 33):
"how go matters!" For: "maiden-heads?"[30]

Judged by the critical canons, Dryden's *Troilus and Cressida* is much looser than his *All for Love*. There is neither unity of time nor unity of place, though both rules are less violently disregarded than they were by Shakespeare. The action is more unified by reason of Dryden's ending. The principle of strict separation of tragedy from comedy is not, and of course could not be, observed. Dryden has intensified both kinds, broadening the comedy of Pandarus and Thersites, which he makes considerably less ironical, and heightening the tragedy of the lovers. As we have seen, in common with most Englishmen, Dryden flouts the injunction against scenes of violence. Poetic justice, we may suppose, is not violated, since the lovers had only the benefit of Pandarus and dispensed with that of clergy. But it is not emphasized by Dryden, who evidently sympathizes with the rectitude of their intentions.

Technically I must own that this play seems to me to be far superior to *All for Love*. Dryden shows in the earlier play utter incapacity for anything but simple confrontations. In *Troilus and Cressida*, this is still a frequent recourse, but there is also expert handling of triangle scenes, as well as competent management of the crowded stage.

As he hints in his preface, Dryden had become still more amenable to Shakespeare's style than he had been a year earlier, and there is far less of Drawcansir in Troilus than in Antony. Taking his *Troilus and Cressida* by and large, it is, in my opinion, next to Shadwell's *Timon of Athens*, the best — the least objectionable, that is — of the violent alterations.

And I am even willing to hazard further, that in some respects Dryden's version is better, as an actable play, than Shakespeare's.

On the other hand, as a study of human passions, and I am thinking here not only of the lovers but of the Grecian chieftains, Dryden's adaptation is conventional and unconvincing—to read. I believe it would be convincing on the stage. What a pity it is that of the treasures of the Elizabethan and Jacobean drama we see only occasional performances of eight or ten plays by one writer, and that after his time till Sheridan's the English drama is now unrepresented in our theatre by a single piece. The historian who must attempt to evaluate the drama of the past without checking his conclusions from a seat in the theatre, or still better from a place in the wings, is working in the dark. How unfortunate that our college theatres have become, so far as they are worth attention at all, largely experimental. I suspect that their audiences are much more bored with their offerings from freakish Continental schools than they would be with judicious selections from the superbly actable repertory of the English theatre of the seventeenth century.

Notes to Chapter VI

1. It was entered in the *Stationers' Register*, January 8, 1670 (Roxburghe ed., ii, 407), and appears in the *Term Catalogue* for February, 1670 (Arber's ed., i, 26).
2. Max Rosbund thinks that a safe conclusion regarding which of the Folios Dryden used cannot be drawn, but he inclines to F 3 (*Dryden als Shakespeare-Bearbeiter*, Halle a. S., 1882, pp. 9, 10). Otto Witt is convinced that the source is F 3, but his text of the adaptation was Q 1701 (*The Tempest, or The Enchanted Island. A Comedy by John Dryden. 1670. The Sea-Voyage. A Comedy by Beaumont and Fletcher. 1647. The Goblins' Tragi-Comedy by Sir John Suckling. 1646. in ihrem Verhältnis zu Shakspere's "Tempest" und den übrigen Quellen*, Rostock, 1899, pp. 7–10). On pp. 64–68 Witt gives a table showing the extent to which Dryden uses Shakespeare's dialogue.
3. Delius suggests that this occupation for a ruling scion was too degrading in the loyal opinion of the adapters (*Shakespeare Jahrbuch*, iv, 16).
4. There is a derisive reference to this in *The Rehearsal* (II, v). Mr. Bayes informs his actors that "you dance worse than the angels in Harry the Eight, or the fat spirits in The Tempest, i' gad."
5. This phrase became almost proverbial.
6. His charge against Fletcher's *The Custom of the Country* is a fine red herring across the trail; there are smuttier passages in his own plays. Indeed I do not hesitate to assert that one of Dryden's songs is smuttier than anything in any Elizabethan drama I have read.
7. This is Elze's view (*Shakespeare Jahrbuch*, iv, 152). Delius refers (*Ibid.*, xx, 70) to "Dryden's Löwenantheil an diesem Machwerk." Cf. also *Ibid.*, iv, 11. This opinion is shared by Witt and Rosbund. Mr. Summers takes the contrary view (*Shakespeare Adaptations*, p. xli); but later (*Ibid.*, p. cviii) he says that, along with *Troilus and Cressida*, this version of *The Tempest* "came from the pen of a dramatist of a genius supreme and unsurpassed." Williams (*Sir William Davenant's [Literary] Relation to Shakespeare*, p. 61) assigns authorship to D'Avenant, but without convincing reasons. Professor Nettleton (*English Drama of the Restoration and Eighteenth Century*, p. 56) thinks "most of the work belongs to D'Avenant," but gives no reason.
8. Hermann Grimm, "Shakespeare's Sturm in der Bearbeitung von Dryden und Davenant," *Fünfzehn Essays*, Berlin, 1875, pp. 183–224. See p. 206.
9. "wörtlich."
10. Summers, *Shakespeare Adaptations*, pp. xlix-liii.
11. Scott–Saintsbury ed. of Dryden's Works, iii, 102. A passage in Dryden's *An Essay on the Grounds of Criticism in Tragedy* (*Troilus and Cressida*, Q 1679, sig. b [1]) reveals his appreciation of Shakespeare's Caliban — and the limitations of that appreciation.

12. *Review of English Studies*, i, 327–330 (July, 1925). His position is attacked by Mr. D. M. Walmsley, *Ibid.*, ii, 463–466 (Oct., 1926). See also Mr. Thorn-Drury's rebuttal, *Ibid.*, iii, 204–208 (April, 1927) and Mr. Walmsley's rejoinder, *Ibid.*, iii, 451–453 (Oct., 1927). Mr. Thorn-Drury appears to be wrong in attempting to explain Shadwell away, but right in answering negatively Mr. Lawrence's question, "Did Thomas Shadwell Write an Opera on *The Tempest?*" (*Studies in the Elizabethan Playhouse* [First Series], pp. 193–206.) I came to the same conclusion in my Harvard dissertation (unpublished, 1923), in so far as Mr. Lawrence's question implies that Shadwell's version departs extensively from the D'Avenant–Dryden comedy. Dr. A. S. Borgman, in *The Dramatic Works of Thomas Shadwell* (Harvard dissertation, unpublished, 1919, p. 114), pointed out (as does Mr. Walmsley) that the reason why Dryden himself did not make the new changes was that he had bound himself to write for the other house, the Theatre Royal.
13. Jaggard, *Shakespeare Bibliography*, p. 709.
14. Professor Strunk lists 27 passages, comprising 119 lines, imitating the text of *Antony and Cleopatra*, and 10 others, of 39 lines, imitating passages in other Shakespearean plays. Strunk's ed. (Belles Lettres series) of Dryden's *All for Love* and *The Spanish Fryar*, pp. xliv, xlv.
15. Entered in the *Stationers' Register*, Jan. 31, 1678 (Roxburghe ed., iii, 56).
16. *All for Love*, Q 1678, sig. b 4 *verso*.
17. *Ibid.*, p. 35.
18. *Ibid.*, sig. b 1 *verso*.
19. Friedrich Hannmann suggests that the artifice is assigned by Dryden to Alexas because Cleopatra has twice before employed ruses to retain Antony, and the adapter was unwilling to use a similar device again. (F. Hannmann, *Dryden's tragödie "All for Love or the World well Lost" und ihr Verhältnis zu Shakespeare's "Antony and Cleopatra,"* Rostock, 1903, pp. 64, 65.) A better reason is Dryden's "elevation" of Cleopatra's character.
20. Cf. this metaphor with *Antony and Cleopatra*, V, ii, 356–358,

    "Come thou mortal wretch,
    With thy sharpe teeth this knot intrinsicate,
    Of life at once vntye."

21. Q 1678, pp. 77, 78.
22. Dryden's Works, ed. Scott–Saintsbury, v, 315.
23. Entered in the *Stationers' Register*, April 14, 1679 (Roxburghe ed., iii, 83), *Term Cat.*, Nov., 1679 (Arber's ed., i, 370).
24. See Jaggard, p. 477, who lists Elkanah Settle's *The Siege of Troy* among the editions and alterations of *Troilus and Cressida*. Settle's piece deals with the fall of Troy, and is in no way connected with Shakespeare's play.
25. Zenke gives a list of the passages in Shakespeare's play used by Dryden (*Dryden's Troilus and Cressida im Verhältnis zu Shakespeare's Drama*, Rostock, 1904, pp. 33–36). Zenke deals with structural alter-

ation and refers his readers to Rosbund's *Dryden als Shakespeare-Bearbeiter* (Halle a. S., 1882), for further material.

26. Genest suggests (he has been followed by other writers) that this change was made "to please the Ladies rather than the Critics" (i, 267). Unfortunately for this theory, we have no evidence that the frail dames of the Merry Monarch's court even pretended to be shocked by a tale of infidelity. The rule of consistency in characterization probably determined Dryden's alteration, which was therefore chiefly for the purpose of pleasing the critics, himself included.
27. With his customary generosity he gives Betterton credit for suggesting it. See his remarks on this scene in the Preface, sig. a 1. It is indebted to the quarrel between Brutus and Cassius and also to that between Agamemnon and Menelaus in Euripides's *Iphigenia in Aulis*.
28. *Julius Caesar*, II, ii. There is also a reminiscence of *Julius Caesar*, I, ii, 199. Cf. *Troilus and Cressida*, Q 1679, p. 60: "You know my name's not liable to fear."
29. That Dryden used the Folio is indicated by his inclusion of certain passages not given in the Quarto, *e. g.*, II, iii, 59–65. Cf. Q 1679, p. 25. It is also shown by the identity of certain readings in Q 1679 with the Folios text, to the exclusion of Q 1, *e. g.*, IV, i, 8, "within" for (Q 1) "wherein," the correct reading. Cf. Q 1679, p. 31. After I had arrived at this conclusion I found that Delius declares Dryden's source to be the Folios text. *Shakespeare Jahrbuch*, iv, 23, 24. Rosbund (*Dryden als Shakespeare-Bearbeiter*, pp. 10–14) thinks that Dryden collated the Quarto. Zenke (*Dryden's Troilus and Cressida im Verhältnis zu Shakespeare's Drama*, p. 15) denies Dryden's use of the Quarto and concludes that his source is F 1.
30. Rosbund, part iii, gives a detailed account of Dryden's verbal changes.

CHAPTER VII

TATE'S ADAPTATIONS

1. King Lear

FOR half a century after the death of Sir William D'Avenant, every one of the poets laureate took a hand in improving Shakespeare. We have already examined the alterations of D'Avenant and Dryden, and have noticed Shadwell's operatic version of *The Tempest.* I shall discuss Shadwell's *Timon of Athens* in the next chapter. And now comes Nahum Tate, a little condescendingly, but not reluctant in patronage of an unlaurelled Elizabethan. The name of this adapter lives in the hymnals. His treatment of Shakespeare's lines is even worse than his doggerel rendering of David's — the pompous substantive, "Tatefication," has been coined expressly to describe his bungling.[1]

Though apparently not the first acted, Tate's *Lear* was the first written of his adaptations; this is evident from the epistle dedicatory to his *Richard II.* It was printed in quarto in 1681, the year of its production at Dorset Garden.[2] The epistolary dedication is one of a number of documents in which the Restoration adapters explain their mental processes. Tate confesses to embarrassment in finding it necessary to provide dialogue for the old characters in his new scenes. But this humility is not evident as he deals with structure:

> I found the whole . . . a Heap of Jewels, unstrung and unpolisht; yet so dazling in their Disorder, that I soon perceiv'd I had seiz'd a Treasure. 'Twas my good Fortune to light on one Expedient to rectifie what was wanting in the Regularity and Probability of the Tale, which was to run through the whole A Love betwixt Edgar and Cordelia, that never chang'd word with each other in the Original. This renders Cordelia's Indifference and her Father's Passion in the first Scene probable. It likewise gives Countenance

to Edgar's Disguise, making that a generous Design that was before a poor Shift to save his Life. The Distress of the Story is evidently heightned by it; and it particularly gave Occasion of a New Scene or Two, of more Success (perhaps) than Merit. This Method necessarily threw me on making the Tale conclude in a Success to the innocent distrest Persons: Otherwise I must have incumbred the Stage with dead Bodies, which Conduct makes many Tragedies conclude with unseasonable Jests.[3] Yet was I Rackt with no small Fears for so bold a Change, till I found it well receiv'd by my Audience; and if this will not satisfie the Reader, I can produce an Authority that questionless will. *Neither is it of so Trivial an Undertaking to make a Tragedy end happily, for 'tis more difficult to Save than 'tis to Kill: The Dagger and Cup of Poyson are alwaies in Readiness; but to bring the Action to the last Extremity, and then by probable Means to recover All, will require the Art and Judgment of a Writer, and cost him many a Pang in the Performance.*

Mr. Dryd. Pref. to the Span. Fryar.

In seeking to motivate Cordelia's failure to speak out, Tate recognizes the structural weakness of Shakespeare's play from a realistic point of view, which, of course, is precisely the point of view it is fatal to adopt. Nor does his happy ending bring aught but outrage to King Lear, whose bitter cup seemed less significant to the adapter than the billing and cooing of Cordelia and Edgar.

In the prologue Tate announces his ethical purpose, anticipating Mr. Bernard Shaw's prediction that the theatre must replace the church as the custodian of morals. The clergy are accused of plotting in the Whiggish interest; thus *Lear*, like Tate's other alterations, is linked with the political troubles.

ACT I [4]

The play begins with Edmund's soliloquy (I, ii, 1–22), Gloster having already been apprised of Edgar's apparent disloyalty, as is explained in an original scene between Kent and Gloster. Then comes the partition scene (I, i, 32 f.). As the court enters, Edgar and Cordelia exchange amorous speeches. Shakespeare's dialogue is then employed, though in mangled form. France does not appear in this version. Cordelia's motive is now her desire to offend Lear in order that Burgundy may reject her. The King knows of her love affair; he supposes Edgar a bad lot. Kent is banished, and Burgundy refuses Cordelia.

Thus, to line 207, the action runs as in Shakespeare. At that point all go out except Edgar and Cordelia. Edgar then woos her with some assurance, but Cordelia will not hear him. Her answer is typical of Tate's idiom; notice also his tripping measures:

Cord. When, Edgar, I permitted your Addresses,
I was the darling Daughter of a King,
Nor can I now forget my royal Birth,
And live dependent on my Lover's Fortune.
I cannot to so low a fate submit,
And therefore study to forget your Passion,
And trouble me upon this Theam no more.
Edg. Thus Majesty takes most State in Distress!
How are we tost on Fortune's fickle flood! [5]
The Wave that with surprising kindness brought
The dear Wreck [6] to my Arms, has snatcht it back,
And left me mourning on the barren Shore.
Cord. This Baseness of th' ignoble Burgundy [*Aside*
Draws just suspicion on the Race of Men,[7]
His Love was Int'rest, so may Edgar's be
And He but with more Complement dissemble;
If so, I shall oblige him by Denying: [8]
But if his Love be fixt, such Constant flame
As warms our Breasts, if such I find his Passion,
My heart as gratefull to his Truth shall be,
And Cold Cordelia prove as Kind as He. [*Exit.*

Now the Bastard bustles in, warns his brother, and shoves him out. Gloster then appears and we have the scene of the forged letter (the remainder of I, ii, 30 f.). Though the heroic play was supposed to be defunct, Drawcansir was still at large; he appears for a moment in Gloster's speech urging Edmund to "wind me into him." Tate's addition gives a specific reason for this injunction:

That I may bite the Traytor's heart, and fold
His bleeding Entrals on my vengefull Arm.

Gloster makes his exit after line 111, as in Shakespeare; but instead of Edmund's cynical comment on his father's credulity we have more exposition: the villain plans to deceive his father again by placing him where he can overhear an interview with Edgar. Edmund then goes, and the disguised Kent comes in for Shakespeare's I, iv, his engagement by Lear; this is greatly reduced, though not much altered. Oswald is haled back by Kent. The Fool is entirely excised from Tate's version. For the most part the action runs as in Shakespeare, though with great condensation and the omission of many speeches. Lear departs shortly after Albany's appearance and does not reënter. Except for the brief comments of Goneril and Albany, the act ends on Lear's curse. Thus we do not learn of the message to Regan.

ACT II

The second act begins as in Shakespeare with the beguiling of Edgar and Gloster. Curan does not appear. Kent and Oswald enter before Regan and Cornwall: thus Shakespeare's II, i, and II, ii, are telescoped. Kent chases Oswald off the stage to make way for the entrance of the ducal party. Cornwall gives no reason for their visit to Gloster; instead he commands sports and revels. Oswald (who is called simply a Gentleman) now rushes back, pursued by Kent, and we pass to Shakespeare's II, ii, 43 f.

Shakespeare's scenes iii and iv follow at once, as in the original. As he tells us in the dedicatory epistle, Tate thinks Edgar's assumption of his rags unjustified by the sordid instinct of self-preservation. Accordingly, Edgar heroically meditates suicide, but refrains because Cordelia is in distress. To preserve himself for her service he condescends to assume a disguise. When Lear inquires for his daughter we learn that she is at a masque. He does not leave the stage. The action runs along as in Shakespeare, with the speeches much reduced, up to line 285; the act ends with Lear's departure into the storm.

ACT III

Act III begins with Shakespeare's III, ii, Lear on the heath, scene i being omitted. This great passage is grievously reduced and altered; without the Fool it is but a faint echo of its original. It is followed by a new scene in Gloster's palace; Edmund soliloquizes and reveals his lust for the "proud imperial Sisters." Tate, albeit he dabbled in pious psalmody, emphasizes this feature of the story and writes it up *con amore*. "Two Servants from several Entrances deliver him each a Letter."

Gloster then comes in, announces his intention of revolting, and entrusts Edmund with despatches. The Bastard declares, in a long aside, his purpose of betraying his father, and at a distance overhears him interview Cordelia, who wants to die with the King. Gloster informs her of his rebellion, and departs. Still overheard by Edmund, she bids Arante, a colorless confidante, to get her a disguise, that she may seek her father on the heath. It is there that she occupies the interim which in Shakespeare's play she spends in France. Edmund is a heavy villain, and has designs on everyone:

> Provide me a Disguise, we'll instantly
> Go seek the King: — ha! ha! a lucky change. . . .
> I'll bribe two Ruffians that shall at a distance follow,
> And seise 'em in some desert Place, and there
> Whilst one retains her t'other shall return
> T' inform me where she's Lodg'd; I'll be disguis'd too.
> Whilst they are poching for me I'll to the Duke
> With these Dispatches, then to th' Field
> Where like the vig'rous Jove I will enjoy
> This Semele in a Storm, 'twill deaf her Cries
> Like Drums in Battle, lest her Groans shou'd pierce
> My pittying Ear, and make the amorous Fight less fierce.

No wonder this play was popular, with a program of villainy like that.

We next return to the heath, for the scene before the hovel (III, iv). This is telescoped with a badly mangled version of III, vi, the scene in the farmhouse. The fantastic trial of the sisters is excised. Finally Edgar withdraws, while Gloster and Kent take the King away to shelter. Cordelia and Arante [9] now arrive (luckily for them) before the hut, followed by the two ruffians, who seize them. At their shrieks, Edgar rushes out and drives away their captors. He reveals his identity, and is rewarded by Cordelia with the declaration of her love. I quote a few speeches as a fair sample of the curious mixture of extravagance and bathos that composes Tate's style.

> *Cord.* Come to my Arms, thou dearest, best of Men,
> And take the kindest Vows that e're were spoke
> By a protesting Maid.
> *Edg.* Is't possible?
> *Cord.* By the dear Vital Stream that baths my Heart,
> These hallow'd Rags of thine, and naked Vertue,
> These abject Tassels, these fantastick Shreds,
> (Ridiculous ev'n to the meanest Clown)
> To me are dearer than the richest Pomp
> Of purple Monarchs.

The scene now changes to the palace and Gloster's punishment (III, vii). Edmund pretends to more sensibility than in Shakespeare, since before he goes he sheds a few tears over his father's plight. Goneril does not appear in this scene. To spare his feelings, Cornwall orders Edmund to withdraw, and in an aside Regan bids him seek a certain grotto. The action of Gloster's punishment runs as in Shakespeare, though it is shortened. The scene ends in a long soliloquy by the blinded man; he determines to show himself to the populace, arouse them against the Duke, and then throw himself from some precipice,

Whence my freed Soul to her bright Sphear shall fly,
Through boundless Orbs, eternal Regions spy,
And like the Sun, be All one glorious Eye.

ACT IV

We now see the grotto of dalliance. The scene being drawn discloses "Edmund and Regan amourously Seated, Listning to Musick." Their conversation signifies terms of complete intimacy. Regan gives her lover a ring, and he reciprocates with a picture of himself. In pulling it from his pocket, he inadvertently drops a note, which is read by Regan after he goes. Of course it is from Goneril. An officer arrives with news of the rebellion.

The next scene shows the meeting of Edgar and Gloster (IV, i). As they set out for Dover, they are met by Cordelia and Kent, who seek the King. Gloster urges Kent, whose identity is now revealed, to lead the rebellion.

The scene changes to Goneril's palace. We learn that Edmund is still with Regan, that Goneril has taken her affairs out of her husband's hands, and finally that Cornwall is dead.

The next scene is tagged "Field Scene." It begins with Shakespeare's IV, vi, the supposed ascent of Dover cliff. This whole scene, including the appearance of Lear, and the killing of Oswald, is somewhat reduced but not greatly altered. It is followed by IV, vii, both altered and reduced; the place is of course not the French camp, since there is no foreign invasion. Following Lear's exit the act closes with a warlike speech by Cordelia.

ACT V

The last act opens with an original camp scene in which the plot thickens desperately. Goneril instructs an attendant to prepare a poisonous draught for her sister, who is soon to arrive as Goneril's guest at a banquet. We next hear Edmund's speculation (altered from his soliloquy, V, i) on the future course of his amours. He has already enjoyed Regan, and Goneril thus becomes more attractive. The next scene, in "a Valley near the Camp," is Shakespeare's V, ii. After Edgar leaves, his father soliloquizes, regretting that he is no longer able to take his customary share in the bloody work. The rest of the scene remains practically unchanged.

Next comes an altered version of V, iii. It begins with the entrance of Albany, Goneril, Regan, and Edmund, with Lear, Cordelia, and Kent as prisoners. Albany gives strict injunctions for their good treatment; but in an aside Goneril directs their execution. Edmund, accordingly, instead of telling what he has done with them, as in Shakespeare, begins to argue for their despatch; and, as in Shakespeare, is snubbed by the Duke. The first speeches of the royal ladies are left, but their controversy is then halted; Albany does not reveal his knowledge of the true situation. He is a much less interesting character in Tate than in Shakespeare.

The quarrel over Edmund's affections is terminated by the entrance of the disguised Edgar with his challenge (V, i, 38 f.). This he delivers orally, and the trial is appointed at once. All go out except the prisoners and their guards. We now have the identification of Kent with Caius, and an altered version of Lear's speech (V, iii, 9–17),

> We too alone will sing like birds i' th' cage.

Goneril orders their immediate execution. With the other dignitaries she has come in for the trial. Edgar is recognized as soon as he enters, and his guilty brother is terrified. Their speeches of defiance are greatly altered; Edmund's bastardy is the chief theme. After his fall, and Albany's denunciation of Goneril, Edgar and the Duke go out, while Goneril and Regan remain to quarrel over their dying lover. Regan's boast that she has enjoyed him maddens her sister, who retorts by revealing the poisoning. But Regan announces that she has poisoned Goneril. Edmund declares he loved them both, and dies happy.

The final scene shows a prison. Lear is asleep with his head in his daughter's lap when the assassins enter. Cordelia begs to be strangled first, but as the soldiers begin their task, Lear "snatches a Partizan, and strikes down two of them; the rest quit Cordelia, and turn upon him. Enter Edgar and Albany"—in the nick of time. The former's remarks would cause almost anyone to desist from murder:

> *Edg.* Death! Hell! Ye Vultures hold your impious Hands,
> Or take a speedier Death than you wou'd give. . . .
> My dear Cordelia, Lucky was the Minute
> Of our Approach, the Gods have weigh'd our Suffrings;
> W' are past the Fire, and now must shine to Ages.

Albany assigns the whole kingdom except his marriage-portion to Lear, who gives it to Cordelia. Edgar brings the news of her sisters' deaths. Lear bestows his blessing on the lovers, and proposes to retire with Gloster and Kent to some cool cell where they may cheerfully pass in calm reflection the little remainder of their lives. The play ends with a mealy-mouthed speech by Edgar:

> Divine Cordelia, all the Gods can witness
> How much thy Love to Empire I prefer!
> Thy bright Example shall convince the World
> (Whatever Storms of Fortune are decreed)
> That Truth and Vertue shall at last succeed.

Before reviewing the play as a whole, let us notice a few samples of the verbal alteration. Tate worked more freely than either D'Avenant or Dryden; where the earlier adapters would have been content to change a word or two, Tate would often cut loose and retain practically nothing of Shakespeare's. On the other hand, when he did retain Shakespeare's diction he was less apt than either of his predecessors to tamper with it.

Yet that is not saying much. There are many cases of such tampering, a few of which I shall now cite. The text first quoted is in each case that of the Quarto of 1681.[10] Lines are numbered to agree with Dr. Furness's New Variorum Edition. Words replaced are cited from the Praetorius facsimile (London, 1885) of Q 2 (Butter, 1608). Tate's source is certainly the text of the Quartos, not of the Folios, and seems to be Q 2, but there are many exceptions, including Folio corrections, which point to some attempt at collation or to the existence of another text in the theatrical library.[11] This may be a good point for Professor Nicoll. The reason why Quarto 2 was not exclusively used is, of course, its archaic character.

Grammatical corrections are fairly numerous. Example:

II, ii, 111 (Q 1681, p. 16): "lately." For: "late."

Many changes are modernizations. Examples:

II, iv, 54 (Q 1681, p. 19): "Spleen." For: "mother."
II, iv, 180 (Q 1681, p. 21): "confirms." For: "approues."
III, ii, 44 (Q 1681, p. 24): "Frightens." For: "gallow."

A zeal for clearness accounts for many others. Examples:

I, i, 54 (Q 1681, p. 3):
"more than words can *utter*."
For: "wield the matter."

I, i, 122, 123 (Q 1681, p. 5):
"and in her tender Trust
Design'd to have bestow'd my Age at Ease!"
For: "and thought to set my rest
On her kinde nursery."

Elegance seems to have been cherished less by Tate than by either of his laureate predecessors. Yet there are some changes which seem due to it. Examples:

I, i, 90, 91 (Q 1681, p. 4):
"I can't dissemble."
For: "I cannot heaue my heart into my mouth."

III, ii, 14 (Q 1681, p. 24):
"Rumble thy *fill*." For: "belly full."

The literalization of figurative language and the toning down of impassioned flights could not, of course, operate extensively in a play dealing with madness. Tate frequently refigures, however, and there are occasional cases of literalization. Example:

II, ii, 15 (Q 1681, p. 14):
"white liver'd." For: "lilly liuer'd."

Scores of changes seem to be purely capricious. Examples:

I, i, 121 (Q 1681, p. 5): "Rage." For: "wrath."
IV, i, 74 (Q 1681, p. 43): "Poverty." For: "misery."

Tate's version held the stage for a century and a half. Even Dr. Johnson defended his changes, on the ground that the original tragedy is too terrible and that innocence is better rewarded on the stage than afflicted. In vain the voice of Addison was raised in advocacy of the original play; he believed that in Tate's version it had "lost half its beauty." [12]

In the light of the critical canons, this adaptation is a curious hodge-podge. The unities of time and place are disregarded, but the action is more closely knit by the Edgar–Cordelia love story. The excision of the Fool recognizes the principle of strict separation. Like Dryden, Tate cared nothing for the dictum against scenes of violence; we shall find in his version of *Coriolanus* no horror too gory for him. Contrary to the neo-classical rule that love should be kept out of tragedy, it becomes in Tate's *Lear* the chief motivating force. In Shakespeare we catch glimpses of the sinister affections of the two elder sisters — enough to show us that other dark currents of passion are seething past. Tate not only amplifies these hints, but creates a new love story, equal in importance to the fortunes of Lear. These are not happy changes. The scenes dealing with the Edmund–Goneril–Regan triangle are highly voluptuous; and Cordelia's more decorous passion does not improve her character. She becomes, in fact, almost a Lydia Languish, as in the over-refinement of her feelings in her feigned indifference to Edgar (Act I).

Worst of all is the so-called happy ending. In Tate's alteration the principle of poetic justice receives the most pitiable sacrifice in all the English drama. The preservation of Lear is best condemned in the very words of Shakespeare: "Vex not his ghost," cries Kent, as that tormented spirit languishes,

> Vex not his ghost, O let him passe,
> he hates him much, that would vpon the wracke
> Of this rough world stretch him out longer.

2. King Richard the Second

Tate's second revision of Shakespeare was also printed in 1681;[13] there was a second edition ten years later. The play lived, as we have seen, but two days on the stage. In his epistle dedicatory Tate gives rein to his resentment:

> I am not ignorant of the posture of Affairs in King Richard the Second's Reign, how dissolute then the Age, and how corrupt the Court; a Season that beheld Ignorance and Infamy preferr'd to Office and Pow'r, exercis'd in Opressing, Learning and Merit; but why a History of those Times shou'd be suppress as a Libel upon Ours, is past my Understanding. 'Tis sure the worst Complement that ever was made to a Prince. . . .

In depicting King Richard, Shakespeare, says Tate, was faithful to history, but the adapter has been at pains to "elevate" him:

> I have every where given him the Language of an Active, Prudent Prince. Preferring the Good of his Subjects to his own private Pleasure. . . . Nor cou'd it suffice me to make him speak like a King (who as Mr. Rhymer says in his Tragedies of the last Age considered, are always in Poëtry presum'd Heroes) but to Act so too, viz. with Resolution and Justice. Resolute enough our Shakespear (copying the History) has made him, for concerning his seizing old Gaunt's Revennues, he tells the wise Diswaders,

Say what ye will, we seize into our Hands
His Plate, his Goods, his Money and his Lands.

But where was the Justice of this Action? This Passage I confess was so material a Part of the Chronicle (being the very Basis of Bullingbrook's Usurpation) that I cou'd not in this new Model so far transgress Truth as to make no mention of it; yet for the honour of my Heroe I suppose the foresaid Revennues to be Borrow'd onely for the present Exigence, not Extorted. . . .

My Design was to engage the pitty of the Audience for him in his Distresses, which I cou'd never have compass'd had I not before shewn him a Wise, Active and Just Prince. Detracting Language (if any where) had been excusable in the Mouths of the Conspirators . . . but I wou'd not allow even Traytors and Conspirators thus to bespatter the Person whom I design'd to place in the Love and Compassion of the Audience. . . .

Further, to Vindicate ev'n his Magnanimity in Regard of his Resigning the Crown, I have on purpose inserted an intirely new Scene between him and his Queen, wherein his Conduct is sufficiently excus'd by the Malignancy of his Fortune, which argues indeed Extremity of Distress, but Nothing of Weakness.

Yet, complains Tate, "a positive Doom of Suppression *without Examination*" ended the play's run on the third day. And this despite the fact that "Every Scene is full of Respect to Majesty and the dignity of Courts, not one alter'd Page but what breaths Loyalty."

Turning from political to aesthetic considerations, the adapter excuses his introduction of comic relief, which he

judg'd necessary to help off the heaviness of the Tale, . . . though less agreeable to strickness of Rule; [this change is] confirm'd by our Laureat's last Piece, who confesses himself to have broken a Rule for the Pleasure of Variety.* The Audience (says he) are grown weary of melancholly Scenes, and I dare prophesie that few Tragedies (except those in Verse) shall succeed in this Age if they are not lightned with a course of Mirth.

*Epst. Ded. to the Span. Fryar.

ACT I

Tate begins with Shakespeare's opening scene, which is not greatly altered, though speeches are reduced and rearranged and there is a good deal of minor tampering with diction. Scene ii follows, as in Shakespeare; it begins with an original soliloquy by the Duchess. Gloster's opening speech is transposed and follows the Duchess's lamentation. Immediately after, York comes in. Only slightly comic in Shakespeare, he is broadly so in Tate; he is simply a funny fat man. Like his brother, he refuses to take up the Duchess's cause.

The third scene shows the pavilion at the lists.[14] It is little altered. The speeches are cut down and there is some verbal tampering, but not much. Richard's exit speech is taken from Shakespeare's next scene (I, iv, which Tate omits); it is composed of lines 38–40 of Green's advice to prosecute the war in Ireland, and line 42 of Richard's decision to go there in person. The parting of Gaunt and Bolingbroke is cut down to 20 lines from 57; it is largely original with Tate and is a deplorable change, for instead of the emphasis on the human side of the parting Tate allows Bolingbroke to express his already meditated designs on the throne. But with this exception there is no serious structural alteration.

ACT II

Omitting Shakespeare's I, iv, in which Richard actually expresses his longing for his uncle's death, a species of royal turpitude that was too much for Tate's loyalty, Act II opens as in Shakespeare at the deathbed of John of Gaunt. The old lion's eulogy of England is nearly all excised, I suppose because it contains serious charges against Richard; eight lines of it are introduced later, in the King's presence. In its stead, the comic York expresses forebodings of disaster. Tate gives him Richard's lines in the preceding scene (I, iv, 24–34) descriptive of Bolingbroke's cultivation of the commons. York's part is also fattened with exposition of the rebellion in Ireland, and includes what looks like a topical hit on the court of Charles II:

all goes worse and worse in Ireland, Rebellion is there on the Wing, and here in the Egg; yet still the Court dances after the French Pipe, Eternal Apes of Vanity: Mutiny stirring, Discipline asleep, Knaves in Office, all's wrong.

Gaunt's warning to the King is echoed by York; Richard meekly accepts their correction, thanks them for it, and puts up a pious petition for his uncle's long life. As Tate points out in his preface, the King seizes the revenues only temporarily:

> Be Heav'n our judge we mean him nothing fowl
> But shortly will with interest restore
> The Loan our sudden streights make necessary.

Piercy, that is, young Hotspur, is added to the group of lords who remain to plot, and is given some original lines and some stolen from those of his associates.

Scene ii (not so marked) corresponds to Shakespeare's II, ii, 67 f.; the Queen's conversation with the King's favorites and the exposition there given of the rebellion are omitted. The scene begins with Bushy's line, "Despair not Madam," which is spoken by a lady in waiting. York cuts a ridiculous figure; to the Queen's demand that he "speak comfort," he replies (in prose):

> Comforts in Heav'n, and we are on the Earth, nothing but crosses on this side of the Moon; my heart stews in Choller, I shall dissolve to a Gelly. That your Husband shou'd have no more wit than to go a Knight Erranting whilst Rogues seize all at home, and that I shou'd have no more wit than to be his Deputy at such a proper time: to undertake to support a crazy Government, that can scarce carry my own Fat.

The scene ends with his exit, since Bushy, Green, and Bagot do not appear in Tate's version. This reduction of casts is typical of the altered versions.

Scene iii follows in reduced form. It begins seven lines before the arrival of Ross and Willoughby, who according to Tate bring the news of the dispersal of the Welsh royalists. Berkeley is not among Tate's characters. York enters eight lines after Ross and Willoughby, and addresses his hypocritical nephew in excellent (Shakespearean) blank verse, which is highly inconsistent with his previous utterances. To Bolingbroke's protest against the confiscation York reiterates Tate's palliation:

> Thy words are all as false as thy Intents,
> The King but for the Service of the State,
> Has Borrow'd thy Revenue for a time,
> And Pawn'd to me his Honour to repay it,
> Which I as Gaunt Executour allow'd.

This explanation fails to satisfy the heir; he arrests his uncle, and the scene closes with York's reproaches.

Scene iv is an original low comedy scene in which the rabble, consisting of "a Shoomaker, Farrier, Weaver, Tanner, Mercer, Brewer, Butcher, Barber, and infinite others with a Confused Noise" debate the respective merits of a republic and a commonwealth, and then engage in a free-for-all fight, some shouting "no Laws, no Laws, no Laws," and others, "Laws, Laws, Laws." Bolingbroke and his forces come in. Young Piercy is all for sweeping the rabble aside. But Bolingbroke is too politic for such methods; the mob is easily swayed by his flattery. He makes the mistake of pretending not to desire the crown; but when he sees the temper of the crowd, quickly retrieves himself and professes his readiness to "take the burden of the State." The leader of the mob counsels him not to be chicken-hearted, and, now secure in his ascendency, Bolingbroke exemplifies this advice by ordering the leader hanged; the act ends with the shouts of the rabble for their new hero.[15]

ACT III

Shakespeare's II, iv, the dispersal of Salisbury's Welsh troops, is omitted by Tate, the necessary exposition having been given. Shakespeare's III, i, is also omitted, since the King's favorites do not appear in Tate's version. The third act begins, therefore, with Shakespeare's III, ii, Richard and his adherents before Berkeley castle. The scene is greatly cut down. After Richard's prediction that the rebels will melt away, Carlile speaks two lines from the same speech (III, ii, 54, 55), and the fatuous Richard closes the scene with a new couplet:

> Move we secure then in our Royal Right,
> To th' Traytors Executions, not to Fight.

The bad news brought by Salisbury and Scroop is postponed by Tate in order to introduce the Queen's scene in York garden. This it is necessary to move forward, since Tate intends to bring the Queen to Richard's side while he is still in the field. The second scene, then, of this act is a grievously abridged version of Shakespeare's III, iv, the Queen and the Duchess of York exchanging original speeches of apprehension. The whole scene is verbally altered.

Scene iii takes us back to Shakespeare's III, ii, where Tate's III, i, ended. The place is a heath, where Richard is met successively by Salisbury and Scroop with their news of disaster. Richard's great speech of despair, beginning

> No matter where, of comfort no man speake,

is cut from 34 to 24 lines, and badly garbled besides. The scene is prolonged after the news of York's capture (as it becomes in Tate), by the entrance of the Queen, the Duchess of York, and their train. The scene then turns into a love passage between the unhappy monarch and his consort, who assures him:

> This Kingdom yet, which once you did prefer
> To the worlds sway, this Beauty and this Heart
> Is Richards still, millions of Loyal thoughts
> Are always waiting there to pay you homage.
> That glorious Empire yields to you alone,
> No Bullingbrook can chase you from that Throne.

At this tender invitation, Richard incontinently orders:

> We'll march no farther, lead to th' Castle here,

a change of plan which, in view of the King's political situation, reminds us of the celebrated simile of Mr. Bayes in *The Rehearsal*.

Scene iv continues with Shakespeare's III, iii, Bolingbroke's appearance before Flint castle, and Richard's surrender. Piercy is already present with his father; it is Ross who comes with the report of the castle's strength. York is much more loyal and defiant in Tate's version than in the original. Speeches are reduced and altered; otherwise the scene is little changed.

ACT IV

In place of the accusation of Aumerle as guilty of Gloster's death, and the subsequent quarrel between him and Surrey, Fitzwater, and Piercy, Tate gives us several short scenes emphasizing the new interests he has brought into the plot. The first is between Aumerle and his father. Both are hostile to Bolingbroke, York in prose and Aumerle in blank verse. The usurper has sent for York to seek his counsel, but the old man refuses to go. He retires, and the Duchess comes in, and urges her son to restrain his father's rashness.

Next the Queen appears, "supported by Ladies." She is evidently the only person unaware of the King's decision to abdicate, but she prophesies evil none the less. The King now enters, dressed in mourning. The attendants are dismissed, and he tells the Queen of his decision. She implores him to die rather than yield the Crown. He answers in typical Tatese:

> Permit me briefly to recount the steps,
> By which my Fortune grew to this distress.
> Then tell me, what cou'd Alexander do
> Against a Fate so obstinate as mine.

The Queen "Weeps over him," and inquires whether none will strike for "an injur'd King." Richard will not hear of further attempts, and the loving couple sadly separate.

Scene ii is Shakespeare's IV, i, beginning with line 107. York's announcement of Richard's willingness to abdicate is given to Northumberland. There is little other alteration, except in diction, to the end of the scene. York then draws a fine distinction, in terms of current political philosophy, between royalty and the King's person. He is thus able to promise obedience to King Henry IV, though he reserves the right to pity Richard. The latter remains on with Carlile, to whom he counsels patience. There is no suggestion of a counter-revolution.

ACT V

The first two scenes of this act are transposed by Tate. The first is Shakespeare's V, ii, beginning with the description of the contrasting receptions of Richard and Henry by the populace. This is assigned to Aumerle, not to York. The latter comes in and protests he cannot blame his son for grieving. On top of that profession, and most inconsistently with York's position during the whole play up to this point, his discovery of his son's complicity is as in the original. The scene as altered is played in a much lower key. To the Duchess's passionate remonstrance,

> Hadst thou groan'd for him, York, as I have done,

the fat man cleverly replies,

> And art e'en like to groan for him again. Away.

The transposition of this scene with Shakespeare's V, i, gives longer suspense for the fate of Aumerle, since that scene intervenes between his discovery and his pardon.

Scene ii follows Shakespeare structurally, but the dialogue is rewritten. The Queen has put on mourning; for

Thus dead in Honour, my Lord and I [16]
Officiate at our own sad Funeral.

Instead of strengthening her dejected Lord, Tate's Queen invites him to

Lean on my Brest whilst I dissolve to Dew,
And wash thee fair agen with Tears of Love.

The height of the ridiculous is scaled in Richard's last speech before Northumberland and the Guards tear them asunder:

Rich. Now Heaven I thank thee, all my Griefs are paid!
I've lost a single frail uncertain Crown,
And found a Virtue Richer than the World:
Yes, Bird of Paradise, wee'll pearch together,
Sing in our Cage, and make our Cell a Grove.

Enter Northumberland, Guards.

North. My Lord, King Bullingbrook has chang'd his Orders,
You must to Pomfrett Castle, not to th' Tower;
And for you, Madam, he has given Command
That you be instantly convey'd to France.

King. Must I to Pomfrett, and my Queen to France?
Patience is stale, and I am weary ont 't [*sic*],
Blood, Fire, rank Leprosies and blewest Plagues. . . .

Permit is a favorite verb with Tate; he begins Richard's concluding speech with it:

Permit yet once our Death-cold Lips to joyn,
Permit a Kiss that must Divorce for ever,
I'll ravish yet one more, farewell my Love!
My Royal Constant Dear farewel for ever!
Give Sorrow Speech, and let thy Farewell come,
Mine speaks the Voice of Death, but Thine is dumb.

Critics (like Mr. Shaw) of Shakespeare's romantic incorrigibility should study the Restoration versions to learn, not that Shakespeare was unromantic, but that his good sense usually restrained his romanticism. Compared with the tragic writers of the Restoration, and for that matter with the nineteenth-century romantics, Shakespeare seems severely realistic, austere, and classical.

The third scene is Shakespeare's V, iii, the pardoning of Aumerle. York is even more disgusted with the King's clemency than is Shakespeare. In the speech with which he ends the scene Henry includes his hint that the murder of Richard would be acceptable. Thus Shakespeare's brief scene of exposition (V, iv) becomes unnecessary; its omission is doubtless an improvement.

The last scene begins, like Shakespeare's V, v, with Richard's long soliloquy, though this is curtailed. An amazing example of Restoration taste is incorporated in this passage:

A Table and Provisions shewn.

What mean my Goalers [*sic*] by that plenteous Board?
For three days past I've fed upon my Sighs,
And drunk my Tears; rest craving Nature, rest,
I'll humour thy dire Need and tast this food,
That only serves to make Misfortune Live.

Going to sit, the Table sinks down.

Apparently the patrons of Dorset Garden insisted that some use should be made of the mechanical features of that stage, whatever the subject of the play. It is difficult to see why else table-sinking should be introduced here. Its employment in *The Tempest* must have scored a tremendous hit, the delight of which lasted long after it had ceased to be a novelty.

The interview with the trusty groom (V, v, 67–94) is omitted in favor of the arrival of letters from the Queen. The King is in the seventh heaven and sits down to answer them when

Enter Exton and Servants.

[*Richard*] Furies! What means this Pageantry of Death?
Speak thou the foremost Murderer, thy own hand
Is arm'd with th' Instrument of thy own Slaughter,
Go thou and fill a room in Hell,
Another Thou. [*Kills 4 of them.*

But, despite this extraordinary prowess, the scene ends as in Shakespeare with Richard's death and Exton's repentance.

Scene v is Shakespeare's V, vi; York does not appear in it. Henry's remorse is more outspoken, and so more "loyal."

Structurally Tate has made few serious alterations. The most important is Bolingbroke's winning of the rabble. This is amusingly done and probably acted well enough. More serious is the "elevation" of Richard's character, a feat on which Tate plumes himself in his preface. As a matter of fact, it spoils the play. The fall of Shakespeare's Richard would not be so tragic if he were only a weakling; his energy in the earlier scenes makes his collapse more striking. We cannot sympathize greatly with Tate's Richard, whose only virtues are negative. The adapter tries to engage our sympathy for the lover, but the picture is overdrawn and Richard becomes uxorious. The Queen, instead of being his foil in the last act, is merely a feminine counterpart of her husband. York is the only other character that suffers alteration. He is not elevated, but degraded to a buffoon.

Of verbal tampering there is a good deal, yet not so much as in either D'Avenant's or Dryden's alterations. Here again Tate works with a freer hand. The following illustrations of his changes are characteristic. The text first cited is in each case that of the Cambridge edition (Clark and Wright, vol. iv, 1864). Lines are numbered to agree with this edition, on which I have relied for variant readings except in the case of Q 5, which I have collated by means of the Praetorius facsimile (1887). Words replaced are cited from the latter text.

That Q 5, issued in 1634, is Tate's source I cannot state certainly, not having made an exhaustive collation. The pre-Wars texts of *Richard the Second* fall into two groups: (1) Q 1, 2, 3, 4; (2) Fs, Q 5. Q 5 is printed from the Folios text. Tate's alteration was printed in 1681; its source is certainly group (2), and probably Q 5.[17]

Tate was no such man of parts as Dryden or even D'Avenant, and his changes were not guided by principles so clearly distinguishable. Yet some categories can be set up. Modernization accounts for many of the adapter's changes. Examples:

I, i, 4 (Q 1681, p. 1):
"th' Impeachment lately charg'd."
For: "the boysterous late appeale."

III, ii, 36 (Q 1681, p. 25):
"*Desponding* Cousin." For: "Discomfortable."

Metrical considerations account for other changes. Example:

IV, i, 148 (Q 1681, p. 41):
"Prevent [it], resist it, stop this breach in Time." Om. Q 1681, followed by Pope.

Efforts to clear up the meaning are less numerous in Tate than in either D'Avenant or Dryden, but I have noticed a few changes which appear to have that object. Examples:

II, iii, 84 (Q 1681, p. 19): "feign'd." For: "deceivable."

V, iii, 35 (Q 1681, p. 50):
"To win thy *future* Love I pardon Thee."
For: "after-."

The same is true of elegance. Tate's was not an elegant mind. But the following passage seems to be a feeble attempt to rise above earthly diction:

IV, i, 184, 185 (Q 1681, p. 41):
"Now is this Crown a Well wherein two Vessels
That in successive Motion rise and fall."
For:
Now is this Golden Crowne like a deepe Well,
That owes two Buckets filling one another."

But by far the greatest number of Tate's changes appear to be simply capricious. Examples:

I, i, 8: "sifted." For: "sounded."

I, i, 12: "sound." For: "sift."

I, i, 92 (Q 1681, p. 3): "Combate." For: "battel."

III, ii, 39 (Q 1681, p. 25):

"Then Thieves and Robbers *do securely Range.*"

For: "raunge abroad unseene."

III, ii, 45, 46 (Q 1681, p. 25):

"Dismantled from the Cloak of Night, stand bare,
And Tremble at their own Deformity!"

For:

"(The Cloake of Night being pluckt from off their backes)
Stand bare and naked, trembling at themselves."

Cf. Tate's second line with Shakespeare's *Richard III*, I, i, 27:
"And descant on mine own deformity."

III, iv, 29 (Q 1681, p. 26): "Peaches." For: "Apricocks."

III, iv, 34 (Q 1681, p. 26): "Sprigs." For: "sprayes."

Many other examples might be cited. Trifling of this sort is not so serious as the bold mangling of D'Avenant and Dryden, but it is hardly less discreditable.

Taking the play as a whole, Tate's structural changes seem to be motivated, chiefly, by his desire for "elevation." The unities are no more observed than in Shakespeare; there is more comedy; and there is no attempt to dodge scenes of violence. Tested by the canons Tate's version is a wretched failure; it conforms only in its elevation of its hero's character; and this in fact degrades him no less than the elevation of Cleopatra and Cressida at the hands of Dryden. As in his *Lear*, Tate emphasizes the love motive above all else, and here the sinister influence of the heroic play is once more visible.

A cleverer policy on the part of the court would have allowed Tate to produce his play unmolested, for it would undoubtedly have died as speedy a natural death as did his next Shakespearean venture. But censors have rarely been distinguished for their cleverness.

3. The Ingratitude of a Commonwealth, or the Fall of Caius Martius Coriolanus

Tate's third and last attempt to improve a Shakespearean drama also had a political inspiration. *Coriolanus*, Professor Odell points out, "seemed destined to be launched, with new trimmings, during or after each of England's successive politico-civic upheavals; Dennis so set it forth after 1715, and Thomson, after the '45."

The Ingratitude was printed in quarto in 1682.[18] Tate's dedicatory epistle to this play is much briefer than those to his *Lear* and his *Richard II*. He owns that he has again

> launcht out in Shakespear's Bottom. Much of what is offered here, is Fruit that grew in the Richness of his Soil; and what ever the Superstructure prove, it was my good fortune to build upon a Rock.[19]

This time, he carefully points out, the satire is unmistakably for the Whigs.

> Upon a close view of this Story, there appear'd in some Passages, no small Resemblance with the busie Faction of our own time. And I confess, I chose rather to set the Parallel nearer to Sight, than to throw it off at further Distance. . . . Where is the harm of letting the People see what Miseries Common-Wealths have been involv'd in, by a blind Compliance with their popular Misleaders: Nor may it be altogether amiss, to give these Projecters themselves, examples how wretched their dependence is on the uncertain Crowd. Faction is a Monster that often makes the slaughter 'twas designed for; and as often turns its fury on those that hatcht it. The Moral therefore of these Scenes being to Recommend Submission and Adherence to Establisht Lawful Power, which in a word, is LOYALTY.

As always in these alterations, the number of characters is greatly reduced; in this case, to eleven.

ACT I

There is no structural alteration up to the point of the entrance of the Messenger with news from the Volscian war. The senators do not come in; the Messenger announces Martius's appointment as Cominius's second, in place of Titus Lartius, who is supposed to be dead and does not appear in Tate's version. The reluctance of the citizens to go to war is emphasized rather deftly by Tate. The colloquy of the tribunes is reduced from 28 lines to 11.

Shakespeare's I, ii, in which Aufidius makes his first appearance, is omitted by Tate, who passes directly to Shakespeare's I, iii, the Roman women. The prose of the opening speeches is rewritten as blank verse. Thus Shakespeare:

> Then his good report should haue beene my Sonne, I therein would haue found issue. Heare me professe sincerely, had I a dozen sons each in my loue alike, and none lesse deere then thine, and my good Martius, I had rather had eleuen dye Nobly for their Countrey, then one voluptuously surfet out of Action.

But Tate:

> Then—
> His Glory shou'd have been my Darling Son:
> Now by Minerva, had the Indulgent Gods
> Blest me with Twenty Sons, as much Belov'd
> As my brave Martius; I had rather Lose them All
> In Chase of Glory, and their Country's Cause,
> Than One, i' th' Surfeit of voluptuous Peace.

Tate's Virgilia is more outspoken in her pacifism than Shakespeare's. Valeria turns out to be a Restoration coquette. She enters "Gawdily and Fantastically Drest, follow'd by Six or Seven Pages." Her airs and graces are amusing enough, but hardly suit their surroundings. No mention is made of Young Martius, though the lad is introduced by Tate later on in the play.

Scene iii is Shakespeare's I, iv, 8 f. (I number with Neilson's

Cambridge edition), the attack on Corioli, the wager being omitted. It is followed by Shakespeare's I, v, the spoil-laden soldier. I, vi, the arrival of Martius at the camp of Cominius, is left out by Tate, who also omits I, vii, at the gates of Corioli. He goes instead to I, viii, the encounter of Martius with Aufidius. This is followed by Shakespeare's I, ix, the entitling of Martius. Tate seems to have missed Shakespeare's effective stroke of characterization near the end of the scene, when the lordly Martius so lightly lets go by the name of his former host. Yet it seems incredible that this should have gone over Tate's head; perhaps he excised it as a means of elevating his hero's character. Shakespeare's last scene, showing Aufidius's hatred, is also cut by Tate. This compression of the events of the fighting into two scenes instead of six is justifiable, and, on a picture stage, perhaps necessary. Tate has omitted nothing essential to his story, though his tampering with the phrasing is constant and deplorable.

ACT II

The second act opens directly with the return of Coriolanus to Rome (Shakespeare's II, i, 179 f.), omitting Menenius's skirmish with the tribunes and the proud and anxious talk of the women. The triumphal entry is thus much less effective than in Shakespeare, since no suspense is created. The conspiracy of the tribunes is abbreviated. Immediately after their resolution (at Shakespeare's II, i, 275) the scene opens and shows the Senate sitting (II, ii); the preliminaries between the officers are omitted, and the scene begins with Coriolanus's remonstrance against the eulogies of his wounds (II, ii, 71 f.). Typical of Tate's condensation is the reduction of Cominius's speech from 41 lines to 25.

The final scene is Shakespeare's II, iii, the solicitation of votes. The debate before Coriolanus's entrance is shortened, and there is much verbal alteration throughout the whole scene.

ACT III

The third act begins as in Shakespeare, with the tribunes' warning (III, i, 24 f.) and the broil between the parties. It is followed by III, ii, much altered. This takes place, not in the house of Coriolanus, but in a street, where Volumnia is met "by Valeria, passing by in a Chair." This talkative dame babbles not unamusingly, and goes on her way rejoicing. Then the patricians appear and we have III, ii. It is immediately followed by Shakespeare's III, iii, 39 f., the people entering the street.

The next scene, Coriolanus's parting from his family and friends (IV, i), is not tagged by Tate; probably the scene did not change and the farewell was said in the street. The adapter possessed a remarkable facility in the invention of imprecations, and Volumnia is assigned in this scene a number of mouth-filling curses. Tate brings in, rather effectively, the young son of Martius, who begs to accompany his father into exile.

ACT IV

We now pass directly to the arrival of Coriolanus at the enemy's city (IV, iv). Both Shakespeare's intervening scenes, Volumnia baiting the tribunes (IV, ii), and the expository scene on the highway (IV, iii), are omitted. In Tate, however, it is to Corioli, not to Actium, that the exiled general goes. He recognizes Aufidius's house without assistance, and (presumably) the scene draws and reveals its interior. We then have Shakespeare's IV, v. The dispute with the servants is much shortened. Immediately after the conclusion of the scene, we are introduced to Nigridius, a broken Roman officer in the service of Aufidius, whom he inflames with jealousy at the warmth of Coriolanus's reception.

The next scene is Shakespeare's IV, vi, the arrival of the news of Coriolanus's treachery. It is greatly abbreviated, though it is telescoped with a reduced version of Shakespeare's V, i, in which Menenius consents to visit the renegade.

Next comes V, ii, the repulse of Menenius, considerably altered. The sentinels are omitted. On the other hand, Tate manages to crowd into this scene all the Roman efforts to soften Coriolanus. The first of these are in dumb show. Menenius's plea is shortened and turned from prose into blank verse.

After his repulse, the invaders are about to attack the walls, but are met by the family of Coriolanus. The scene is, of course, Shakespeare's (V, iii), but how differently phrased! It begins:

> *Cor.* Look there, my Mother, Wife, and little Darling,
> Are come to Meet our Triumph on its way,
> And be Spectators of our keen Revenge. . . .

He greets his wife:

> Life of my Life, Fly to me? O a Kiss.

For several speeches the unthinkable proposition is implied that Coriolanus does not know why the women have come. Thereafter Shakespeare's structure is retained, though his diction is mutilated.

ACT V

Tate's last act is brief, but he packs it full of surprise and violence. Shakespeare's V, iv, the arrival of the news of peace, is omitted. On the other hand, Shakespeare's V, v, the honored return of the ladies, furnishes Tate with another excuse for Valeria's babbling; she did not join their mission, and now affects the rôle of committee of welcome. Virgilia receives a letter from Menenius warning her that Nigridius is plotting her husband's ruin. The women determine to return and save him, though how that could possibly have been accomplished Tate does not trouble to suggest.

The next scene is original with the adapter. In voluptuous

accents Aufidius confides to Nigridius his passion for Virgilia. News comes that with Volumnia and Young Martius she has entered Corioli. Aufidius orders them seized.

The final scene is in the palace, where the Volscian lords are met in council. It follows Shakespeare's V, vi (though it is much condensed) up to the assassination of Coriolanus, who manages to wound Aufidius. Nigridius comes in with news of an imminent battle between the legions of the two generals.

All rush out except Aufidius, Nigridius, and Coriolanus. The first now tells the dying Roman that Virgilia is in his power. I quote his speech despite its brutality, because it affords a curious view of the pious Tate.

> I charge thee Dye not yet, till thou has seen
> Our Scene of Pleasures; to thy Face I'll Force her;
> Glut my last Minuits with a double Ryot;
> And in Revenges Sweets and Loves, Expire.

Virgilia is brought in wounded; the piteous sight is too much for the ravisher and he dies. Coriolanus now inquires:

> What means that purple Dew upon thy Breast?

Virgilia replies:

> 'tis a Roman Wound,
> Giv'n by Virgilia's Hand, that rather chose
> To sink this Vessel in a Sea of Blood,
> Than suffer its chast Treasure, to become
> Th' unhallowed Pyrates Prize.

With a tender farewell she dies, and Coriolanus begs that "Some kind God descend t' inform me" where Volumnia and his son may be.

Nigridius responds, gloating over his former commander's plight, that the boy has been "Mangled, Gash't, Rack't, Distorted." Coriolanus asks how the torturer disposed of him: "Didst eat him?" Nigridius answers:

> Having kill'd your old Menenius,
> Off'ring his feeble Vengeance, streight I threw

> The Tortur'd Brat, with Limbs all broke . . .
> Into Volumnia's Arms, who still retain'd
> Her Roman Temper; till with bitter Language,
> And most insulting, added to her Suff'rings;
> I rous'd her silent Grief, to loud Disorder. . . .

Mark Coriolanus's phrasing of his agony:

> Convultions! Feavers! blewest Pestilence!
> Sleep on Virgilia. . . .

Enter Volumnia Distracted, with Young Martius under her Arm.

We now witness a mad scene, in which Volumnia raves at great length (one of her speeches contains 23 lines), but certainly does not turn thought and affliction, not to mention passion or hell, into either favor or prettiness. At last she snatches a partisan from one of the guards, kills Nigridius with it, and runs off.

But she has dropped the boy. And now succeeds a really "sweet bit," as Mr. Odell calls it, between Coriolanus and his son. The pathos is artificial, and the insistence on physical torture is too painful; but the little scene is affecting, none the less. At last the boy dies and so does Coriolanus, who clasps with one arm the body of his wife, and with the other his son's.

Naturally, the Epilogue is spoken by Valeria.

The verbal changes made by Tate are of the same order as those we have noticed in his *Lear* and his *Richard II*. It hardly seems worth while to list further examples. Tate worked less on a principle than either D'Avenant or Dryden. Consequently more of his changes seem made without rhyme or reason, while on the other hand he frequently retains phrases which his predecessors would almost certainly have altered.

His play follows Shakespeare's with a reasonable degree of fidelity up to the catastrophe. Tate then cuts loose completely and turns a respectable tragedy into an unpleasant reminder of the old tragedy-of-blood. He evidently aimed at giving his audience a last act they would not easily forget; accordingly he works in a sword combat with the death of both the principals, an attempted rape, a suicidal demise, a mad scene, and a juvenile expiration.

Like Shakespeare's play, Tate's violates all the canons. The unities of time and place are disregarded by both. The unity of action is more observed by Shakespeare than by Tate, whose Valeria scenes are irrelevant to the plot. These also go a long step beyond Shakespeare's in permitting the mingling of comic with tragic. The last scene is one of horrid violence. Poetic justice is flouted by Tate even more than by Shakespeare. Again the love motive is emphasized. Rape is a favorite device with Tate; he uses it in both *Lear* and *The Ingratitude* without the slightest warrant in either source. In spite of this morsel the latter play was a failure; but in the former the poetaster scored a success which more than compensated. Shakespeare's *Coriolanus* seems never to have appeared on the Restoration stage.

Notes to Chapter VII

1. Ward (*Camb. Hist. Eng. Lit.*, viii, 41) describes Tate as "a painstaking and talented writer who, with enduring success, adapted *King Lear.*" The *D. N. B.* bluntly calls him a poetaster.
2. It appears in the *Term Catalogue* for May, 1681 (Arber's ed., i, 440).
3. Had the audience indulged in witticisms over Dryden's corpse-paved ending for *Troilus and Cressida*, two years before?
4. For elaborate tables showing Tate's use of Shakespeare's lines, see R. Erzgräber, *Nahum Tate's und George Colman's Bühnenbearbeitungen des Shakespeare'schen King Lear*, Weimar, 1897, pp. 40–44.
5. Shades of Pyramus and Thisbe!
6. An exquisite trope for Cordelia!
7. In spite of the fact that she has counted on it, and has directed her conduct accordingly!
8. A rather casuistical paradox.
9. Erzgräber (p. 52) points out that the introduction of the confidante was probably due to French influence. Certainly it was more decorous for Cordelia to make her sweet avowal in the presence of a chaperone.
10. This was reprinted in 1689, *c.* 1690, 1699, *c.* 1710, 1712, 1717, 1729 1733, 1745, 1749, 1750, 1756, 1757, 1759, 1760, 1761, 1763, 1767, etc. etc. See Jaggard, pp. 356 f. It has recently been reprinted by Mr. Montague Summers in his *Shakespeare Adaptations*, 1922.
11. Erzgräber (p. 14) concludes that Tate's sources are Q 2 and F 3.
12. *Spectator*, No. 40 (April 16, 1711). Cited by Furness, v, 477.
13. It appears in the *Term Catalogue* for June, 1681 (Arber's ed., i, 451). William Allwardt (*Die englischen Bühnenbearbeitungen von Shakespeares King Richard II;* Rostock dissertation, Doberan, 1909, p. 11) concludes that Tate's sources were F 1 and F 3.
14. Professor Odell errs in stating that this scene is omitted (Odell, i, 58).
15. Allwardt (p. 20) suggests that Tate's reason for interpolating this scene was to show Bolingbroke in an unfavorable light, thus preparing the audience for his treachery to Richard. It was, rather, chiefly to portray the fickleness of the mob, a favorite theme of "loyal" writers at this time.
16. Tate had a positive genius for falling into tripping measures at solemn moments.
17. For the evidence see my unpublished Harvard dissertation (1923), pp. 457, 458.
18. *Term Catalogue*, Feb. 1682 (Arber's ed., i, 473).
19. Another instance of Tate's genius for absurd metaphor.

CHAPTER VIII

MISCELLANEOUS ADAPTATIONS BEFORE 1700

1. Lacy's Sauny the Scot, or The Taming of the Shrew

THE alterations of D'Avenant and Dryden have more historical significance than those of their successors. This is true of the first because he inaugurated the vogue, and of the second because he dominated his age. The extraordinary success of Tate's *King Lear* seems to justify, despite the relative unimportance of his other versions, a separate chapter on his share in Restoration revision. There are, moreover, interesting problems connected with the work of the earlier adapters, and it has seemed wise to treat their versions in some detail. Similar questions are less numerous in the case of the later alterations. In this chapter and the next, we shall merely glance briefly at the chief features of the remainder. These are in general less amenable to consideration in the light of contemporary canons of criticism. More detailed treatments, valuable chiefly for their tabulations, are afforded in nearly every case by German doctoral dissertations. To these suitable reference will be made as each play is discussed. All I shall attempt to do is to place these adaptations before the reader in order that his picture of the whole course of Restoration tampering may be complete.

To proceed in chronological order, the first of these miscellaneous productions was one of the most popular, at least in its own day. Since we always like to commence in an optimistic frame of mind, I quote the verdict of Mr. Montague Summers, who characterizes it as "a good bustling farce." It was printed in 1698 with the following title-page: "Sauny the

JOHN LACY AS SCRUPLE, GALLIARD, AND SAUNY

Scott: or, The Taming of the Shrew: A Comedy. As it is now Acted at the Theatre-Royal. Written by J. Lacey, Servant to His Majesty. And Never before Printed. Then I'll cry out, Swell'd with Poetick Rage, 'Tis I, John Lacy, have Reform'd your Stage. Prol. to Rehers. London, Printed and Sold by E. Whitlock, near Stationers-Hall. 1698."[1]

Vincke erroneously pronounces this version to be without important alteration.[2] It is in fact one of the most violently altered of them all. In the first place, Lacy turns the verse of Shakespeare's play into prose; in the second, he translates it from Elizabethan into Restoration idiom; in the third, he introduces violent structural changes. The opening speeches illustrate the first two of these improvements:

Enter Winlove [*Lucentio*], *and his Man Tranio.*

Win. I Am quite weary of the Country Life; there is that Little thing the World calls *Quiet*, but there is nothing else; Clowns live and die in 't, whose *Souls* lye hid here, and after Death their *Names:* My Kinder Stars (I thank 'em) have Wing'd my Spirit with an Active Fire, which makes me wish to know what Men are Born for, to Dyet a Running Horse, to give a Hawk casting, to know Dogs Names; These make not Men; no, 'tis Philosophy, 'tis Learning, and Exercise of Reason to know what's good and Virtuous, and to break our Stubborn and Untemper'd Wills, to Choose it; This makes us Imitate that Great Divinity that Fram'd us.

Tran. I thought you had Learn't *Philosophy* enough at *Oxford*, what betwixt *Aristotle* on one side, and *Bottle-Ale* on the other, I am confident you have arriv'd at a Pitch of Learning and Virtue sufficient for any Gentleman to set up with in the Countrey, that is, to be the Prop of the Family.

ACT I[3]

Lacy's version omits the Induction. The scene proceeds as in Shakespeare; Baptista becomes Beaufoy; Katharine, Margaret; Bianca, Biancha; Hortensio, Geraldo; Gremio, Woodall; and Biondello, Jamy.

ACT II

Shakespeare's I, ii (Petruchio's entrance and the conspiracy to get the Shrew married off) begins Lacy's second act. The principal change in characterization now appears; Sauny (Grumio) becomes the leading rôle. Mr. Summers notes that "Maidment and Logan, who ought to speak with authority on the point, say that 'the language of Sauny . . . is not Scotch in its idiom or apparent pronunciation, but savours strongly of the meridian of Doncaster, Lacy's birthplace.'"[4] That Lacy did not intend Sauny's speech to be taken for genuine Scots is indicated by the opening speech of Act II:

> *Pet.* Sirrah, leave off your Scotch, and speak me *English*, or something like it.
>
> *Saun.* Gude will I Sir.

Sauny, then, is trying to speak English, but naturally introduces many Scotch expressions. The result is exactly what Petruchio predicts—"something like it." As for the name Sauny, it is nothing more than a corruption of the common nickname, Sandy.[5] Mr. Summers suggests that Lacy may have taken the name from "Sander" in Shakespeare's source, the old *Taming of a Shrew*, but this hardly seems likely.

In Lacy's hands this character becomes even more the buffoon than in Shakespeare. His lines are greatly coarsened; many of them are thoroughly disagreeable. So with Petruchio; the good-humored avowal of his mercenary intentions becomes an unmanly boasting of his indifference: "If she be Rich, I care not if she want a Nose or an Eye, any thing with Money."

The second scene is Shakespeare's II, i. The delightful impudence of Petruchio's proposal to the harassed father is omitted, his entrance being delayed till the other suitors have made their offerings, after which Sauny comes in and hands over the supposed music-master. This is a shameless fattening of the title rôle at Petruchio's expense. Sauny remains on for the tempestuous wooing scene, in which he takes a hand himself. The closing speeches illustrate the change in tone:

Pet. Hold, get me a Stick there Sauny; by this hand, deny to Promise before your Father, I'll not Leave you a whole rib, I'll make you do 't and be glad on 't.

Marg. Why you will not Murther me Sirrah? you are a couple of Rascals, *I* don't think, but you have pickt my Pockets.

Saun. I'se sooner pick your tang out O' your head, nor pick your Pocket.

Petruchio's exit at the conclusion of this scene was not theatrical enough to suit Lacy; in *Sauny* the mad lover insists on being seen to his horse; accordingly he drags Margaret off the stage, Sauny bringing up the rear. That this spoils the effect of Petruchio's next exit, after the wedding, Lacy seems not to have suspected.

ACT III

The third act runs along as in Shakespeare. Winlove is not, like Lucentio, a classical scholar, but M. Mawgier, a professor of French. Bianca obliges with a song by the supposed music-master. Toward the end of the second scene, which ought to end with Petruchio's violent departure with his bride, Lacy tacks on Shakespeare's IV, ii, Tranio's deception of Geraldo by showing Bianca's partiality for Winlove. Geraldo, unlike Hortensio, throws off his disguise and abjures Bianca to her face. Another of Lacy's altered characters is Snatchpenny, "A rare old Sinner in the Temple Cloysters," who ill supplies the place of Shakespeare's "ancient engle coming down a hill." He is avowedly a rascal, ready to sell his cheating services to the highest bidder.

In scene iii we have Shakespeare's IV, i, the arrival of the honeymooners at the house in the country. It ends with Sauny's retrieving of the mutton (after Petruchio has dragged Margaret off to the bridal chamber) and a complacent but incredibly vulgar assurance that he has dined well.

Scene iv. Finally, we have an original scene actually presenting the bridal chamber. This replaces Petruchio's amusing and splendidly actable soliloquy. Petruchio orders Margaret to disrobe. She asks him to send his men away and summon her maids. His reply is to order Sauny to undress her. Then, changing his mind, he proclaims the bed unfit for their reception and resolves to sit up all night. He orders in beer and tobacco and forces his bride to partake of both. The scene ends as she bursts into tears and the tamer renews his threats.

ACT IV

Lacy's fourth act begins with Shakespeare's IV, iii. Again Lacy anticipates a later device, this time by changing Petruchio's insistence on Margaret's thanking him for the meat to a demand that she recognize it as, not a pullet, but a piece of veal. This change robs the roadside scene and Petruchio's insistence on the moon of much of their effectiveness. The Haberdasher is omitted, and so is Petruchio's mock-sermon on the unimportance of fine clothes. This is one of his most comic speeches; it was sacrificed, presumably, to make room for Sauny's gibberish.

Scene ii is Shakespeare's IV, iv, the introduction of the impostor to Bianca's father. Lacy adds a slight complication by making Woodall appear, suspect a device, and bribe Winlove to turn the lady over to him.

Next follow the roadside scene and Shakespeare's V, i. The plotting of Woodall results in an addition to the latter. Immediately after Winlove elopes with Bianca, Woodall appears "with 3 or 4 Fellows," ready to "seize on her, and Clap her into a Chair." He continues to wait, during the appearance of Sir Lyonell (Vincentio) and his attempts to secure recognition. Sir Lyonell is actually arrested and led off by Tranio, and the stage is cleared for Winlove's return with his bride and the disappointment of Woodall, who goes out swearing vengeance, and returns with Sir Lyonell, Beaufoy, and the rest. The scene then proceeds as in Shakespeare till the end, when a brief reconciliation is staged between Margaret and Bianca.

ACT V

The last act is violently altered and quite replaces Shakespeare's V, ii, his final scene, which is pure resolution. In a confidential interview with her sister, Margaret announces her intention, now that she is at her father's house, of revenging herself:

> I'll muster up the Spight of all the Curs'd Women since Noahs Flood [6] to do him Mischeif, and add new Vigour to my Tongue; I have not par'd my Nails this fortnight, they are long enough to do him some Execution, that's my Comfort. . . . I'll make Petruchio glad to wipe my Shoes, or walk my Horse, ere I have done with him.

That hero now appears, boasting to Winlove of Margaret's gentleness. He attempts to show off as the complete tamer, but with no success. Margaret finally relapses into sullen silence, vowing she will not speak at all. The scene is punctuated by Sauny's comments. He is finally dispatched by Petruchio in search of a barber, who pretends that Margaret is ill and must have a tooth drawn, but is beaten out of the room by her. Petruchio's next move is to assume that she is dead. A bier is brought in; as they start to place her on it she speaks and professes submission.[7]

Geraldo now appears, announcing his nuptials. The wager is made at this point, and, as in Shakespeare, Kate's obedience wins for Petruchio. Her superb speech to the recalcitrant brides is reduced by Lacy to two lines. The whole concludes with a dance, after which the following lines are spoken by Petruchio:

> Now let us in, and Eate, the Work is done,
> Which neither Time nor Age can wear from Memory;
> I've Tam'd the Shrew, but will not be asham'd,
> If next you see the very *Tamer Tam'd*.

The reference is to Fletcher's sequel to Shakespeare's *Shrew*, entitled *The Woman's Prize; or, The Tamer Tamed*, in which a second wife turns the tables on Petruchio. Evidently it was often, and perhaps regularly, played after each performance of *Sauny*.

It would be absurd to discuss this vulgar adaptation of the delightful Elizabethan farce in the light of the critical canons. The most serious of Lacy's changes in character is the transformation of Petruchio from a madcap to a brute. The chief problem which confronts the actor who assumes this rôle in a humanitarian age is how to play it vigorously and still keep the sympathy of the audience.[8] Yet Shakespeare cleverly insures Petruchio of that sympathy at the outset, by exhibiting Katharine's display of temper in the opening scene. The Petruchio must study to hold this sympathy till the final curtain; he must be spirited and even rough; but his hearty good humor must flow repeatedly across the footlights, so that his audience shall never forget that his harshness to Katharine is assumed, though for a definite purpose. This is accomplished in modern productions of Shakespeare's play by the use of asides of laughter and by the introduction of new business, by means of which Shakespeare's Petruchio makes himself agreeable to the audience. Lacy's Petruchio would not be tolerated on a modern stage, and that Restoration audiences thought his jocular brutality amusing is an impressive index to the taste of that refined age.

One of the most amazing things about Shakespeare is the delicacy with which he treats his heroines. Such grossness as he allows is merely verbal. Petruchio's taming campaign affords numerous opportunities for indecent innuendoes, but Shakespeare passes them all by. Not only is his depiction of that stormy honeymoon entirely free from licentiousness, but he actually takes us along with him: we do not pause to speculate concerning the more intimate relations of Katharine and Petruchio. To that extent is sex ignored, save that Curtis tells us Petruchio is in his wife's chamber "making a sermon of continency to her." That is all; the hint is enough to satisfy the realist, while the general reader forgets it immediately. Compare with this handling, Lacy's bedroom scene, in which coarse buffoonery is mingled with downright indecency.

Margaret is almost as violently changed. She is no longer the wilful beauty, but a squalling virago. Other parts suffer similar degradation. Most egregious is the turning of Shakespeare's Pedant into the pitiful rogue, Snatchpenny.

As for Lacy's changes in plot, we have already discussed the bedroom scene. The other violent alteration is the episode of the barber and the bier in Act V. Shakespeare's play is essentially farcical, but it borders on comedy. Lacy's fifth act is preposterous and extravagant, even for farce.[9]

And yet — this is the sad conclusion with which we shall end our description of several of these plays — the adaptation drove its original off the stage. The thing survived till Garrick's time, when the great actor but uncertain critic recast Shakespeare's play into a three-act affair in which the Lucentio subplot is omitted. This version is still sometimes acted by amateur organizations. It was not driven from the professional stage till 1886, when Augustin Daly revived Shakespeare's play, with that sterling actor, the late John Drew, as Petruchio, and Ada Rehan, perhaps the greatest Katharine of all time, in the title rôle.

2. Shadwell's Timon of Athens, The Man-Hater

Our next author has the misfortune of living for posterity chiefly in the verses of a bitter enemy, instead of in his own. "The True-blue Protestant poet" on whom the vitriolic talents of John Dryden played with excoriating vigor is only now reviving from the satirist's awful charge that Shadwell "never deviates into sense." We have already noticed his operatic embellishment of the D'Avenant–Dryden version of *The Tempest.*

His *Timon of Athens* is mentioned by Downes among the chief plays acted at Dorset Garden between 1671 and 1682, when the patent companies united: "'T was very well Acted, and the Musick in 't well Perform'd; it wonderfully pleas'd the Court and City; being an Excellent Moral."[10] This adaptation was printed in 1678,[11] and, according to Jaggard, went through eleven editions before Tonson issued the first separate edition of Shakespeare's *Timon* in 1734. My references are all to Q 1678.[12]

In dedicating his revision to the Duke of Buckingham, Shadwell declares that "It is the more worthy of you, since it has the inimitable hand of Shakespear in it, which never made more Masterly strokes than in this. Yet I can truly say, I have made it into a Play." No cast of characters is given.

ACT I

Scene i. Shadwell begins with a soliloquy by Demetrius (Flavius), explaining his master's straits. In Shakespeare the revelation is more effective because it is deferred till after Timon has appeared in his magnificence. Of the suitors the poet appears first; he is brought up to date — for he deals in heroic verse, and Shadwell uses him to ridicule that now discredited form:

Poet. The last thing I presented my Noble Lord was Epigram:
But this is in Heroick style.
Dem. What d'ye mean by style? that of good sence is all alike;
that is to say, with apt and easie words, not one too little
or too much: And this I think good style.
Poet. O Sir, you are wide o' th' matter! apt and easie!
Heroicks must be lofty and high sounding;
No easie language in Heroick Verse;
'Tis most unfit: for should I name a Lion,
I must not in Heroicks call him so!

Dem. What then?
Poet. I'de as soon call him an Ass. No thus —
The fierce Numidian Monarch of the Beasts.
Dem. That's lofty, is it?
Poet. O yes! but a Lion would sound so baldly, not to be
Endur'd, and a Bull too — but
The mighty Warriour of the horned Race:
Ah — how that sounds!
Dem. Then I perceive sound's the great matter in this way.
Poet. Ever while you live.
Dem. How would you sound a Fox as you call it?
Poet. A Fox is but a scurvey Beast for Heroick Verse.
Dem. Hum — is it so? how will a Raven do in Heroick?
Poet. Oh very well, Sir.
That black and dreadful fate-denouncing fowl.

At the end of the scene appears one Nicius, who turns out to be Timon's prospective father-in-law.

After all have departed, Timon meets Evandra, his mistress. She and Melissa, his betrothed, are Shadwell's chief contribution to the new version.[13] Evandra is deeply in love with Timon, but she is not merely the puppet of a ruling passion. She recognizes her predicament, and uses every argument to convince Timon that he ought not to marry her rival, whom she accuses of a mercenary motive. Timon is strikingly portrayed as keenly desirous of acting the cad, but held in check by his natural honesty and love of truth. The dialogue, while not highly distinguished, is vigorous and spirited. Evandra finally succeeds in extracting Timon's promise to continue loving her, and the act closes with his lament for the brevity of passion.

ACT II

The opening of the second act introduces us to the third side of the triangle, the bride-to-be. Melissa is an amusing jade, whom we catch in the act of making up for the festivities at Timon's house. She is as far from our notion of a true classical dame as Tate's Valeria; her opening speeches instantly betray a Restoration coquette. Timon comes to urge her not to delay their marriage. She refuses to hasten the date, but swears eternal constancy.

Shadwell's second scene is Shakespeare's I, ii, the feast; it occupies the remainder of Act II. Thus Shadwell's first two acts get on with the plot only as far as to the end of Shakespeare's Act I; this is due, of course, to the two new scenes, Timon and Evandra, and Timon and Melissa. During the course of the dinner Timon successfully pleads with the senators for the recall of Alcibiades. Melissa is among the guests, and so is her rival, the unhappy Evandra.

Finally all the guests depart except Evandra, who takes her last farewell of Timon. Her lover is remorseful and assures her that

I can love two at once, trust me I can.

But she disdains to "be fed with crumbs"; she offers to stab herself, but is prevented by Timon. After her departure Demetrius appears and reminds the audience of his master's ruin.

ACT III

Shadwell's third act begins with Shakespeare's II, ii, 133 f., Timon informed of his real state. This is followed by an original scene in "the Porch or Cloister of the Stoicks." Apemantus rails; then Timon's servants appear and we see his rejection by his friends (III, i). The next scene shows Melissa's reception of the news of his poverty. At this highly psychological moment Alcibiades returns in disguise, and their former love is renewed.

The following scene is also original with Shadwell; it replaces Shakespeare's III, iv, 80 f. Timon learns of his friends' desertion, and of the persistence of his creditors. Finally, Shadwell brings the friends on the stage, and exhibits them confronted by Timon, to whom they make excuses as they hurry away. This effective scene is, however, unduly prolonged. The last persons to appear are Melissa, who cuts her lover, and Evandra, who comes to offer him her savings, but is tenderly dismissed. In the meantime Demetrius has informed the friends that Timon is as prosperous as ever, and in the next scene we have the mock banquet. In Shadwell's version the viands are toads and snakes.

ACT IV

As in the original, Act IV begins with Timon outside the walls. Scene ii shows us, instead of the grief of his servants, the senate debating Alcibiades's unauthorized return. A violent quarrel ensues, and Alcibiades is again banished.

The third scene is Shakespeare's IV, iii, Timon in the woods, and his discovery of the gold. This passage is reduced from forty-seven lines to twenty-three. The entrance of Alcibiades on his expedition against Athens is reserved by Shadwell till the last act. Instead, the faithful Evandra appears in search of her lover. At first she fails to recognize in the unkempt creature the curled darling of Athenian society. She proffers money and jewels, to which she has converted part of her estate. She attempts in vain to persuade Timon to return to Athens, and then insists on sharing his exile. He shows her the treasure, employing the lines omitted by Shadwell from the opening speech of this scene.

As in Shakespeare, Apemantus comes in. So do not, however, either the Banditti or Timon's steward. Finally the Poet, the Painter, and the Musician arrive (V, i), but their scene with Timon is greatly reduced. After they have been stoned out, Timon and Evandra lie down to rest. Who should now appear but Melissa! She has heard of the gold, and attempts to win Timon back again. Evandra remonstrates, and the rival ladies express unflattering opinions of each other. Timon threatens to beat Melissa if she stays; she thereupon retires, and the scene ends with a tender passage between the lovers.

ACT V

The greater part of the last act is Shadwell's. It begins with Timon's speech commencing

> Timon hath made his everlasting Mansion,
> Upon the beached Verge of the Salt Flood.

This passage is addressed to Evandra, who tries to turn his thoughts from death. Now the recreant friends appear; in the name of the Senate they invite Timon back to Athens and offer him the command against Alcibiades (Shakespeare's V, ii). He refuses, and the ambassadors run off as Alcibiades and his mistresses come in.[14]

Shakespeare's IV, iii, 48 f., then follows. After its conclusion the scene changes to the walls of Athens (V, iv) and the rebel's triumph. It ends with the submission of the senate, for Timon's death, instead of being related, is shown in the next scene, another of Shadwell's additions. Timon bids Evandra live happily and then dies, whereupon she stabs herself.[15] The final scene takes us back to Athens. Melissa turns once more to Alcibiades, but he now knows her real character and spurns her. Apemantus is haled in for railing against the army, but is pardoned for the sake of Socrates. The false friends of Timon appear with halters about their necks and beg mercy, which is granted. Alcibiades mounts the pulpit and announces the overthrow of the Four Hundred. Finally a messenger, as in Shakespeare, brings the news of Timon's death.

On the whole, I am inclined to rate this adaptation as the best, or at any rate the least objectionable, of the Restoration alterations. Shadwell's boast was that he had made his original into a play; the claim is hardly exaggerated. The addition of the love story not only adds greatly to our interest in the central figure, but exercises throughout the play a unifying force, which brings the Alcibiades subplot into closer relation with the main theme. The Shakespearean ending is lame, and while Shadwell has not mended the death of Timon, except by showing it instead of narrating it, he is able to offer a convincing conclusion by a stronger use of the Alcibiades plot.

The weak point in Shadwell's version is the "humours" character, Melissa. She is so consistently in the mercenary key that she is not always convincing. Evandra is possibly too violent a contrast; subtler characterization of both women would vastly improve the play.

Shadwell seriously alters the character of Flavius, who in Shakespeare is loyal to Timon throughout. His successor, Demetrius, is shrewd enough to desert ship. This unwelcome change is doubtless due to the invention of Evandra; since Timon had one faithful friend, the adapter thought it more effective to number the steward among the recreants.

The unities are not seriously regarded in this version; in fact, the unity of place is more frequently violated than in the original. Comic and tragic are not separated, and Evandra's violent death defies the neo-classical standard. Nor is poetic justice observed.

I have said little concerning Shadwell's diction. He works in this play with a free hand, but when he retains Shakespeare's lines he generally does so without serious alteration. His own style has a certain rude vigor, which, while it is almost as far from Shakespeare's as anyone's, is preferable to the ineptitudes and inanities of Nahum Tate, and the vandalism of D'Avenant.

3. Ravenscroft's Titus Andronicus, or the Rape of Lavinia

As a tribute to the strong stomach of the British constitution Shakespeare's *Titus* has few equals; but Ravenscroft's version is unquestionably one of them. Like several other adaptations staged between the years 1678 and 1682, it was called into being by the political troubles, as the author frankly avows in the address "To the Reader" of the Quarto of 1687.[16] This preface is uncommonly important because it affords one of the few extant bits of evidence bearing on the problem of original authorship.

> I have been told by some anciently conversant with the Stage, that it was not Originally his, but brought by a private Author to be Acted, and he only gave some Master-touches to one or two of the Principal Parts or Characters; this I am apt to believe, because 'tis the most incorrect and indigested piece in all his Works; It seems rather a heap of Rubbish than a Structure.—However as if some great Building had been design'd, in the removal we found many Large and Square Stones both usefull and Ornamental to the Fabrick, as now Modell'd: Compare the Old Play with this, you'l finde that none in all that Authors Works ever receiv'd greater Alterations or Additions,[17] the Language not only refin'd but many scenes entirely New; Besides most of the Principal Characters heighten'd, and the Plot much encreas'd.

Ravenscroft goes on to congratulate himself on its success in the theatre. His most important changes are as follows.

ACT I

The first act is practically unaltered. It is divided into three scenes, ending as follows: (1) with the submission of Saturninus and Bassianus (Shakespeare, I, i, 63); (2) with the meeting of Titus and Marcus (I, i, 178); (3) with the kidnapping of Lavinia (I, i, 289).

ACT II

Ravenscroft's second act begins with Shakespeare's I, i, 290, Titus's encounter with his son, and continues with some condensation, but little alteration, through Shakespeare's II, i, that is, through the plot against Lavinia.

ACT III

Ravenscroft's third act omits Shakespeare's II, ii, the meeting of the hunters, and begins with Aaron's soliloquy and the hiding of the gold (II, iii). The scene proceeds as in Shakespeare until the arrival of Quintus and Martius. They are not accompanied by Aaron but have sought the place in response to a decoy letter. They do not fall into the pit, but are gazing down into it when the Emperor comes in, guided by "Aron." This method of getting the victims to the pit's brink is more plausible than Shakespeare's; Aaron's sudden departure in the original play is not convincing. Tamora's letter of accusation is marked in Ravenscroft's text with quotation marks, indicating that it was not read on the stage. With these exceptions the scene is little altered; it is followed without a break by Shakespeare's II, iv, Marcus's encounter with the mutilated Lavinia.

ACT IV

Ravenscroft's fourth act opens with Shakespeare's III, i, but slightly changed, either verbally or structurally. Titus considerately, but inexplicably, leaves the stage to have his hand cut off. Between the execution of this barbarity and the appearance of the messenger with the heads of Titus's sons, Ravenscroft introduces Shakespeare's IV, i, the pursuit of Junius (Young Lucius) by Lavinia, and the writing in the sand. This is accomplished with an arrow instead of a staff. The appearance of the child affords an opportunity for some innocent prattle, which the Restoration playwrights always delight in.

> *Titus.* Lucius is not yet gone far:
> But presently he goes to Banishment.
> *Junius.* How far is that Grandfather?
> *Titus.* A Long Journey —
> *Junius.* And must I go with him or stay with you?
> *Titus.* I am going yet a Longer Journey Child.
> *Junius.* But whither Grandfather Titus.
> *Titus.* From whence I came —.

This is hackneyed stuff, to be sure, and not very profound. But it has the air of profundity, and doubtless was effective on the stage.

The boy "pudles in the Sand with the arrow"; this is the cue for Titus (not Marcus) to write with it, and after him Lavinia. As soon as the names become known, the heads of Titus's sons are brought in. The scene proceeds as in Shakespeare's III, i, and ends with the departure of Lucius and the family procession, in an improved form. Lavinia does not carry her father's severed hand between her teeth; this important member is entrusted to young Junius, who is initiated early, perhaps to prepare him for his dangerous task in the next act.

ACT V

The scene at Titus's house (III, ii) is omitted; so is the shooting to the gods, and the finding of the messages by Tamora's sons (IV, ii). The act begins with Shakespeare's IV, ii, 52, the appearance of the "Black-a-more-Child." The woman is accompanied by her husband, who is told to wait outside. Aaron is not present at first. The child is not newly born, but has been in charge of a Nurse, who has just died. After the murder of the woman, her husband reappears in pursuit of Aaron. This scene is followed at once by Shakespeare's IV, iv, the Emperor's reception of Titus's arrows. The Clown is omitted. Hard on the heels of the report of the rebellion Titus rushes in, demanding justice. He gives up the quest and determines to seek revenge instead.

This affords Tamora a cue for her impersonation, which follows immediately, and in the presence of all (Shakespeare's V, ii). She arranges for the banquet and offers hostages; for his part, Titus hands over young Junius as his pledge. After Titus leaves, the well-coached boy begins to scatter handfuls of gold. The curiosity and cupidity of Demetrius and Chiron are aroused; they ask the boy to show them where he got it. Pretending complete innocence, he leads them off to seek his grandfather's garden, where, after the discovery of the treasure, they intend to kill their guide.

The next scene is Shakespeare's V, i, greatly reduced, the camp of the Goths. It is not marked as a separate scene. Neither is the scene that follows, the sons of Tamora in Titus's garden. Decoyed by Junius, they are led into the trap and seized, as in Shakespeare's V, ii. Lavinia and her father describe the fate which awaits the guilty princes; their throats are not, however, cut before the audience. The next scene, again undistinguished from what precedes it, is new; it exhibits Aaron captured and sentenced to the rack.

Next comes Shakespeare's V, iii. Titus does not appear as cook. After he has killed his daughter, Aaron is "discover'd on a Rack." Before the very eyes of the spectators he writhes in torment, but repeatedly shakes his head in token of his determination not to speak. Tamora inquires for her sons; whereupon:

A Curtain drawn discovers the heads and hands of Dem. and Chir. hanging up against the wall. Their bodys in Chairs in bloody Linnen.

Tam. O dismall sight!
Tit. But here their hearts and Tongues.
No dish but holds some part of which y'ave fed.
And all the Wine y'ave drunk mixt with their blood.

As in Shakespeare, Titus stabs the Empress, and is stabbed by the Emperor, whom in turn Lucius strikes down. All this while Aaron is on the rack. Marcus now threatens him with the death of his child, whereupon he agrees to confess all. This is from Shakespeare's V, i. Marcus promises to spare the boy and even to bring him up. Aaron then confesses, but in the presence of Tamora, who, like the Emperor, still lives. She asks for the child, now her only son, and when it is brought to her stabs it, reproaching the Moor for blabbing. She dies, cursing him. Whereat:

Aron. She has out-done me in my own Art—
Out-done me in Murder — Kill'd her own Child.
Give it me — I'le eat it.

This is too much for Saturninus, who promptly expires. Lucius is proclaimed Emperor; his first act is to sentence Aaron to be both burned and racked to death. As the play ends, "the Fire flames about the Moor."

In spite of Ravenscroft's boast that he has refined Shakespeare's language, his verbal tamperings are not important. There are occasional modernizations or simplifications such as *Empire* for *empery* and *call* for *accite*, but there is nothing like the systematic improvements of D'Avenant, Dryden, and Tate. Passages are not rare in which whole speeches occur without alteration.

Nor are Ravenscroft's structural changes so extensive as he implies in the address "To the Reader." There is no change in characterization. The "new scenes" have already been described. Nor, except for the letter to Titus's sons, and the use of the boy Junius as a decoy for Tamora's sons, has anything of importance been added to the plot. The principal change is the reservation of Aaron's most lurid scene to the end of the play. Sending him up in smoke is, as tragedy-of-blood technique, infinitely better than merely assuring him of even the most hellish torments. One wonders how the thing was staged. He must have been a bold man who elected to play Aaron. But perhaps a dummy was dexterously substituted, as in the feats of our intrepid movie actors.[18]

4. Otway's The History and Fall of Caius Marius

The title of this ostensibly classical tragedy gives no hint of its true nature: the play is based on *Romeo and Juliet*. That passionate pair are whisked away from the glowing streets of Renaissance Verona and plunged, hissing-hot, into the chastely frigid atmosphere of republican Rome. It is true that there they distinctly warm up their environment; yet Otway's play remains, on the whole, the most absurdly incongruous of all the Restoration versions.[19]

The first edition of *Caius Marius* (1680) [20] was reprinted in 1692, 1696, and 1703. In the Prologue, spoken by Betterton, Otway frankly confesses his indebtedness; the following lines are sandwiched in between a wistful reference to Maecenas and a lament, with which the Prologue closes, that the King is not patronizing the theatres as was his wont. Shakespeare found favor at the court of James, and

> Therefore he wrote with Fancy unconfin'd,
> And Thoughts that were Immortal as his Mind.
> And from the Crop of his luxuriant Pen
> E're since succeeding Poets humbly glean.
> Though much the most unworthy of the Throng,
> Our this-day's Poet fears h' has done him wrong.
> Like greedy Beggars that steal Sheaves away,
> You'll find h' has rifled him of half a Play.
> Amidst this baser Dross you'll see it shine
> Most beautifull, amazing, and Divine.

A not unworthy tribute. How different this strain from D'Avenant's, Dryden's, Tate's, and Shadwell's! It is a pleasant thought that the greatest follower of the old tragic tradition was not so sure that Shakespeare needed improving as that he himself needed support. Otway's adaptation is, in fact, less a reworking of Shakespeare's material than a bold appropriation of it for new purposes.

ACT I

The play opens with an agreement among the patricians, headed by Metellus (Capulet) to make Sylla (Paris) consul instead of Marius (Montague). The latter is aware of their plan, and, vowing hatred for all of Metellus's name, commands his son, who loves Metellus's daughter Lavinia (Juliet), to renounce her. This act is almost entirely Otway's own except for a brief dialogue in which Sulpitius (Mercutio) rallies Young Marius (Romeo) on his love.

ACT II

Otway's second act begins with the announcement to Lavinia that she must marry Sylla. This scene is dominated by the Nurse; Lavinia's mother is not in the play, and so it is Metellus himself who commands his daughter to accept his choice.

Next comes the balcony scene. It begins with Shakespeare's II, i, Sulpitius and Granius (Benvolio, but Young Marius's brother) in search of the lover. Since Young Marius is in love with Lavinia when the play begins, it is by her charms that Sulpitius attempts to conjure his friend. In debate over the scenic significance of the line, the commentators have neglected the marvellous dexterity by which the tone of the scene is changed by Shakespeare from banter to high seriousness — in nine words:

> He jests at scars that never felt a wound.

Now the adapter begins his deadly rephrasing:

> He laughs at Wounds that never felt their smart.

This stupid change does not stand alone in this scene, for Otway makes fearful hash of the deathless music of the lovers' speeches.

The final scene of Act II occurs in the Forum, where the election of the consul turns into a factional fight, in which Marius, represented as a thoroughly unprincipled demagogue, is victorious. This and similar scenes were inspired by the vogue for dramatic satire of the follies of the rabble. The hero of the fight in the Forum is the bloodthirsty Sulpitius, who kills with his own hand Young Pompey, the consul's son.

ACT III

Young Marius rouses from his amorous dreams and sends a challenge to Sylla, who is at the city's walls with an army. We learn from an interview between Young Marius and the

Nurse, who is accompanied by Clodius (Peter) with his fan, that the lovers have been secretly married, and that Young Marius is to visit his wife during the coming night. He confesses the marriage to his father. The old warrior is enraged, and Young Marius agrees not to seek his bride till he has his father's consent.

Next comes Shakespeare's III, ii, Lavinia waiting for the night. Finally, we have a pitched battle in the Forum; the plebeian party is beaten by Sylla, and its leaders are captured and banished. Marius Senior is gratified by his son's behavior and bids him employ with Lavinia the night which precedes his exile.

ACT IV

The fourth act opens with a mangled version of the bedroom scene, transferred to the garden. Having parted from her husband, Lavinia determines to follow him into exile. The scene then changes to the fields outside the city, where the banished demagogues wander hungrily, pursued by patrician troops. Lavinia joins the former, and with fruits she has gathered saves the life of her father-in-law. Martha, a Syrian prophetess, tells Marius that the aristocratic party is splitting into factions, and he is soon joined by Cinna, one of the consuls. Marius Junior, who has been momentarily off stage for no particular reason, reappears to tell of Lavinia's capture by the aristocrats, who have taken her back to Rome. At her father's house she is rescued from the marriage to Sylla by the potion of a Priest of Hymen (Friar Lawrence), who promises to inform Young Marius. The act closes as she drinks it.

ACT V

In the final act, Marius Senior, before the walls of Rome, receives the submission of the senate. The next scene shows the discovery of Lavinia's seeming death. We then witness the plebeian reprisals. Marius Junior happens by the church-yard, and there is told of Lavinia's supposed death, but why the Priest had failed to warn him of the truth is not explained. He visits the apothecary and procures poison. In the final scene, at the monument, the Priest sends off the letter and then proceeds to break open the tomb, when Marius (who, of course, does not receive the letter) arrives and, supposing him to be a robber, kills him.[21] After he "pulls down the side of the tomb,"—an interesting clue to the producer's method of coping with the difficulty of representing both the inside and outside of the monument,—young Marius drinks the poison, but before he dies Lavinia wakes, and for a few moments the lovers are reunited. It is unnecessary to suppose that Otway is here following an older version of the story; this change would suggest itself to any adapter.

Marius Senior and his men rush in, pursuing Metellus, whom they cut down. Lavinia stabs herself with his sword. A messenger informs Marius that Sylla has returned at the head of an army and has been joined by the rabble. Sulpitius comes in mortally wounded and, as Marius is led off by Sylla's guards, ends the wretched business thus:

> *Sulpit.* A Curse on all Repentance! how I hate it!
> I'd rather hear a Dog howl than a Man whine.
> *Gran.* You're wounded, Sir: I hope it is not much.
> *Sulpit.* No; 'tis not so deep as a Well, nor so wide as a Church-door. But 'tis enough; 'twill serve; I am pepper'd I warrant, I warrant for this world. A Pox on all Madmen hereafter. If I get a Monument, let this be my Epitaph:
> Sulpitius *lies here, that troublesome Slave,*
> *That sent many honester men to the Grave,*
> *And dy'd like a Fool when h' had liv'd like a Knave.*
> [*Ex. omnes.*

And, agrees the reader, time they did.

Of this abominable mixture of Roman and Renaissance, I am not aware that anything encouraging can be said. The execution of Otway's project is as grotesque as its conception. The

Romans are struck now by a Roman thought, now by an Elizabethan; and, as in the following passage, they can pass at will from the sobriety of the republican stoic to the airy lightness of Shakespeare's gay Italians:

Sulpit[*ius*]. Is not this better now than whining Love?
Now thou again art Marius, son of Arms,
Thy Father's Honour, and thy Friends Delight.
[*Enter Nurse and Clodius.*
Mar[*ius*]. *Jun*[*ior*]. Sulpitius, what comes here? a Sail, Sulpitius.
Sulpit. A tatter'd one, and weather-beaten much.
Many a boistrous Storm has she bin toss'd in,
And many a Pilot kept her to the wind.
Nurse. Clodius.
Clod. Madam.
Sulpit. Madam.
Nurse. My Fan, Clodius.
Sulpit. Ay, good Clodius, to hide her Face.

This from the toged consuls!

Nor is it possible to condone the poetic losses entailed by Otway's trimming down of the dialogue. The Queen Mab speech appears thus, as delivered by Sulpitius:

Oh! the small Queen of Fairies
Is busy in his Brains; the Mab that comes
Drawn by a little Team of smallest Atoms
Over mens Noses as they lie asleep,
In a Chariot of an empty Hazel-nut
Made by a Joiner Squirrel: in which state
She gallops night by night through Lovers brains.
And then how wickedly they dream, all know.
Sometimes she courses o're a Courtier's Nose,
And then he dreams of begging an Estate.
Sometimes she hurries o're a Souldier's Neck,
And then dreams he of cutting forrein Throats,
Of Breaches, Ambuscado's, temper'd Blades,
Of good rich Winter-quarters, and false Musters.
Sometimes she tweaks a Poet by the Ear,
And then dreams he
Of Panegyricks, flatt'ring Dedications,
And mighty Presents from the Lord knows who,
But wakes as empty as he laid him down.

The rough Sulpitius, commander of the Marian guards, is given these and many more of Mercutio's lines, but not the airy nothings that decorate and almost hide, but do not, that fine and noble nature. There is no excuse for this mistreatment of the "prince of cats" speech:

Gran[*ius*]. Why, what is Sylla?
Sulpit[*ius*]. A most courageous Captain at a Congee:
He fights by measure, as your Artists sing,
Keeps Distance, Time, Proportion, rests his Rests,
One, two, and third in your Guts.
Oh! he's the very Butcher of a Button.

As for the critical canons, the play violates all the unities, and allows the intermingling of comic with tragic. Poetic justice is of necessity outraged. Scenes of violence abound; several of them are conducted on a large scale with a Forumful of desperate fighters. In spite of this, the incidents of the historical tragedy are dull; and the passages quoted show how completely Otway fails to recapture the Shakespearean lyrical phrasing. He has, moreover, completely ignored the element of fate, which in Shakespeare's play hangs over the star-crossed lovers throughout their course. His version of their misadventured piteous overthrows does not move us as does Shakespeare's dark but tender story of

The fearful passage of their death-marked love.

5. Crowne's The Misery of Civil War

By 1680 factional emotion in England was at a high pitch, and the two great parties were distinct and active. "Little starched Johnny Crowne" was nothing if not "loyal," though it was not to the rigidity of his politics but the stiffness of his cravats that he owed his nickname. Neither his three years' sojourn in America nor his attendance at Harvard University had liberalized his political views; there was never a more servile flatterer of royalty than the author of the following blasphemous lines from the epilogue to his court masque (produced in 1675), *Calisto, or The Chaste Nymph*, addressed to the Merry Monarch:

> You, Sir, such blessings to the World dispense,
> We scarce perceive the use of Providence.

Crowne was one of the foremost popular dramatists of his day, with half-a-dozen comedies and twice that number of tragedies to his score. Of the former his *Sir Courtly Nice* held the boards for a hundred years; it has recently been reprinted by Mr. Montague Summers in *Restoration Comedies*. His versions of *Henry VI* belong among the political dramas.

The Misery was printed in 1680; its appearance in the *Term Catalogue* indicates publication between February and May.[22] The following year it was reissued as *Henry the Sixth, the Second Part; or, The Misery of Civil War*.

The prologue points the political moral of the play:

> This Poet, (though perhaps in Colours faint)
> Those scurvy Joys does in all Postures Paint
> Fools take in pelting out each others Brains:
> A joy, for which this Nation oft takes pains.
> If any like the Ills he shews to day,
> Let them be damn'd and let them damn the Play.

Also in his prologue, Crowne denies quite disingenuously his indebtedness to Shakespeare:

> For by his [the author's] feeble Skill 'tis built alone,
> The Divine Shakespear did not lay one Stone.

This is an egregious misstatement, for Crowne's *Misery* has not the slightest claim to be considered as an independent play or even as an imitation. It is a bare-faced adaptation — its author's shameless mendacity is hard to account for.[23] The following summary of the plot indicates both Crowne's indebtedness to Shakespeare and his own inventions.

ACT I

The play begins past the middle of Shakespeare's *Second Part* (IV, vi) with the lordly Cade at London-stone, commanding the conduits. To it is annexed the portion of IV, ii, in which the rebel displays his contempt for scholarship by ordering the Clerk of Chatham to execution. The unfortunate setter of boys' copies is, however, designated merely Scrivener. To this is also added an abridged version of IV, vii, in which Lord Say is also condemned.

The scene is further protracted by an extensive arraignment by Cade of the nobility and gentry. This is original with Crowne. The rabble are more specific in their allegations than in *Henry VI;* various professions are stigmatized, and numerous atrocities are definitely projected. Finally Old Clifford appears for a reduced version of IV, viii; as in the original, the mob is easily swayed. The scene ends with young Clifford and his men, who engage the rebels. As a whole the scene is a not unskilful blending of several in *Henry VI*, though in the process of telescoping we lose the climactic and ominous effect of the original. When he uses *Henry VI*, Crowne commonly takes over the lines without serious change.

The next scene is in a tent; it corresponds to *2 Henry the Sixth*, IV, ix; the mob, however, does not come in. It begins with an alteration of the corresponding speech (by King Henry) in Shakespeare's play. I reproduce it that the reader may observe Crowne's style as an adapter:

Shakespeare: [24]

> Was euer King that ioy'd an earthly Throne,
> And could command no more content then I?
> No sooner was I crept out of my Cradle,
> But I was made a King, at nine months olde.
> Was neuer Subiect long'd to be a King,
> As I do long and wish to be a Subiect.

Crowne (Quarto 1680, p. 9):

> Never had King less joy in Throne than I,
> Nor more misfortune. Heaven was pleas'd to set
> My Cradle on the top of humane Glory,
> Where I lay helpless, open to all Storms.
> My Childish hand, not able to support
> My Fathers Sword, dropt the victorious point,
> And let fall all the Lawrels that adorn'd it,
> And French and English fell a scrambling for 'em,
> So lost I France; now am I threatned too
> By wicked Rebels, with the loss of England.
> Cade and his Rebels drive me from my City,
> Plantagenet seek's to drive me from my Kingdom.

The Cliffords now appear; the younger (not Iden) has killed Cade. A hot shot is fired at the Whigs when Young Clifford, referring to the approach of Richard of York under color of forcing ministerial changes, sententiously observes:

> The constant Vizard of Rebellion.
> Rebellion is so foul and grim a Monster,
> That those that mount the horrid Beast, are forc'd
> To cover it all o're with gaudy Trappings.
> They mark it in the Forehead with white starrs,
> Pretences Heavenly, and Innocent.

2 H. VI, IV, x, Iden's fight with Cade, is of course omitted. So is the first part of the following scene (V, i); instead, Duke Richard appears with his sons at Henry's tent. Margaret accuses him of treason, whereupon Clifford tries to arrest him. The Duke, offering his sons as bail, demands Clifford's authority. Upon the latter's reply, "In the Kings name," Plantagenet bursts out in the best style of the Restoration heavy:

> Then I'll unfold my self.
> Know hitherto I've been like a dark Cloud,
> Where scorching heat has been ingendring Thunder:
> The grumbling and the rowling you have heard,
> But now the deadly bolt shall light among you.
> I am your King.

Hen. Ha!

The fling at Richard Crookback is extended by Crowne to his elder brother Edward, whom Old Clifford taunts with his sexual irregularities. Having expounded his claim, and produced his three sons, Richard of York finally plays Warwick as his trump card. The bold Earl is also coarsened in Crowne's hands.

> *Pl*[*antagenet*]. Inform the ignorant world who is King of England,
> *War.* Whom my sword pleases.

He assures Henry, with unblushing bravado,

> Your Father warlick Henry, I confess,
> Had in desert what he did want in Title.
> But merit makes no lawful claim to Crowns,
> For if it did, I wou'd be King of England.

Once again, Crowne points his dialogue closer to his own times:

> *War.* The duke of Lancaster's no King of mine.
> *Y*[*oung*]. *Cl*[*ifford*]. Whence hast thou this? from Lawyers, and from Scriblers? . . .
> Damn thy pedantick Treason; thou art as far
> From wit as honour, and that's far enough.
> Who stopps a River's head up, drie's the stream;
> Thou hast divided thy self from thy King,
> The spring of honour, so thou hast no honour.
> But art a heap of dirty pesantry
> Fit only to manure a brave mans fortune;
> A straying Beast, with the Devil's mark upon thee,
> Rebellion, and I'll send thee to thy owner.

The scene ends with an appeal to arms. It is greatly expanded from the original, obviously in order that loyal sentiments may have full scope.

ACT II

The first scene of the second act begins with *2 H. VI*, V, ii, the killing of old Clifford by York; they come in fighting and have only four lines between them. Clifford's death is delayed till after his son's entrance, in whose arms he expires: this is a good dramatic stroke. The dialogue is chiefly from the original. Crowne continues to broaden the characterization. Edward's special weakness is twice reëmphasized:

> I must confess, I fought with more dispatch;
> 'Cause had the Battle lasted, 'twould have spoil'd
> An assignation that I have to night.
> . . . .
> I well approve this speedy March to London,
> For there to Night I hope to meet my Mistress.

The last of these excerpts is Edward's exit speech. Lady Grey is introduced at this point, rather aptly; her husband has fallen on the Lancastrian side, and she seeks him on the field. To her charms Warwick falls an immediate victim, and he woos her with a heartless plainness that disgusts her.

The next scene introduces a new element, in a typical Restoration intrigue situation. It begins with the stage direction: "Enter Edward, pulling in Lady Elianor Butler." Unlike our modern playwrights, who can drop the curtain or stop cranking the camera, the Restoration deviser of ultra-passionate scenes had for decency's sake always to arrange for a plausible exit. In this case Richard Crookback is heard off stage summoning his wayward brother.

The final scene is a reduced version of *3 H. VI*, I, i, Henry's recognition of the Duke as heir. A good touch is the introduction of Rutland; Richard bids his sons take up, if he falls, the Yorkist claims.

ACT III

The pathetic episode of Rutland's death is still further worked up by Crowne in the first scene of this act (*3 H. VI*, I, iii). The Duke takes a tender farewell of the boy, who is soon afterwards killed, as in the original. The fall of York himself (*3 H. VI*, I, iv) comes in the same scene. Crowne piles on the agony, again to good theatric advantage. Clifford fights the Duke, overcomes him, and has raised his arm to kill him when Margaret arrives and orders the rebel's life prolonged. Not content with exhibiting the crimsoned napkin, she has Rutland's body brought in, after which York is killed, as in the original.

The second scene begins with the anxiety of the Duke's sons for news of him (*3 H. VI*, II, i). Edward's apprehension is forgotten when Lady Elianor Butler appears in a riding-dress; a true heroic mistress, she has sought her princely lover in the field. The latter now has a single thought — Clerk Saunders's:

> To speak the truth, mine is a scurvy destiny,
> The Enemy is in my Father's Castle,
> And I've no Beds of Down, on Golden Bed-steads
> Under plum'd Canopies, t' embrace my Love in;
> My Destiny will be to lye to night
> On some Straw-bed, under some low thatch'd Roof,
> And thou shalt share it; what if the chil wind
> Blow on us? it will make us lye the closer;
> Or what if we shou'd lye on the cold Earth?
> It was our Grandsire Adam's Bridal Bed,
> 'Twas there he gave the start to all mankind.

In brief, the lady consents, and the amorous princeling bears her off.

We are then shown two scenes, quite unconnected with the plot, in which the miseries of civil war are vivaciously presented. The first, at a cottage, reveals a band of soldiery looting and raping. As if that were not enough to make a Whig think twice, "The Scene is drawn, and there appears Houses and Towns burning, Men and Women hang'd upon Trees, and Children on the Tops of Pikes."

Into this unpleasant landscape Richard and Warwick next thrust themselves, Edward and "a woman" looming in the offing. The last is temporarily dismissed, and Edward advances and confesses that

I've been to night a happy, but great sinner.
Starting to gallop for the Crown, my destiny
Flung in my way brighter temptations,
Than were all Atalanta's Golden Balls,
That had it cost a Kingdom and my life,
I cou'd not but have stoop'd to take 'em up.

Reproached by Richard and Warwick he asks forgiveness, but announces that he is King. Warwick threatens to go over to the Lancastrians, but is appeased by Edward's news that his activities have included the bringing up of Clarence and his troops.

Richard, as well as Warwick, has been recalcitrant and is now rebuked by Edward in a speeech which, like one I have already cited, seems written with Charles II and Shaftesbury in the mind of the loyal dramatist:

A King is a strong Tower on a high Rock,
And it is dangerous to storm him openly;
So at a mighty distance they break ground
And cast up earth, that is by subtle tricks
They raise the dirty crow'd, and behind them
They lie secure from Royal battery.
There if they find any unguarded place,
About the King, they use it most unmercifully.
My heart to beauty always lies too open,
And that infirmitie thou givest no quarter;
Though thou who censurest me, because sometimes,
I shed some vacant hours among fair Women,
Wou'dst shed the blood, or of thy Friend or King,
Or [o]f thy Father, were he now alive,
To gain a Crown, for there is thy chief Lust.

Edward easily turns the tables on his sulky associates. He reminds Warwick of the wooing of Lady Grey on the field of St. Albans, and to Richard's extreme mortification proves that paragon of chastity a hypocrite by calling in the woman with whom he had entered —

A Peasant's dirty Daughter, whom thou keep'st,
By whom thou hast a little tawny Bastard.

By this strange performance he apparently cements the loyalty of both Warwick and Gloucester, and in high spirits the Yorkists move off toward the next battlefield. I need not remind the reader that this scene is chiefly Crowne's.

ACT IV

We now pass to *3 H. VI*, II, v, Henry on the battlefield, and the episodes of the fathers and sons. We lose, thus, the fight between Richard Crookback and Clifford. Instead, the wounded Clifford comes in, but does not die (*3 H. VI*, II, vi) until he has actually heard the Yorkists' taunts. Richard mocks him bitterly, and then:

> *Geo[rge of Clarence]*. No answer? prithee swear as thou wast wont.
>
> *War[wick]*. He's dead I'm certain, if he does not swear.

Clifford obligingly responds, "Damnation on you all —" and dies; the scene ends with Warwick's commission for France and the fair Bona. The later course of Clarence is made clearer by the introduction at this point of his request for the hand of Warwick's daughter.

The next scene is Crowne's. In it Warwick returns to his wooing of Lady Grey. He gives her a month to make up her mind, swears he will have her anyway, and sets off for France. In utter abhorrence, the lady determines to seek protection of King Edward. We then have an abridged and altered version of *3 H. VI*, III, ii, in which Edward determines to marry her. True to Restoration interests, the triangle created in the preceding scenes must be further exploited. Accordingly, Crowne introduces another original scene. The solemnization of the royal marriage is ending when the forsaken Lady Elianor Butler rushes in and denounces her faithless lover. This, however, is nothing to what happens next, for Warwick, who has not been to France at all, now appears and arrests Edward.

ACT V

The fifth act opens with an adaptation of *3 H. VI*, IV, vi, the Lancastrian triumph and the appointment of Clarence and Warwick as protectors. A short scene follows (original with Crowne), showing Edward and Richard entering London in disguise. Another original scene follows. This is the double wedding of Warwick's daughters; the bridegrooms are, of course, the Prince of Wales and the Duke of Clarence. The Yorkists now break into the palace (*3 H. VI*, V, i); Clarence has never really changed sides; he has pretended loyalty to the Lancastrians in order to win Warwick's daughter.

The next scene is the field. Lady Elianor appears in man's habit, challenges Edward, and falls. Edward's next conquest is Warwick, and then we have the stabbing of the Prince (*3 H. VI*, V, v). Crowne's coarsening hand is shown again at the end of this scene, when Richard bluntly declares his intention of killing Henry.

The final scene is a delirious amplification of *3 H. VI*, V, vi, the murder of the King. To him sleeping enters the Ghost of Richard II, who naturally takes an uncomplimentary tone in describing the doomed monarch's grandfather. The Ghost's homily is pointed finally at the moral of the play:

> When e're Oh! England,
> Thou hast a mind to see thy Cities fir'd,
> Thy people slaughter'd, and thy Country desolate,
> Send all the dirty Traytours in the Kingdom
> To climb the Royal Rights, and Throne invade,
> Then a high road for vast destruction's made.

Then "the Ghost goes out and enters with soft Musick one clad in a white Robe." This gracious spirit assures the King of immortal joy, and introduces a song, sung by heavenly spirits. They vanish, and Gloucester comes in and dispatches the King. Edward next arrives and is duly horrified; and with a last, long, lingering invective against civil war the play ends:

But I believe I'm safe, England, by this time,
Has had enough of Rebels, and Usurpers. . . .

Geo[*rge of Clarence*]. That's all a Nation gets by Civil War.

Ed[*ward*]. Yes, with the Prodigal they learn, 'tis better
Obeying their Kings, the Fathers of their Country,
Than run and wast their Fortune and their Liberties,
And do the drudgeries of proud Usurpers. . . .
A Monarch's Right is an unshaken Rock,
No storms of War nor time can wear away,
And Wracks those Pirates that come there for prey.

Crowne's *Misery*, then, is a condensed adaptation of *2 Henry the Sixth*, Acts IV and V, and the whole of *3 Henry the Sixth*. Throughout the borrowed portions of his work Crowne has coarsened and broadened both plotting and characterization. Henry is weaker, Edward more voluptuous, Warwick more arrogant, Margaret more ferocious, Clarence more treacherous, Richard more shameless. On the other hand, Crowne has made some progress toward unifying the disjointed scenes of his original. He has taken pains to motivate more carefully, or at least to make motivation more apparent earlier in the play. He has seen the chance for occasional theatric or even dramatic strokes overlooked by Shakespeare, and has brought them off with a good deal of skill. And finally, he has infused the plot with love.

Samples of his diction have been quoted; it is in no way distinguished. On the other hand, it is a cut far above D'Avenant's or Tate's. If he never says a thing brilliantly, at least he never writes grotesquely.

As for the critical canons and conventions, he has paid them no heed, and we need not discuss their application to his work. All in all, his version is probably a better play structurally than his original; but in matters of diction and of characterization his changes are, for the most part, contemptible.

6. Crowne's Henry the Sixth, the First Part

In *The Misery* Crowne's virus was chiefly for the Whigs; he now announces, in dedicating to Sir Charles Sedley the Quarto of 1681,[25] that his purpose is to satirize "the most pompous fortunate and potent Folly, that ever reigned over the minds of men, called Popery." The same high mission is alluded to in his prologue:

> To day we bring old gather'd Herbs, 'tis true,
> But such as in sweet Shakespears Garden grew.
> And all his Plants immortal you esteem,
> Your Mouthes are never out of taste with him.
> Howe're to make your Appetites more keen,
> Not only oyly Words are sprinkled in;
> But what to please you gives us better hope,
> A little Vineger against the Pope.

Concerning the extent of his indebtedness to Shakespeare, Crowne is both more specific and more mendacious in this play:

> I called it in the Prologue Shakespear's Play, though he has no Title to the 40th part of it.[26] The Text I took out of his Second Part of Henry the Sixth, but as most Texts are serv'd, I left it as soon as I could. For though Shakespear be generally very delightful, he is not so always. His Volumn is all up-hill and down; Paradise was never more pleasant than some parts of it, nor Ireland [*sic*] and Greenland colder, and more uninhabitable than others. And I have undertaken to cultivate one of the most barren Places in it. The Trees are all Shrubs, and the Men Pigmies, nothing has any Spirit, or shape; the Cardinal is duller than ever Priest was. And he has hudled up the Murder of Duke Humphry, as if he had been guilty of [it] himself, and was afraid to shew how it was done: But I have been more bold, to the great displeasure of some, who are it seems ashamed of their own mysteries, for there is not a Tool us'd in the Murder of Duke Humphry in this Play, but what is taken out of their own Church Armory, nor a word put into the mouth of the Cardinal and his foolish Instruments, but what first dropt from the Heads that adorn their own Church Battlements.

Crowne's play is based on *2 Henry the Sixth*, Acts I, II, and III.[27] I shall confine my account to a summary of its plot and the citation of a few passages to illustrate Crowne's verbal changes.

ACT I

The play begins, not with Suffolk's surrender of the Queen, but with the complaints of Humphrey to the other lords (I, i). Thus the clash of the two rival personalities is not at once presented; the dropping of the paper is a good "point" that is ill omitted. The vigor and terseness of the original lines are lost in the process of expansion. Cf. *2 H. VI*, I, i, 107–112:[28]

> I Vnckle, we will keepe it, if we can:
> But now it is impossible we should.
> Suffolke, the new made Duke that rules the rost,
> Hath giuen the Dutchy of Aniou and Mayne,
> Vnto the poore King Reignier, whose large style
> Agrees not with the leannesse of his purse,

and Crowne's *Henry the Sixth, The First Part*, p. 2:

> No, 'tis not gone indeed, but all the sluces
> Are pulling up, and it is going fast.
> 'Tis pouring out apace in Provinces;
> The new made Duke of Suffolk gives whole Provinces
> To buy the King a Wife, Anjou and Maine
> Are frankly given to the Queen's poor Father
> King Regnier, whose high and flowing style
> Dwells far above the Banks of his low Purse,
> But he must have these Provinces to fill it.
> Of such low value, in this Duke's esteem,
> Is all the purchase of our Blood, that he
> Will give it all away for Blushing Cheeks.

Immediately after the conspiracy is formed against the Duke, follows without change of scene the revelation of the Duchess's ambition (I, ii). This in turn is merged with *2 H. VI*, I, iii, the scene of the petitioners. Hard upon the Queen's tirade against Eleanor, Humes [*sic*] enters and betrays her to Suffolk, and with Margaret's gratification the act ends.

ACT II

The second act begins with the council on the regency of France (*2 H. VI*, I, iii, 104 f.). As in his other adaptation, Crowne constantly broadens and coarsens character. One need not, with Professor Odell, regard Margaret as actually Hyrcanian, to feel that the strength of her personality needs no emphasis. Crowne thought otherwise; the following speech is typical of his methods:

> Is this a King that speaks? or some poor Pilgrim,
> That having lost his way, seates himself ignorantly
> Down in a Throne, and does not know 'tis one.
> And falls a Preaching to the gaping Multitude.
> Oh! What a Prince is this to sway three Kingdoms? }
> And what a Husband's this for a young Queen? } *Aside.*

Eleanor, too, must needs be more strongly characterized. And so, when the pack turn on Humphrey with their charges of extortion, the Duchess bursts out with:

> So! so! my Dress becomes a Crime of State;
> Shortly I do believe you will Arraign
> My Necklaces and Bodkins of High Treason.

After the Horner episode all go out but the Cardinal, who remains for a soliloquy, explaining his villainous purposes, and slightly reminiscent of Edmund's reflections on legitimacy. The following scene is Crowne's version, not much altered, of *2 H. VI*, I, iv, the surprisal of Eleanor and her conjuring crew.

Next comes II, i, the return from hawking and the episode of the unlucky Simpcox. Crowne here adds to his salad a dash of his boasted vinegar, for the impostor proves to be in league with the Abbot of St. Albans and a regiment of holy friars. The scene ends with a brief love passage between Suffolk and the Queen.

ACT III

The third act begins with the original II, ii, the acceptance by Salisbury and Warwick of York's claim to the throne. Next comes II, iii, the sentence of Eleanor. The fight between Horner and Peter is merely narrated; the former appears and confesses. Thus room is made for a protraction of the scene, another love passage between Suffolk and Margaret. The last scene is II, iv, the Duchess's penance.

ACT IV

The fourth act opens with Shakespeare's III, i. The expansion of the original's 92 lines (prior to Gloucester's appearance) to Crowne's 175 is characteristic of the adapter's efforts to spin out his three acts of material into a four-act play, for this is one of the rare Restoration departures from the five-act form.

Next comes, without change of scene, an original passage, the murder of Gloucester, which Crowne shows instead of narrating. The scene is a long one, and there are three and a half pages of chatter by the assassins before the crime is committed. These are devoted to more of Crowne's vinegar, for the villains are fired by religious ardor, as well as by lucre. The Cardinal himself has two conversations with them, full of unscrupulous and transparent sophistries. The hirelings finally muster up sufficient zeal to strangle the Duke in his chair, before which a curtain is then drawn.

We have next, still without change of scene, a version of III, ii, in which Suffolk brings the King the terrible news. Finally the curtain is drawn, and the corpse exhibited. The action then follows the original with the revolt of the commons and the intrusion of Warwick and Salisbury. Needless to say, the parting of Suffolk and the Queen is prolonged and made much more tender.

Finally, we have the scene in the Cardinal's bedchamber (III, iii, of *2 H. VI*). This is expanded from 33 lines to 106;

it is greatly coarsened. "The Ghost of Duke Humphry appears and goes out, the Cardinal falls into a Swoon." The Murderers now come in and add to the dying man's torments by sneering at his "Infallibility." Then the King and the rest appear for the original scene.

Last comes the Queen's reception of the news of Suffolk's death; this scene is, of course, Crowne's own, though it is suggested by *2 H. VI, IV*, iv, 1–18. A gentleman brings the bloody head, and Margaret indulges in a long and tiresome tirade. Finally the King comes in with the news of Cade's rebellion, and the play ends with the decision to flee from London.

There is still less to be said for this play than for the other. Not even a more unified structure results from Crowne's tampering. There are fewer departures from the original, which is, after all, as Professor Odell suggests, a pretty good three-act play as it stands.[29] Crowne has discarded the obvious artistic development in favor of his political aims. Surely the figure to set off against Humphrey is Suffolk; as we have seen, Crowne fails to make them clash vividly in his first scene. Again, the play should end with Suffolk's gallant death for the fair name of Margaret; instead, Crowne narrates it. He has chosen, instead of Suffolk, the Cardinal, in order that his religious animus may have full expression. To this end, also, the three wordy Murderers. So strong is the anti-Roman flavor of Crowne's dramatic salad that it was highly disrelished by the Court; Crowne tells us in his preface to *The English Friar* that the piece was finally suppressed.

7. D'Urfey's The Injured Princess, or the Fatal Wager

The versatile Tom D'Urfey's improvement of Shakespeare's *Cymbeline* was printed in quarto in 1682.[30] Several of the characters' names are changed. Posthumus becomes Ursaces; Iachimo, Shattillion; Imogene, Eugenia; Helen, Clarina.

ACT I

Omitting the laborious exposition of the two gentlemen, the play opens with Shakespeare's I, i, at the parting of Eugenia and Ursaces. The trickery of the Queen is omitted; she is frankly her stepdaughter's enemy. I, iii, follows at once, Eugenia's interview with Pisanio. D'Urfey's diction is partly his own and partly Shakespeare's. A good example of his style as an adapter is Eugenia's speech to Pisanio, *Cymbeline*, I, iii, 25–37:[31]

> I did not take my leaue of him, but had
> Most pretty things to say: Ere I could tell him
> How I would thinke on him at certaine houres,
> Such thoughts, and such: Or I could make him sweare,
> The Shees of Italy should not betray
> Mine Interest, and his Honour: or haue charg'd him
> At the sixt houre of Morne, at Noone, at Midnight,
> T' encounter me with Orisons, for then
> I am in Heauen for him: Or ere I could,
> Giue him that parting kisse, which I had set
> Betwixt two charming words, comes in my Father,
> And like the Tyrannous breathing of the North,
> Shakes all our buddes from growing.

Cf. *The Injured Princess*, p. 5:

> I did not take my leave of him, but had
> Most pretty things to say, ere I cou'd tell him
> How I would think of him at certain hours
> Such thoughts, and such — ere I could make him swear,
> The Gallian Beauties never should betray
> My Interest, or his Honour, or have charg'd him
> At the sixth hour of Morn, or Noon, or Midnight,
> To bless me with his Greeting: Or ere I could
> Give him a parting Kiss, which I had set
> Between two charming words, comes in my Father,
> And like the stubborn blast o' th' stormy North,
> Nipp'd all my Buds from blowing.

The "Shees of Italy" become "Gallian Beauties" because Ursaces goes to his friend, Beaupre, in France. Again without change of scene, Shakespeare's II, i (violently altered), follows; this is Cloten's absurd exposure of his want of wit. Nearly all the dialogue is D'Urfey's. A Jachimo appears in this scene; but he has nothing of Shakespeare's character, being merely the Prince's boon companion. Again without change of scene, there ensues a violently altered version of I, v, the Queen's determination to poison Eugenia; the Doctor does not appear, nor does Pisanio.

The second scene of D'Urfey's play is I, iv, of Shakespeare's, the "fatal wager." Its postponement was dictated by the scenic exigencies of the new stage. Ursaces's host is Beaupre; Iachimo becomes an opinionated Frenchman, Shattillion; the other member of this group is Don Michael, a Spaniard. The scene is greatly reduced.

ACT II

D'Urfey's second act begins with a scene, partly his own, partly based on I, v, in which Cymbeline and Pisanio quarrel over the merits of Ursaces. After the former leaves, the Queen treacherously assures Pisanio of her good will and summons the Doctor, who, as in the original, informs us in soliloquy that the drug is harmless.

The second scene is a version of I, vi, Eugenia's reception of Shattillion. The dialogue is coarsened, but the characterization is unchanged. Finally we have an original scene (unnumbered) between Pisanio and the Queen, who presents her enemy with a "rich Cordial." He surmises her villainy. Eugenia, likewise, comes under his suspicion; he has seen "a tall, hot-blouded, fluttering Fellow" leaving her apartment.

> I always thought her innocent,
> Pray Heaven she prove so; for if the Woman's
> Fickle Devil once seize her,

Like a huge Stone she rowls the steepy Hill,
Not to be stopp'd by Conscience, Force, or Skill.

This passage is a fair sample of D'Urfey's style.

The next scene is Shakespeare's II, ii, the bedroom scene, considerably reduced.

ACT III

The first scene of this act is not set off from the last of the one preceding. It is Shakespeare's II, iii, almost entirely altered; the talk is not of gambling, but of the Prince's appearance. The direction specifies "Flutes and a Song here." Let us hope that the most exquisite of aubades was retained by D'Urfey. Eugenia enters at once, and a condensed version of the remainder of the scene ensues. Pisanio does not appear; one of the women is sent to search for the bracelet.

The second scene takes us back to France and Ursaces's reception of Shattillion's report (*Cymbeline*, II, iv). It is considerably reduced and (like the original) is followed by the brief scene of Ursaces's despair. In D'Urfey's version the letter to Pisanio is mentioned, and we know that Ursaces has written, urging his friend to kill his wife.

Scene iii is Shakespeare's III, iii, the first appearance of Belarius and the Princes; the dialogue is somewhat altered. Upon the withdrawal of the hunters, Pisanio comes in with Eugenia, who is already in masculine attire. Pisanio has a letter in his hand, and only now learns of Eugenia's supposed inconstancy, which he credits without difficulty. This corresponds to *Cymbeline*, III, iv, but is mostly original with D'Urfey. Pisanio prepares to carry out Ursaces's command; Eugenia pleads for her life. Unconvinced of her innocence, but loath to kill her, Pisanio abandons her to her fate. He leaves, however, the Queen's cordial to sustain her.

ACT IV

The first scene of the fourth act shows us the Queen's rage when Eugenia's flight is discovered. The unfortunate Clarina, Pisanio's daughter, is charged with connivance, and is handed over to Jachimo to be taken out into the country and raped as punishment — a sweet Restoration touch! The Romans, the reader will have noticed, have not yet been introduced by D'Urfey; we now hear news of their landing at Milford Haven. Scene ii is an alteration of *Cymbeline*, III, vi, Eugenia's discovery of the cave.

Scene iii replaces Shakespeare's IV, i, in which we see Cloten in pursuit. D'Urfey concocts an original scene of highly unclassical violence. First Pisanio walks across the stage on his doubtful way back to the court. Then Cloten appears in Ursaces's clothes, along with "Jachimo dragging in Clarina in a mean Habit." Attracted by her cries, the victim's father returns. Cloten is highly pleased; he orders Jachimo to proceed before Pisanio's face. But the old hero kills the villain, though he falls down with him. Cloten nimbly disarms Pisanio and puts out his eyes; Clarina escapes, pursued by Cloten.

The fourth scene is Shakespeare's IV, ii, Cloten's appearance at the cave. It proceeds, though greatly reduced, about as the original. We learn during its course (and thus much earlier than in *Cymbeline*) of the Queen's death. The dirge is omitted.

ACT V

The first scene of the last act is an altered version of Shakespeare's V, i, Ursaces's soliloquy. It is followed by an expansion of V, ii, a certain amount of exposition being necessary, since the Romans' object has not yet been explained. Shakespeare's V, iii, is omitted; Ursaces does not revert to the Romans, but is honored by Cymbeline. Accordingly, Ursaces not being thrown into prison, Shakespeare's V, iv, with the vision, is omitted.

Instead we pass at once to the defeated Romans, and the entrance of Lucius, Shattillion, and the disguised Eugenia, who are, however, still uncaptured. This portion of the scene is D'Urfey's own. So is the part that follows; for Shattillion, disguised as a Briton, attempts to make his way through the victorious army. He meets Ursaces, who recognizes him. Shattillion clears Eugenia's name, whereupon the perplexed Ursaces challenges and kills him. Dying, he convinces his slayer of the princess's innocence. Ursaces tries to fall on his sword but is prevented by the Britons, who arrest him.

In the third and final scene Ursaces is brought before the King, in the presence of the Roman prisoners. As in the original, Eugenia reveals herself. Then follows new matter by D'Urfey. The blinded Pisanio is led in by Clarina, and the full measure of Cloten's baseness, as well as the manner of his death, is revealed. Finally, Cymbeline's sons are made known, and the general pardon is promulgated.

D'Urfey, then, follows Shakespeare's structure pretty closely. His most serious changes are the simplification (certainly at the cost of force) of the last act, and his addition of the Jachimo–Clarina–Pisanio plot.

At least one can say for D'Urfey's play that the fifth act is much more succinct than Shakespeare's. But little more can be said for it. On the other hand, Shakespeare's *Cymbeline* is not among those plays about which one feels outraged by the adapter's clumsy hand. Much of it is botchwork, and its plethora of ungainly expositions, as well as its unconscionably protracted dénouement, ill accords with those matchless songs and lyric passages with which it is so plentifully sprinkled.

8. The Fairy Queen

The prologue to the first edition of this opera (1692) [32] is of particular interest because it protests against that ancient nuisance, the presence of spectators on the stage:

But that this Play may in its Pomp appear;
Pray let our Stage from thronging Beaux be clear.
For what e're cost we're at, what e're we do,
In Scenes, Dress, Dances; yet there's many a Beau,
Will think himself a much more taking show.
How often have you curs'd these new Beau-skreens,
That stand betwixt the Audience and the Scenes?
I asked one of 'em t'other day — *Pray, Sir,*
Why d'ye the Stage before the Box prefer?
He answer'd — *Oh! there I Ogle the whole Theatre,*
My Wig — my Shape, my Leg, I there display,
They speak much finer things than I can say.
These are the Reasons why they croud the Stage;
And make the disappointed Audience rage.

The preface is a plea for the encouragement of native opera.

The Fairy Queen follows the action and dialogue of *A Midsummer Night's Dream* with reasonable faithfulness up to the third act, when the mechanicals gather in the wood.[33] The scenes are greatly reduced, but the lines are not grievously tampered with. The most serious changes are the excision of those speeches in the first scene which refer to Theseus's marriage (Hippolita does not appear in *The Fairy Queen*), the addition to the first mechanicals' scene of Bottom's remonstrances (*M. N. D.*, III, i, 8–71),[34] and the discording of the melodious lullaby (*M. N. D.*, II, ii) in favor of some new songs of little merit. The staging of this scene is of some interest.

Enter Titania, and her Train.

Tit. Take Hands, and trip it in a round,
While I Consecrate the ground.
All shall change at my Command,
All shall turn to Fairy-Land.

The Scene changes to a Prospect of Grotto's, Arbors, and delightful Walks: The Arbors are Adorn'd with all variety of Flowers, the Grotto's supported by Terms, these lead to two Arbors on either side of the Scene, of a great length, whose prospect runs toward the two Angles of the House. Between these two Arbors is the great Grotto, which is continued by several Arches, to the farther end of the House.

There are two songs, a "Composition of Instrumental Musick, in imitation of an Eccho," a "Fairy Dance," and a "Dance of the Followers of Night."

Early in the third act the most radical change occurs. For the last act the adapter had conceived something far more magnificent than the amateurish performance of Pyramus and Thisbe; and so the rehearsal in the greenwood consists of the interlude which is actually presented in Act V of *M. N. D.* Those agreeable objections of Bottom and their still happier solutions have already been added to the first Act, and so we begin at once with the Prologue, Robin Goodfellow taking up the comment originally allotted to the Athenian aristocrats. Bottom is not metamorphosed till after the rehearsal is broken up; this is accomplished, after Thisbe's death, by Robin, who rushes in among the actors.

The action then proceeds as in the original (though the dialogue is severely cut) till Oberon learns of Titania's infatuation. As in Shakespeare, Demetrius and Hermia then come in, but now they say nothing, merely crossing the stage. Again as in the original, Oberon sends Robin to find Helena; but before he can return, the adapter brings in Titania, Bottom, and the Fairies. This is really *M. N. D.*, IV, i, but instead of Bottom's varied employment of his elvish servitors Titania commands,

> prepare a Fairy Mask
> To entertain my Love; and change this place
> To my Enchanted Lake.

The Scene changes to a great Wood; a long row of large Trees on each side: A River in the middle: Two rows of lesser Trees of a different kind just on the side of the River, which meet in the middle, and make so many Arches: Two great Dragons make a Bridge over the River; their Bodies form two Arches, through which two Swans are seen in the River at a great distance.

[Enter a Troop of Fawns, Dryades and Naides.

Follows a song, excellent in its own genre, and deliciously incongruous here:

If Love's a Sweet Passion, why does it torment?

The stage direction continues:

While a Symphany's Playing, the two Swans come Swimming on through the Arches to the bank of the River, as if they would Land; there turn themselves into Fairies, and Dance; at the same time the Bridge vanishes, and the Trees that were Arch'd, raise themselves upright.

Four Savages, fright the Fairies away, and Dance an Entry.

[Enter Coridon, and Mopsa.

These pastoral personages sing a duet, and then come "A Song by a Nymph," "A Dance of Hay-Makers," and another song, after which Bully Bottom breaks the spell by demanding a peck of provender, though not, for some reason, a bottle of hay. This ends the third act of *The Fairy Queen*.

The fourth act goes back to the lovers again (*M. N. D.*, III, ii, 105 f.), and Oberon squeezes the magic juice on the sleeping Demetrius's eyes. The action then proceeds as in the remainder of Shakespeare's III, ii, though the dialogue is greatly reduced. The first 51 lines of Act IV are of course omitted, and the action continues without a break through the rest of IV, i, and the restoration of sanity to Titania. Upon her waking, another mechanical marvel is sprung:

The Scene changes to a Garden of Fountains. A Sonata plays while the Sun rises, it appears red through the Mist, as it ascends it dissipates the Vapours, and is seen in its full Lustre; then the Scene is perfectly discovered, the Fountains enrich'd with gilding, and adorn'd with Statues: The view is terminated by a Walk of Cypress Trees which lead to a delightful Bower. Before the Trees stand rows of Marble Columns, which support many Walks which rise by Stairs to the top of the House; the Stairs are adorn'd with Figures on Pedestals, and Rails; and Balasters on each side of 'em. Near the top, vast Quantities of Water break out of the Hills, and fall in mighty Cascade's to the bottom of the Scene, to feed the

Fountains which are on each side. In the middle of the Stage is a very large Fountain, where the Water rises about twelve Foot.

Then the 4 Seasons enter, with their several Attendants.

There is a song by one of the latter. Then, "A Machine appears, the Clouds break from before it, and Phoebus appears in a Chariot drawn by four Horses." After much singing, and another dance, Puck applies the herb to the sleeping lovers, and the act ends.

The fifth act begins with the entry of Theseus and his train (*M. N. D.*, IV, i, 116). The adapter was vouchsafed grace enough to preserve "My hounds are bred out of the Spartan kind" almost intact; indeed, his treatment of the text, while ruthless in excision, is commendable in its lack of verbal improvements. The action proceeds as in the original, though we do not see the play performed.

An exception to this adaptation's freedom from vandalism is the Duke's speech on Imagination:

I never could believe
These Antick Fables, nor these Fairy toys.
Lovers, and Lunaticks have pregnant brains.
They in a moment by strong fancy see
More than cool reason e're could comprehend.
The Poet, with the mad-man may be joyn'd.
He's of imagination all made up,
And see's more Devils, than all Hell can hold.
Can make a Venus of an Ethiop.
And as imagination rolls about,
He gives the airy Fantasms of his Brain,
A Local habitation, and a name.
And so these Lovers, wandring in the night,
Through unfrequented ways, brim full of fear,
How easie is a Bush suppos'd a Bear!

But this sort of tampering is infrequent.

Hard on the heels of this speech Oberon, Titania, Robin, and their train appear and address the aristocrats, the while is heard "Fairy Musick sent . . . to cure your Incredulity." The rest of the scene is new. "Juno appears in a Machine drawn by Peacocks. . . . While a Symphony Plays, the Machine moves forward, and the Peacocks spread their Tails, and fill the middle of the Theater." Juno sings, and then ascends. Next:

While the Scene is darken'd, a single Entry is danced; Then a Symphony is play'd; after that the Scene is suddainly Illuminated, and discovers a transparent Prospect of a Chinese Garden, the Architecture, the Trees, the Plants, the Fruit, the Birds, the Beasts quite different from what we have in this part of the World. It is terminated by an Arch, through which is seen other Arches with close Arbors, and a row of Trees to the end of the View. Over it is a hanging Garden, which rises by several ascents to the top of the House; it is bounded on either side with pleasant Bowers, variours Trees, and numbers of strange Birds flying in the Air, on the Top of a Platform is a Fountain, throwing up Water, which falls into a large Basin.

A Chinese Enters and Sings [in praise of the primitive].

He is soon joined by a Chinese woman, also conspicuously vocal. Together they proclaim that in perfect happiness "thus wildly we live." To demonstrate that Nature's Simple Plan is best, "Six Monkeys come from between the Trees, and Dance."

Next in order is a duet in honor of Hymen, who thereupon appears and sings. He has hardly ended when:

Six Pedestals of China-work rise from under the Stage; they support six large Vases of Porcelain, in which are six China-Orange-trees. . . . The Pedestals move toward the Front of the Stage, and the Grand Dance begins of Twenty-four Persons; then Hymen and the Two Women sing together. . . . A Chinese Man and Woman dance. . . . The Grand Cho. . . . All the Dancers join in it.

The piece is concluded by a page of dialogue between Oberon and Titania, who drop informally into Restoration idiom and present their compliments to the Wits, Critics, Sharpers, Beaux, and Cits as pertly as in any epilogue.

Embellishments of the sort I have been detailing do not

call for serious criticism. Ridicule is easy; but let not the modern playgoer cast a stone at either the pedestals of China-work or the monkey ballet. I quote from the program of *Midsummer Night's Dream* (here the alteration began with the first word of the title), as produced in the Hollywood Bowl by the Motion Picture Directors Association on October 7, 1922. (It was a play, not a motion picture.) This must have been one of the queerest adaptations in the history of the play; I make only a few excerpts from the cast of characters:

The Timarch of Athens, Marc Antony, The Rulers of the World (Assyria, Britain, Chaldea, Egypt, Greece, Hindu [*sic*], Norseland, Rome), The Great Lovers of the World (Aspaspia [*sic*], Calypso, Faustina, Helen of Troy, Salome, Sheba), the Goddesses of Olympus (Aphrodite, Diana, Isis, Juno, Lilith, Minerva, Cleopatra [*sic*]), Tom Mix and His Pony Tony.

To be sure, this is an extreme case, and even here one cannot deny that Miss Mae Murray as Aphrodite is less foreign to that magical wood near Athens than anyone could possibly be as either a Chinese vocalist or a monkey. But the difference, I submit, is in degree, and not in kind.

Notes to Chapter VIII

1. Jaggard notes editions in 1698, 1708, 1714, and 1731. (*Shakespeare Bibliography*, pp. 457 ff.)
2. *Shakespeare Jahrbuch*, ix, 41. Miss Bartlett, quite as unwarrantably, calls it "a burlesque on the *Taming of the Shrew.*" (Henrietta C. Bartlett, *Mr. William Shakespeare*, p. 79.)
3. A minute account of the plot is given by Eberhard Moosmann, *John Lacy's Sauny the Scot. Eine Bearbeitung von Shakespeare's The Taming of the Shrew aus der Restaurationzeit*, Halle, 1901. Cf. F. Weber, *Lacy's Sawny the Scot und Garrick's Catharinè and Petruchio im Verhältnis zu ihren Quellen*, Rostock, 1901. Weber finds it difficult to ascertain the exact source of Lacy's text, but concludes that it was probably either F 1 or Q 1631. He plausibly suggests that a mixture of readings may have arisen from Lacy's familiarity, as an actor, with the text, which he doubtless knew by heart (Weber, p. 16).
4. Montague Summers, *Shakespeare Adaptations*, p. xxix.
5. *N. E. D.*, *s.v.* "Sandy" and "Sawney."
6. One would like to recognize here an allusion to the shrew of the medieval Flood plays, but it seems unlikely.
7. The introduction of the coffin was doubtless suggested by the last scene (V, iv) of Fletcher's *The Woman's Prize.*
8. I speak from personal experience with this rôle.
9. Professor Odell (i, 40) states that much of Lacy's new material recurs in the farce-opera, *A Cure for a Scold*, 1735. In his *Serious Remonstrance*, Arthur Bedford makes a terrific attack on *Sauny the Scot:* "A late Comedy, call'd Sawny the Scot, is said in the Title-Page to be altered and improv'd by a Servant to his Majesty. But notwithstanding these Improvements and Alterations, it is full of most dreadful Oaths, and horrid Curses. The Name of GOD is ridiculed by a paltry Footman, almost as often as he speaks. The Alterations seem to be made In the Devil's Name, according as it is expressed in the Play itself. The pretended Reformation shews us to be ripe for utter Destruction; and he who will compare this Performance with the Original, will find it ten times more the Child of Hell than the first. But the Moral in either is good for nothing. The Original in Shakespear is free from Cursing; but it is frequently added in the other by way of Improvement. The Original doth make an Oath by a Creature the most solemn of all Oaths. It doth not jest upon Adam, Eve or Noah, or the Sacred Scriptures; neither doth it ridicule saying Grace before Meat, with the Devil's Name to it, like the late Alterations. The Original hath no praying to the Devil, no Ejaculation in his Name, and no drolling upon an Article of our Faith, like the other. Grumio in Shakespear is but once uncivil to his Mistress, which seems to be by his Master Petruchio's Order. He makes use of the Name of GOD but twice, and (these things excepted) is seldom out of Character. He argues, *Was it fit for a Servant to use*

his Master thus? But Sawny is rude and impertinent to both Master and Mistress, and indeed upon all occasions. He swears, he curses, he adjures in the Devil's Name, and ridicules the Name of GOD; he prays to the Devil, and is continually talking of him. He burlesques the Articles of our Faith, and exposes Religion. And perhaps for these Reasons he is honoured to have his Name in the Title-Page, which was omitted in the Original." (Arthur Bedford, *A Serious Remonstrance In Behalf of the Christian Religion, against The Horrid Blasphemies and Impieties which are still used in the English Play-Houses, to the great Dishonour of Almighty GOD, and in Contempt of the Statutes of this Realm. Shewing their plain Tendency to overthrow all Piety, and advance the Interest and Honour of the Devil in the World; from almost Seven Thousand Instances, taken out of the Plays of the present Century, and especially of the five last Years, in defiance of all Methods hitherto used for their Reformation*, London, 1719. See pp. 371–373.) I refrain from giving the 208 page and line references cited by Bedford in support of his accusations.

10. Downes, p. 37.
11. *Stationers' Register*, Feb. 23, 1678 (Roxburghe ed., iii, 58).
12. Oscar Beber (*Thom. Shadwell's Bearbeitung des Shakespeare'schen "Timon of Athens,"* Rostock, 1897, p. 14) concludes that Shadwell's source was F 3.
13. Beber (p. 21) thinks that the introduction of these women indicates that Shadwell went back independently to some earlier version of the story, as well as to Shakespeare. But this innovation would be the first to occur to any Restoration dramatist.
14. Professor Odell (i, 48) is wrong in stating that Alcibiades's mistresses are omitted. See Q 1678, pp. 75 f. Their names are now Phryne and Thâis.
15. Professor Odell (i, 47) thinks Timon poisons himself. The text is not clear, but I doubt if that is what Shadwell means by Timon's answer to Evandra when she urges him to take some cordial:

    "I have taken the best Cordial, Death, which now
    Kindly begins to work about my Vitals."

    See Q 1678, p. 81.
16. The Harvard copy lacks two leaves — those containing the "Address to the Reader," and the last two pages of the text of the play. The Boston Public Library's copy is in good condition. Fritz Bake (*Ravenscrofts Bearbeitung des Shakespeareschen "Titus Andronicus,"* Rostock, 1907, pp. 14, 15) fails to reach a satisfactory conclusion as to Ravenscroft's source. The Quarto of 1687 is listed in the *Term Catalogue* for Feb., 1687. (Arber's ed., ii, 188.)
17. As a matter of fact, the play is not (relatively) greatly altered.
18. Except that the excision of the Clown conforms to the principle of strict separation, this adaptation has no relation to the critical canons.
19. Willy Schramm (*Thomas Otway's "The History and Fall of Caius Marius" und Garrick's "Romeo and Juliet" in ihrem Verhältnis zu*

Shakespeare's "Romeo and Juliet" und den übrigen Quellen, Greifswald, 1898, p. 7) states that for the classical portion of his play Otway used North's Plutarch. He accepts (p. 7, n. 2) the (in my opinion untenable) theory of Ludwig Fränkel (*Zeitschrift für Vergleichende Litteraturgeschichte und Rennaissance-Litteratur*, N. F. III (1889–90), p. 184), that Otway also made use of Luigi da Porto or Bandello, or Luigi Groto. Schramm (pp. 8 f.) concludes that Otway employed either Q 4 or Q 5 of Shakespeare's play.

20. *Term Catalogue* for Nov., 1679 (Arber's ed., i, 370).
21. Schramm (p. 43) points out that the appearance of Young Marius at the tomb is unmotivated, since he has not received news of Lavinia's death before.
22. Arber's ed., i, 394. Gustav Krecke (*Die englischen Bühnenbearbeitungen von Shakespeares "King Henry the Sixth,"* Rostock, 1911, pp. 17–20) concludes that Crowne's source for both his versions was F 3.
23. It has been suggested (*e. g.*, by Dr. A. F. White, *John Crowne His Life and Dramatic Works*, Cleveland, 1922, p. 109; cf. Lounsbury, *Shakespeare as a Dramatic Artist*, p. 369) that public ignorance of Shakespeare made Crowne's deception feasible. But the critics knew Shakespeare even before 1709. Krecke (pp. 84, 85) tabulates Crowne's lines. He finds 75 derived literally from Shakespeare, and 2718 Crowne's own *or adapted*.
24. Text from *Henry VI* is quoted from the *National Shakespeare* facsimile of the First Folio. My numbering agrees with Neilson's Cambridge ed.
25. It appears in the *Term Catalogue*, Nov., 1681 (Arber's ed., i, 462), along with the reissue of *The Misery*. Gustav Krecke (*Die englischen Bühnenbearbeitungen von Shakespeares "King Henry the Sixth,"* Rostock, 1911, pp. 17–20) concludes that Crowne's source for both versions was F 3.
26. Krecke (pp. 50, 51) tabulates Crowne's original lines and those derived from Shakespeare. He finds 215 taken literally from Shakespeare, and 2649 of Crowne's own. The latter include, however, adapted lines.
27. Captain Jaggard errs in listing it under *I H. VI*.
28. Text from *Henry the Sixth* from the *National Shakespeare* facsimile of F 1. My numbering agrees with Neilson's Cambridge ed.
29. Odell, i, 64.
30. Friedrich Lücke (*Über Bearbeitungen von Shakespeares "Cymbeline,"* Doberan, 1909, p. 13) states that he is unable to decide which of the Folios D'Urfey used as his source. Q 1682 appears in the *Term Catalogue* for May and Nov., 1682 (Arber's ed., i, 485, 509).
31. My numbering agrees with Neilson's Cambridge ed. Shakespeare's text is quoted from the *National Shakespeare* facsimile of F 1.
32. *Stationers' Register*, Nov. 2, 1691 (Roxburghe ed., iii, 393).
33. Professor Marjorie H. Nicolson has very kindly collated for me the British Museum copies of Quartos 1692 and 1693. The opening scene of the second edition consists largely of the rehearsal scene of

Shakespeare, which in the first edition was partly omitted and partly combined with the actual performance of the interlude. The fairies, but not the lovers, are also introduced in Act I; more is made of the boy as the cause of the fairy rulers' quarrel. There are no further changes of importance, except the insertion of new songs in Acts III and IV.

34. My numbering agrees with Furness's New Variorum Ed., vol. x.

CHAPTER IX

MISCELLANEOUS ADAPTATIONS FROM 1700 TO 1710

1. GILDON'S MEASURE FOR MEASURE, OR BEAUTY THE BEST ADVOCATE

CHARLES GILDON, critically prominent as an apologist for Shakespeare, took a hand in the last flurry of Restoration alteration with

Measure for Measure, or Beauty the Best Advocate. As it is Acted at the Theatre in Lincolns-Inn-Fields. Written Originally by Mr. Shakespear: And now very much Alter'd; With Additions of several Entertainments of Musick. London . . . 1700.

Gildon's name does not appear on the title-page, nor is it signed to the dedicatory epistle. The adaptation has, however, long been attributed to him,[1] and there seems to be no reason to doubt his responsibility.

After complaining of the patronage given the rival company at Drury Lane, the prologue announces the source of the adapter:

> Hold; I forgot the Business of the Day;
> No more than this, We for our Selves, need say,
> 'Tis Purcels Musick, and 'tis Shakespears Play.

Yet Gildon borrowed extensively from D'Avenant's *The Law against Lovers*, though he nowhere records the fact. On the other hand, he sloughs off many of D'Avenant's changes. His principal accomplishment is the restoration of Mariana. The following summary of his structure shows the extent of his dependence on his sources, as well as the new twists he gives the plot.

ACT I

The opening lines of the play are an excellent sample of the adapter's style:

Lucio. What, Balthazar Return'd from the Wars?
Bal. Ev'n as you see, Friend Lucio, spight of Bullets
Now Mars is gon to take a Nap till Spring;
I, that hate Idleness, seek other Warfare:
Love, Love, my Lucio, Love; this Winter Season
Will find me Work; and, if there are, in Turin,
But Eyes, of any Colour, Blew, Gray, Black,
My Courage will Attack 'em.

The scene, then, remains, as in *The Law against Lovers*, not Vienna, but Turin. We learn that the Duke has gone away incognito, and that Angelo has ordered enforcement of the unpopular law. We also hear that Claudio has been arrested, and that the good Escalus has prepared an entertainment "to sweeten [Angelo's] Sour Temper." The scene is thus far a condensation of all the exposition of the original Act I, though only a portion of the dialogue is borrowed.

Angelo and Escalus now enter for a version of II, i (of both *Measure for Measure* and *The Law against Lovers*). The comic characters, however, are (with the exception of Lucio in this first scene) entirely excised, including Benedick and Beatrice, who do not appear in Gildon's adaptation at all. This scene is telescoped with a version of *Measure for Measure*, II, ii (in *The Law against Lovers* the latter part of the same scene, Folio 1673, part ii, p. 285), Isabella's first plea to Angelo. The soliloquy in which the latter reveals his lust may be compared with the corresponding passages in *Measure for Measure* and *The Law against Lovers*.

Measure for Measure, II, ii (F 1, Lee's facsimile, p. 68):

From thee: euen from thy vertue.
What's this? what's this? is this her fault, or mine?
The Tempter, or the Tempted, who sins most? ha?
Not she: nor doth she tempt: but it is I,

That, lying by the Violet in the Sunne,
Doe as the Carrion do's, not as the flowre,
Corrupt with vertuous season: Can it be,
That Modesty may more betray our Sence
Then womans lightnesse? hauing waste ground enough,
Shall we desire to raze the Sanctuary
And pitch our euils there? oh fie, fie, fie:
What dost thou? or what art thou Angelo?
Dost thou desire her fowly, for those things
That make her good? oh, let her brother liue:
Theeues for their robbery haue authority,
When Iudges steale themselues: what, doe I loue her,
That I desire to heare her speake againe?
And feast vpon her eyes? what is 't I dreame on?
Oh cunning enemy, that to catch a Saint,
With Saints dost bait thy hooke: most dangerous
Is that temptation, that doth good vs on
To sinne, in louing vertue: neuer could the Strumpet
With all her double vigor, Art, and Nature
Once stir my temper: but this vertuous Maid
Subdues me quite: Euer till now
When men were fond, I smild, and wondred how.

The Law against Lovers, II, i (D'Avenant's *Works*, Folio 1673, part ii, p. 287):

From all, but from thy virtue maid!
I love her virtue. But, temptation! O!
Thou false and cunning guide! who in disguise
Of Virtues shape lead'st us through Heaven to Hell.
No vitious Beauty could with practis'd Art
Subdue, like Virgin-innocence, my heart.

Measure for Measure, or Beauty the Best Advocate, I, i (Quarto 1700, pp. 6, 7):

From thee — ev'n from thy Virtue.
What's this I feel? Is it her fault or mine?
The Tempter, or the Tempted? Who sins most? Ha!
Not She; nor does She Tempt, but it is I,
That lying by the Violet, in the Sun,
Corrupt, like Carrion, by his friendly Beams,
But Ripen not like the Flower into Sweets.
Can Virtue win us more to Vice, than Vice?
Oh! fie! fie! fie! What dost thou Angelo?

> Is it her Virtue, that thou lov'st? oh! no!
> Thou false and deluding Guide, who in Disguise
> Of Virtues shape, leadst us thro' Heav'n to Hell!
> No Vicious Beauty cou'd with Practis'd Art,
> Subdue my Heart like Virgin Innocence.

The last of these passages is not to be commended without qualification, but at least it is better than D'Avenant's version of the speech.

At this point in *Beauty the Best Advocate* the adapter cuts loose with the first part of "The Loves of Dido and Aeneas, a Mask, in Four Musical Entertainments." This is the offering of Escalus; but, though Angelo listens patiently, his soul is not soothed, and with a (new) speech to that effect the act closes.

ACT II

The second act is located, likewise, in the palace. In scene i we have Isabella's second plea to Angelo and her rejection of his proposal (*M. for M.*, F 1, II, iv, pp. 69 f.; *L. against L.*, III, i, F 1673, part ii, pp. 290 f.). Scene ii brings the second part of Escalus's entertainment. Now the mechanical wonders are sprung: "The Spirit of the Sorceress descends to Aeneas in likeness of Mercury." "The Cave rises." "At the end of the Dance Six Furies Sinks."

Scene iii is the first outside the palace; this is a version of the expository scene at the prison between the disguised Duke and Friar Thomas (*M. for M.*, I, iv, F 1, pp. 63 f.; *L. against L.*, I, F 1673, part ii, p. 279). This is telescoped with the interview with Julietta (*M. for M.*, II, iii, F 1, pp. 68 f.; *L. against L.*, II, F 1673, part ii, p. 288). But before Julietta comes in, Claudio is introduced for an original scene in which we learn the astonishing news that the lovers were duly joined in lawful wedlock. Unfortunately the priest, Father Pierre, has returned to his native monastery in France, and the cruel Angelo refuses to wait for a letter from him.

ACT III

Next comes the scene in which Claudio, assured by the disguised Duke of certain death, learns of Angelo's proposal to his sister (*M. for M.*, III, i, F 1, pp. 71 f.; *L. against L.*, III, F 1673, part ii, pp. 297 f.). A certain amount of suspense is added to the situation because Claudio appears to vacillate, though he is really heroic, as in D'Avenant. He phrases the outburst on death as follows (Q 1700, p. 23; cf. p. 146, above):

> Oh! Sister, tis to go we know not whither;
> To lye a kneaded Clod in the dark Grave,
> And have this sensible warm motion end.
> Or rotting get another of crawling Worms;
> That springs from every part of our Corruption.
> The Spirit perhaps must bathe in fiery Floods,
> Or shiver in shrilling Regions of rib'd Ice:
> Or be imprison'd in the viewless Winds;
> And blown with restless Violence round about
> This pendant World, or if condemn'd like those
> Whom our uncertain Thoughts imagine howling.
> Oh! 'tis too horrible, and the most loath'd Life,
> That Age, or Ach, or Want, or Imprisonment
> Can lay on Nature is a Paradise,
> To what we fear of Death.

In general, Gildon's text is closer to the original than is D'Avenant's; yet he uses much of D'Avenant's diction as well as much of his own.

This interview is followed, as in both the earlier plays, by the Duke's conversation with Isabella. Gildon restores the Mariana strand of the plot, though he makes Angelo actually wedded to the deserted woman. The last scene changes to the palace again, in order to introduce part iii of the Purcell masque. At its close Isabella appears, tells Angelo she comes to urge her suit, and is ordered to follow him to another place.

ACT IV

The first scene of the fourth act is in a room of Angelo's. It is an amusing passage, for it is no other than D'Avenant's original scene (*L. against L.*, F 1673, part ii, pp. 314 f.), with the old Laureate's creaking couplets laboriously uncoupled into blank verse. The diction is practically identical — except for the rhyming words, and a certain amount of condensation. As in D'Avenant, Angelo offers jewels; but, not as in D'Avenant, Isabella accepts them — on behalf, of course, of Mariana. The scene ends with Isabella's promise to be at the Royal Grotto, and Angelo's that there shall be no light.

Scene ii is Shakespeare's IV, i, Mariana's acceptance of the Duke's scheme. It is somewhat altered, but not greatly; and "Take, oh take those lips away" is restored intact. Isabella turns over the jewels to Mariana.

Scene iii is a version of Shakespeare's IV, ii, the receipt of the treacherous order for Claudio's execution. Of course the Clown and Abhorson are excised. Gildon adds a new passage of farewell between the wedded pair.

ACT V

The fifth act is again at the palace. It begins with a version of Shakespeare's IV, iv, the reception by Angelo and Escalus of the news of the Duke's impending return. Immediately after Angelo's soliloquy, the Duke enters (Shakespeare's V, i). The action proceeds (in condensed form) as in the original, up to Mariana's accusation of Angelo. Thereupon the Duke orders the jewels exhibited and substantiates her story. In swift succession now follow the sentence and pardon of Angelo, and the appearance of Claudio and Juliet. As in Shakespeare, the Duke hints at his own marriage with Isabella. Finally, we have the fourth entertainment, with further mechanical feats.

As Professor Odell has pointed out, this version belongs to the genre of *The Fairy Queen*. The plot is reduced to its lowest terms, and room is thus made for singing, dancing, and the mechanical marvels. In comparison with the elaborate effects of *The Fairy Queen*, however, Gildon's version of *Measure for Measure* fails to thrill. The piece has the sole merit of being less violently altered from Shakespeare's comedy than was D'Avenant's version.

2. Cibber's King Richard III

Another (future) Laureate now takes the centre of the stage with the longest-lived of all the alterations of Shakespeare. On the whole, Cibber's adaptation is a fair acting version, here and there touched up with extremely effective theatrical flourishes; but it is a thing of patches, if not of shreds, for it pilfers from *1* and *3 Henry the Sixth*, *Richard the Second*, *2 Henry the Fourth*, and *Henry the Fifth*. Perhaps the most notable of Cibber's interpolations are, however, the two famous gags:

> Off with his head. So much for Buckingham,

and

> Richard's himself again.

The play was first published in quarto in 1700.[2] The dedicatory epistle is a piece of servile flattery; it is addressed to Henry Brett, the same who afterwards became involved in the fortunes of Drury Lane. There is a short preface, chiefly occupied with a complaint against the censoring of the first act, and Cibber's acknowledgment of his source.

ACT I

The first scene, "A Garden within the Tower," is expository. Stanley and Tressell describe to King Henry the battle of Tewksbury. At the end of the scene Richard appears and delivers a condensed version of the opening soliloquy of Shakespeare's play. The lines are for the most part untampered with. In an addition to this speech Richard declares his intention of seeking the crown, and that his first step "shall be on Henry's Head." The second scene is practically Shakespeare's *3 Henry the Sixth*, V, vi, the murder of Henry.[3]

ACT II

Act II begins with an interview at St. Paul's between Tressell and Stanley, introducing Richard's designs on Anne. Then comes the funeral of Henry (I, ii). Anne's first speech shows the unreliability of Cibber's declaration that he has italicized borrowed passages. It consists of the first five lines of Shakespeare's *1 Henry the Sixth*, I, i, almost *literatim;* but Cibber, instead of italicizing, has used the inverted comma, indicating his own phrasing of Shakespeare's thought.

The action proceeds as in Shakespeare's play, but with many new passages. Anne is more easily won; and indeed Richard himself is more romantic. His reservation, "not all so much for love," Cibber omits. Clarence does not appear in Cibber's version; nor does Margaret, or Hastings.

Passing over several scenes, Cibber next goes to the mourning for Edward (II, ii); the dialogue is mostly new. Richard's soliloquy (after Buckingham's exit) is an amusing sample of Cibber's tragic vein:

> Thus far we run before the wind — Let me see,
> The Prince will soon be here — let him — the Crown!
> O yes! he shall have twenty, Globes, and Scepters too
> New ones made to play withall — But no Coronation!
> No! nor no Court flies about him, no Kinsmen —
> — Hold ye! — where shall he keep his Court! —
> — Ay! — the Tower.

ACT III

We now pass to the entry of the young Prince Edward, in a scene (III, i) of which less than a third of the lines are Shakespeare's. The next five of Shakespeare's scenes are omitted; in their stead we have an original scene between Richard and Anne. The latter laments her marriage and pauses to hear a song intended to soothe her. She then delivers a nutshell version of Henry the Fourth's great soliloquy on sleep. Now comes Richard, and we learn that his loves are not wholly political but in part romantic:

CIBBER AS LORD FOPPINGTON

Ap[illegible]l the 24 : 1714

To the Child [illegible] Richard the Third

five Shillings

B. Booth

Cibber

Rob Wilks

MRS. SMITH'S BILL

Ha! still in tears; let 'em flow on; they're signs
Of a substantial grief — Why don't she die?
She must; My Interest will not let her live.
The fair Elizabeth has caught my Eye,
My Heart's vacant; and she shall fill her place.

The ill-mated couple exchange regrets and recriminations. Then follows a fairly faithful version of Shakespeare's III, vii, the citizens' offer of the crown to the hypocritical Protector.

ACT IV

The fourth act opens with a version of Shakespeare's IV, i. The two princes are present, as well as Elizabeth, the Duchess of York, and Anne, besides Stanley, who brings the news that Anne is now Queen. An effective stroke is the tearing of the children from their mother.

The scene then changes to the Presence and we have a version of IV, ii, the check to Buckingham. Shakespeare's following scene, Richard's meeting with the queens, is postponed; instead we have the murder of the princes actually represented. Their childish terror is prolonged by their waking before the murderers enter.[4] Then follows a very short version of the meeting of Richard with Queen Elizabeth and the Duchess of York, Margaret of course being omitted. It is perhaps worth noting that the most famous line of this scene, Cibber's interpolation,

Off with his head. So much for Buckingham,

is italicized by Cibber as borrowed from Shakespeare. Does this mean that the gag was already on the stage before his time?

ACT V

Shakespeare's scene i, the last moments of Buckingham, is omitted. Instead, we begin with the pitching of the rival camps on Bosworth Field. Next comes the appearance of the ghosts, but only those of Henry VI, the little princes, and

Anne; they address Richard alone, Richmond's tent not being shown. The action proceeds as in Shakespeare, with the dialogue greatly altered and reduced. Richmond's oration is whittled down and otherwise mangled. A portion of Henry the Fifth's great harangue beginning,

> Once more into the breach, dear friends, once more,

is put into the mouth of the future Henry VII. Richard's address is also shortened and mangled. The dialogue throughout the battle scenes is chiefly Cibber's.

In general, the reader will have noticed that Cibber has omitted scenes in which Richard does not appear, and has keyed up the central figure. On the other hand, the character lacks the intellectual malignity of Shakespeare's — he even succumbs to love. The adapter's intention is evidently to exhibit him as a complete monster — hence the quite unnecessary scene in which he coolly tells Anne that he no longer loves her. The cast of characters is greatly reduced, and the number of scenes is also curtailed. In these respects Cibber's version is an improvement. Yet, even if we can do without Clarence and Stanley, we cannot spare the terrible figure of Margaret. Worst of all is the dialogue: Cibber was not a tragedian, and his attempts to write outside the borders of comedy are as absurd as some of his contemporaries found his acting when it strayed beyond them.

3. Granville's The Jew of Venice

George Granville, first Baron Lansdowne, was a successful, though not a prolific, dramatist. *The She-Gallants*, a comedy, and *Heroic Love*, a tragedy, were both popular and esteemed by critics. So was *The Jew of Venice*, produced shortly before its author went into political life. To him John Dennis dedicated his essay on Shakespeare in the following terms:

For to whom can an Essay upon the Genius and Writings of Shakespear be so properly address'd, as to him who best understands Shakespear, and who has most improv'd him.[5]

Granville's adaptation appeared in quarto in 1701.[6] In an "Advertisement to the Reader" the author apologizes for undertaking it:

The Foundation of the following Comedy being liable to some Objections, it may be wonder'd that any one should make Choice of it to bestow so much Labour upon: But the judicious Reader will observe so many Manly and Moral Graces in the Characters and Sentiments, that he may excuse the Story, for the Sake of the Ornamental Parts. Undertakings of this kind are justify'd by the Examples of those Great Men who have employ'd their Endeavours the same Way. . . . The Reader may please moreover to take Noti[c]e, (that nothing may be imputed to Shakespear which may seem unworthy of him) that such Lines as appear to be markt, are Lines added, to make good the Connexion where there was a necessity to leave out; in which all imaginable Care has been taken to imitate the same fashion of Period, and turn of Stile and Thought with the Original. What other Alterations have been requisite as to the change of Words, or single Lines, the Conduct of Incidents, and Method of Action throughout the whole Piece, to bring it into the Form and Compass of a Play, would be superfluous to examin, every Reader being able to satisfy himself, if he thinks fit, by comparing.

Granville's remarks, it occurs to me, strengthen the contention which I have elsewhere maintained,[7] that *The Merchant of Venice* probably dropped out of the theatrical repertory not many years after its original production, and was almost certainly not acted on the Restoration stage.

In the prologue, a dull piece written by "Bevill Higgons, Esq.," a kinsman of Granville's, "The Ghosts of Shakespear and Dryden arise Crown'd with Lawrel," complimenting each other profusely. Shakespeare is constrained to say:

These Scenes in their rough Native Dress were mine;
But now improv'd with nobler Lustre shine;

The first rude Sketches Shakespear's Pencil drew,
But all the shining Master-stroaks are new.
This play, ye Criticks, shall your Fury stand,
Adorn'd and rescu'd by a faultless Hand.

Dryden's shade concludes with a clumsy reference to his own attempts to improve Shakespeare, a complaint that when alive he starved, and a plea to

Indulge the Pledges I have left behind.

For Granville devoted the receipts to the needs of Dryden's son.

The cast of characters is greatly reduced, only nine being named. In printing his text, Granville indicates the new lines by inverted commas, though many of those unmarked are grievously tampered with.

ACT I

The play begins at Shakespeare's I, i, 86,[8] as follows:

Anto. I Hold the World, but as a Stage, Gratiano,
Where every Man must play some certain Part,
And mine's a serious one.

The exposition continues much as in the original, but the adapter's hand plays havoc with the beautiful speeches of Bassanio and Antonio. That matchless passage in which Portia's name is first mentioned is thus rendered by the impudent improver:

Then briefly thus. In Belmont is a Lady
Immensly rich, and yet more fair than rich.
And vertuous as she's fair; sometimes from her Eyes
I have receiv'd kind speechless Messages.
Her Name is Portia: you have heard her Fame,
From the Four Corners of the World; the Winds
Blow in, from every Coast, adoring Crowds;
The watry Kingdom, whose ambitious Head
Spets in the Face of Heaven, is no Bar
To aemulous Love, as o're a Brook they come
To Anchor at her Heart: Her Sunny Locks
Hang on her Temples, like a golden Fleece,

> For which these many Jason's sayl in Quest.
> O my Antonio, had I but the Means
> To hold a Rival-Place with one of 'em.

As outrageous garbling, this, as any we have met with since the days of Tate's activity.

As in the original, the scene changes to Belmont, and we have a mangled version of I, ii. The German suitor is turned into "Myn Heer van Gutts, the Dutchman," by way of compliment to the contemporary rival. There is no reference to Bassanio.

Still following Shakespeare, we have next a version of I, iii, Shylock's first scene. While far from intact, his lines are less tampered with than those of the first two scenes.

ACT II

Granville's second act begins with Shakespeare's II, v, 14, Shylock's departure for his appointment with Bassanio. Morocco and the two Gobbos are entirely omitted in this version. Next come scenes v and vi, the elopement. The first four scenes of this act were cut to make room for a new one: "Scene opens, and discovers Bassanio, Antonio, Shylock, and others, sitting, as at an Entertainment. Musick playing: During the Musick, Gratiano enters, and takes his place."

The scene, happily, is brief; it consist of a series of healths. The first is to friendship; this is Antonio's. Then Bassanio gives Portia. Gratiano follows:

> Mine's a short Health: Here's to the Sex in general;
> To Woman; be she black, or brown, or fair;
> Plump, slender, tall, or middle-statur'd —
> Let it be Woman; and 'tis all I ask.

Whereupon Shylock:

> I have a Mistress, that outshines 'em all —
> Commanding yours — and yours tho' the whole Sex:
> O may her Charms encrease and multiply;
> My Money is my Mistress! Here's to
> Interest upon Interest.

Antonio demurs, commanding that no music shall play to grace this sordid toast. He adds that music always makes him sad. This affords Bassanio an excuse for a practically unaltered version of Lorenzo's speech on music (V, i, 80 f.). On which persuasion we are to suppose that Antonio consents to see the masque that follows.

This is entitled *Peleus and Thetis.* [9] Curiously enough, no mechanical marvels are provided, nor is there dancing; it is chiefly a musical affair. Upon its termination Bassanio takes a tender farewell of Antonio.

ACT III

We now pass directly to Shakespeare's III, ii, the winning of Portia. We thus lose the scenes which prepare us for Antonio's letter to Bassanio and, what is more important, make Shylock the superb creation that he is.

The next scene is III, iii, Antonio in the Jailor's charge, without, however, Salanio, who like Salarino does not appear in Granville's version. Two of the great speeches from Shakespeare's III, i, those beginning, "To bait fish withal," and "Why there, there, there, there, a diamond gone," are here introduced, (comparatively) little tampered with.

ACT IV

As in Shakespeare, the fourth act is the trial. Again Shylock's speeches, while reduced, are almost free from garbling. Bassanio's part is fattened at the expense of Gratiano, who loses the speech beginning, "O be thou damn'd." On the other hand, the "quality of mercy" speech is both reduced and mangled. A slight alteration in the action is introduced: as the Jew is about to execute the bond, Bassanio draws to protect his friend; the Duke angrily orders his arrest, when Portia shows her hand. The rest of the scene proceeds as in the original.

ACT V

The fifth act, though verbally garbled, and greatly reduced, follows the action of the original.

A deal of ink has flowed about the question of this Jew of Granville's. In the first place, let it be understood that the adapter has not altered Shylock's character. And his diction, though reduced in quantity, is otherwise almost intact. Even in the new scene, when Shylock offers his toast to money, there is nothing out of harmony with the character as drawn by Shakespeare, especially since Shylock has drunk at least three toasts before offering his own. There is, then, no warrant for condemning Granville (as some have done) for writing Shylock down.

Granville's *Jew* cannot, therefore, be cited as proof positive that the stage tradition was a farcical Shylock. He appears in this version only four times — when the bargain is struck, at Bassanio's feast, with the Jailor, and at the trial; but he is essentially unchanged in character. Nor does the mere assignment of the rôle to the comedian Dogget indicate anything more than that the performance was not tragic. Which is in fact all Rowe's reference in 1709 implies.[10] The Restoration comedians, *teste* Cibber, knew how to achieve that mingling of pathos with humor which the severer of the historical critics seem reluctant to recognize in the old theatres. Dogget was what we should call to-day a character actor; he may have played Shylock as a comic spectacle — I hope he did. But there is no evidence that he caricatured him. And even if there were, let me reiterate that the absence of any record of performance for the hundred years previous would nullify any effort to use the Granville *Jew* as evidence concerning Elizabethan interpretation of the rôle.

In general, Granville's play is contemptible enough. The interpolated masque is absurd; it was the merest pandering to a ridiculous fashion of the moment. On the other hand, the number of transitions from Venice to Belmont has been reduced, though at the cost of much excision of *dramatis personae*. To sum up, the version is a rude sketch of the main structure of *The Merchant of Venice*, chiefly clothed, except for Shylock's speeches, in abominably garbled dialogue.

4. Dennis's The Comical Gallant, or The Amours of Sir John Falstaff

Like *Beauty the Best Advocate*, *The Comical Gallant* was the work of a well-known critic. Like Gildon, too, Dennis was one of Shakespeare's defenders. His play failed on the stage and appeared in the same year (1702) in quarto, with a dedicatory epistle to Granville accounting for the current "Taste, in Poetry, and the Causes of the Degeneracy of it."

Dennis tells us that his intention of altering *The Merry Wives* was received in two ways: one party considered the original incapable of improvement, the other thought it "so despicable" as to be unworthy of Dennis's attention. Against the latter view the adapter argues (1) that the play pleased Elizabeth and "was written at her Command, and by her direction, and she was so eager to see it Acted, that she commanded it to be finished in fourteen days; and was afterwards, as Tradition tells us, very well pleas'd at the Representation"; (2) that the wits of Charles II's time admired *The Merry Wives;* (3) that

> after so long an acquaintance as I had with the best Comick Poets, among the Antients and Moderns, I might depend in some measure upon my own Judgment, and I thought I found here three or four extraordinary Characters, that were exactly drawn, and truly Comical; and that I saw besides in it some as happy touches as ever were in Comedy: Besides I had observed what success the Character of Falstaffe had had, in the first part of Harry the Fourth. And as the Falstaffe in the Merry Wives is certainly superiour to that of the second part of Harry the Fourth, so it can hardly be said to be inferior to that of the first.

For in the second part of Harry the Fourth, Falstaffe does nothing but talk, as indeed he does nothing else in the third and fourth Acts of the first part. Whereas in the Merry Wives, he every where Acts, and that Action is more Regular, and more in compass than it is in the first part of Harry the Fourth. 'Tis true, what he says in Harry the Fourth is admirable; but action at last is the business of the Stage. . . .

Dennis next gives his reasons for thinking *The Merry Wives* open to improvement: (1) the speed at which it was written; (2) its little success on the stage in Charles II's time, Slender by Wintersell being the only real hit; (3) specific faults in the play. These he finds to be the lack of unified action, there being three plots, several superfluous scenes, and a style often "forced and affected, whereas the Dialogue in Comedy ought to be as free as the air." In his alteration he has "endeavoured to Correct the foresaid Errours."

I have made everything Instrumental to Fenton's Marriage, and the whole to depend on one common Center, which I believe was hardly in the power of every Writer to perform.[11] I have added to some of the parts in order to heighten the Characters, and make them show the better. I have above all things endeavoured to make the Dialogue as easie and free as I could. For in Comedy, which is an Image of common Life, every thing which is forc'd is abominable. In short, I have alter'd every thing which I dislik'd, and retain'd every thing which I or my Friends approved of, excepting something of Justice Shallow in the first Scene of the Play, which I omitted for two Reasons, the one was because I could not bring it into the same design with the rest, the second because I knew nobody who would be capable of Acting that Character, unless those who would be otherwise employed.

Dennis's next paragraph is even more confident:

Thus, Sir, I have endeavoured to convey two things by you to the General Reader, the one, that this Comedy is not so Despicable as to be Incapable of Improvement; the other, that it is not so admirable, as not to stand in need of any. Whether, Sir, I have improv'd it or no I leave it to you to determine, whether the Scene between the Wives in the first Act be altered for the better or the worse, whether that between Falstaffe and Ford in the second Act is aptly contriv'd to give occasion to an excellent Actor to show himself; whether that between Falstaffe and the Wives in the third Act be wholly without art, and whether that between Falstaffe and Ford in the fourth Act, may be said to be truly Comical.

The adapter next passes, by way of finding fault with the player who acted Falstaff, to a consideration of the two general objections to the piece: that the characters are low, and that they are obsolete. Disposing of these cavils, he takes up objections to specific scenes; these we shall recur to at the proper time. Finally, he launches into a jeremiad on the cause of contemporary degeneracy. It is not so clear from his remarks that Dennis was an intelligent critic as that the failure of his play had got under his skin.

The following summary of the plot shows the nature of his alterations. The play, it should be noted, is wholly in prose.

ACT I

The version begins with an original scene between Fenton and mine Host of the Garter, who is completely in his confidence. The dialogue is expository and sets before the audience the triple suit for Anne Page. The latter soon appears. A few lines of the dialogue at this point exhibit its general character:

Fent. Can I then have the happiness to see you at last, unkind Mrs. Page!

Mrs. P. Well! Are you not the most ungrateful Man upon Earth, to upbraid me with unkindness, when I do and suffer so much for you? Have not both my Parents forbid me the very sight of you, upon pain of their mortal displeasure. And is it a small proof of my esteem for you, that I give you, in disobeying their orders?

Fent. But have I not a greater right to you than either of your Parents can claim? Are you not mine by a Sacred Vow that was solemnly made, both in the Face of Earth and of Heav'n.

Mrs. A. The thought of that Vow distracts me.

It is hardly necessary to quote more of this "easy and free" dialogue to convince the reader that Dennis did not improve his original. Fenton informs Anne that he has prevailed on the Host of the Garter to persuade Falstaff that Mmes. Page and Ford are in love with him; he has also bribed two of the fat knight's men to acquaint the two husbands of their master's intentions. By this intrigue Fenton hopes to create a sufficient disturbance to enable him to elope with Anne.

A version of I, i, follows, the arrival of Shallow, Slender, Evans, and Simple. The scene is greatly reduced, and the dialogue frightfully mutilated. Next come Falstaff, Pistol, and Nym, not, however, for the quarrel with Shallow, which is not mentioned; instead we have a version of I, iii, the discharge of the henchmen. A brief scene follows in which the Host incites Dr. Caius to fight Sir Hugh, and then comes Dennis's version of II, i, the first scene between the Wives. As in the original, this is followed by Pistol's and Nym's betrayal.

ACT II

The second act begins with II, iii. So far the scene has not changed from Windsor Park. We next go to the Garter for a version of II, ii, Falstaff's first interview with "Master Broom." It is interrupted, not preceded, by the invitation of Mrs. Ford; the messenger is not Dame Quickly but Mrs. Dorothy Tearsheet. The whole scene is greatly coarsened. Falstaff mistakes Ford's jealous transports, and thinks to please him by whetting his appetite; the dialogue is unquotable. The scene now changes to the Park, where the trembling Evans awaits his enemy. This scene is considerably reduced.

ACT III

The third act opens with Shakespeare's III, iii, Falstaff's first call on Mrs. Ford. The place of meeting is the Bull Inn, kept by Mrs. Ford's brother. Mrs. Page is not present when the scene opens. As in the original, she furnishes the interruption — but with a difference! For she appears disguised as "Captain Dingboy." With Falstaff behind a screen, this jaunty cavalier makes impudent love to Mrs. Ford, and, the fat knight's name being mentioned, mocks at him, and ascribes two scandalous affairs to him. These are too gross for Sir John, who whips out from behind the screen and is about to chastise the stripling when a servant dressed like a soldier arrives to tell the Captain of the death of an officer he has pistolled. Discovery of the supposed Captain's valor cools Falstaff's ardor at once. The fiery officer consents to spare Sir John's life only in case he agrees to stand sentry while Mrs. Ford retires to her chamber with the conqueror. Falstaff gladly consents.

Next comes the return of Ford, and the action proceeds as in the original, except that, after the servants have gone off with the basket, Mrs. Page, still as the Captain, and aided by her disguised servants, beats Ford. The latter, getting away from the servants who have been holding him, rushes at her; her peruke falls off, and she runs out, discovered.

ACT IV

The fourth act begins with a short scene in which the Host of the Bull tells Ford that Sir John was actually in the house. Then follows Dennis's version of III, v. It is typical of the clumsiness with which he has put his adaptation together that, although Ford knows that the Captain was only Mrs. Page, Dennis attempts to extract more humor from the situation by making him believe, for a while, Falstaff's story of his wife's infidelity with that officer. In the following scene the Host sets him right. As a device for resolving Ford's doubts the Host suggests anticipating Falstaff's appearance at Herne's Oak, for this is the next rendezvous, the second visit to Mrs. Ford being omitted.

In an interview between Fenton and Anne, we now learn that the former has contrived the whole affair; he has persuaded his aunt, Mrs. Ford, to induce Mrs. Page to grant another interview. He now advises Anne, most tediously, concerning the plans of her mother and her father, and his own plan for circumventing them. Here is a sample of their love-making:

Fent. Can't you guess?
Mrs. A. Not I really.
Fent. Why before morning you are to have me in your Arms.
Mrs. A. Why you have been drinking, Mr. Fenton.
Fent. Not a drop.

Next comes Slender's wooing; all this is an adaptation of Shakespeare's III, iv.

ACT V

The last act begins with IV, iv, greatly reduced and altered. Ford, of course, is not present. This scene is telescoped with V, ii, iii, and v, as the various parties converge on Herne's Oak. Though we have been led to expect Ford, it is Falstaff who appears as Herne. The first intimation that all is not well is a "Terrible Symph." As Falstaff runs out, maskers rush in and chase him; they return, not with Falstaff, but with Ford, disguised like him. It is Ford, then, who endures the pinches of the fairies, and hears the terrible symphony as well as a song in two stanzas and two choruses.

Finally the Host brings in Falstaff, who proceeds to lecture Ford on the folly of his jealousy. The frantic husband now professes that the beating has cured his mind. Falstaff, however, comes in for the rebuke of Sir Hugh (text: "Caius") and the mockery of all. The unravelling of Anne's elopement is inordinately spun out; it is enlivened by a fight between Slender and Dr. Caius. We learn that the lovers are not yet married; they frankly ask the consent of Anne's parents. The Fords promise a settlement on Fenton, and all ends happily.

As I hope the reader is by this time convinced, Dennis's version is a contemptible compound of farce and smut. That its author thought well enough of it to dignify it with a preface examining the causes of degeneracy in poetical taste is not creditable to his critical faculty. But after all, the play died immediately; and if anyone but the adapter mourned, I have not seen the record of his sorrow.

5. Burnaby's Love Betrayed, or The Agreeable Disappointment

The last alteration of Shakespeare for many years was this play of Burnaby's, based on *Twelfth Night*.[12] It was published in quarto in 1703. In his preface Burnaby admits the appropriation of "Part of the Tale of this Play . . . and about Fifty Lines." The latter he marks with inverted commas.

ACT I

Villaretta denies suitors, even the Duke of Venice; though, unlike Olivia, she is not unhappy. Most of the play is prose. A fair sample of Burnaby's blank verse is the first speech of Moreno, the Duke:

> Madam, I come to prove Moreno's Fate:
> This Day has been propitious to our Race;
> My Father on it triumph'd o'er the Turks,
> And gain'd the lost Morea to the State.
> Moreno's Fortune may be great as his,
> If Heaven and Villaretta will be kind.

Burnaby is no more inspired in prose; witness the following lines of Drances, an unfortunate substitute for Sir Toby:

> Ha! ha! my Kinswoman and I, you must know, divide the House; all under-ground is mine; the whole Region of Mirth and Claret. I can't look upward without a Trespass — Ha! ha! I happened to whisper her House-maid, that I had fallen in love with one Morning at Prayers, and she sent her to the Devil immediately, for I never saw her after.

Drances is friendly to the Duke's suit. In order to "beat down" his kinswoman's pride, he has told the Butler (Malvolio–Aguecheek) of Villaretta's supposed infatuation.

The second scene is at the Duke's. The disguised Viola, in a clumsy scene of exposition with Laura, her servant, informs us that she appears thus, as the page Caesario, for love of the Duke, whom she saw in France two years ago. None of the dialogue in this act is taken from Shakespeare.

ACT II

"Scene opens, and discovers Moreno on a Couch, and Caesario kneeling by." The exquisite lyrics of the original did not suit with Burnaby's mood; he introduces two conventional quatrains of complaint against Orinda. The three lines beginning,

> If music be the food of love, play on,

now follow, introducing a version of Shakespeare's II, iv. The scene is not long: after Moreno's opening speech Caesario's confession follows almost at once. Only seven of Shakespeare's lines are employed.

The scene now changes to Villaretta's. Dromia is introduced, a coquettish old lady who is calling on Villaretta. We next have a version of I, v, almost wholly in original dialogue.

The next scene is on "the Ryalto" (III, iii). Sebastian, following his sister in another ship, saw her vessel sink, as he supposed, shortly before his own foundered. He was picked up by Rodoregue (Antonio). A new character is Pedro, Sebastian's clownish servant. Next comes a brief version of II, ii, in which a footman, not the butler, brings Caesario the ring.

ACT III

The third act opens with an original scene corresponding to *Twelfth Night*, II, v, in which, for the edification of Dromia and Emilia, Villaretta's woman, who are hidden behind a screen, Drances further beugiles the fatuous butler, Taquilet. Caesario comes in and, much against the butler's will, is received by his lady. Then follows a scene corresponding to the latter part of Shakespeare's III, i, in which the supposed page denies the lady his love. Next comes a short passage between Villaretta and Emilia, with a song by the latter; and then we have Burnaby's version of part of III, iv, the attack on Caesario. Drances instigates the jealous Taquilet to challenge his rival; Caesario draws on the butler, who flees. As Drances draws in his turn, Rodoregue appears, like Antonio, rescues her, and is arrested, as in the original. Next comes a new scene, in which Laura tells Caesario that Villaretta has sent for the Duke's physician; Caesario decides to impersonate him, in order to learn for certain whether she is really averse to the Duke.

ACT IV

An original scene opens the fourth act; Villaretta, feigning illness, receives the disguised "Caesario," who learns that she really loves "him." The scene now changes to the Rialto (IV, i). "Villaretta's Footman," in lieu of the accomplished Feste, summons Sebastian, who is set upon by Drances and Taquilet, and found by Villaretta, as in *Twelfth Night*. Pedro remains on for a few moments, during which he attempts to court Emilia, but is repulsed. Next comes a short original scene between Caesario and the Duke, who promises to free Rodoregue. The final scene is Shakespeare's IV, iii, Sebastian's acceptance of Villaretta's proposal.

ACT V

The last act begins in most exciting fashion. "Enter several running over the Stage, crying out stop Thief — After which, Enter Rodoregue," who has escaped but is recaptured by some soldiers. The Duke now appears with Caesario, whom Rodoregue persists in mistaking for Sebastian. Villaretta comes in, and proclaims her love for Caesario, whom the Duke thereupon "Offers to Stab. . . . Vill. steps between, and Laura Enters and holds his Arm," and tells him that Caesario is a woman.

Finally the Priest and Sebastian come in, the mystery is solved, and the play ends with a masque, which is not printed.

On the whole, this version is perhaps the dullest of all the alterations we have considered. The dialogue is almost wholly new, and quite undistinguished. The character of Viola is not altered, nor is the Duke's. But Drances is no Sir Toby; nor can Taquilet pass muster for either Malvolio or Sir Andrew. The deception is a mere episode and is left unfinished, the whole interest of the fifth act being the pairing off of the lovers. Thus the last of the alterations, like the first, is typical of the Restoration versions in its exaltation of love to heights untouched by the original author. If Shakespeare seems in the age of Shaw distressingly romantic, he is almost frigidly chaste in comparison with the adapters of the final decade of our study.

Notes to Chapter IX

1. *E. g., Biographia Dramatica* (ed. 1812), I (i), 277.
2. *Term Catalogue*, Feb., 1700 (Arber's ed., iii, 173). Richard Dohse (*Colley Cibbers Bühnenbearbeitung von Shakespeares Richard III*, Bonn, 1897) thinks that Cibber chiefly used the Folios text, but that he must have seen the Quartos as well, since he uses passages not in the Folios.
3. For a more detailed account, including specific references to sources, see the monograph of Alice I. Perry Wood, *The Stage History of Shakespeare's King Richard the Third*, pp. 76–100. There is, however, no reason to suppose that Cibber went back to the Chronicles.
4. Dr. A. C. Sprague (*Mod. Lang. Notes*, xlii, 29–32) has found that in later editions this scene is omitted.
5. John Dennis, *An Essay on the Genius and Writings of Shakespear* (1712), sig. A 3 *verso.*
6. On June 17 (Nicoll, *Early 18th Century Drama*, p. 333). It was several times reprinted. See Jaggard, p. 394. Otto Burmeister (*Nachdichtungen und Bühneneinrichtungen von Shakespeare's Merchant of Venice*, Rostock, 1902, p. 19) is inclined to think that Granville's source was Quarto 2. I have not collated exhaustively, but I have reason to believe the source was probably F 4.
7. In "Shylock and the Historical Method," a paper read at the 1926 meeting of the Modern Language Association of America. The Jordan ballad, often cited, has no relation to the stage.
8. My numbering agrees with Furness's New Variorum Ed.
9. It was omitted in later revivals of this play. (Odell, i, 79.)
10. "But tho' we have seen that Play Receiv'd and Acted as a Comedy, and the Part of the Jew perform'd by an excellent Comedian, yet I cannot but think it was design'd Tragically by the Author." (Cited by Furness, *The Merchant of Venice*, New Variorum Ed., p. 421.)
11. And so he has, but his connecting links are far-fetched and unconvincing.
12. Vincke (*Shakespeare Jahrbuch*, vol. ix) fails to give this play in his bibliography of the alterations. Jaggard (p. 281) lists Burnaby's version under *All's Well* as based partly on that play and partly on *Twelfth Night*. With Odell (i, 83), I am unable to find traces of *All's Well*.

CHAPTER X

UNALTERED QUARTOS

1. The Players' Quartos of Othello

THE popularity of *Othello* with readers is attested by its frequent appearance in quarto up to the date of Rowe's edition (1709). The last pre-Restoration issue was the Third Quarto (1655), a rather poor reprint of the Second (1630), though it contains some corrections from the Folios. According to Mr. Jaggard, editions appeared between 1660 and 1710 as follows: 1670, 1674, 1681, 1687, 1695, 1697, 1701, 1705. Of these I have examined four, the Quartos of 1681, 1687, 1695, and 1705. The others may have existed, but it seems unlikely. Mr. Jaggard follows Lowndes in listing editions in 1670, 1674, 1697, and 1701 altered or edited by Dryden; but neither of these bibliographers gives his authority. The catalogues of the British Museum and the Boston Public Library do not mention these editions.[1] The Quartos of 1687, 1695, and 1705 are reprints of Quarto 1681, the only changes being minor errors and occasional corrections of misprints.

This version is not an alteration.[2] It is a fair text, based, as I shall show, on the Second Quarto (1630). The following examples will serve to exhibit typical variants.[3] The majority are palpably misprints. The numbering of my citations agrees with that of the New Variorum Edition (vol. vi) of Dr. Furness, whose notes of variant readings of the Folios and of the pre-Restoration Quartos I have employed. I have, however, collated the Second Quarto (1630) independently. In each case the passage first quoted gives the text as it appears in Quarto 1681, after which the significant variants are given.

I, ii, 38: "*Janus* I think no." For: "By *Ianus*."

II, i, 100: "Hail to *the* Lady." For: "thee."

II, i, 345: "Knaveries plain *ace* is never seen, till us'd." Sense could unquestionably be made out of this, but unfortunately the other Restoration Quartos show that the change is only a misprint, by correcting it to *face*.

II, ii, 243: "If partiality *assigned*." For: "If partially *affin'd*." The Quartos all read "partiality," but "assigned" occurs only in the Restoration Quartos.

IV, ii, 37: "Your Mistress, your Mistress." For: "Your mystery, your mystery." Perhaps this is an emendation due to the editor's misunderstanding of the extended trope which is the key to Othello's language in this scene.

The next two variants may be blundering efforts to improve grammar, rather than misprints:

I, iii, 156: "that he *bid* me tell it." For: "bade."

II, i, 230: "That ere our hearts *should* make." For: "shall."

The only changes I have noticed that appear to be genuine attempts to improve the old text are the following, and the first of these may be only a misprint.

III, iii, 221: "Away at once with love *and* jealousie." For: "*or*." Of course Shakespeare's meaning is spoiled: On the proof (as a result of the test) there is no more but this: Away at once with love (if she is guilty) or jealousy (if she is innocent). The reading of 1681 looks like an emendation due to a misunderstanding of "proof" as "proof of guilt."

The second and last passage seems to be an attempt at simplification, though here again careless printing may be a sufficient explanation:

I, iii, 101: "some nine *moneths* wasted." For: "*Moones*." Qs 1687, 1695, and 1705 correct to "months."

In view of the character of these changes, and their infrequency, I have no hesitation in pronouncing quite absurd the time-honored identification of the name of Dryden with these texts. It is impossible that the author of the altered *Troilus and Cressida*, the mangled *Tempest*, and the perverted *All for Love* should have touched *Othello* without leaving a trace. And trace there is none.

The source of Quarto 1681 (and indirectly, therefore, of those of 1687, 1695, and 1705) is the Second Quarto (1630). I shall not burden the reader with the citations which prove that Q 1681 follows the earlier Quartos without reference to the Folios. Nor with those which establish the source as falling in the second of the two groups formed by the pre-Restoration Quartos: (1) Q 1; (2) Q 2 and Q 3.

Elimination of Q 1 is easy, since in numerous passages Q 1681 agrees with Qs 2, 3, to the exclusion of Q 1.[4] There are, to be sure, still other passages which show agreement between Q 1681 and Qs 1, 2, to the exclusion of Q 3. But I have found no passages which show agreement with Q 1 to the exclusion of Q 2. It is clear, then, that Q 1 must be counted out, and our range has narrowed to Qs 2, 3.

The reader should bear in mind that our separation of the three Quartos into two groups is not in the least dependent on the relation of Q 1681 to them. Q 3 is derived from Q 2, which varies considerably from Q 1. Thus the subsequent passages I shall cite, though some contain identities between Q 1 and Q 2 and disparities between Q 2 and Q 3, do not alter the fact of the difference between Q 1 and Q 2 or of Q 3 as derived from the latter. All that we now have to do is to rule out Q 3, to exhibit the derivation of Q 1681 from Q 2, since the source is either Q 2 or Q 3. Again there is no difficulty in reaching a decision.[5]

I, ii, 15, 16: "a voice potential,
As double as the *Dukes*."
So Q 2, but Q 3: "Duke."

I, ii, 17: "grievance." Folios and Qs 1, 2: "greeuance"; but Q 3: "greevances."

I, ii, 21: "My *services* which I have done the Signiory."
So all except Q 3, which reads: "service."

I, iii, 106: "In speaking *for* my self." So Q 2. Q 3: "of."

I, iii, 127: "Without more certain and more *overt* test."
So Qs 1, 2. Q 3 has been changed to agree with the Folios: "ouer."

II, i, 10: "when *mountain* melt on them."
So Q 2. Q 1: "the huge *mountaine* mes lt;" Q 3 and Folios: "mountaines."

II, i, 213: "If after every tempest, *come* such calmness."
So all except Q 3, which has: "came."

II, ii, 68: "*Nay my* sick fool Roderigo." For: "now my."
Q 2 reads: "noy mw," the *w* and *y* having been transposed by the compositor. The editor of 1681 instead of *transposing*, *corrected*, as he thought.

My contention is that this person, so far from being a poet laureate, was no more than a compositor or proof-reader, and that his version was set up directly from the text of 1630. It probably represents Hart's acting version, and its appearance (this is a guess, of course) may be due to renewed public interest in *Othello* about the time when that actor succeeded to the great title rôle.

That the Restoration text should not be derived from the last pre-Restoration Quarto seems at first a little puzzling. But the solution is not difficult and helps, I think, to confirm the accuracy of the term "Players' Quartos" as applied to these Restoration editions. The latter derive, as a rule, not from the Folios but from the pre-Wars Quartos. I feel reasonably confident that when a printer wished to issue a new separate edition he sent to the players for a copy of their latest text. This opinion is supported by the case of *Othello*. When Q 3 appeared in 1655 the theatres were closed, and so it did not supersede the previous Quarto in the theatrical library. The publisher of 1681 printed, therefore, from *the last Players' Quarto*, that of 1630, since Q 3 was not, in any sense, a Players' Quarto at all.

2. The Bettertonian King Henry IV, with a Note on The Sequel of Henry the Fourth

The title-page of Betterton's version (published in 1700) is as follows:

K. Henry IV. With the Humours of Sir John Falstaff. A Tragi-comedy. As it is Acted at the Theatre in Little-Lincolns-Inn Fields by His Majesty's Servants. Revived, with Alterations. Written Originally by Mr. Shakespear. London. . . . 1700. . . .[6]

The fact that no Part is indicated in this title appears to be a clue to the real situation. It seems likely that of the *Henry IV* material Betterton produced only this play, and that our various references to the performance of *Henry IV* are all to this version of *Part One*. It is, as a matter of fact, not an alteration at all, but an acting edition cut for the stage.

Before considering it further, we shall do well to glance at the piece hitherto commonly linked with it, though I believe incorrectly, *The Sequel* of *c.* 1719. Its title-page reads:

The Sequel of Henry the Fourth: With the Humours of Sir John Falstaffe, and Justice Shallow. As it is Acted by His Majesty's Company of Comedians, at the Theatre-Royal in Drury-Lane. Alter'd from Shakespear, by the late Mr. Betterton. London: Printed for W. Chetwood . . . [n. d.].

This edition is in octavo. The date is usually said to be 1719; *e. g.*, Catalogue of the British Museum, Catalogue of the Barton Collection in the Boston Public Library, *Biographia Dramatica*, and Jaggard (p. 332). Genest, however, asserts that it must have been printed after December 17, 1720.

The cast of characters includes Barton Booth as King Henry, Wilks as the Prince, Theophilus Cibber as Clarence, Mills as Falstaff, Colley Cibber as Shallow, Penkethman as Feeble, Bowman as Chief Justice, and Norris as Pistol. This list looks away from any connection with Betterton.

Shakespeare's Induction is omitted, and also the opening scene of conference among the rebels. The action begins with

Falstaff, the Page, and the Chief Justice. It then proceeds exactly as in the original,[7] though with severe but warrantable and skilful cutting of dialogue, up to the parting of Northumberland from his lady. This scene is omitted entirely, and the beguiling of Falstaff immediately follows Prince Hal's proposal of it. The next scene, with the apostrophe to sleep and the King's decision for war, is also omitted, and we pass at once to Justice Shallow's house.

Thereafter the play proceeds unaltered (except for reduction of dialogue) up to the conclusion of the fighting. The editor of *The Sequel* was not unmindful of the beauty of the great apostrophe already noted as missing, and inserts it in somewhat garbled form at the end of the next scene, the first in which the King appears after the battle.

The following scene (Falstaff *et al.* at Justice Shallow's) is omitted. Instead we have the next scene at Shallow's (F 1, V, iii). It is followed by F 1, V, ii, in which we learn of the King's death and see the new ruler's new behavior. Poor Doll's discomfiture is left out, and the next scene is the rebuff to the fat knight. To this is added a version of *Henry the Fifth*, I, i, the undertaking of the adventure in France.

In fine, the play is hardly more than a well-cut acting version of *2 Henry IV*, with the addition of an adaptation of *Henry V*, I, i, and some, but not much, verbal tampering. That the cutting was done by Betterton is not impossible, but I incline to doubt it. If it had been produced about the same time as his stage version, *King Henry IV*, (1) why was that play so entitled? (2) why was the publication of *The Sequel* delayed for twenty years? (3) why has no reference been found to Betterton's producing *The Sequel?*

It appears, then, that our various references to the acting of *Henry IV* in the decade 1700–1710 are probably all to the stage version of *Part One*, printed in 1700.

With his customary and invariably charming enthusiasm

Dr. Doran calls the Bettertonian version an "unhallowed outrage." We must recognize the justice of the adjectival portion of this impeachment, for hallowed the version certainly is not. The present writer, either on the stage or in the study, has never seen an acting version of Shakespeare that appealed to him as consecrated in the slightest. But *outrage* is too harsh a name for what is really a perfectly respectable stage version. One must deplore, to be sure, the loss of many a line that only Shakespeare could have written; yet this editor was no tamperer. Almost without exception the text is faithful, except for cutting, to that of the Folios — it is not, like most of the Restoration versions, derived from the last pre-Wars Quarto, in this case the Quarto of 1639.

The action proceeds without structural alteration up to (F 1) Act III, scene i, of *1 Henry the Fourth;* in Betterton's version this is chopped off (Q 1700, p. 32) immediately after the agreement on parcelling the land, the "schooling" of Hotspur and the entrance of the ladies being cut. There is no further structural change till (F 1) Act IV, scene iv, the brief expository scene in which the Archbishop of York appears. This is excised. The action is thereafter unchanged till (F 1) Act V, scene iii, the first part of which is omitted. It begins (Q 1700, p. 52) with the entrance of Hotspur. There is no other structural change.

While I have not collated the texts exhaustively, I can safely assert that there is practically no tampering with Shakespeare's language. Even the stage directions of the Folio are followed verbatim. It is a pleasure to report that Thomas Betterton, if like any actor he was willing to cut scenes and parts of scenes, did so sparingly; and that, unlike some of his literary betters, he did not feel that overmastering urge to improve Shakespeare's diction. Since *The Sequel of Henry the Fourth* does tamper with language, even though not extensively, we have still another reason against attributing it to Betterton. In my opinion the two versions are probably not from the same hand.

3. The Players' Quartos of Julius Caesar, with a Note on the Altered Version of 1719

In an article in the *Library* Miss Bartlett has examined the Players' Quartos of *Julius Caesar* with great care.[8] Her conclusions are briefly as follows. *Julius Caesar* was printed separately for the first time in 1684; Quartos 2, 3, 4, and 5 are undated; Quarto 6 is dated 1691. Q 6 is practically a line-for-line reprint of Q 1. Qs 1–4 are all much alike, evidently set up one from another, and differing only as the carelessness or peculiarities of the various printers caused this or that slight variation. Q 5, however, is different; it is better printed, and has fuller stage directions. It appears to be derived from the Fourth Folio, the others apparently being from the First. Thus we have three groups of Quartos: (1) Qs 1–4, from F 1; (2) Q 5, from F 4; and (3) Q 6, from Q 1.

Before I saw Miss Bartlett's definitive study I had examined the four Quartos at the Boston Public Library (1684, 1691, and two undated) and had concluded that Q 1 must be the edition of 1684. That the edition incorrectly dated by bibliographers 1680 and (at the Boston Public Library) 1681 could not have been printed in those years is evident from the cast, which includes Betterton, Smith, and other members of the Duke's company. This fixes the date of the first edition as at least after the united company had opened at Drury Lane, on November 16, 1682. As Miss Bartlett says, there is no reason to suppose that *Julius Caesar* was thereupon produced at once. There can be little doubt that the edition of 1684 was the first separate printing, and that it appeared in response to renewed public interest in the play because of Betterton's revival.

The Restoration text is not an alteration. The most serious change gives Marullus's lines (I, i) to "Caska," in spite of their manifest incompatibility with his character as drawn by Shakespeare. A similar economy puts Cicero's language in the storm into the mouth of Trebonius (I, iii). The printer, however, was careless and failed to make all the changes; the inconsistent lines survive in all the four Quartos which I have seen. Caska addresses Trebonius (I, iii, 6–8) as follows:

> O *Cicero*,
> I have seen Tempests, when the scolding Winds
> Have riv'd *thy* knotty Oaks.

Again, I, iii, 43, we find:

> Farewell Trebonius. [*Exit Cicero.*

That this edition slavishly follows the Folios is shown by the following passages:

II, ii, 54: "We *hear* two Lyons litter'd in one day."
III, i, 47: "And turn pre-Ordinance, and first Decree,
Into the *Lane* of Children."

These blunders would surely have been noticed by any editor who had the vaguest intention of establishing a text. They are retained in the four Quartos I have seen.

Professor Odell supposes that the Quarto of 1684 represents the acting version of Hart and Mohun.[9] Strictly speaking, it is not exactly an acting version, since it is an excellent printing of the Folios text. It probably represents Betterton's revival of the play after the union; on the other hand, it was doubtless the text received from Hart and Mohun. The version of the King's Company had presumably always been that of Folio 1; when *Julius Caesar* was first printed therein it was, of course, from the text in the hands of the old King's Company. No separate edition having been issued, this had never been superseded in their library. Thus we find Q1 in 1684 deriving from F 1.

In 1719 an edition of *Julius Caesar* appeared with the following title-page:

The Tragedy of Julius Caesar: With the Death of Brutus and Cassius; Written Originally by Shakespear, And since alter'd by Sir William Davenant and John Dryden late Poets Laureat. As it is now Acted by His Majesty's Company of Comedians at the Theatre Royal. To which is prefix'd, The Life of Julius Caesar, abstracted from Plutarch and Suetonius. London. . . . M.DCC.XIX . . .[10]

The edition of 1719 appears in the first volume of "A Collection of Plays by Eminent Hands; in Four Volumes. . . . London . . . 1719." It seems to be a stage version. The following cast is given: Mills, Julius Caesar; Walker, Octavius; Wilks, Antony; Booth, Brutus; Elrington, Cassius; Bickerstaffe, Caska; Bowman, Flavius; Shepard, Decius; W. Wilks, Metellus; W. Mills, Messala; Wilson, Cinna; Oates, Pindarus; Williams, Soothsayer; Bowman, Jr., Trebonius; Kay, Servant to Antony; Johnson, Miller, Norris, Cross, Plebeians; Norris, Jr., Lucius; Mrs. Horton, Calphurnia; Mrs. Porter, Portia.

Before offering my conclusions as to the authorship of this adaptation, I present some of its typical changes. In the first place, the reduction of dramatis personae in the interests of economy, which as we have seen was begun in the edition of 1684 by assigning Marullus's speeches to "Caska," is continued in the version of 1719. "Caska" also takes over the lines of Titinius in the scenes at Philippi, and in that gallant gentleman's place dies his very Roman death. Cicero, as in 1684, is absorbed by Trebonius. Still further, the Soothsayer takes the speeches of Artemidorus.

In the second place, there are many cuts of lines, phrases, and words. Some of these are due to exigencies of the stage. Others indicate a desire to excise language and ideas unsuited to the elevation of tragedy:[11]

III, i, 123, 124: "And let us bathe our Hands in Caesar's Blood, [Vp to the Elbowes,] And all besmear our Swords." Tragedy was no place for the funny-bone. "all" is introduced, of course, to mend the hiatus left by the excision.

Other omissions seem due to misunderstanding of the text:

I, iii, 31, 32: "let not Men say,
[These are their Reasons,] They are Natural."

III, i, 175: ["who else is ranke."]

III, i, 223: ["Most Noble, in the presence of thy Coarse,]
Had I . . ." *etc.*
Here the punctuation, and, one may add, a certain lack of imagination, produced what seemed to the editor of 1719 a hopeless crux.

As for the textual alterations, some are mere modernizations. Examples:

I, ii, 228: "whilst." For: "whiles."[12]

III, i, 36: "first." For: "presently."

Others are more or less unsuccessful attempts to improve grammar. Examples:

I, iii, 49: "Cassius, what *a* Night is this." "a" is inserted by the editor of 1719.

II, i, 103: "Know I these Men, that *came* along with you."
For: "come."

Two changes are amusing examples of subservience to decorum:

I, ii, 187: "Till then, my noble Friend, *depend on* this."
For: "chew upon."

II, i, 347: "To be distemper'd in."
For: "To weare a Kerchiefe."

There is a curious example of prudery, reminiscent, one must confess, of D'Avenant:

II, i, 330: Portia has stabbed herself in her *Arm*, not her *Thigh.*

Of the remainder of the changes some are wanton, some are ridiculous, and some are rather clever. Here I have grouped the changes which alter the sense, or at least color it:

II, i, 95: "For if thou *put* thy Native Semblance on."
For: "path."

II, i, 136: "So let high-*seated* Tyranny range on."
For: "sighted," anticipating Theobald's conjecture.

II, i, 144: "falter." For: "palter."

II, ii, 15, 16: "the things that *threaten* me
Ne're *look* but on my Back."
For: "threaten'd" and "look'd," anticipating Hudson's emendation.

III, i, 45: "Crouchings." For: "couchings."

III, ii, 115: "And Men have lost their *Reasons*."
For: "Reason." Brutus's speech, just preceding this, is set up as if it were verse.

III, ii, 130: "And none so *proper* to do him Reverence."
For: "poore."

V, v, 3, 4: "let us *rest here*." For: "rest on this Rock."
Ergo, a "practical" rock was not among the properties.[13]

In the same scene (V, v) *Volumnius* becomes *Popilius*.

V, v, 7: "Come hither Lucilius."
For: "Sit thee down, Clitus." It is *Lucilius*, not *Clitus*, throughout. As we have seen, the rock was not there and therefore could not be sat upon.

V, v, 25: The Ghost of Caesar has appeared to Brutus not "this *last* Night," but "this *same* Night." This change was made because the Ghost was actually introduced at Philippi.

V, v, 83: "He only in a *Generous* honest thought."
For: "generall."

So far it is evident that the alterations, while often irritatingly stupid, are not of a very serious character. I have reserved the most considerable changes till last.

Act IV closes (in 1719) in true Ercles's vein. The Ghost disappears; whereupon:

Brut. Sure they have raised some Devil to their aid,
And think to frighten Brutus with a shade.
But e're the night closes this fatal Day,
I'll send more Ghosts this visit to repay.

This Ghost of Caesar is, in the version of 1719, an apparition of its word, for, true to its promise to drop in at Philippi, we see it confronting Brutus there in all its gruesome glory.

In V, iii, there is much alteration of Shakespeare's lines. Both Cato's speeches (105 and 109, 110) and consequently the fine touch of the crowning of Cassius, are cut. Lines 106–108 are transferred, slightly altered, to the end of Brutus's speech of mourning. Brutus has directed, "Leave us a while."

After his concluding remark over the body:

Enter Caesars *Ghost* —

Ghost. Cassius, my three and thirty wounds are now reveng'd.
Brut. What art thou, why com'st thou.
Ghost. To keep my word, and meet thee in Philippi fields.
Brut. Well, I see thee then.
Ghost. Next, ungrateful Brutus, do I call.
Brut. Ungrateful Caesar, that wou'd Rome Enthral
Ghost. The Ides of March Remember — I must go,
To meet thee on the burning Lake below [*Sinks*.
Brut. My Spirits come to me — Stay thou bloody
Apparition, come back, I wou'd converse
Longer with thee — 'tis gone, this fatal shadow
Haunts me still.
Brut. Come, let's to the field — Flavius, set our
Battles on — and Romans, yet e're night,
We shall try fortune in a second fight.
Take off Cassius.
[*Alarm here. Exeunt*.

I find it impossible to believe that John Dryden perpetrated these half-hearted couplets.

Finally, lines 39–79 of V, v, are omitted in favor of the following:

Brut. Why do you stay to save his Life
That must not live.
Luc. After you, what Roman wou'd Live?
Brut. What Roman wou'd not live, that may
To serve his Country in a nobler day.
You are not above a pardon, tho' Brutus is.
Luc. I'm not afraid to die.

Brut. Retire, and let me think a while.
Now one last look, and then farewel to all.
That wou'd with the unhappy Brutus fall.
Scorning to view his Country's Misery,
Thus Brutus always strikes for Liberty.
[*Stabs himself.*
Poor slavish Rome farewel, Caesar now be still.
I kill'd not thee with half so Good a will.
[*Dies.*

Enter Anthony, Octavius, Messala, and Soldiers.

Anth. Whom mourn you over?
Luc. 'Tis Brutus.
Mess. So Brutus shou'd be found — I thank
Thee Brutus, that thou hast prov'd
Messala's saying true.

Antony then begins his final speech:

This was the noblest Roman of 'em all.

Now there have been laureate poets capable of these lines, but again I submit that John Dryden was not one of them.

The ascription of this version to D'Avenant and Dryden was rejected as long ago as the *Biographia Dramatica* of Baker,[14] and perhaps it is flogging a dead horse to expound one's reasons for sharing that view.

Suggestive as some of these changes and omissions are of D'Avenant's technique in revision, he could scarcely have had a hand in this version because the play was the exclusive property of Killigrew's company till long after his death. Furthermore, we have the text of 1684, which we have just examined. These changes do not appear in that edition, nor in the edition of 1691. How they crept into the text may best be described in the eloquent trope of Genest, who characterizes the promptbook as a "sink of corruption."

The limits *of composition* of this version are thus 1691 and 1719. Sometime during those years the play was altered; but that any of the changes I have recorded were made before 1691 seems impossible in view of their absence from the edition of that year. The Quarto of 1691, as we have seen, was printed from Quarto 1 (1684). In my judgment this is proof positive that the acting text was unchanged during those years.

I should not care to deny the possibility that here and there Dryden may be responsible for an altered detail. But that this text represents an edition by him is unthinkable; first, from the character of most of the verse; and second, because he would scarcely have confined his serious alteration to the fifth act.

4. Some General Observations

It is evident, then, that the adapted versions seen on the Restoration stage greatly outnumber the unaltered revivals. Not till the Romantic influence crept into the English theatre in the middle of the eighteenth century was there any serious attempt on the part of the actors to get back to Shakespeare. Garrick took several steps in that direction, and his successors among the actor-managers, several more. But they all — Irving as much as any — regarded the plays as adaptable to the improved stage instead of recognizing that the only reason for the existence of the stage is to produce plays.

I would not deny the possibility that in another generation our theatre may develop a new art, synthetic of the rest. But even when we grant that certain contemporary experiments are extremely interesting, what has that fact to do with the staging of Shakespeare? It is not hostile to the theatre of to-day, nor even to that of to-morrow, to point out that every dramatic piece ought to be approached as far as possible in terms of its own time. Not merely to satisfy the antiquary's whim, but because we confine our pleasures when we neglect, not to dwell in the past, but to enjoy occasional excursions into its vast and various provinces.

We do not wish our dramatists to-day to give us blank-verse tragedies, but only a few quite extraordinary persons have wanted to produce Shakespeare rewritten in modern prose. Yet, with no more reason, *Hamlet* has been done in modern dress and with modern properties. It is not that doublet and silk hose are more dignified or more colorful than knickers and plaid hose, or a rapier more dramatic than a pistol. The supreme reality is the play, and everything else should be subordinated to the one end of staging it with the least possible loss of the dramatist's intention. That will call for the finest sort of discrimination as the director determines which Elizabethan feature is essential to that intention and which is merely distracting or superfluous. To pronounce the modernized production successful in this respect—to insist, that is, that *Hamlet* stands revealed by it as a modern play—is sheer perversity. *Hamlet* is Elizabethan, not modern: this age neither sees ghosts nor feels obliged to obey their vengeful orders. If this production of *Hamlet* made the play modern, it did precisely what it should not, and was in fact a menace to the morals of all the youth who saw it.

If, on the other hand, the end of Shakespearean production is to set forth the actual, the historical, play, then the means must be, not necessarily a replica of the Elizabethan stage, but some use of its methods. The two essentials are, first, a simplicity of setting and vivacity of acting which will guarantee full scope for the lines; and, second, rapidity of pace and the overflowing of scene into scene. If these can be accomplished on a picture stage, and with the great advantages derivable from modern lighting used not to make pictures but to illuminate, well and good. But the producer must tax the resources of his stage for the play, not mangle the play to suit his stage.

Any modern stage would be taxed by an attempt to realize the opening scene in *The Tempest*, or the siege and battle scenes of the histories. Since Shakespeare's method was impressionistic, since he laid on his lines the burden of establishing his audience's conviction, would it not be better on the whole to leave it to the lines, which support it so brilliantly that any stage picture of them is a hopeless disappointment? The actors love their trappings, of course; but lately they have had to economize on scenery. Economic pressure has at this point been helpful to art; several recent productions have used a simply draped stage and tried to keep the action rapid and unbroken. But not yet, though nearly three hundred years have passed, have we got wholly free of the Restoration attitude toward revision, or indeed of the Restoration versions themselves.

I need not recapitulate the results of this study of the text of these Quartos. For the most part they are independent of the Folios, and they are always close to the theatre. Unfortunately they have no light to shed on the problem of the true text. Yet they exercised some influence on subsequent editors. Rowe and Pope, for instance, fail to distinguish sharply between pre- and post-Restoration editions, and a number of their so-called emendations are really incorporations of Restoration improvement.

It is, I think, impossible to exaggerate the harm these versions have done, not only in the long career of some of them on the stage, but also because they inaugurated the fashion of adaptation. What caused the original vogue is not easy to summarize. It has long been held that the impulse came from the influx of French neo-classical standards, according to which Shakespeare's technique is clumsy if not barbarous. For the critical canons and their influence on his position in the late seventeenth and the eighteenth century the reader should consult Professor Lounsbury's *Shakespeare as a Dramatic Artist.*

As we have seen, the adapters paid occasional but inconsistent heed to "the rules." Here and there, largely by excision of minor plots and numerous characters, they improve the unity of the action. The crowded stage was no longer demanded by the audience, and the change in original composition was naturally followed in adaptation. The zeal for dramatic economy, abetted of course by financial considerations, sometimes went to absurd lengths, and we find two quite incompatible Shakespearean characters forcibly joined by the improver. Most of the adaptations show a reduction in dramatis personae of between twenty and fifty per cent. The average number of characters is about one third less than in the original.

There are also reductions of Shakespeare's violations of the unities of time and place. The last of these improvements, however, was chiefly conditioned, not by the canons, but by the requirements of the new stage. The strict separation of tragedy and comedy, one of the most obnoxious and artificial of the rules, received many sacrifices, chief among them Lear's Fool. On the other hand, the injunction against scenes of violence was frankly flouted, and poetic justice fared little better.

Yet, though we must not minimize foreign and critical pressure, it seems clear that the natural development of the English drama and theatre was more influential on the course of Shakespearean representation. For one thing, the vogue of the heroic play left unmistakable traces in the acting versions, especially D'Avenant's, Dryden's, and Tate's, whose heroes sometimes drop their Shakespearean masks for Drawcansir's.

Most important of all, and directly responsible for the most violent mangling, was the emphasis in production on the material. Scenery and machines — to these were often sacrificed, not only their verbal equivalents in the original, — those descriptive passages in which Shakespeare paints his backgrounds more effectively than any designer from Inigo Jones to Robert, — but also the human values, the direct yet subtle clash of character on character which, far more than situation, makes his scenes so actable. The Restoration versions show an immense increase in the number and length of stage directions.

Another influence on revision was less pervasive than the scenic and mechanical innovations, but in certain plays was as disastrous to Shakespeare. Being Restoration products, the adaptations show the license of the time. Not that Shakespeare is an exceptionally pure author. And sometimes the changes serve to display that wicked wit whose charm bears authority for its own pardon. But there is much in the altered texts that lacks all charm. It is depressing to notice that the most unpleasant of the degraded versions, the Restoration *Tempest*, came from the pen of the greatest genius of the age.

Of slighter importance, but potent for a few years, was the motive of loyalty, which influenced particularly the altered versions of 1678–1682. Again we find the practices of independent composition reflected in the adaptations. When original dramas were written in order to denounce the Whigs and flatter the Court, it is not surprising to find Shakespeare's historical plays employed to exhibit the ingratitude of commonwealths and the miseries of civil war.

As for the changes in diction, I have ventured to group some of the altered passages under such heads as modernization, simplification, refinement, grammatical correction, clarification, and subservience to decorum. But many of the revisions seem capricious. That the adapters felt no restraint is understandable enough. Reverence for the text of a stage play is a relatively modern refinement — the mere thought of it would have made Shakespeare laugh. No more ruthless tamperer ever lived than he, and he might be the first to reprehend the scholar's anxiety. Which does not mean that the scholar is wrong. By Shakespeare's fruits (and by little else) we know him, and care not for his predecessors' injuries. And by their fruits, such as they are, we must weigh the Restoration improvers.

Concerning their efforts as a whole I am not aware that anything good can be said, though, as we have seen, there is occasional merit in detail. Dryden has been justly praised for his ending of *Troilus and Cressida*, and Shadwell for the love story of Timon. But after all, what makes Shakespeare's best plays so great is not the cleverness with which he put them together, however masterly (sometimes) his handling of exposition, complication, contrast, suspense, surprise, and the other tricks of the trade. The plays are great because their characters were executed by an incomparable observer of human nature, and because their lines were endowed by the world's finest poet. I do not see why we should expect anyone except a keener observer or a better poet to be capable of improving to any considerable extent their characterization and diction. Structure is another and an accidental matter, dependent on stage and age and climate and a local technique. What avails it that the adapter has tinkered up a bit of plotting more neatly for a special stage, if he has obscured a great character or spoiled a great phrase?

It is an amusing whirligig of literary time that the chief satisfaction to be derived from reading these stage versions of Shakespeare is the new beauty they lead us to recognize in their originals. The Restoration adapters thought of the great Elizabethan almost as a sort of noble savage. How aware of himself he was, who shall say? At least we can be sure he was no exquisite: he was of the earth, earthy. That accounts for some of both the merits and the defects of his work. But not for *him*. His was not exactly an over-refined audience, and he had to play to it. He met it on its own level, which was where the Restoration men had to meet their audience; but unlike them he led it, in his greatest moments, to something like the level of his own high heart and mind.

NOTES TO CHAPTER X

1. Henry B. Wheatley ("Post-Restoration Quartos of Shakespeare's Plays," *Library*, 3d ser., iv, 237–269) says he can find no authority for the existence of these editions or their ascription to Dryden. Lowndes is followed, also, by H. T. Hall (*Shakspere's Plays: The Separate Editions of, with the Alterations Done by Various Hands*, Second Edition, Cambridge, 1880, p. 74), who states that eight editions of Dryden's revision were published. He fails to locate any copy or to give his authority.
2. Otto Bobsin, in his dissertation, *Shakespeare's Othello in englischer Bühnenbearbeitung* (Rostock, 1904), ignores the Restoration Quartos, both in his list of editions and in his account of altered versions.
3. I have not listed all the variants. I have tried, however, not to omit any passage of unusual significance or interest, or any tending to controvert my conclusions.
4. For the material passages see my Harvard dissertation, unprinted, pp. 176, 177.
5. Here I have also collated Q 3 independently.
6. Besides the edition of 1700, Jaggard lists one of *c.* 1710, but fails to locate any copy. Wheatley lists only 1700. I reprint portions of my article, "Improving Shakespeare," *P. M. L. A.*, xli, 727–746 (Sept., 1926).
7. The adapter follows the text of the Folios, not of the Quarto of 1600. This aberration from the normal practice of the Restoration reworkers may be explained by the relatively archaic condition of the old Quarto. The editor of *The Sequel* is almost invariably faithful to his source, except for occasional modernizations. Walter Wrage (*Englische Bühnenbearbeitungen von Shakespeares "King Henry IV. Part I*," Hamburg, 1910, p. 32) is positive that the source is F 4.
8. "Quarto Editions of *Julius Caesar*," *Library*, 3d ser., iv (April, 1913), 122–132.
9. Odell, i, 38.
10. Copies of this version are rare. I have used a photostatic reproduction of the British Museum copy. The Sheffield *Julius Caesar* I shall not discuss. It was not printed till after the play under consideration, nor was it a stage version, but a pseudo-classical imitation conceived in the closet. In order to secure a technical unity the author broke it into two parts of five acts each.
11. My numbering agrees with that of Dr. Furness's New Variorum Ed. (vol. xvii). Text quoted is in each case from the edition of 1719, except bracketed text, which is given according to that of the Folios.
12. Rowe had already made this change (1709).
13. A stage direction on page 12 orders "[Ring down."
14. *Biog. Dram.*, ed. 1812, ii, 353. Cf. H. Fischer, "Gibt es einen von Dryden und Davenant Bearbeiteten Julius Cäsar?" *Anglia*, viii, 415–418.

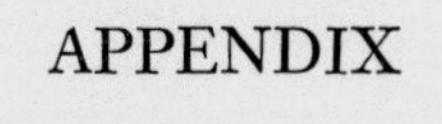

APPENDIX

APPENDIX

A LIST OF PUBLIC THEATRES AND THE COMPANIES APPEARING IN THEM FROM 1660 TO 1710

COCKPIT IN DRURY LANE (not to be confused with the King's private Cockpit theatre in Whitehall Palace):
- Cockpit
  - Rhodes's Company: *c.* March, 1660–*c.* Oct. 8, 1660
  - United Cockpit Company: *c.* Oct. 8, 1660–Nov. 4, 1660
  - Beeston's Company: Nov. 5, 1660 (?)–?

RED BULL
- Old Actors: ?–*c.* Oct. 8, 1660
- " " : Nov. 5, 6, 7, 1660
- Remnant of Rhodes's Company (?) : ?

SALISBURY COURT
- Whitefriars
- Blackfriars (?)
  - Beeston's Company: ?–*c.* Nov. 4, 1660
  - D'Avenant's Company: Nov. 15 (?), 1660–*c.* June, 1661

VERE STREET
- Clare Market
- Gibbons's Tennis Court
- The Theatre
- Lincoln's Inn Fields
- King's
- Killigrew's
  - King's Company: Nov. 8, 1660–*c.* May 6, 1663

[FIRST] LINCOLN'S INN FIELDS
- Portugal Row
- The Duke's
- The Opera
- D'Avenant's
  - Duke's Company (D'Avenant's): late June, 1661–*c.* Nov. 8, 1671
  - King's Company (Killigrew's): Feb. 26, 1672–*c.* March 25, 1674

[FIRST] THEATRE ROYAL IN DRURY LANE
- The King's
- Theatre Royal
- Theatre in Drury Lane
- Brydges Street
- Covent Garden
  - King's Company: May 7, 1663–Jan. 25, 1672

DORSET GARDEN
The Duke's
The Queen's
Salisbury Court
Duke's Company: Nov. 9, 1671–*c.* Nov. 15, 1682
(Thereafter used occasionally by the Theatre Royal till its destruction in 1709.)

[SECOND] THEATRE ROYAL IN DRURY LANE
Theatre Royal
Drury Lane
Brydges Street
King's Company: March 26, 1674–*c.* Nov. 15, 1682
United Patent Company: Nov. 16, 1682–Dec. 28, 1694
Rich's Remnant: April 4, 1695–Jan. 14, 1708
Rich's United Patent Company: Jan. 15, 1708–June 4, 1709
Collier's Patent Company: Nov. 23, 1709–Nov. 5, 1710
Wilks–Cibber–Dogget Management: Nov. 6, 1710–

[SECOND] LINCOLN'S INN FIELDS
Little Lincoln's Inn Fields
New Theatre in Lincoln's Inn Fields
Betterton's Seceding Company: April 30, 1695–March 31, 1705

HAYMARKET
Seceding Actors under Vanbrugh: April 9, 1705–summer of 1706
Swiney's Company: Oct. 15, 1706–Jan. 10, 1708
Swiney's Management of Opera: 1708–1709
Seceding Actors under Swiney: Sept. 15, 1709–*c.* Nov. 5, 1710

BIBLIOGRAPHY

BIBLIOGRAPHY

A. First Editions of the Altered Versions

1. The D'Avenant-Dryden *Tempest*.

   The Tempest, or the Enchanted Island. A Comedy. As it is now Acted at his Highness the Duke of York's Theatre. London, Printed by J. M. for Henry Herringman at the Blew Anchor in the Lower walk of the New Exchange. MDCLXX.

2. D'Avenant's *The Law against Lovers*.

   Pp. 272–329 of Part II of The Works of Sr William D'avenant Kt Consisting of Those which were formerly Printed, and Those which he design'd for the Press: Now Published Out of the Authors Originall Copies. London: Printed by T. N. for Henry Herringman, at the Sign of the Blew Anchor in the Lower Walk of the New Exchange. 1673.

3. D'Avenant's *Macbeth*.

   Macbeth, A Tragedy. With all the Alterations, Amendments, Additions, and New Songs. As it's now Acted at the Dukes Theatre. London, Printed for P. Chetwin, and are to be Sold by most Booksellers, 1674.

4. The D'Avenant-Dryden-Shadwell operatic *Tempest*.

   The Tempest, or the Enchanted Island. A Comedy. As it is now Acted at his Highness the Duke of York's Theatre. London, Printed by T. N. for Henry Herringman, at the Blew Anchor in the Lower Walk of the New Exchange. MDCLXXIV.

5. D'Avenant's *Hamlet*.

   The Tragedy of Hamlet Prince of Denmark. As it is now Acted at his Highness the Duke of York's Theatre. By William Shakespeare. London, Printed by Andr. Clark, for J. Martyn, and H. Herringman, at the Bell in St. Paul's Church Yard, and at the Blew Anchor in the Lower Walk of the New Exchange, 1676.

6. Dryden's *All for Love*.

   All for Love: or, The World well Lost. A Tragedy, As it is Acted at the Theatre-Royal; And Written in Imitation of Shakespeare's Stile. By John Dryden, Servant to his Majesty. Quanquam O—! In the Savoy: Printed by Tho. Newcomb, for Henry Herringman, at the Blew Anchor in the Lower Walk of the New Exchange. 1678.

7. Shadwell's *Timon of Athens*.

   The History of Timon of Athens, the Man-Hater. As it is acted at the Dukes Theatre. Made into a Play. By Tho. Shadwell. Licensed, Feb. 18. 1677/8. Ro. L'Estrange. London, Printed by J. M. for Henry Herringman, at the Blue Anchor, in the Lower Walk of the New Exchange, 1678.

BIBLIOGRAPHY

A. First Editions of the Altered Versions

1. The D'Avenant–Dryden *Tempest:*
   The Tempest, or the Enchanted Island. A Comedy. As it is now Acted at his Highness the Duke of York's Theatre. London, Printed by J. M. for Henry Herringman at the Blew Anchor in the Lower-walk of the New-Exchange. MDCLXX.
2. D'Avenant's *The Law against Lovers:*
   Pp. 272–329 of Part ii of The Works of S[r] William D'avenant K[t] Consisting of Those which were formerly Printed, and Those which he design'd for the Press: Now Published Out of the Authors Originall Copies. London: Printed by T. N. for Henry Herringman, at the Sign of the Blew Anchor in the Lower Walk of the New Exchange. 1673.
3. D'Avenant's *Macbeth:*
   Macbeth, A Tragaedy. With all the Alterations, Amendments, Additions, and New Songs. As it's now Acted at the Dukes Theatre. London, Printed for P. Chetwin, and are to be Sold by most Booksellers, 1674.
4. The D'Avenant–Dryden–Shadwell operatic *Tempest:*
   The Tempest, or the Enchanted Island. A Comedy. As it is now Acted at his Highness the Duke of York's Theatre. London, Printed by T. N. for Henry Herringman, at the Blew Anchor in the Lower Walk of the New-Exchange. MDCLXXIV.
5. D'Avenant's *Hamlet:*
   The Tragedy of Hamlet Prince of Denmark. As it is now Acted at his Highness the Duke of York's Theatre. By William Shakespeare. London: Printed by Andr. Clark, for J. Martyn, and H. Herringman, at the Bell in St. Paul's Church-Yard, and at the Blue Anchor in the lower Walk of the New Exchange. 1676.
6. Dryden's *All for Love:*
   All for Love: or, The World well Lost. A Tragedy, As it is Acted at the Theatre-Royal; And Written in Imitation of Shakespeare's Stile. By John Dryden, Servant to his Majesty [Quotation]. In the Savoy: Printed by Tho. Newcomb, for Henry Harringman, at the Blew Anchor in the Lower Walk of the New-Exchange. 1678.
7. Shadwell's *Timon of Athens:*
   The History of Timon of Athens, the Man-Hater. As it is acted at the Dukes Theatre. Made into a Play. By Tho. Shadwell. Licensed, Feb. 18. 1678/7. Ro. L'Estrange. London, Printed by J. M. for Henry Herringman, at the Blue Anchor, in the Lower Walk of the New-Exchange, 1678.

8. Dryden's *Troilus and Cressida:*

Troilus and Cressida, or, Truth Found too Late. A Tragedy As it is Acted at the Dukes Theatre. To which is Prefix'd, A Preface Containing the Grounds of Criticism in Tragedy. Written by John Dryden Servant to his Majesty. [Quotation.] London, Printed for Jacob Tonson at the Judges-Head in Chancery-lane near Fleet-street, and Abel Swall, at the Unicorn at the West-end of S. Pauls, 1679.

9. Otway's *Caius Marius:*

The History and Fall of Caius Marius. A Tragedy. As it is Acted at the Duke's Theatre. By Thomas Otway. [Quotation.] London, Printed for Tho. Flescher, at the Angel and Crown in S. Paul's Church-yard. 1680.

10. Crowne's *Misery of Civil War:*

The Misery of Civil-War. A Tragedy, As it is Acted at the Duke's Theatre, by His Royal Highnesses Servants. Written by Mr. Crown. London, Printed for R. Bentley, and M. Magnes, in Russel-Street in Covent-Garden, 1680.

11. Crowne's *Henry the Sixth, The First Part:*

Henry the Sixth, The First Part. With the Murder of Humphrey Duke of Glocester. As it was Acted at the Dukes Theatre. Written by Mr. Crown. London, Printed for R. Bentley, and M. Magnes, in Russel-Street, in Covent-Garden. 1681.

12. Tate's *King Lear:*

The History of King Lear. Acted at the Duke's Theatre. Reviv'd with Alterations. By N. Tate. London, Printed for E. Flesher, and are to be sold by R. Bentley, and M. Magnes in Russel-street near Covent-Garden, 1681.

13. Tate's *Richard II:*

The History of King Richard The Second Acted at the Theatre Royal, Under the Name of the Sicilian Usurper. With a Prefatory Epistle in Vindication of the Author. Occasion'd by the Prohibition of this Play on the Stage. By N. Tate. [Quotation.] London, Printed for Richard Tonson, and Jacob Tonson, at Grays-Inn Gate, and at the Judges-Head in Chancery-Lane near Fleet-street, 1681.

14. Tate's *Ingratitude:*

The Ingratitude of a Common-Wealth: Or, the Fall of Caius Martius Coriolanus. As it is Acted at the Theatre-Royal. By N. Tate. [Quotation.] London, Printed by T. M. for Joseph Hindmarsh, at the Black-Bull in Cornhill. 1682.

15. D'Urfey's *Injured Princess:*

The Injured Princess, or the Fatal Wager: As it was Acted at the Theater-Royal, by His Majesties Servants. By Tho. Durfey, Gent. London: Printed for R. Bentley and M. Magnes in Russel-street in Covent-Garden, near the Piazza. 1682.

16. Ravenscroft's *Titus Andronicus:*
Titus Andronicus, or the Rape of Lavinia. Acted at the Theatre Royall, A Tragedy, Alter'd from Mr Shakespears Works, By Mr. Edw. Ravenscroft. Licensed, Dec. 21, 1686. R. L. S. London, Printed by J. B. for J. Hindmarsh, at the Golden-Ball in Cornhill, over against the Royal-Exchange. 1687.

17. *The Fairy Queen:*
The Fairy-Queen: an Opera. Represented at the Queen's-Theatre By Their Majesties Servants. London, Printed for Jacob Tonson, at the Judges-Head, in Chancery-Lane. 1692. [Advertisemetn.]

18. Lacy's *Sauny the Scot:*
Sauny the Scott: or, The Taming of the Shrew: A Comedy. As it is now Acted at the Theatre-Royal. Written by J. Lacey, Servant to his Majesty. And Never before Printed. [Quotation.] London, Printed and Sold by E. Whitlock, near Stationers-Hall. 1698.

19. Gildon's *Measure for Measure:*
Measure for Measure, or Beauty the Best Advocate. As it is Acted At the Theatre in Lincolns-Inn-Fields. Written Originally by Mr. Shakespear: And now very much Alter'd; With Additions of several Entertainments of Musick. London: Printed for D. Brown, at the Black Swan without Temple-Bar; and R. Parker at the Unicorn Under the Royal-Exchange in Cornhill. 1700.

20. Cibber's *Richard III:*
The Tragical History of King Richard III. As it is Acted at the Theatre Royal. By C. Cibber. [Quotation.] London, Printed for B. Lintott at the Middle Temple-Gate, in Eleet-street, and A. Bettesworth at the Red-Lyon on London-Bridge. [1700. Advertisement.]

21. Granville's *Jew of Venice:*
The Jew of Venice. A Comedy. As it is Acted at the Theatre in Little-Lincolns-Inn-Fields, by His Majesty's Servants. London, Printed for Ber. Lintott at the Post-House in the Middle Temple-Gate, Fleetstreet, 1701. [Advertisement.]

22. Dennis's *Comical Gallant:*
The Comical Gallant: or the Amours of Sir John Falstaffe. A Comedy. As it is Acted at the Theatre Royal in Drury-lane. By his Majesty's Servants. By Mr Dennis. To which is added, A large Account of the Taste in Poetry, and the Causes of the Degeneracy of it. London, Printed, and Sold by A. Baldwin, near the Oxford Arms in Warwicklane. 1702.

23. Burnaby's *Love Betrayed:*
Love Betray'd; or, The Agreable Disappointment. A Comedy. As it was Acted at the Theatre in Lincolns-Inn-Fields. By the Author of The Ladies Visiting-Day. [Quotation.] London: Printed for D. Brown at the Black-Swan without Temple-Bar, F. Coggan in the Inner-Temple-Lane, Fleet-Street, W. Davis at the Black-Bull, and G. Strahan at the Golden-Ball against the Exchange in Cornhill. 1703.

B. Bibliographies and General Works on the Altered Versions

1. Henrietta C. Bartlett, *Mr. William Shakespeare*, New Haven, 1922.
2. Thomas P. Barton, *Shakespeariana*, MS. in the Boston Public Library.
3. Henry T. Hall, *Shakspere's Plays: The Separate Editions of, with the Alterations done by various hands*, 2d ed., Cambridge (England), 1880.
4. W. H. Hudson, "Early Mutilators of Shakespeare," *Poet-lore*, iv (June–July, 1892), 360–371.
5. William Jaggard, *Shakespeare Bibliography*, Stratford-on-Avon, 1911. The altered versions are not listed separately but appear chronologically like regular editions of the original plays.
6. Frederick W. Kilbourne, *Alterations and Adaptations of Shakespeare*, Boston, 1906.
7. Thomas R. Lounsbury, *Shakespeare as a Dramatic Artist*, New York, 1901.
8. Allardyce Nicoll, *Dryden as an Adapter of Shakespeare*, London, 1922, pp. 26–34.
9. George C. D. Odell, *Shakespeare from Betterton to Irving*, New York, 1920. (See vol. i.)
10. "Stage Adaptations of Shakespeare," *Cornhill Magazine*, viii (July, 1863), 48–58.
11. Montague Summers, *Shakespeare Adaptations*, London, 1922.
12. G. F. Vincke, "Bearbeitungen und Aufführungen Shakespeare'scher Stücke vom Tode des Dichters bis zum Tode Garrick's," *Shakespeare Jahrbuch*, ix (1874), 41–54.
13. H. B. Wheatley, "Post-Restoration Quartos of Shakespeare's Plays," *Library*, 3d series, iv, 237–269.

C. Works on Adaptations of Single Plays

1. Antony and Cleopatra:

   Delius, N. "Dryden und Shakespeare," *Shakespeare Jahrbuch*, iv, 6–40. See pp. 22 f.

   Hannmann, F. *Dryden's Tragödie "All for Love or the World Well Lost" und ihr Verhältnis zu Shakespeare's "Antony and Cleopatra,"* Rostock, 1903.

   Rosbund, M. *Dryden als Shakespeare-Bearbeiter*, Halle a. S., 1882.

2. Cymbeline:

   Lücke, F. *Über Bearbeitungen von Shakespeares "Cymbeline,"* Doberan, 1909.

3. King Henry the Fourth, Part One:

Wrage, W. *Englische Bühnenbearbeitungen von Shakespeares King Henry IV. Part 1*, Hamburg, 1910.

4. King Henry the Sixth:

Krecke, G. *Die englischen Bühnenbearbeitungen von Shakespeares "King Henry the Sixth,"* Rostock, 1911.

White, A. F. *John Crowne His Life and Dramatic Works*, Cleveland, 1922.

5. King Lear:

Erzgräber, R. *Nahum Tate's und George Colman's Bühnenbearbeitungen des Shakespeare'schen King Lear*, Weimar, 1897.

6. King Richard the Second:

Allwardt, W. *Die englischen Bühnenbearbeitungen von Shakespeares "King Richard the Second,"* Doberan, 1909.

7. King Richard the Third:

Dohse, R. *Colley Cibbers Bühnenbearbeitung von Shakespeares Richard III*, Bonn, 1897. (*Bonner Beiträge*, ii, 1–61.)

Sprague, A. C. "A New Scene in Colley Cibber's Richard III," *Mod. Lang. Notes*, xlii, 29–32 (Jan., 1927).

Wood, Alice I. P. *The Stage History of Shakespeare's King Richard the Third*, New York, 1909.

8. Macbeth:

Delius, N. "Shakespeare's Macbeth und Davenant's Macbeth," *Shakespeare Jahrbuch*, xx, 69–84.

Weber, G. *Davenant's Macbeth im Verhältnis zu Shakespeare's Gleichnamiger Tragödie*, Rostock, 1903.

Williams, J. D. E. *Sir William Davenant's Relation to Shakespeare. With an Analysis of the Chief Characters of Davenant's Plays*, Liverpool, n. d.

9. Measure for Measure:

Elze, K. "Sir William Davenant," *Shakespeare Jahrbuch*, iv, 121–159. See pp. 153 f.

Illies, G. *Das Verhältnis von Davenants 'The Law against Lovers' zu Shakespeares 'Measure for Measure' und 'Much Ado about Nothing,'* Halle a. S., 1900.

See also Williams's dissertation, under No. 8, above.

10. Merchant of Venice, The:

Burmeister, O. *Nachdichtungen und Bühneneinrichtungen von Shakespeare's Merchant of Venice*, Rostock, 1902.

11. Much Ado about Nothing:

See under *Measure for Measure*.

12. Romeo and Juliet:

Schramm, W. *Thomas Otway's "The History and Fall of Caius Marius" und Garrick's "Romeo and Juliet," in ihrem Verhältnis zu Shakespeare's "Romeo and Juliet" und den übrigen Quellen*, Greifswald, 1898.

13. TAMING OF THE SHREW, THE:

Moosmann, E. *John Lacy's Sauny the Scot. Eine Bearbeitung von Shakespeare's The Taming of the Shrew aus der Restaurationzeit. (1667.)*, Halle a. S., 1901.

Weber, F. *Lacy's Sauny the Scot und Garrick's Catharine and Petruchio im Verhältnis zu ihren Quellen*, Rostock, 1901.

14. TEMPEST, THE:

Clarke, Sir Ernest. "The Tempest as an Opera," *Athenæum*, August 25, 1906, pp. 222, 223.

Grimm, H. "Shakespeare's Sturm in der Bearbeitung von Dryden und Davenant," *Fünfzehn Essays*, 1875, pp. 183–224.

Lawrence, William J. "Did Thomas Shadwell write an Opera on 'The Tempest'?" *The Elizabethan Playhouse and Other Studies* [First Series], 1912, pp. 193–206.

Witt, O. *The Tempest, or The Enchanted Island. A Comedy by John Dryden. 1670. The Sea-Voyage. A Comedy by Beaumont and Fletcher. 1647. The Goblins' Tragi-Comedy by Sir John Suckling. 1646. in ihrem Verhältnis zu Shakespere's "Tempest" und den übrigen Quellen*, Rostock, 1899.

See also Delius's article and Rosbund's dissertation, under No. 1, above.

15. TIMON OF ATHENS:

Beber, O. *Thom. Shadwell's Bearbeitung des Shakespeare'schen "Timon of Athens,"* Rostock, 1897.

16. TITUS ANDRONICUS:

Bake, F. *Ravenscrofts Bearbeitung des Shakespeare'schen "Titus Andronicus" "Titus Andronicus or The Rape of Lavinia." 1687*, Rostock, 1907.

17. TROILUS AND CRESSIDA:

Zenke, H. *Dryden's Troilus und Cressida im Verhältnis zu Shakespeare's Drama und die übrigen Bearbeitungen des Stoffes in England*, Rostock, 1904.

See also Delius's article and Rosbund's dissertation, under No. 1, above.

D. SELECT BIBLIOGRAPHY OF WORKS ON THE RESTORATION THEATRE

Adams, Joseph Quincy. *The Dramatic Records of Sir Henry Herbert, Master of the Revels, 1623–1673*, New Haven, 1917.

——. *Shakespearean Playhouses*, Boston, 1917.

Aston, Anthony. *A Brief Supplement to Colley Cibber, Esq; his Lives of the late Famous Actors and Actresses*, reprinted in Lowe's ed. of Cibber's *Apology*, II, 297 f.

Baker, David Erskine. *Biographia Dramatica; or, A Companion to the Playhouse. . . . Originally compiled, to the year 1764, by David Erskine*

Baker. Continued thence to 1782, by Isaac Reed, F. A. S. And brought down to the End of November 1811, with very considerable Additions and Improvements throughout, by Stephen Jones, 3 vols., London, 1812.

Baker, H. Barton. *History of the London Stage and its Famous Players, (1576–1903)*, London, 1904.

Cambridge History of English Literature, vol. viii, chaps. 5, 6, 7.

Campbell, Lily B. *Scenes and Machines on the English Stage during the Renaissance*, Cambridge (England), 1923.

Cibber, Colley. *An Apology for the Life of Mr. Colley Cibber Written by Himself*, ed. Robert W. Lowe, 2 vols., London, 1889.

Davies, Thomas. *Dramatic Miscellanies*, 3 vols., London, 1784.

Doran, Dr. [John]. *Their Majesties' Servants: Annals of the English Stage from Thomas Betterton to Edmund Kean*, ed. Robert W. Lowe, 3 vols., London, 1888.

Downes, John. *Roscius Anglicanus, or, an Historical Review of the Stage*, ed. Joseph Knight, London, 1886.

Evelyn. *Diary and Correspondence of John Evelyn, F. R. S.*, 4 vols., London, 1889.

Fitzgerald, Percy. *A New History of the English Stage from the Restoration to the Liberty of the Theatres, in Connection with the Patent Houses*, 2 vols., London, 1882.

Flecknoe, Richard. "A Short Discourse of the English Stage," *Love's Kingdom*, London, 1664.

Genest, John. *Some Account of the English Stage from the Restoration in 1660 to 1830*, 10 vols., Bath, 1832. See vols. i and ii.

Gildon, Charles. *A Comparison between the Two Stages*, London, 1702.

Halliwell-Phillipps, James Orchard. *A Collection of Ancient Documents Respecting the office of Master of the Revels, and other Papers Relating to the Early English Theatre, from the Original Manuscripts formerly in the Haslewood Collection*, London, 1870.

Hotson, J. Leslie. "George Jolly, Actor-Manager: New Light on the Restoration Stage," *Studies in Philology*, xx, 422–443 (Oct., 1923).

——. *Sir William Davenant and the Commonwealth Stage*, Harvard dissertation, 1923, unprinted.

Ingleby–Smith–Furnivall–Munro. *The Shakspere Allusion-Book*, vol. ii, New York, 1909.

Langbaine, Gerard. *Momus Triumphans*, London, 1688.

——. *An Account of the English Dramatick Poets*, Oxford, 1691.

Langbaine–Gildon. *The Lives and Characters of the English Dramatick Poets*, London, n. d. (*c.* 1699).

Lawrence, William J. "A Forgotten Restoration Playhouse," *Englische Studien*, xxxv, 279–289.

——. "The Origin of the English Picture-Stage," *The Elizabethan Playhouse and Other Studies, Second Series*, Philadelphia, 1913.

Lounsbury, Thomas R. *Shakespeare as a Dramatic Artist, with an Account of his Reputation at Various Periods*, New York, 1901.

Lowe, Robert W. *Thomas Betterton*, London, 1891.

Malone, Edmond. *An Historical Account of the Rise and Progress of the English Stage*, London, 1803. (This material also appears in the Variorum Ed. of 1821.)

McAfee, Helen. *Pepys on the Restoration Stage*, New Haven, 1916.

Nicoll, Allardyce. *A History of Restoration Drama 1660–1700*, Cambridge (England), 1923.

——. *A History of Early Eighteenth Century Drama 1700–1750*, Cambridge (England), 1925.

Odell, George C. D. *Shakespeare from Betterton to Irving*, 2 vols., New York, 1920.

Pepys's *Diary*, ed. H. B. Wheatley, 9 vols., London, 1893–1896.

Sprague, Arthur Colby. *Beaumont and Fletcher on the Restoration Stage*, Cambridge (Massachusetts), 1926.

Summers, Montague. *Shakespeare Adaptations*, London, 1922.

Thaler, Alwin. *Shakspere to Sheridan*, Cambridge (Massachusetts), 1922.

Thorn-Drury, G. *A Little Ark Containing Sundry Pieces of Seventeenth-Century Verse*, London, 1921.

——. *Some Seventeenth Century Allusions to Shakespeare*, London, 1920.

——. *More Seventeenth Century Allusions to Shakespeare*, London, 1924.

Ward, Adolphus William. *A History of English Dramatic Literature to the Death of Queen Anne*, new and revised ed., 3 vols., London, 1899.

Wood. *The Life and Times of Anthony Wood, antiquary*, ed. Andrew Clark, 5 vols., Oxford, 1891–1900.

Wright, James, *Historia Histrionica* (1699). Reprinted by Lowe, Cibber's *Apology*, vol. i, pp. xix–li.

INDEX

INDEX